Policy Analysis and Pub... ~..~.~~

Policy Analysis and Public Choice

Selected Papers by William A. Niskanen

William A. Niskanen

Chairman, Cato Institute, Washington DC, US

THE LOCKE INSTITUTE

Edward Elgar

Cheltenham, UK • Northampton, MA, USA

Published by
Edward Elgar Publishing Limited
Glensanda House
Montpellier Parade
Cheltenham
Glos GL50 1UA
UK

Edward Elgar Publishing, Inc.
136 West Street
Suite 202
Northampton
Massachusetts 01060
USA

Paperback edition 2004

A catalogue record for this book
is available from the British Library

Library of Congress Cataloguing in Publication Data

Niskanen, William A., 1933–
    Policy analysis and public choice : selected papers by William A.
Niskanen / William A. Niskanen
    (The John Locke series)
    Includes bibliographical references and index.
    1. United States — Economic policy.   2. Government spending policy—
United States.   3. Social choice—United States.   I. Title.
    II. Series: John Locke series in classical liberal political
economy.
    HC103.N57   1998
    339.973—dc21   97–29956
                                                                                          CIP
ISBN 1 85898 702 4 (cased)
      1 84542 092 6 (paperback)

Printed and bound in Great Britain by MPG Books Ltd, Bodmin, Cornwall

For my daughters

Contents

Contents

Figures

Tables

1. A personal note: from technocrat to political economist

RAND

In September 1957, on completing my graduate studies in economics at the University of Chicago, I started work as a staff economist at the RAND Corporation in Santa Monica, California. RAND was my first job choice for two reasons: I had little interest in a conventional academic career, and I felt that I owed the military some time because I had had a college student deferment during the Korean War. At that time, I had no reason to anticipate that I would work as a defence analyst for the next 13 years or that this first job choice would lead to such a diverse and rewarding professional career.

For a young economist, RAND was an exciting place to work. The professional firmament was full of bright stars, some then apparent and others more visible later. Armen Alchian, Charles Hitch, Roland McKean, Steve Enke and David Novick had been developing and applying the techniques of cost-effectiveness analysis and programme budgeting to defence problems for some years. George Danzig had developed linear programming as a useful analytic tool. Herman Kahn and Albert Wohlstetter were profound analysts of broader issues. Others of my generation, such as Alain Enthoven and Harry Rowen, later had positions of substantial responsibility. The other new economist in my project and my sometimes programmer, William Sharpe, later won the Nobel prize for his work with Harry Markowitz on portfolio theory. For its time, RAND also had a large computer that was slower and less reliable than my current PC.

I was assigned to the transportation project of the logistics department of the economics division. The general objective of this project was to identify the most efficient combination of airlift, sealift and forward storage to support the deployment of conventional forces to meet a range of potential regional threats. For most of the next five years, I worked to develop ever larger linear programming models of the military air transport system, work that led to a classified report (coauthored with Don Fort) published in 1963. Along the way, I had the opportunity to complete my doctoral dissertation on 'The demand for alcoholic beverages' and to develop a 'proposal for a smog tax' for the Los Angeles region.

OFFICE OF THE SECRETARY OF DEFENSE

After the election of John Kennedy as President and his appointment of Robert McNamara as Secretary of Defense, a number of RAND colleagues and I packed our bag of new professional tools and moved to Washington. Charles Hitch was appointed as the Defense Controller, and he created a new Office of Systems Analysis headed by Alain Enthoven. This was the group sometimes called the 'whiz kids', a term that had also been used to describe the group of young financial analysts, including Robert McNamara, hired by the Ford Motor Company after World War II. I worked for this office on military transportation issues for several months in the summer of 1961 and joined this office in the summer of 1962, later to be appointed the Director of Special Studies. Most of my work in this position was on continental air defence and Army ground forces. This was a heady experience for a young analyst, the opportunity to work on important problems and report to the most senior relevant government official; at the end of each year, we would write a draft memorandum to the president on each of our programme areas. Initially, this was a seductive experience. In a very rank-conscious organization, my civilian rank at age 29 was equivalent to that of a brigadier-general, and we often had access to McNamara ahead of a queue of generals and senior defence contractors. Only later did I understand why we were often regarded as 'smart alec brats'.

Fortunately, this was also a maturing experience. The implicit mindset of a technocrat is optimistic but naive – a faith that all that stands between current conditions and a state of bliss is the opportunity to present your analysis to an official with sufficient authority to implement your recommendations. Work in the Pentagon undermined that illusion rather quickly. The most important problems are not amenable to linear programming and were often handled rather badly; most of the less important problems were managed satisfactorily by much simpler techniques. Many decisions are made on the basis of criteria not even considered by the analyst. Also, with access to highly classified information, I came to recognize that our government sometimes lies to us about important events:

- the initial story about the abortive Bay of Pigs invasion was clearly a cover;
- the official story about the October missile crisis was at least, deceptive;
- the official stories about the assassinations of John Kennedy and Martin Luther King are still not very convincing; and
- the Tet Offensive was a military victory for US forces but the critical political victory for the communist Vietnamese.

Over the 1960s, I became so sceptical about government pronouncements that I suspected that the television images of the first moon landing were staged in some warehouse. Somehow I survived the 1960s as a sceptic but not a cynic, more realistic about public officials and political processes, recognizing that some major mistakes are by 'the best and the brightest', but still optimistic that ideas matter, that good analysis can improve policy decisions even if neither necessary nor sufficient in many cases. For me, that was the beginning of wisdom, the difference between a technocrat and a policy analyst.

INSTITUTE FOR DEFENSE ANALYSES

The second stage of my professional career began in November 1964 when I was appointed director of the economic and political studies division of the Institute for Defense Analyses (IDA), like RAND a federal contract research institute working primarily for the Department of Defense. Over my tenure at IDA this division addressed a wide range of defence issues plus important early studies of the supersonic transport, the war on poverty and the housing programme. I also organized, supervised and taught a graduate programme in defence economics for military officers, a programme the officers completed at the University of Maryland. I came to value my relations with military officers, whether as clients, colleagues or students; most of them have a sense of both dedication and realism too often lacking among my other professional contacts.

As it turned out, I was a good manager but I did not find it especially rewarding. I quickly discovered that the secret of being a good research manager is to hire bright people and give them only the most general guidance. Somewhat by accident, some of those I hired – Steve Hoenack, Peter Ordeshook, Gordon Tullock and Donald Wittman – had made or would later make important contributions to the economic analysis of political behaviour, a field now termed public choice. My interaction with these and other fine scholars on this staff led me to start thinking about applying formal economic analysis to the structure and processes of government. Despite my primary responsibilities, this was a surprisingly productive period for my own research. My IDA publications include such early papers as 'The combination of strategic offense and defense forces', 'Soviet responses to U.S. threats', and the 'productivity of major military forces in Vietnam'. Over time, however, more of my research was addressed to the decision processes in the Department of Defense. Gordon Tullock first suggested that I distil my developing views about bureaucracy in a 1968 article, and most of my last year at IDA was committed to writing my book on *Bureaucracy and Representative Government*. My IDA years were rewarding in several dimensions, and I remain personal friends with many of those who worked with me there.

OFFICE OF MANAGEMENT AND BUDGET

In October 1970, I returned to the government as the assistant director for evaluation in the new Office of Management and Budget (OMB). The prospects were encouraging; the Nixon administration had appointed a first-rate team to administer this important agency. George Shultz was the director and the other appointees included Caspar Weinberger, Jim Schlesinger, Ken Dam and Don Rice; each of whom was later appointed to one or more cabinet or other high federal positions. As a group, we made an awful botch of things as party to a rapid growth of domestic spending and regulation and the implementation of comprehensive wage and price controls. My professional mood soured further on realizing that the wage and price controls were designed, supported and first implemented by economists who had been professors or students at the University of Chicago! I left OMB one week before Watergate to spend the summer writing a monograph on 'Structural reform of the 'federal budget process' for the American Enterprise Institute (AEI).

BERKELEY

My first academic appointment was as professor at the new Graduate School of Public Policy at the University of California, Berkeley, where I started teaching in September 1972. The dean was Aaron Wildavsky, probably the wisest and most productive policy analyst of my generation and a good friend until his untimely death. My primary responsibility was to design and teach the basic introduction to policy analysis, and I also had the opportunity to teach courses in public choice, law and economics, and welfare policy.

For me, Berkeley was not an especially productive research environment because I could not reconcile the demands of research and being a conscientious teacher. My major study during that period was 'Cities and schools' (with Mickey Levy), an analysis of the effects of the municipal and education codes of the State of California. During this period, I also had my first contact with then-Governor Ronald Reagan, a contact that led me into the movement for constitutional tax limitation and a later federal appointment. My major reward from my period at Berkeley is still accumulating with interest – a recognition that many of my students are now mature scholars and policy analysts in responsible positions.

FORD

In July 1975 I resigned a one-sided lifetime contract at Berkeley and started work as the director of economics at the Ford Motor Company, a position that could be terminated at any time without cause and without notice. As it turned out, I was fired from this position five years later without cause but with some notice. In the meantime, this was a very rewarding period. I learned a lot quickly about the role of business economists, the auto industry, the effects of regulation, and the similarities and differences of work in a large private firm and bureau; I would never teach the conventional theory of the firm again after this experience. Most of my professional work was proprietary – economic and industry forecasting, the analysis of regulations, advise on the use of new risk-management techniques, and so on – but I also had the opportunity to write several professional papers included in this book.

One rewarding sideline was to chair the committee that wrote an amendment to the constitution of the State of Michigan that tightened the rules affecting state and local fiscal decisions; this amendment was promoted by popular initiative and was approved by Michigan voters in 1978. I also continued to work with a national committee to promote similar amendments in other states and the first effort to design and promote a similar amendment to the federal Constitution.

In the late 1970s, the Ford management was running scared about Japanese competition and, for the first time, sought temporary trade protection. I was a minor casualty of that decision. On leaving Ford, I returned to California to teach briefly at the Graduate School of Management at the University of California, Los Angeles. I have no regrets about my adventure as a business economist, and I still maintain contact with some of my former colleagues at Ford.

COUNCIL OF ECONOMIC ADVISERS

Duty calls! In April 1981 I returned to Washington, this time as a member of the Council of Economic Advisers in the new Reagan administration. I served in this position for the next four years, the last nine months as acting chairman of the Council. Again, most of my professional work was proprietary, in part because I found that any public article or comment risked a political controversy. My responsibility was to advise the White House on the whole range of macroeconomic policies. This was a turbulent, controversial and important period in the history of American economic policy. I will not summarize this experience here, however, because it is described at length in my book on *Reaganomics*.

CATO

So far, my professional life had been somewhat footloose. I counted up the years that I had worked in Washington, however, and decided to stay. In April 1985 I joined the Cato Institute, then a small, young, energetic, libertarian policy institute. My position as both chairman of the board and a staff economist looks awkward on paper, but it is not. Ed Crane, Cato's very able founder and president, raises most of the financing and makes most of the management decisions. My primary roles as the senior scholar have been internal quality control, editor of *Regulation* magazine for seven years, and my own research. This has been the longest that I have worked for any institution and the longest period that I have had the opportunity to write for a general policy or professional audience. This has been a very productive period for both Cato and for me. Cato has grown into one of the larger, more visible policy institutes, now with a dramatic new building, without losing our energy or succumbing to 'the beltway mentality'. We have helped to slow the Leviathan, even if it is not yet tamed. My professional work at Cato has been characteristic of that in the community of policy institutes: my book on *Reaganomics*, editing *Regulation*, some articles for professional journals, numerous articles and editorials for other publications, congressional testimony, frequent speeches, organizing forums and conferences, occasional radio and TV spots, and providing policy context for journalists. One wonders why anyone would pay us for an activity that is so enjoyable. At this stage, I hope to continue such activities as long as health and motivation hold out.

A REFLECTION

My first 40 years as a professional economist involved two quite different careers and two somewhat complementary specialities.

For 24 years I was employed in government, a defence research firm, or in an industrial firm. Most of my professional work during these years was proprietary, with limited opportunity to write for a broad professional or policy audience. Each of these positions, however, was a marvellous learning experience, exposing me to problems and perspectives shared by few other economists. This experience made me a different economist than if I had chosen a conventional academic career, affecting my choice of problems and the perspective of my writing for a broader audience. In retrospect, the decision to start my career at RAND was fortunate.

For 16 years I have been employed as a professor or in a policy institute. This has given me much more opportunity to write for a broader audience; most of the articles in this book, for example, were written during these years. At the same time, one's opportunity for continued learning in these environments is limited to the usual forms of interaction within the same profession. My occasional switch from one of these careers to the other was usually rewarding in both directions, in one case the challenge of new problems and in the other the opportunity to recharge my batteries.

My two professional specialities have evolved into policy analyst and political economist. As a policy analyst, I focus on the activities of government with the somewhat naive optimism that good analysis may change these activities for the better. As a political economist, or public choice scholar, I focus on government as an institution, the structure of incentives and constraints that affect the decisions of voters, politicians and bureaucrats. Public choice is often described as 'politics without romance'. And the study of public choice has led me and many public choice scholars to a quite possibly exaggerated pessimism about our political institutions. Although the characteristic moods of the policy analyst and the political economist are quite different, these two perspectives can be complementary. The conflict of these moods need not lead to schizophrenia. Public choice can add political realism to policy analysis, and the occasional success of policy analysis in changing the activities of government can add more optimism that the institutions of government may also be changed for the better. My own balance of these moods has evolved into one of optimism about the possible and pessimism about the probable.

ABOUT THIS BOOK

This book is a collection of articles and notes that I have written over the past 30 years, the majority of them written during the past 12 years at Cato. The articles selected are representative of my writing on policy analysis and public choice but do not include the following longer studies:

- 'The demand for alcoholic beverages', my PhD dissertation at the University of Chicago completed in 1962.
- *An Analysis of Military Air Transportation*, a RAND report published in 1963.
- *Bureaucracy and Representative Government*, published in 1971 and reprinted, with my other major articles on bureaucracy, as *Bureaucracy and Public Economics* in 1994.
- 'Structural reform of the federal budget process', a report published by the American Enterprise Institute in 1973.
- 'Cities and schools', a report for the Local Government Reform Task Force in California in 1974. Chapter 8 of this book is based on a part of this study.
- *Reaganomics*, published in 1988. Chapters 13–15 of this book are based in part on material from this record.
- All my articles or notes published in *Regulation* during my period as editor.
- 'Autocratic, democratic, and optimal government', an article published in 1997. This article is not included because I am now expanding this topic into a book.

The articles included in this book address a range of subjects and may be coherent only in my own mind. In any case, I trust that they are informative and interesting to the reader. I ask your understanding that any 'his' could also be a 'her' unless clearly referring to a specific person. These articles have been edited but not updated.

I am indebted, of course, to many people too numerous to mention who provided support for the articles in this book. For the preparation of this book I am specifically indebted to Cato president Ed Crane for tolerating my internal sabbatical, my secretary Pat Felder for her long and faithful service, my interns James Hawken and Paul Levitan for their temporary tolerance of dogwork, and to the Locke Institute director Charles Rowley for his encouragement and counsel.

PART I

Policy Analysis

2. An irreverent perspective on the case for federal chartering of corporations*

INTRODUCTION

The case for federal chartering of corporations is based on:

twelve phantom footnotes,
eleven alleged abuses,
ten factual errors,
nine false analogies,
eight irrelevant precedents,
seven silly syllogisms,
six unrealistic expectations,
five legal myths,
four catch phrases,
three real concerns,
two serious misconceptions,
and a partridge in a pear tree.

I

I shall spare the poor partridge.

II

The first serious misconception is that corporations are 'private governments'. An observation that corporations are not organized like democratic governments leads to a conclusion that corporations are not accountable and a recommendation that corporations should be organized like democratic governments. The observation is largely correct,

* This chapter is the text of a paper presented at a symposium on the federal chartering of corporations at the American Enterprise Institute, 21 June 1976.

the conclusion is generally wrong, and the recommendation seems to have been the original premise.

It is most important to recognize the powers that a corporation does *not* have. A corporation cannot finance its activities by taxation or by printing money. A corporation cannot recruit labour services by conscription or by by an appeal to patriotism and public service. A corporation cannot use force to extend its market area, constrain competition, or defend against a takeover bid. In short, a corporation does not have *any* of the characteristic powers of a government.

Governments in our national community are organized as representative democracies. Although this form of government has served us moderately well, representative democracy is an expensive time-consuming form of organization and there is no obvious reason to extend it to other institutions that do not have the characteristic powers of a government. Our political history suggests that representative democracy is neither a necessary nor a sufficient instrument to assure responsiveness, avoid major error, minimize the personal abuse of power, or to induce efficiency. The Army and the Post Office, the nation's two largest employers, are federally chartered corporations, in effect, and do not provide attractive models of the way other institutions should be organized.

The second major misconception is that corporations are 'creatures of the state'. A concept has developed that the existence of a corporation is somehow dependent on special rights that only a government can confer. A casual acceptance of this concept leads to a conclusion that the government should extract some concessions concerning the organization and behaviour of corporations in exchange for these rights. Again, the concept that leads to this type of conclusion is incorrect. A corporation is a specific form of voluntary association. Limited liability, the one distinctive attribute of a corporation, is a voluntary agreement between a corporation and its creditors and is in no way dependent on a right granted by government. The attributes of perpetual life and legal entity are not unique to corporations. Any form of private organization – a marriage, a church, a fraternal organization, a partnership, a corporation – is based on a voluntary agreement among people for a specific purpose. Governments have a long history of requiring the *registration* of such organizations and of extracting a little revenue as a registration fee. All of these organizations could exist without any special rights granted by the government, and one cannot infer from the practice of governments in requiring registration that any grant of rights is necessary to the formation and survival of these organizations. (One should also not be surprised that people wishing to form such organizations prefer registration in those states that extract the minimum registration fee and restrictions on their behaviour.) Indeed, the proposal for federal charter-ing seems to be based on a medieval concept that all rights inhere in the state, and that any form of private association is based on a concession of rights by the state. Our national community, in contrast, is based on the principle that all rights inhere in the people and that any powers of the government are based on a limited delegation of these rights by voters.

III

A corporation deserves to be evaluated on the basis of three real concerns:

- How well does it serve the interests of its shareowners, creditors, employees and suppliers?
- How well does it serve the interests of its customers?
- How well does it serve the interests of those people who are not party to a voluntary agreement with the corporation?

The advocates of federal chartering of corporations have not offered any evidence that federal charters for large corporations would increase their responsiveness or accountability to these groups. It is also difficult to prove the contrary, but the advocates of a radical restructuring of large corporations clearly should bear the burden of proof.

The substantial differences in corporate law among states provides the basis for a potential study that bears on these concerns. Two facts are uncontested: the State of Delaware law bearing on corporate charters least constrains the organization and activities of corporations, and many firms that are now large have chosen to incorporate in Delaware. These facts lead the advocates of federal chartering to conclude that the Delaware law is 'bad' law, that is, that it does not serve the interests of the other affected parties. The fact that the Delaware law serves the interests of the organizers of corporations (and the state treasurer), however, is not sufficient proof that the interests of other groups are not served. The following questions, for example, could be studied:

- Do Delaware corporations have a lower price/earnings ratio than other corporations?
- Are they more subject to default and bankruptcy?
- Do Delaware corporations pay lower wages or have poorer work-ing conditions?
- Are their prices higher, or the quality of their products lower?

- Do Delaware corporations pay lower total taxes?
- Do they make a lower contribution to the affected local communities?
- Are managers of Delaware corporations more subject to violations of the law?
- Do the activities of Delaware corporations involve higher pollution per unit of output?

As far as I know, there is not one study that has addressed these questions. I have not done such a study either, but I am willing to make a small wager that the evidence would not support an affirmative answer to any one of the above questions. The advocates of federal chartering have developed no evidence of the relation between the provisions of a corporate charter and the alleged abuses by corporations. Even Washington lawyers should be obliged to provide *some* evidence to support their case.

My primary point is that the responsiveness and accountability of corporations are primarily determined by market conditions and by sections of the law other than those affecting the corporate charter. The interests of shareowners and creditors are primarily protected by a competitive, liquid market for corporate financial instruments and by competition for corporate control (a number of recent and proposed antitrust measures, unfortunately, reduce the competition for corporate control by establishing barriers to mergers, even when they would not increase concentration in any product market). The interests of employees are primarily protected by competition in the labour market. Similarly, the interests of consumers are primarily protected by competition in the product market. Government has an important role to assure corporate responsiveness to these groups, primarily by avoiding legal barriers to competition and entry and by vigilant antitrust action against private collusion and restrictions on entry. Some government role is also required to assure an efficient use of common environmental resources. Pollution inherently involves the use of some common resource without the consent of all affected parties, and neither corporations nor any other type of organization will voluntarily reduce pollution in the absence of some collective institution for allocating our scarce common resources.

Federal charters for corporations would not resolve any of these concerns and would exacerbate some. The only interests that federal charters would clearly serve are those who would substitute political and bureaucratic control of a major part of the American economy for the discipline of voluntary agreements under competitive conditions. Americans have a healthy suspicion about large organizations, and continued vigilance is important to avoid collusion among large corporations or with the government. Federal chartering, by transforming large corporations into instruments of the state, would *reduce* the diffusion of power that is essential to a community of free people.

IV (*ET SEQ.*)

Alas, my time is up. I so much wanted to discuss those phantom footnotes.

3. Crime, police and root causes[*]

It could probably be shown by facts and figures that there is no distinctly native American criminal class except Congress. (Mark Twain)

Congress, in a frenzy of competitive machoism and with little regard for the Constitution or common sense, recently passed another election-year crime bill. The Violent Crime Control and Law Enforcement Act of 1994 substantially federalized criminal law, increased sentences for a wide range of crimes, banned some semiautomatic rifles, and authorized about $30 billion in additional spending for police, prisons and a range of exotic social programmes. A major premise of the act, for which there is surprisingly little evidence, is that more police and prisons would reduce crime. A minor premise, for which there is even less evidence, is that federal grants for everything from sensitivity training to midnight basketball would also reduce crime!

The act is an outrage. Let me count the ways:

1. Some of its provisions are inconsistent with the Constitution and the historical limits on the powers of the federal government. A major recent federal publication summarizes the constitutional perspective:

    The U.S. Constitution reserves general police powers to the States. By act of Congress, Federal offenses include only offenses against the U.S. Government and against or by its employees while engaged in their official duties, and offenses which involve the crossing of State lines or an interference with interstate commerce.[1]

    This act, however, establishes federal penalties for most murders and for a wide range of other crimes already subject to state law. Moreover, the act substantially reduces the discretion of state judicial officers by making the new grants for prisons conditional on a state law that violent criminals serve at least 85 per cent of their sentence and by establishing a mandatory life sentence for those convicted of

* Reprinted by permission from the Cato Institute, First published as Cato *Policy Analysis*, No. 218, 14 November 1994.

three serious violent crimes or drug offences. The premise on which Congress asserted those powers is that crime is a nationwide problem and that guns, drugs and criminals move across state lines. On that premise, no area of American life is immune to a similar assertion of federal powers.

2. Some provisions are an abuse of civil liberties. In cases involving sexual assault or child molestation, the rules of evidence are changed to permit evidence on the defendant's prior behaviour. Juveniles convicted of violent crimes or serious drug offences are to be subject to an additional sentence of up to ten years if they are also members of street gangs. Aliens convicted of an 'aggravated felony' are to be denied a deportation hearing.

3. Some provisions are counterproductive. A federal death penalty is established for four crimes not involving murder (that may be unconstitutional). A third conviction for a serious offence not involving murder is punishable by life imprisonment, a longer sentence than for most murders. Such increases in the penalties for less heinous crimes *reduce* the incremental penalty for more heinous crimes.

4. The ban of 19 types of semiautomatic rifles is purely symbolic (and may also be unconstitutional). The banned rifles are not functionally different from hundreds of still-legal rifles, the aggregate of which is used in about 1 per cent of crimes involving a gun. No one contends that this ban will reduce the crime rate. The ban is hotly contended, primarily because its supporters hope and its critics fear that it will serve as precedent for a broader ban of semiautomatic rifles.

5. Most of the social programmes financed by the act (about one-third of the total funding) are likely to be worth less than their cost. Few, if any, of those programmes would be approved if subject to a stand-alone vote, and most of the funds are to be spent for activities with only a token relation to crime prevention. Larry Sherman, president of the Crime Control Institute, describes the programmes as 'untested drugs. Nobody has evaluated any of these ideas to see whether they are safe and effective'.[2] Advocates of these programmes should explain why an explosion of similar programmes since 1960 has not reduced the crime rate.

6. And finally, the 1994 act is unnecessary. Crime is a nationwide problem but does not require a national solution. More police in California, for example, do not reduce the crime rate in New York. More likely, to the extent that criminals are mobile, state and local governments may have *too strong* an incentive to spend on public safety activities, reducing the local crime rate at the expense of increasing the crime rate in other jurisdictions. Moreover, the large

high-crime states such as California, New York, Illinois and Florida will receive a *smaller* share of the $9 billion in earmarked funds than their proportionate share of federal taxes.[3]

The report of the conference committee concludes that 'individual states and localities find it impossible to handle the problem by themselves' and that 'the Congress finds that it is necessary and proper to assist the States in controlling crime'.[4] Crime is a serious problem in much of the United States. The federal government, however, lacks the constitutional authority, the incentive and the information to address the problem of local crime and has no more resources than are available to the states. Moreover, to the extent that the best combination of measures to reduce crime is unknown or differs among jurisdictions, it is especially important to decentralize decisions on the crime problem. For those reasons, the Violent Crime Control and Law Enforcement Act of 1994 is wrong on all counts.

SOME COMMON QUESTIONS

Most of us have become inured to Congress's making law without a factual basis. In drafting the recent crime bill, however, Congress had little to work with: there are reams of data that document the daily tragedies of crime in America but surprisingly little evidence on what changes in government policy would reduce the crime rate.

In 1991 state and local governments spent $75.5 billion on public safety. That sum financed about 700 thousand police, the incarceration of 1.1 million people, and the associated legal and judicial system. The numbers of police and prisoners per capita have both somewhat more than doubled since 1960, primarily in the past 15 years. That about exhausts the hard data on the subject.

One might hope that the record would provide evidence bearing on the following types of questions:

- Has the substantial increase in the number of police and prisons since 1960 significantly reduced the crime rate?
- Will the small increase in the number of police and prisons authorized by the 1994 crime bill significantly reduce the crime rate?
- What conditions, other than the public safety system, most affect the crime rate?

As it turns out, there is surprisingly little evidence that bears on those questions. In approving the 1994 crime bill, members of Congress were talking tough, but they were flying blind.

This chapter summarizes a statistical analysis that provides some tentative answers to those questions.

MEASURING CRIME

The US Department of Justice provides two measures of the level and composition of crime in the United States. The Uniform Crime Report (UCR) summarizes the number of index crimes reported to (and recorded by) police. The index violent crimes are murder, rape, robbery and aggravated assault. The index property crimes are burglary, larceny and auto theft. The data on reported crimes are based on reports by local law enforcement agencies (those reports now cover 98 per cent of the population), are summarized by political jurisdiction and the nation, and have been prepared on a consistent basis since 1960.

The National Criminal Victimization Survey (NCVS) reports estimates of the numbers of victims of major crimes. The estimates of violent crimes include rape, robbery, aggravated assault and simple assault. The estimates of property crimes include larceny (theft) from individuals (with or without contact), household burglary, household larceny and auto theft. Those estimates are based on an annual survey of 66 thousand households (with a 96 per cent participation rate); are summarized by type of locality, major census region and the nation; and have been prepared on a consistent basis since 1973.

It is important to understand the difference between those two measures. The UCR reports the number of *reported incidents* of crime; the NCVS reports the *estimated* number of *victims* of crime. Moreover, the coverage is quite different. For example, the NCVS includes an estimate of simple assault but does not include estimates of murders, crimes against commercial property, or crimes of which the victim was less than 12 years old. The primary reason, however, that the number of reported crimes is much smaller than the number of estimated crimes is that a large share of the estimated crimes is not reported to the police. The NCVS estimates are probably a more accurate measure of the *level* of crime, but those estimates, unfortunately, have limited value as a data base for analysis because they are not reported at a jurisdictional level for which data on public safety activities and other conditions are also available. For that reason, most studies of crime, as well as media reports, are based on the reported crime data – with an understanding, it is to be hoped, that crime reporting rates are not constant over time or across jurisdictions.

HAS THE CRIME RATE INCREASED?

The press, public opinion polls and politicians regularly reflect the perception that crime, especially violent crime, has increased rapidly. That perception may be correct, and it is consistent with the time series on reported crime. The more surprising finding is that the estimated rates of both violent and property crime have *declined* over the past 20 years. Table 3.1 summarizes the long-term trends in both the reported and the estimated crime rates.[5]

The two aggregate measures of crime in the United States tell very different stories. The reported crime rates support the perception that crime has increased rapidly. The aggregate reported crime rate more than doubled in the 1960s and more than doubled again in the 1970s. Since 1980 the reported violent crime rate has increased more slowly, and the reported property crime rate has declined slightly.

The estimated crime rates, in contrast, are a bad news, good news story. The bad news is that the total crime rate in the United States is much higher than the crimes reported to police. The good news is that the estimated violent crime rate has *declined* slightly for 20 years and the estimated property crime rate has *declined sharply* since 1980. Moreover, that pattern is more consistent with the reported murder rate (not shown), a crime for which the reporting is most accurate and a consistent series is available for many decades. The reported murder rate has been roughly stable for 20 years and is now about the same as it was in the 1920s and 1930s.

Table 3.1 Crime rates: long-term trends (crimes per 100 000 residents)

Year	Violent		Property	
	Reported[a]	Estimated[a]	Reported	Estimated[b]
1960	160		967	
1973	417	1391	3737	14 341
1980	597	1371	5353	15 016
1991	758	1202	5140	11 465

Notes:
a. Includes reported murders; excludes simple assaults.
b. Excludes commercial burglaries and larcenies.

Sources: Statistical Abstract of the United States, various years, Washington: Government Printing Office; *Historical Statistics of the United States: Colonial Times to 1970*, Washington, Government Printing Office, 1984; and *Criminal Victimization in the United States, 1992*, Washington: Bureau of Justice Statistics, 1994.

By any measure, American crime rates are much higher than those of other high-income countries. Has the actual crime rate increased substantially in the past 20 years? Maybe so, but probably not. Either answer has some very awkward implications. If popular perceptions and the reported crime rates are more accurate indicators of changes in actual crime rates, something is dreadfully wrong with the large, careful survey of victimization – possibly an increased reluctance to report crimes on the government survey. If the estimated crime rates are more accurate, the increase in reported crime rates reflects an increase in reporting rates, not in actual crime rates, and the popular perception of increasing crime appears more like mass hysteria created by or reinforced by the press and politicians.

DO POLICE CAUSE CRIME?

The most perplexing problem with any study of the determinants of crime is that there is a strong *positive* relation between the reported crime rates and the number of police per capita, both over time and across jurisdictions. Figure 3.1 illustrates that relation based on data for the 50 states in 1991.[6]

The observed relation might suggest that police cause crime. There are three reasons, however, why the observed relation is misleading:

1. The number of police may be correlated with other conditions that have a stronger effect on crime than the (presumed) negative effect of police.
2. The number of police demanded in a jurisdiction may be a function of the crime rate; in technical terms, the crime rate and the number of police are jointly determined.
3. The percentage of crimes reported to the police may be a positive function of the number of police.

Conventional statistical techniques are sufficient to address the first two of those effects. If data on the actual crime rates were available by jurisdiction, that would be sufficient to identify the effect on crime of increased police. Only reported crime rates are available by jurisdiction, however, and a strong assumption about the relation between the reporting rate and the number of police is necessary to estimate the effect on actual crime of increased police, an issue addressed in the next section of this chapter.

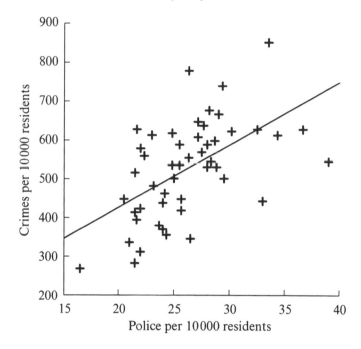

Figure 3.1 Relation between crime and police

Do police cause crime? That question is too important to be left dan-
gling. The analysis reported in the next section, as anticipated, concludes
that more police would reduce the actual crime rate. The positive effect
of more police on the reporting rate, however, appears stronger than the
negative effect on the actual crime rate over a wide range of numbers of
police. For most jurisdictions, more police would probably increase the
reported crime rate even if they reduced the actual crime rate. That
result suggests why most increases in the public safety system are perceived to be futile.

THE SUPPLY OF CRIMES

About 25 years ago economists began to formalize a model of the economics of crime. The major early contributors to the literature were
Gary Becker (1968), now a Nobel laureate, and Isaac Erlich (1973).
More recent contributors to the empirical literature on the economics
of crime include Steven Craig (1987); William Trumbull (1989); and

Helen Tauchen, Ann Dryden Witte and Harriet Griesinger (1993).[7] In retrospect, the central hypothesis of the model seems intuitive: the crime rate is expected to be a negative function of the probability and expected severity of criminal sanctions, a positive function of returns to criminal activity, a negative function of returns to legal activity, and a positive function of the share of the population that may have a relative tolerance of or preference for criminal activity.

The major contribution of that literature has been an accumulation of careful empirical studies that reflect a recognition that the crime rate, the percentage of crimes reported and the level of public safety activities are jointly determined. Those studies provide useful estimates of the effects of increased police *effectiveness* – arrest rates, conviction rates and expected sentences – but they do not provide useful estimates of the effects of increased public safety resources. The early empirical studies were all based on data aggregated at the level of a political jurisdiction. Most of the later studies are based on large special samples of individual data. The two types of data provide somewhat different perspectives on the determinants of crime and are subject to different problems of interpretation. The study summarized in this chapter is similar to the body of early studies based on aggregate data and is new primarily in that it is based on the most recently available data.

The Data

The sample for this study is the set of conditions in the 50 states plus the District of Columbia. All data are for 1991 and are from the *Statistical Abstract of the United States* (1992 and 1993) unless otherwise noted. The supply of crimes, the variable to be explained by the first part of this study, is measured by the logarithm of the reported violent crime rate and the logarithm of the reported property crime rate (both per 100 000 residents). The level of public safety resources is measured by the logarithm of the number of police and the logarithm of the number of corrections employees (both per 10 000 residents). Economic conditions are measured by the logarithm of the average annual income, the male unemployment rate, the employment rate, and the poverty rate (1989). Demographic and cultural conditions are measured by the percentage of the state population living in metropolitan areas, the percentage of births to single mothers, the percentage of church members and the percentage of blacks or Hispanics (all for 1990). Table 3.2 presents the average level and range of those variables.

Policy analysis

Table 3.2 Crime and related conditions by state, 1991

	Minimum	Average	Maximum
Reported crimes per 100000 residents			
Violent	65	758	2453
Property	2472	5140	8315
Public safety employees per 10000 residents			
Police	16.3	28.0	89.0
Corrections	7.5	20.7	77.6
Economic conditions			
Average annual income	$13318	$19091	$25968
Male unemployment rate	2.7	7.0	11.5
Employment rate	49.5	61.6	69.5
Poverty rate (1989)	6.4	13.1	25.2
Demographic and culural conditions (1990)			
Percentage metropolitan	23.9	79.4	100.0
Percentage births to single mothers	13.5	28.0	64.9
Percentage church members	32.6	57.4	80.0
Percentage minority	1.0	21.0	71.3

Source: Statistical Abstract of the United States, 1992 and 1993.

The Statistical Technique

The effects of the level of public safety resources and other conditions on the reported crime rates are estimated by a weighted two-stage least-squares regression. All variables are weighted by the relative population of the state; this increases the relative effect of conditions in the larger states and makes the estimates more representative of average conditions in the nation. The two-stage technique is used to reflect the recognition that crime rates and the level of public safety resources are jointly determined. The instrumental variables include the other independent variables in both crime regressions and in the two regressions on the demand for police and corrections employees (to be described later). It is important to recognize that the estimates from these regressions reflect the *sum* of the effect of conditions on the actual crime rates and the effect on the reporting rates. Given that only reported crime rates are available by jurisdiction, no statistical technique, by itself, can estimate the separate effects. Table 3.3 summarizes the results of the two regressions on the supply of crimes.

Table 3.3 The supply of crimes

	Type of crime	
Condition	Violent	Property
Effects of 1 per cent change		
Police	0.77 (0.32)	0.53 (0.25)
Corrections employees	0.08 (0.20)	0.29 (0.12)
Average annual income	−1.05 (0.41)	−1.01 (0.34)
Effects of 1 percentage point change		
Male unemployment rate	9.11 (2.78)	
Employment rate		3.12 (0.57)
Poverty rate		2.58 (1.05)
Percentage metropolitan	0.91 (0.36)	0.94 (0.23)
Percentage births to single mothers	1.73 (0.51)	
Percentage church membership		−0.51 (0.20)
Percentage minority	1.83 (0.38)	
$\bar{R}^2$		
Weighted	0.999	0.999
Unweighted	0.565	0.596

Note: Numbers in parentheses are standard errors of the coefficients.

Policy analysis

Effects of Police and Corrections

Back to square one. The most disturbing result of these regressions is that a 1 per cent increase in police appears to *increase* the reported violent crime rate by about 0.8 per cent and the reported property crime rate by about 0.5 per cent, even when corrected for other conditions and for the joint determination of crime rates and public safety resources. The most plausible explanation of that result is that the presumed negative effect of more police on actual crime is outweighed by a positive effect of more police on the reporting rate. A strong assumption about the form of the relation between the reporting rate and the number of police and an estimate of the average reporting rate, however, is necessary to separate those effects.

Consider the following model:

$$C = a\,P^{-b}\,X^c, \tag{3.1}$$

$$RC = rC, \tag{3.2}$$

and

$$r = (1 - dP^{-1}), \tag{3.3}$$

where

C = the actual crime rate,

P = the number of police,

X = the set of other conditions that affect the actual crime rate,

RC = reported crime rate, and

r = the reporting rate.

In this case, the estimated elasticity of reported crime in response to the number of police is

$$E = -b + (d/P - d). \tag{3.4}$$

Since the regression yields an estimate of the elasticity of the reported crime rate on the number of police, an independent estimate of parameter *d* is sufficient to estimate parameter *b*. Now for the strong assumption: *if* equation (3.3) is a rough approximation of the relation between the reporting rate and the number of police *and* the reporting rate is independent of the several *X* variables, then parameter *d* can be derived from an estimate of the average reporting rate.

The NCVS provides estimates of the reporting rate for all major crimes except murder. For 1991 the estimated reporting rates for violent crime were 59 per cent for rape, 55 per cent for robbery and 58 per cent for aggravated assault. Assuming that all murders were reported, the weighted average reporting rate for the index of violent crimes was 57.2 per cent. Similarly, the estimated reporting rates for property crime were 50 per cent for burglary, 28 per cent for larceny and 74 per cent for auto theft. The weighted average reporting rate for the index property crimes was 34.4 per cent. Equation (3.3) can then be used to derive parameter *d* from those average reporting rates.

The elasticity of the actual crime rate with respect to the number of police, thus, is the elasticity of the reported crime rate presented in Table 3.3 minus the reporting bias ($d/P-d$). For violent crime, this yields a net effect that is not significantly different from zero. The elasticity of property crime, however, is −1.37 and is strongly significant. This indirect approach to estimating the effect of police on actual crime rates, thus, yields no significant effect on violent crime and a strong negative effect on property crime.[8] More police do make a difference, at least for property crime. The observed positive relation of the reported crime rate and the number of police is misleading, however, in that it reflects primarily a strong positive effect on the percentage of crimes reported.

An increase in the number of corrections employees appears to have no significant effect on violent crime and a small but significant *positive* effect on property crime. Both of those results are disturbing because there is no reason to expect the number of corrections employees to affect the reporting rate. More prison spaces are expected to have three effects: a deterrent effect on those never incarcerated, a sequestering effect on those in prison and some effect on postincarceration behaviour. The first two of those effects should have a combined negative effect on crime. The expected sign of the third effect is less clear. The early prison reform movement expected a prison term to have a negative effect on future criminal behaviour, wishfully calling juvenile jails reform schools and adult prisons penitentiaries. The older, more cynical, perspective regarded prisons as schools for crime. Whatever the combination of those effects, the disturbing evidence of this study is that more prison spaces and more corrections employees do not appear to reduce the reported crime rates.[9] The reasons for this result are not clear. One plausible explanation is that the rapid increase in the number of people imprisoned for drug offences has led to reduced sentences for those likely to commit more serious crimes.[10]

Economic Conditions

In general, as expected, an increase in legal economic opportunities reduces the crime rate. An increase in average annual income appears to reduce both violent crime and property crime by a roughly proportionate amount. An increase of 1 percentage point in the male unemployment rate appears to increase the violent crime rate by about 9 per cent. A 1 percentage point increase in the poverty rate appears to increase the property crime rate by about 3 per cent. The one surprising finding is that a 1 percentage point increase in the employment rate appears to *increase* the property crime rate by about 3 per cent; a plausible explanation is that more homes are vulnerable to burglary and more people vulnerable to theft when more women work outside the home, but more analysis is necessary to explain this strong unexpected finding.

Demographic and Cultural Conditions

Crime rates are especially high in metropolitan areas. A 1 percentage point increase in the share of a state's population that lives in metropolitan areas appears to increase both the violent and property crime rates by about 0.9 per cent, even when controlled for other characteristics of the population. The reason for this effect is less clear; the effect probably reflects a higher productivity of criminal behaviour relative to that of police in metropolitan areas, rather than a higher relative propensity for criminal behaviour of urban residents.

The violent crime rate, in turn, appears to be strongly dependent on the composition of the population. A 1 percentage point increase in births to single mothers appears to increase the violent crime rate by about 1.7 per cent. This effect, of course, is a proxy for more general patterns of social behaviour, not the direct effect, at least for a decade or so, of a current increase in births to single mothers. Similarly, a 1 percentage point increase in the minority (black or Hispanic) population appears to increase the violent crime rate by about 1.8 per cent.

Property crime, in contrast, appears to be related to only one significant behavioural condition. A 1 percentage point increase in church membership appears to reduce the property crime rate by about 0.5 per cent. Controlling for economic conditions and church membership, there do not appear to be any racial or other cultural effects on property crime.

Omitted Variables

Several conditions that are believed to affect crime rates or reporting rates were not included in the final regressions summarized in Table 3.3. A high proportion of crime, for example, is committed by young men. The percentage of the state population aged 18 to 24, however, has no significant effect on either the violent crime rate or the property crime rate. The NCVS reports that the reporting rate is unusually high among home owners and unusually low among Hispanic victims. Those variables also had no significant effect in either regression. 'But you didn't test my favourite explanation!' Yes, you are right. There is bound to be some condition that affects the crime rate or the reporting rate that I did not test. For the moment, that will continue to be the case.

The Test of Time

Do the conditions that explain the variation of crime rates among the states in 1991 help explain the changes in crime rates over time? Not much, is the simple answer. First, it is not obvious that actual crime rates have changed very much, at least since 1973 when the victimization survey was first collected. Most of the increase in the reported crime rate may reflect an increase in the reporting rate. Police per capita and real personal income per capita have roughly doubled since 1960, conditions that should have substantially reduced the actual crime rate. The male unemployment rate, the poverty rate and the percentage of church members are about the same. The employment rate, the percentage metropolitan and the percentage minority have each increased a few percentage points but not by an amount that would explain a substantial increase in the crime rate. The one condition that has changed substantially is the percentage of births to single mothers, increasing from 5 per cent in 1960 to 28 per cent in 1991. If the actual crime rate has increased, that increase appears to reflect some groups' increased tolerance of or propensity for crime, not a reduction in public safety resources or the returns to legal activity.

THE DEMAND FOR POLICE AND CORRECTIONS EMPLOYEES

The other side of the 'market for crime' is the demand for public safety resources. The numbers of police and corrections employees per capita, for example, are expected to be a negative function of their salary, a positive function of the average income in and average federal aid to the jurisdiction, and a positive function of the crime rate.

Again, the sample for this test is the 50 states and the District of Columbia. All data are for 1991. The average monthly salary of local government employees in the state is used as a proxy for the salary of police and corrections employees. All variables are weighted by the relative population of the state. Again, because public safety resources and the crime rate are jointly determined, the two-stage least-squares regression technique is used with the same instrumental variables as in the regressions on the supply of crimes. In this case, the estimates are based on linear regressions on the original levels of each included variable. Table 3.4 summarizes the results of these tests of the demand for police and corrections employees.

Effects of Fiscal Conditions

As expected, state and local governments economize on public safety employees in response to higher salaries. An increase of $100 in average monthly earnings leads to a reduction of about 0.8 police and 0.3 corrections employees per 10 000 residents. At the sample means, the corresponding earnings elasticity is –0.67 for police and –0.33 for corrections employees, both about equal (with sign reversed) to the payroll share of total costs.

The demand for public safety employees is a positive function of both the average income in the state and the per capita federal aid to governments in that state. An increase of $100 in average annual income leads to an increase of about 0.2 police and 0.05 corrections employees per 10 000 residents. At the sample means, the corresponding income elasticities are about 1.4 for police and 0.4 for corrections employees. Local residents apparently have a much stronger demand for police than for prisons.

An increase of $100 per capita in annual federal aid, in contrast, leads to an increase of about 0.5 police and 1.7 corrections employees per 10 000 population. The much higher marginal effect of federal aid on police and, especially, corrections employees reflects the typical 'flypaper' effect of federal aid plus a higher relative demand for prisons. In

Table 3.4 Effect of a 100-unit change on the demand for police and corrections employees

	Police	Corrections
Average monthly earnings	0.77	−0.28
	(0.09)	(0.16)
Average annual income	0.20	0.05
	(0.02)	(0.03)
Average annual federal aid	0.54	1.72
	(0.20)	(0.40)
Violent crime rate	1.02	1.02
	(0.13)	(0.36)
Property crime rate		0.23
		(0.09)
$\bar{R}^2$		
Weighted	0.994	0.978
Unweighted	0.722	0.836

Note: Numbers in parentheses are the standard errors of the coefficients.

summary, state and local governments will spend much more federal grant money on police and prisons than they would spend if the money came from state or local taxes. Measured by the interests of local residents, spending for police and prisons financed by federal grants is worth less than it costs.

Effects of the Crime Rate

The demand for police appears to be a function of the violent crime rate but not of the property crime rate. An increase of one reported violent crime per 100 000 residents leads to an increase of about one police officer per 10 000 residents. In this case, the coefficient on the actual crime rate is equal to the reporting rate times the estimated coefficient on the reported crime rate. At the sample mean, the elasticity of the demand for police with respect to the actual violent crime rate is about 0.16. A comparison with the supply of crime estimates suggests an interesting paradox: the

Policy analysis

demand for police appears to be a function of the violent crime rate, but more police appear to have no effect on that rate. The demand for police, in contrast, does not appear to be a function of the property crime rate, even though additional police would substantially reduce that rate. The reasons for that combination of findings are not clear.

The demand for corrections employees appears to be a function of both the violent crime rate and the property crime rate. An increase of one violent crime per 100 000 residents leads to an increase of about one corrections employee per 10 000 residents, and an increase of one property crime per 100 000 residents leads to an increase of about 0.2 corrections employee per 10 000 residents. Again, the effect of the actual crime rate is equal to the reporting rate times the estimated coefficient on the reported crime rate. At the sample means, the corresponding elasticities are about 0.21 for violent crime and about 0.20 for property crime.

In summary, an increase in the actual crime rate leads to a far smaller proportionate increase in public safety employees, increasing the number of crimes per police and corrections employee. That pattern, by reducing the percentage of crimes cleared by arrest and conviction and by reducing the expected sentence, appears to feed on itself. An increase in crime, by straining the resources of the public safety system, reduces the expected sanctions on criminal behaviour.

POLICY IMPLICATIONS

The major lesson of this study is how little is known about the actual level of crime, the effects of the public safety system, and the effects of other policies that affect crime.

The victimization survey provides an estimate of the actual level of crime at the national level, but the estimates based on that survey are strongly inconsistent with the data on reported crime. And estimates of actual crime are not available for state and local jurisdictions.

More police appear to increase the reported crime rate, but that observed effect is probably due to a strong effect of the number of police on the percentage of crimes reported. Controlling for that reporting rate effect, an increase in police appears to have no significant effect on the violent crime rate and a roughly proportionate negative effect on the property crime rate. More prisons and corrections employees appear to have no significant effect on the violent crime rate and a small positive effect on the property crime rate. The reason for the latter finding is not clear because there is no reason to expect that the reporting rate is a function of the number of corrections employees. There is strong popular support for a police-and-prisons strategy to reduce crime but surprisingly little supporting evidence.

Economic growth reduces many problems. An increase in real per capita income appears to reduce both the violent and property crime rates by a roughly proportionate amount. The economic conditions of specific groups are also important. An increase in the male unemployment rate has a strong positive effect on the violent crime rate, and an increase in the poverty rate has a strong positive effect on the property crime rate. For reasons that are less clear, an increase in the general employment rate appears to increase the property crime rate. The implication of those findings is that an economic growth strategy may more effectively reduce crime than a public safety strategy, especially if it leads to higher employment and income for teenage males, minorities and the poor.

Both the perpetrators and the victims of crime are increasingly concentrated among minority groups in the inner cities. Over time, the two conditions most strongly correlated with the increase in reported crime are the unemployment rate for teenage males and the percentage of infants born to single mothers. And the results of this study, based on state data for 1991, are roughly consistent with the effects of those conditions over time. Both of those conditions have increased sharply. As of 1954 (the first year for which such data were collected), the black teenage unemployment rate was about the same as the rate for white teenage males; since then, the black rate has increased to more than twice the white rate. The increase in the percentage of births to single mothers is a more general condition. Since 1960 that rate has increased from 2 per cent to 22 per cent for whites and from 22 per cent to 68 per cent for blacks. The reasons for the increase in those two conditions are not clear, and the policy changes that would reduce those conditions are even less clear. But those two conditions should be the focus of any targeted crime prevention programme. Economists may not have the best judgement on these issues, because they appear to reflect a substantial change in cultural values across generations.

The most important policy advice, given the surprising paucity of evidence about what works, is to *decentralize* decisions on the public safety system and on crime prevention programmes. Our federal system provides a continuous natural policy experiment if the federal government stays out of the way. If you do not know where the fish are, cast your net broadly. If you do not know what works, do not do the same thing everywhere. Experiment with a variety of policies and be prepared to learn from the experiments in other jurisdictions. Most important, local governments should experiment with different ways of deploying police and state governments with different types of sanctions for nonviolent crimes. Moreover, for those who still care, that approach would be more consistent with the letter and spirit of the Constitution. That is why the next step on crime should be to repeal the Violent Crime Control and Law Enforcement Act of 1994.

NOTES

1. *Statistical Abstract of the United States, 1993*, Washington: Government Printing Office, 1994, p. 189.
2. Quoted in 'Crime bill is target of GOP attack', *Miami Herald*, 10 August 1994.
3. 'Crime bill losers', *Wall Street Journal*, 19 August 1994. Calculation by Stephen Moore of the Cato Institute.
4. *Conference Report on the Violent Crime Control and Law Enforcement Act of 1994*, Washington: Government Printing Office, 1994, p. 391.
5. The estimated violent crime rate reported in Table 3.1 has been revised from the published rate by adding the reported murder rate and subtracting the estimated rate of simple assaults; that makes the coverage identical to the reported rate. The estimated property crime rate has not been revised, and the coverage is smaller than that of the reported property crime rate by the amount of commercial property crime.
6. The observation for the District of Columbia, with the nation's highest murder rate and 89 police per 10 000 residents in 1991, is literally off the chart. A similar relation between the reported crime rate and the number of corrections employees is even stronger and tighter.
7. Gary Becker, 'Crime and punishment: an economic approach', *Journal of Political Economy*, March–April 1968; Isaac Erlich, 'Participation in illegitimate activities:a theoretical and empirical investigation', *Journal of Political Economy*, May–June 1973: 521–67; Steven Craig, 'The deterrent impact of police: an examination of a locally provided public service', *Journal of Urban Economics*, **21**, 1987: 298–311; William N. Trumbull, 'Estimations of the economic model of crime using aggregate and individual level of data', *Southern Economic Journal*, **26**(2), October 1989: 423–39; and Helen Tauchen, Ann Dryden Witte and Harriet Griesinger, 'Criminal deterrence: revisiting the issue with a birth cohort', National Bureau of Economic Research Working Paper No. 4277, February 1993.
8. Two other statistical approaches were tried in an attempt to estimate the effect of police on the actual (but unknown) crime rates. One approach was to use a weighted nonlinear regression with the logarithm of the reporting rate equation $(1 - dP^{-1})$ as an independent variable. The other approach was to estimate the actual crime rate by dividing the reported rate by $(1 - dP^{-1})$ and then using a weighted two-stage regression on the estimated actual rate. Those two approaches yielded small negative but insignificant estimates of the effect of police on violent crime, with an estimated elasticity of –0.2 and little change in the other coefficients. Those two approaches yielded strongly negative and significant estimates of the effect of police on property crime, with estimated elasticities of –1 and –1.5 and some changes in the other coefficients. In the absence of data on actual crime rates, there is no one best way to estimate this relation, but the general consistency of the results of the three approaches is encouraging.
9. The number of prisoners per capita and the number of corrections employees per capita are closely correlated and essentially interchangeable in statistical analysis.
10. David Kopel, 'Prison blues: how America's foolish sentencing policies endanger public safety', Cato Institute Policy Analysis No. 208, 17 May 1994.

4. The defence resource-allocation process*

INTRODUCTION

Department of Defense budgets were approximately $50 billion a year from fiscal year 1962 to fiscal year 1965 – an amount representing 8 to 10 per cent of the US gross national product. This chapter summarizes and evaluates the process of determining the total defence budget and the allocation of funds among the major defence activities. The gross characteristics of the present defence programme are outlined, the programme-change process is described, and several general problems of defence management are identified.

It is important to recognize that the focus of this chapter is upon the decisions to provide military forces, not upon the decisions to use these forces as an instrument of US policy – upon resource allocation, not upon resource utilization. The complex decision process by which US military forces are controlled, operated, deployed and committed interacts, over a period, with the resource-allocation process, involving some of the same people and component organizations. But is beyond the scope of this chapter to describe and evaluate the short-run resource-utilization process.

THE DEFENCE PROGRAMME

US military forces are now more powerful and flexible than at any time in our peacetime history, and a major share of the credit for the improved capabilities of these forces must be granted to the eighth Secretary of Defense, Robert S. McNamara. The defence programme – representing the aggregate of existing and planned military forces, support activities,

* Reprinted by permission from Stephen Enke (ed.), *Defense Management*, Englewood Cliffs, NJ: Prentice-Hall, 1967, pp. 4–22.
  This was my first article published for a general readership.

and funding – is also subject to greater control by McNamara than was the case with any of his predecessors. What are the primary instruments that McNamara and his principal assistants have used to shape and control the defence programme? What are the historical and institutional reasons for the use of these instruments? Most importantly, perhaps, what part of the substantial recent improvement in the capabilities of US military forces represents the personal contribution of McNamara and his assistants, and what part is attributable to the use of these new instruments of programme control?

The basic directive governing the defence programme defines clearly and forcefully the primary instrument of programme control:

> The 'Five Year Force Structure and Financial Program, is the official program for the Department of Defense. The programming system, outlined herein, will provide the means for submission, review, record keeping, and decision making on the DoD program. The planning, programming, resource, material, and financial management systems of all DoD components will be correlated with the programming system set forth herein.[1]

The Five-Year Program is a set of tables, updated quarterly, which presents the officially approved level of military forces and support activities, manpower and funding. These characteristics of the defence programme are displayed and controlled in two critical dimensions:

- *output* – related information by major mission and activity, and
- *time* – related information for several prior years, the current fiscal year, and a subsequent five-year period.

These two dimensions of control represent the major changes from the type of programme control that existed prior to 1961. Until that time, Congress and the Department of Defense had exercised programme control through appropriations by military service and by input category for a single fiscal year. Although Congress still exercises its primary control of the defence programme in this way, the Department of Defense analyses, formulates and controls the defence programme by the mission and activity categories for a five-year planning period: funding by service and input categories is a byproduct of the present defence programme rather than its basic building block.

The Historical Basis

Some lessons from recent history will better explain the reason for this fundamental change in the dimensions of defence-programme control. If these new concepts of programme control are now so important, how did the US until 1961 (and other nations up to the present) manage defence programmes with any effectiveness? In retrospect, the reason is clear: *resource control by component organizations provides an adequate basis for programme control only if there is a strong separation of missions by organization.* This condition prevailed until the end of World War II, but considerable interservice mission competition developed in the postwar period.

Until the end of World War II, the Army, Navy and (Army) Air Force each had a single primary mission. The primary Army mission was that of sustained land combat in the European and Pacific theatres. In addition, at the start of the war the Army had maintained a small coast artillery force (which rapidly lost importance) and also operated the troopships throughout the war. The primary Navy mission was that of sea combat against other naval forces; the Navy also provided the coastal defence against submarines and supported the movement of troops and cargo to the theatres. Even the Marines and the air forces presented less competition to the similar Army and Air Force forces than that which developed in the postwar period; the Marines were used primarily as navy-supported assault forces and only in the Pacific theatre; and the carrier air forces were used primarily against other naval forces and for support of assault operations beyond the reach of land-based tactical air forces. The primary Air Force mission was tactical air support of land combat in both theatres; during the course of the war the Air Force also developed forces for the strategic air mission against the German and Japanese heartlands and also operated a small air-transport force. For the most part, the services had different types of forces and, even for similar forces, noncompetitive mission responsibilities.

After World War II, this separation of mission responsibilities broke down as a consequence of the rapid development of military technology and the different character of the potential military opposition. Each of the services developed forces in new mission areas as a hedge against changes in strategic concepts and military technology. An attempt to limit interservice competition, was made in the Key West Agreement of 1947, but this agreement was rapidly – and understandably – undermined.

The Army, until recently, had been least successful in broadening its mission base; and, as a consequence, its existence as a major force was threatened by the 'massive retaliation' strategy following the Korean War. During the late 1950s, they based an unsuccessful case for operation of the strategic missile force upon their development of the intermediate-range Jupiter missile and upon the doctrinal argument that 'missiles are artillery'. The Army did develop effective surface-to-air missile systems for continental defence, a substantial force of light aircraft and helicopters, and a forward stockage posture to complement the airlift and sealift forces. Sustained land combat is still the primary Army mission, however, and at present this service is the only one characterized by a single dominant mission.

The Navy, whose position was threatened by the absence of a significant Soviet surface navy, was most successful in broadening its mission base. They developed an effective contribution to the strategic offence forces, first with the carrier air forces and subsequently with the Polaris missile submarines; they also developed substantial antisubmarine forces to defend coastal waters and to protect sealift to the theatre where the large Soviet submarine force would be a threat. The Marines have been partly transformed from a navy-supported assault force to a more independent, sustained land-combat force. The carrier air forces have been reoriented to provide tactical air support for land combat in all theatres.

The Air Force, believing that the dominance of the strategic offence had been proved by the World War II strikes against the German and Japanese heartlands, concentrated for a long time after World War II on long-range delivery vehicles and nuclear weapons. During the late 1950s, however, the Air Force developed a substantial continental air-defence force and, more recently, a substantial tactical air force and airlift force.

At present, antisubmarine warfare is the only mission which is the single responsibility of one service (the Navy, in this case). The separate service contributions to each of the other missions are sufficient to present effective competition for a larger part of the mission resources.

The Administration and Congress recognized the major operational problems raised by interservice competition for a given mission and passed the Defense Reorganization Act of 1958. This Act established Unified Commands on a mission and theatre basis with the primary responsibility for operational control of associated forces. It did not, however, address the major problems presented by this competition regarding the planning and control of the defence programme. During the late 1950s, there was a growing recognition that the civilian administration of the Department of Defense had been losing control of the central political element of the defence programme – the allocation of resources among missions. The traditional role of the political and management processes had been inverted: the allocation of resources among missions, properly a political decision, was being made primarily by the services; the allocation of resources within missions, properly a management decision, was often being made in the political arena.

Several major controversies among the services on how to perform a given mission became public issues that were resolved only by bargaining and fiat.

Two substantially different solutions were developed during the late 1950s to correct this situation. The first proposed solution, linked with some of most distinguished names in the eastern business and legal community, would have eliminated service competition by creating a single service or by reorganizing the services along clearly defined mission lines. (The Soviet military establishment incidentally, is organized along these lines.) This proposal would have maintained programme control by component organization through a significant restructuring of the component organizations.

The second proposed solution, developed primarily by a group of economists the RAND Corporation, involved a change in programme control from a service to a mission base; the services would maintain their present form and would continue to compete with each other for each of the major missions. This proposal was outlined in publications by David Novick[2] in 1954 and 1956 and by Charles Hitch and Roland McKean[3] in 1960. The proposed programme format presented military forces and funding by mission aggregations and funding for major groups of support activities. The mission aggregations were designed to focus the political choices primarily upon the allocation of resources among missions and the management choices primarily upon the allocation within missions. The proposal also presented both forces and funding for a five-year planning period, in order to identify the long-range commitments inherent in the decisions of any one fiscal year.

The Experience Since 1961

After the presidential campaign of 1960, in which the defence programme was a major issue, John F. Kennedy appointed Robert McNamara as Secretary of Defense and Charles J. Hitch as the Defense Comptroller. Before six months had passed, the programme format proposed by the RAND economists became the Five-Year Force Structure and Financial Program, with few changes. This set of tables, originally considered 'the Secretary's book', became the only official programme statement and was soon recognized, with some concern, as a powerful instrument for control of the defence programme. From 1961 to the Vietnam buildup, total defence expenditures increased by about 10 per cent, and the defence programme was substantially strengthened in most major areas. Because these changes to the defence programme and the use of new management techniques are both associated with McNamara's administration of the

Department of Defense, it is understandable that the programme changes
are generally attributed to the management changes. A careful examination of the published information, however, raises the serious question of
whether the major changes to date *are*, in any fundamental way, attributable to the new management techniques.

The nature, magnitude and timing of the major programme changes
can be adequately identified from the annual unclassified statements on
the defence programme by the Secretary of Defense. Table 4.1 presents a
financial summary of the defence programme for the fiscal years 1961 to
1966. The financial summary itself suggests many of the major changes.
The funding information is not conclusive of course, because the
component funding levels are large and major changes could be implemented within a constant mission funding. The detailed force tables that
accompany the financial summary are classified, but the published information is sufficient to identify the major force levels and the timing of the
force-level decisions.

Table 4.1 The defence programme: financial summary by fiscal year

	FY62	FY62 Orig.	FY62 Final	FY63	FY64	FY65	FY66 Prop.
Strategic forces		(total obligational authority, in billions)					
Offence	—	7.6	9.0	8.4	7.3	5.3	4.5
Air and missile defence	—	2.2	2.0	1.9	2.0	1.7	1.6
Civil defence	—	–	0.3	0.1	0.1	0.1	0.2
Total	—	9.8	11.3	10.4	9.4	7.1	6.3
Tactical forces							
General purpose	—	14.5	17.4	17.6	17.7	18.1	19.0
Airlift and sealift	—	0.9	1.2	1.4	1.3	1.5	1.6
Reserves	—	1.7	1.8	1.8	2.0	2.1	2.0
Military assistance	—	1.8	1.8	1.6	1.2	1.2	1.3
Total	—	18.9	22.2	22.4	22.2	22.9	23.9
Support activities							
General support	—	11.4	12.1	13.0	13.7	14.3	14.6
Research and development	—	3.9	4.2	5.1	5.3	5.1	5.4
Retired pay	—	0.9	0.9	1.0	1.2	1.4	1.5
Total	—	16.2	17.2	19.1	20.2	20.8	21.5
Total obligational authority	46.1	44.9	50.7	51.9	51.9	50.9	51.7

The major changes suggested by Table 4.1 are the consequence of two major concerns about the US defence programme – the survivability of the US strategic offensive forces and the adequacy and mobility of US tactical forces – which were raised, beginning in 1956, primarily by informed civilians outside the federal government. The first concern stemmed from the spectacular Soviet missile and space developments beginning in 1956 and the 'intelligence gap' following the May 1960, U–2 incident, which raised serious questions about the survivability of the US strategic offence forces (at that time consisting primarily of a warning-dependent bomber force). The second concern stemmed from the Suez and Hungary crises of 1956 and the Lebanon and Quemoy crises of 1958. These events raised serious doubts whether the US had sufficient tactical forces and mobility to counter military threats that its strategic forces did not deter and for which the use of these forces was clearly purposeless. The Kennedy administration came into office in 1961 with a commitment to correct these problems and already well-developed ideas for changing the defence programme.

It is surprising how quickly these ideas were translated into the defence programme and how few subsequent changes have been made. In late 1960 the Eisenhower administration had prepared a FY 1962 defence budget of $44.9 billion and had left office with a sombre warning about the size of the US military–industrial establishment. During the first few months of 1961, before the existence of the new programme format or a formal programming system, the Office of the Secretary of Defense (OSD) prepared a revised FY 1962 defence budget of $50.7 billion, incorporating many of the force-level decisions still effective. During the remainder of 1961, with the programming system in a formative stage and with service contributions only nominal, OSD prepared a FY 1963 defence budget of $51.9 billion, incorporating most of the major force-level decisions that remained in effect until the 1965 Vietnam buildup.

A review of the FY 1963 defence programme submitted to Congress in January 1962 illustrates how few major changes postdate this programme. Although the Department of Defense, unlike other federal agencies, does not formally develop its programme from a tentative budget estimate, the total defence budget prior to the Vietnam buildup did not change by more than $1 billion (or 2 per cent) from the budgets prepared in 1961. Improvements in the efficiency of defence management, of course, have increased the 'real output' of the defence programme, but the growth of 'output' since 1961 has been essentially constrained by the rate at which economies derived from an improved combination of forces and the cost reduction programme could be realized. Basic decisions on the size of the strategic offence and defence forces reflected in the FY 1963 programme are still effective. The quality of the strategic offence force has been improved, for example, by the recent decisions to procure the FB–111 and the Minuteman II and Poseidon missile systems, but the total numbers of both bombers and missiles are essentially those programmed in 1961. The strategic defence force reflects the still current decision to thin out the air-defence force and strengthen civil defence. The FY 1963 programme includes the aggregate Army, Navy and Marine general-purpose forces that were effective until the recent Vietnam buildup and only a slightly smaller land-based tactical air force; this programme also reflects the basic decisions to strengthen the airlift, sealift and reserve forces and thin out the military-assistance programme. Within a constant number of divisions and tactical air wings, of course, some improvements were made, such as the organization of the air-cavalry division and the development of the A–7 fighter bomber. The growth of the general-support programme (primarily for improved command and control) and the research and development programme were also largely planned at this time.

Since 1961, within a constant total budget, approximately $5 billion has been transferred from the strategic forces to various support activities, and the decisions reflected by this transfer were largely made in this first programme. None of this discussion questions the correctness of the decisions, but it does suggest that the major programme decisions were made on the basis of objectives defined, ideas developed, and analysis performed before the effective use of the new management techniques and, largely, outside the government.

During 1962, the first full year of the programming system, the services responded with enthusiasm to McNamara's open-ended invitation to submit programme-change proposals based on their perceived requirements; the resulting FY 1964 programme differed hardly at all from the FY 1963 programme in either force levels or funding. The services had a direct confrontation with McNamara's analysts for the first time in 1962, and the result was a nearly wholesale rejection of the service proposals. From that year, unfortunately, the analytic process has often been associated with the refutation of service arguments rather than with the initiation and channelling of continued change.

Partly as a consequence of the use of the new programme format and supporting analysis, two major opportunities for substantial improvement in the defence programme have been identified in the past few years: the characteristics of a balanced defence against nuclear attack are now better understood; and the cost of achieving high survival levels is less than that previously estimated. The level and characteristics of an effective nonnuclear defence against a Soviet attack on Europe are also better understood, and the costs are much less than previously estimated. The president and Congress have the basic responsibility for the political choice of whether or not the Department of Defense should provide these capabilities. Both issues are complex and involve other parties, but it is disturbing that the two major programme issues that have developed since 1961 are not yet resolved one way or another. The defence programming system has proved to be an effective instrument of programme control; only some period of external pressure, such as the Vietnam War, will prove whether or not it can be an effective instrument of programme change.

THE DEFENCE PROGRAMME-CHANGE PROCESS

The programme-change process used on the Department of Defense since 1962 merits serious study – whatever one's interpretation of its effectiveness during this period. This is true because similar processes will be adopted by other federal agencies, and there are important lessons to be gleaned from the defence experience by both the advocate and critic. A summary of the programme-budget cycle serves as the best introduction to the characteristics of this process and the role of the component organizations. Table 4.2 presents a schema of this cycle in 1965 for preparation of the FY 1967 programme and budget. A number of important features of this process should be recognized at the outset. First, the annual budget cycle is about eighteen months long (in this case, from August 1964 to January 1966). As a result, the component organizations, for some period, must begin preparation of the following programme before the final decisions on the present programme are made. Second, this process as been changed in some respect every year and will probably be subject to continued periodic change.[4]

Planning

The programme-budget cycle begins in effect in August, eighteen months before the defence programme is presented to Congress and about two years before funds are appropriated. At this time the services and unified commands begin to prepare force recommendations to be reviewed by the Joint Chiefs of Staff (JCS) and presented in the Joint Strategic Objectives Plan (JSOP), Part VI. These recommendations are presumably based on a

Table 4.2 *Department of Defense Program – budget process for preparation of FY 1967 budget*

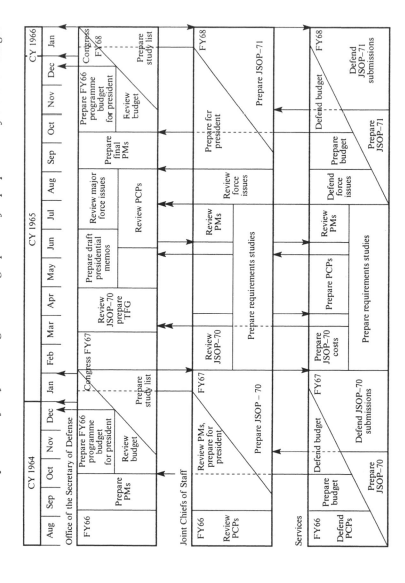

44

review of the world situation, an interpretation of US national security policy, and an agreement on the mission responsibilities of the component organizations. This background work is completed in the prior March–June period and presented in the JSOP, Parts I–V; it reflects the traditional military approach that desired force levels can somehow be derived from the military threat and national policy statements; according to this approach, the costs of military forces determine only the difference between the desired and budgeted force levels. At present, the JSOP, Parts I–V, which include some incisive political analysis, are largely unread and almost totally ignored. The services and unified commands each propose a single array of forces, rather than a menu of alternatives with estimates of the respective military capabilities and costs; the language of these submissions suggests that a specific force level is either 'required' or it is not. The service force recommendations usually reflect an estimate of 'reasonably attainable' budget levels (often about 20 per cent more than the present budget), but it is not clear that force costs enter the determination of the composition of forces. Force recommendations of the unified commands are almost completely unaffected by economic considerations and, as such, are of little value; these submissions to the JSOP (which the Office of the Secretary of Defense does not usually see) are the only formal contribution by the unified commands to the defence programme-change process, with the exception, oddly enough, of their major role in planning the military-assistance programme.

About 15 September, the Joint Staff begins a review of the recent requirements studies and the service and unified command force recommendations as the basis for preparing the JSOP proposed forces. The force levels are now reviewed in three major groups: the strategic offence and defence forces, the general-purpose forces, and the airlift and sealift forces. This review includes a good deal of continued discussion with the military components as well as, in recent years, formal analysis of increasing quality. (This exercise is always hectic, as most of the analysis has to be completed before the final decisions on the present programme are made.) The Chiefs review the force levels and associated costs proposed by the Joint Staff in February and on 1 March transmit their force-level recommendations to OSD in the format of the official defence programme. In some cases, the analysis presented in the JSOP may indicate the relationship of capability and cost for several force levels; the JSOP recommends a single array of force levels, however, unless one service has recommended an alternative level for some forces. In recent years, the aggregate cost of the JSOP recommended forces has been about 20 per cent higher than the present budget.

Programming

The Office of the Secretary of Defense reviews the JSOP in March. In 1965, this review was translated into a set of Tentative Force Guidance (TFG) tables, which provided initial guidance to the services in preparing their Programme Change Proposals (PCPs). The services are directed not to appeal this initial guidance, and they are discouraged from submitting a PCP not in accord with this guidance. Formally, PCPs are used only to review the detailed costs and to update the official programme, not to review the basic force level. In fact, the TFG tables are usually incomplete and subject to change, and many small issues are resolved during the PCP review.[5]

After transmitting the TFG to the Services on 1 April, McNamara and his staff begin preparation of the draft memoranda to the president (PMs) on each major mission area and support activity. These memoranda, of which there are now twelve, cover such topics as the strategic offence and defence forces, the antisubmarine warfare forces, and the research and development programme; they summarize the major force levels proposed, the rationale for choice among these alternatives, and the recommended force levels and funding. These memoranda, which are the basic statement on the defence programme by the Secretary of Defense to the military components and to the president, are explicit, critical, surprisingly honest and based on analysis of generally high quality. McNamara now sends these memoranda to the JCS and services in June for review of the recommended forces; these reviews are sent to OSD during July, and the major remaining issues are resolved by the end of August. The draft memoranda and the military reviews are now the primary decision documents of the defence-programming system, and the exchange among the contesting parties is usually spirited. McNamara has often overruled a majority of the JCS, but seldom has he overruled all the Chiefs on a force-level issue; this places a high premium on consensus with all the consequent bargaining. Although the force-level decisions made through this process are sometimes substantially different from the initial guidance, the services do not prepare new PCPs to implement the change; the decisions are merely transmitted to the services in the standard format for replying to a PCP.

The services and other defence components currently submit Program Change Proposals for all force and support changes above a specified threshold by 15 June. About three hundred PCPs are now submitted, most of which involve programme elements not covered by the Tentative Force Guidance; all but a few of the PCPs are submitted by the services.

The PCPs present the presently approved and proposed force structure, manpower, and funding by programme element, and some supporting analysis is usually attached; the PCP submissions, unfortunately, seldom convey any sense of priority either among submissions or in relation to the base programme. These PCPs are reviewed during the June–August period by the OSD office of primary interest – most of the proposed force changes by Systems Analysis, the logistics changes by Installations and Logistics, the development changes by Research and Engineering, and so on. Decisions on these PCPs are issued by the end of August, and there is no formal procedure for appealing the outcome.

Preparation and review of the PCPs is a considerable and, possibly, unnecessary chore; most of the PCPs involve such minor issues that they could be incorporated in the budget review later in the year. During this same period the major force issues must be resolved by the same offices through the preparation and review of the draft memoranda to the president. This was not always so. During 1962 and 1963, without any Tentative Force Guidance, the PCPs were the primary decision documents, and the draft memoranda to the president were used mostly to summarize the decisions of the PCP review. In order to reduce the number of 'unrealistic' PCPs, OSD initiated the use of the Tentative Force Guidance and greatly increased its role in the programme-change process.

Budgeting

In September, on the basis of the programme decisions made during the parallel review of the draft memoranda to the president and the PCPs, the services prepare the budget for the next fiscal year in the traditional budget categories. OSD and the Bureau of the Budget review the budget submissions during October and November. Presumably, all major decisions should be resolved by this time, but these budget offices initiate about six hundred Subject Issues, identifying areas of potential saving. The Subject Issues are not intended to change the earlier force-level decisions, but they have sometimes undermined the effectiveness of these forces by reducing support resources. Budget-review decisions have a different time horizon from the programme review discussed earlier: the programme decisions generally have a long-term cost basis, whereas budget decisions are based on a single fiscal year. It is often difficult to make a case (in the budget review) for spending resources now to save funds in the future. In any case, this final budget review, reflecting a remarkably detailed understanding of defence expenditures, usually reduces the total defence budget by several billion dollars.

During this same period, the OSD staff is also completing the final draft memoranda to the president based on the August decisions; the statement to Congress by the Secretary of Defense in turn, is based on these memoranda, including the basic organization, style and analysis of these internal documents. The Joint Chiefs of Staff have one more court of appeal – their December visit with the president – at which a number of major programmes have been decided. Such last-minute changes are incorporated in the new budget for transmittal to the president in late December. The Secretary's statement to Congress is usually prepared for presentation late in January.

The last step of a defence programme-budget cycle is, of course, the first step of the next cycle. This step is characteristic of the best features of the present defence-management techniques. On the basis of the problems identified during the cycle just completed, OSD and, more recently, the services, draw up lists of important studies that should be completed to assist the forthcoming programme reviews. The Secretary's project list is received by the JCS and the services in late January, and a six-month study cycle begins. The resulting studies, in turn, form the basis for both support and review of the proposed defence-programme changes. The study process is more subtle and less hurried than the formal programme-change process; and the integration of these two processes may be the most important feature of the new defence-management techniques.

SOME PROBLEMS AND PROPOSED SOLUTIONS

A review of the five-year history of the new defence resource-allocation process reveals three major problem areas:

1. Military components do not effectively express their priorities.
2. The resource-management process is highly centralized.
3. Some of the major defence resources are substantially underpriced and, thus, require special management.

The Problem of Priorities

A recommended defence programme reflects two kinds of judgements: the professional judgement (based on experience or analysis) that a given mission budget should be allocated for certain forces and the political judgement that so much capability is desired and so much should be spent in each mission area. The defence programme proposed by the military components, through the JSOP and PCPs, seldom separate these two kinds of judgement; these documents, which propose a single force level or an array of force levels, do not identify the effect of higher or lower mission budgets on the proposed force composition. The JCS and service force recommendations for a given mission budget merit respect on the basis of the professional judgement of the senior officers of the US military establishment; the force levels and budgets by mission areas proposed by the JCS merit respect on the basis of their political judgement as informed citizens, an issue on which their vote is important but not decisive. There is now no formal mechanism that the military components can use to explicitly state their estimates of the efficient force composition for a given mission budget; as a consequence, the Secretary of Defense has assumed the primary responsibility for these management decisions.

A part of this problem is attributable to McNamara's ambivalent guidance. Without establishing an explicit budget guidance, he has invited the JCS and services, to submit force recommendations based on their perceived requirements – but his decisions have implied that these 'requirements' had better not increase the defence budget. The Department of Defense has operated under a strong implicit budget constraint without making effective use of this constraint as a planning instrument. The military components, however, must bear most of the responsibility for this problem. At present, the only military components whose responsibility spans the major mission areas are the unified commands and the Joint Chiefs of Staff. Most of the force-structure planning outside OSD, however, is performed by the services, which provide only part of the forces in each major mission area (except the antisubmarine warfare forces). The unified commands have no budgets and no planning responsibility for their own forces; a weak attempt by OSD to permit the unified commands to comment on the PCPs was vigorously opposed by the services. With no budgets or planning responsibility, the submissions by the unified command to JSOP (their only formal contributions to the defence programme-change process) have little value.

The JCS have no budget, but they do have a fundamental planning responsibility. The basic limitation on the potential contribution of the JCS is its role as a legislative body, rather than an independent review and analysis group.[6] It consists, after all, of the service Chiefs of Staff, and it should not be surprising that the officers on the Joint Staff are often chosen to represent service positions. In this situation, faced by a strong Secretary of Defense, consensus is more important than objectivity; and consensus is much easier to achieve by proposing larger defence programmes that do not threaten the present position of any component. The consensus usually breaks down under explicit budget constraints in which an improved position of one component clearly threatens the position of other components. In fact, the JCS contribution is greater than this situation implies, but only because individual officers bring to their task considerable energy and devotion to broad national objectives.

The military contribution to the force-planning process would be greatly improved by reorganizing the JSOP to present alternative recommended forces for several mission budgets. For each major mission, a group from the Joint Staff, working with officers from the relevant unified commands and services, would prepare what they believed to be the most efficient combination of forces for three mission budgets – 10 per cent below the current level, equal to the current level, and 10 per cent above. The mission budgets should probably be defined in terms of the five-year programme costs with future costs discounted at a positive rate to discourage transfer of funds to the early years. This mission review group would also evaluate the capabilities of the forces at each budget level, given the programmed level of complementary US and allied forces. This group would present, in the language of economics, a part of the 'supply curve' of the military forces in this mission area. If one service objected to the combination of forces proposed by this group, it would be obliged to prepare alternative combinations for each budget level, evaluate the capabilities, and explain the basis for proposing forces other than those outlined by the mission review group. The recommended forces for three budget levels for each major mission, as modified and approved by the majority of the JCS, would be the primary output of the JSOP. It would also be valuable, but less important, for the JCS to recommend a single array of forces for all missions and the total defence budget that they, as informed citizens, believe the nation should support. The military components include many officers both capable of and interested in making such a contribution, but the nature of the system is such that OSD initiative would probably be necessary to effect this change.[7]

The Problem of Centralization

The substantial centralization of defence management since 1961 is indicated by the grumbling of lower-level managers, the substantial increase in the OSD staff, the small problems for which OSD approval is routinely required, and by the increasing concern about who could succeed McNamara in the role that he has created as Secretary of Defense. The costs of this centralization are suggested by comparing defence management with that of the most efficient (and much smaller) private industrial firms. The primary indictment of the present centralized process, however, is its failure to be an effective instrument of continued change.[8]

The centralization of political decisions regarding the total defence budget and its allocation among missions is the key element of the present decision process and is probably necessary for effective civilian control of the US military establishment. But the centralization of the management decisions regarding the allocation of resources within each mission area is a matter of style. In the short run, this style may not be detrimental so long as the Secretary of Defense and his staff are as capable and hard working as is now the case and so long as the morale and judgement of the lower-level managers are not eroded. The sluggishness of continued programme change, however, suggests that the increased centralization of defence management may already be having a detrimental effect upon national security interests. What important first steps should be considered to reverse the centralization of resource management?

The primary requisite of effective decentralized management is that the objectives of the lower-level managers promote actions that are generally consistent with the objectives of the organization. In a profit-maximizing organization a lower-level manager can be rewarded for efficiency by higher pay or a share of the profits, whether or not his actions lead to an increase or decrease in the resources under his control; in a bureaucratic organization, a lower-level manager is rewarded primarily on the basis of the size of the activity under his control. If the demand for the output of his activity is highly elastic, the manager can maximize the size of his activity, and his own objectives, by efficient management. But if the demand for the output of his activity is highly inelastic, he can garner these rewards through inefficient management. Because the demands for the output of many aggregate defence activities are inherently inelastic, the only way to provide an incentive for efficiency is to divide the aggregate activity among several component organizations and to present each resource manager with competition whose supply curve is highly elastic. Paradoxically, the situation that led to control of the defence programme by missions – the competition among the services in the major mission areas – is the primary requisite for decentralization of the management decisions within each mission area. It is not surprising that there is collusion among component organizations in both industry and government in an attempt to restrict competition among themselves – but such agreements should not be reinforced by public policy. Many of our present tactical concepts and weapons systems are the products of interservice competition. Perhaps the Key West Agreement should be rewritten to encourage each of the services to develop both concepts and weapons systems in any mission area.

The first step towards increasing the management responsibility at lower organizational levels would proceed from the proposed changes in the JSOP outlined above. On the basis of the alternative force levels and budgets for each mission area presented in the revised JSOP, OSD should issue a Tentative *Budget* Guidance for each mission area. In most cases, this Tentative Budget Guidance should be accompanied by a statement of marginal objectives, such as the value of systems that are less dependent on warning relative to those that are more dependent, or the value of present capability relative to future capability. The primary concern about issuing budget guidance by service – that is, that they would reallocate resources among missions – would thus be avoided.

The services would then prepare PCPs that they were prepared to support within the Tentative Budget Guidance for the overall mission. These PCPs would first be transmitted to the Joint Staff mission review group that was responsible for preparing the JSOP forces in this area. This group would evaluate the competing service proposals and again prepare what they believe to be the most efficient combination of forces for this mission, in this case, within the Tentative Budget Guidance; this combination might not be the same as that recommended in JSOP, since the budget level might be different, new information might have developed, or one service might be able to make a better case for its forces in this mission. The programme recommended by this mission review group and the service PCPs would be sent as a package to OSD for review of the competing proposals, the cost estimates and consistency with the earlier guidance on marginal objectives. All the PCPs in each mission area would be reviewed at the same time, first by the Joint Staff and then by OSD. The OSD review should be greatly assisted by the prior Joint Staff review of the mission programme. During the OSD review, the services would have the opportunity to defend PCPs that the Joint Staff group recommends for disapproval. This procedure would substantially change the responsibilities for programme planning – the services and JCS, not OSD, would have the primary responsibility for preparing balanced forces in each mission area, within the political guidance on mission budgets and marginal objectives.

After OSD has completed its review of the programmes recommended by the Joint Staff mission review group and the service PCPs, the services would prepare budgets based on the force-level decisions. Since a final budget review would probably still be valuable, all proposed expenditures not considered by the mission reviews could be incorporated in the budget submission. The memoranda to the president would merely summarize the major decisions and the rationale for choice rather than serve as the primary decision document.

The effectiveness of this procedure depends on the ability of the Joint Staff to serve as a professional, independent review and force-planning group. Some scepticism on this point is justified; but it is characteristic of the US military establishment that capability follows real responsibility, and the challenge and excitement of an important role in the force-planning process should attract the best talent in the system. If this procedure should not work out, the only other obvious way to decentralize the major management decisions would be more radical: to issue the Tentative Budget Guidance to the unified commands and permit them to 'buy' forces from the services. Full exploitation of the 'buyer–seller' device to induce efficient management may, at some time, involve this next step, but institutions that survive do not take giant steps in the dark.

The Problem of Resource Pricing

No organization, however the management responsibilities are divided, can efficiently allocate resources if the prices faced by the decision maker do not reflect the full value of these resources. The Department of Defense, however, acquires and uses several major resources at prices considerably below their full value. The most important examples are military manpower, land and nuclear materials; other minor examples include the electronic frequency spectrum and the airspace. It is not surprising that each of these resources requires special management. In the aggregate, the annual cost of resources used by the Department of Defense, but not entering its expenditure accounts, is probably about $10 billion.

Since 1948, with the enactment of the Selective Service Act, the Department of Defense has chosen to draft some military manpower rather than pay salaries high enough to maintain the desired force levels. As a consequence, the total resource cost of military manpower may be $5 billion a year higher than the explicit expenditures. (McNamara has stated that the additional salaries necessary to eliminate the draft would total $20 billion a year; this total is grossly inconsistent with other evidence but, in any case, reinforces the case for reform of the military-pay structure.) The existence of the draft, by reducing the explicit manpower cost and by selecting personnel without regard for the individual's choice of alternative occupations, distorts both the level and composition of military manpower. A system of selective manpower controls has partially compensated for these distortions, but these controls cannot meaningfully be applied below the service level.

Defence landholdings total about 30 million acres, over 50 per cent of which has been transferred from the public domain. Public land can be acquired by administrative transfer at no cost and private land at the market value exclusive of the value to local governments as a property-tax base. Once acquired, the lease value of the land never enters the expenditure accounts, nor does a service receive credit to its accounts if land is returned to other public use or sold. The acquisition and use of foreign land is particularly distorted; the pertinent activity pays nothing for such land, but the military and economic-aid accounts often bear the high cost of this resource. The Department of Defense usually treats its enormous landholdings as a free good, except during periodic special campaigns (often under congressional pressure) to dispose of particular parcels.

The Department of Defense pays nothing for the development and production of nuclear weapons. Until recently, all parties (except the Bureau of the Budget) were happy with this arrangement; the Department of Defense ordered all the weapons that could be produced, and the Atomic Energy Commission (AEC) managed to produce all the weapons that were ordered. Defence activities are not charged for weapons acquired or in stockpile and are not credited for nuclear material returned. The resulting escalation of defence 'requirements' and AEC capabilities was halted only by the direct intervention of the president and some rather awkward management controls.

One major support activity – military air transport – is seriously underpriced within defence, although the resources used by this activity (except manpower) are correctly priced on transfer from the private sector. This underpricing has led to a substantially greater reliance on airlift for wartime mobility rather than on substitute activities for which the services pay nearly full cost. A few other activities, such as basic training and the defence communications system, are subject to similar problems.

In some cases, the Department of Defense pays considerably more for resources than their value. The most striking examples in recent years are the high premiums for US flag shipping and other US substitutes for goods and services available at a lower price abroad. Such overpricing, usually the result of using the defence budget to support balance-of-payments policy or a domestic-employment objective, also distorts the resource-allocation process.

Ideally, all resources acquired or released by the Department of Defense should be transferred at their full value. Fortunately, improved resource management need not be dependent on this condition. The manpower draft, however undesirable, looks like a permanent feature of our military establishment, and there are many pressures against an explicit accounting for such resources as public land and the frequency spectrum. A satisfactory interim solution for the misallocation resulting from distorted resource prices would be the establishment of annual 'shadow charges' (or credits) for the use of these resources. These shadow charges would be used for all resource-allocation decisions within the Department of Defense, although they would not be included in the formal budget. For example, the manpower costs for each defence activity should be estimated at the level of pay and perquisites that would be necessary in the absence of the draft. All land, both public and private, should be valued at the market value plus the public value as a property tax base, and the land-using activities should be charged an annual lease based on this total value. All defence activities 'using' nuclear weapons should be charged an annual lease on the value of the nuclear materials in the present stockpile, and the fabrication cost plus an annual lease on all new weapons. The component defence organizations should be able to make a case to OSD for an increase in their explicit budgets if they can demonstrate a more than offsetting reduction in these shadow charges; the Department of Defense, of course, should be able to make a similar case to the Bureau of the Budget. The case for such arrangements is not widely appreciated, but the annual value of these 'lost resources' is larger than the cost of any major mission, and the potential savings from good management of these resources would compare with those from the present cost-reduction programme.

CONCLUSION

The substantial improvements in the capabilities of the US military establishment since 1961 should be recognized. The decisions leading to the major improvements, however, were largely made in 1961 and cannot be attributed to the use of the new defence-management techniques. Without questioning the major force-level decisions, certain features of the defence resource-allocation process are subject to criticism. The principal defects are the failure of the military components to state priorities meaningfully, overcentralization at the level of the Secretary of Defense, and unrealistic resource pricing.

This chapter has outlined the major strengths and weaknesses in the defence resource-allocation process with the conviction that both the defence programme and the defence-management process should be subject to continued improvement.

NOTES

1. The Department of Defense Directive Number 7045.1, 30 October 1964. Subject: DoD Programming System Section. I.C.
2. David Novick, 'Efficiency and economy in government through new budgeting and accounting procedures', R–254; and 'A new approach to the military budget', RM–1759, RM–1956, RAND Corporation, 1954.
3. Charles J. Hitch and Roland N. McKean, *The Economics of Defense in the Nuclear Age*, Cambridge, MA: Harvard University Press.
4. Robert Anthony, Hitch's successor as Defense Comptroller, initiated a set of changes in the summer of 1966 which are expected to be fully implemented by July 1967.
5. The Tentative Force Guidance has proved to be both cumbersome and unpopular and is presently being modified.
6. This does not suggest a generic superiority of the analytic process over the bargaining process, rather that the JCS do not represent the appropriate constituency for the resolution of political problems.
7. The present incentive structure within the services, unfortunately, does not reinforce this proposed role of the Joint Staff mission review group. Creation of a special career pattern (or a separate 'purple suit' service) may be necessary for officers who have been assigned to the Joint Staff.
8. The concern expressed by Hitch and McKean is still most relevant:

Decentralization of the decision-making function is an extremely attractive administrative objective – in the military as elsewhere. The man on the spot can act quickly and flexibly. He has intimate first-hand knowledge of many factors relevant to his decisions. Large hierarchical organizations, by contrast, tend to be sluggish and hidebound by rules and regulations. Much of the time and energies are consumed in attempting to assemble, at the center, the information so readily available 'on the firing line'; and since these efforts are never successful, their decisions have to be made on the basis of information both incomplete and stale. Decentralization of decision-making responsibility has the further advantage of providing training, experience, and a testing ground for junior officers. The best way to develop qualities of responsibility, ingenuity, judgment, and so on, and to identify them is to provide genuine opportunities for their exercise. ... Unfortunately the superficial illogicalities of decentralization are more strikingly obvious than the deadening consequences of extreme centralization. (Hitch and McKean (1960) pp. 236–7, 238).

REFERENCES

Committee for Economic Development (1966), *Budgeting for National Objectives*, A Statement by the Research and Policy Committee, New York, January.

Hitch, Charles J. (1965), *Decision Making for Defense*, Berkeley: University of California Press.

Hitch, Charles J. and Roland N. McKean (1960), *The Economics of Defense in the Nuclear Age*, Cambridge, MA: Harvard University Press.

Novick, David (ed.) (1965), *Program Budgeting; Program Analysis and the Federal Budget*, Cambridge, MA: Harvard University Press.

Seligman, Daniel (1965), 'McNamara's management revolution', *Fortune*, **LXXII** (1), July, 117–121.

5. More defence spending for smaller forces*

US defence spending (adjusted for general inflation) is now about 60 per cent higher than it was in 1978 (and about 20 per cent higher than it was in 1968, the peak spending year during the Vietnam War).[1] The buildup from 1979 to 1987 was the largest and longest peacetime increase in real defence spending in US history. At the current real spending level, however, several important elements of the nation's military force are projected to be smaller or more vulnerable in 1990 than they were in 1978.

This chapter examines the characteristics of the defence buildup and addresses the following questions:

- What were the origins of the buildup?
- How was the money spent?
- How did the buildup affect US military capability as measured by changes in force structure, the number and quality of modern weapons, the quality of military personnel and force readiness and sustainability?
- Was the buildup affordable?
- To what extent did the buildup resolve the perceived national security problems at the beginning of the period?
- Was the buildup worthwhile?
- What effects will the buildup have on the US defence budget and programme in the near future?
- What lessons of the buildup period should guide US defence policy during the next administration?

Some of those questions are difficult, and there will continue to be disagreement over the answers, even among defence analysts with access to classified data. A better understanding of the issues by the broader community of public officials and voters, however, is necessary to rebuild a consensus on US defence policy. This chapter is intended to serve that objective.

---

* Reprinted by permission from the Cato Institute. First published as Cato *Policy Analysis*, No. 110, 29 July 1988.

THE ORIGINS OF THE BUILDUP

Real defence spending declined substantially from 1968 to 1978, partly as a result of the reduction of conventional forces following the US withdrawal from Vietnam, the large number of conventional weapons at the end of the war, and the disintegration of the consensus that had guided defence policy from President Harry S. Truman to President Lyndon B. Johnson. Developments elsewhere in the world, however, presented an increasing threat to US security interests. The Soviet Union continued to strengthen its strategic forces, despite several arms control agreements and a long interval of US restraint. Warsaw Pact forces maintained a substantial advantage over NATO forces in central Europe. A series of communist coups in Third World countries was followed by revolutions in Nicaragua and Iran.

The deterioration of international political conditions finally led to a broad bipartisan consensus for a new defence buildup. In May 1977 the United States and its NATO allies made a joint commitment to a 3 per cent annual increase in real defence spending. Although President Jimmy Carter deferred the US response to that commitment, the Soviet invasion of Afghanistan and the Iranian hostage crisis locked in the consensus for the defence buildup. Both presidential candidates in 1980 proposed to sustain the buildup. In a tabular supplement to a major campaign speech in September 1980, Ronald Reagan advocated a 5 per cent annual increase in real defence spending. In January 1981 President Carter, in his last budget, also recommended a 5 per cent annual increase.

One month later, however President Reagan recommended a 9 per cent annual increase – without a major review of national security objectives and prior to the development of a defence programme consistent with such a budget. Congress approved the initial phase of the president's proposed buildup without serious reservations. Although Congress later reduced the proposed defence budgets, real defence outlays increased at a 7 per cent annual rate from fiscal years 1981 to 1986.

The consensus that led to that record peacetime defence buildup, however, has dissolved. Beginning in FY 1986, real defence budget authority has declined each year, and real defence outlays are projected to decline slightly in FY 1988 and FY 1989.[2] It is thus time to review the buildup, as part of the process of determining the future defence budget and programme.

DEFENCE SPENDING DURING THE BUILDUP

Figure 5.1 displays the annual real defence outlays (in FY 1987 dollars) and the annual percentage increases during the buildup period.[3] As the figure illustrates, from FY 1978 to FY 1987 real defence outlays increased by 63 per cent and by about $110 billion. The rate of increase in real defence outlays rose sharply through FY 1982 (the year of the first Reagan budget), declined gradually through FY 1986 and was barely positive in FY 1987.

How was the money spent? The simple answer: with great haste and, apparently, considerable waste. A more thorough answer must be based on an examination of spending by appropriation and mission.

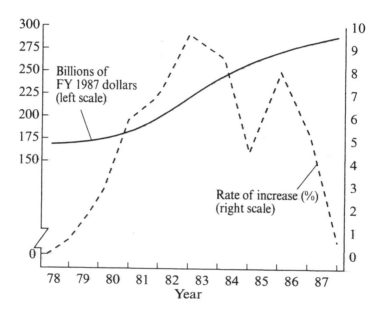

Source: Based on data in *Budget of the United States Government*, FY 1989.

Figure 5.1 Real defence outlays, FY 1978–1987

Outlays by Appropriation

Table 5.1, which displays real defence outlays by appropriation, reveals that spending increases took two quite different paths. The combined real outlays for military personnel, operations and maintenance increased at a 3 per cent annual rate. The combined real outlays for procurement, research, development, testing and evaluation, however, increased at a 10 per cent annual rate. Thus, most of the increase in real defence spending was in outlays for procurement and research and development (R&D). Other Department of Defense (DoD) outlays (for military construction, family housing and revolving funds, minus offsetting receipts) and outlays for defence-related activities by other agencies (primarily the Department of Energy) were much smaller but also increased sharply.

Budget Authority by Mission

Table 5.2 displays real defence budget authority by mission.[4] As it illustrates, the largest increase was in real budget authority for general-purpose forces. Real budget authority for intelligence and communications, airlift

Table 5.1 Real defence outlays by appropriation, FY 1978–1987

	FY 78	FY 87	
Category	Billions of FY 87 dollars		Percentage change
Department of Defense – military			
Military personnel	58.5	72.0	23.1
Operations and maintenance	55.3	76.2	37.8
Procurement	32.9	80.7	145.3
Research, development, testing and evaluation	17.3	33.6	94.2
Other	4.5	10.0	121.7
Total	168.5	272.5	61.7
Other agencies – defence-related activities	3.5	8.0	128.6
Total outlays	172.0	280.5	63.1

Source: Budget of the United States Government, FY 1980 and FY 1989.

and sealift, and administration, however, increased at a higher rate. Real budget authority for training and other activities declined, probably because of the higher quality of recruits and the higher reenlistment rates during the buildup period. On net, however, the share of budget authority allocated to each mission did not change very much.

CHANGES IN US MILITARY CAPABILITY

How did a 63 per cent increase in real defence outlays affect the capability of the nation's military forces? An answer to that question must be based on an examination of changes in force structure, the number and quality of modern weapons, the quality of military personnel, and the readiness and sustainability of the forces.

Force Structure

Table 5.3, which displays changes in the level of active US military personnel and forces by service and by type of force, reveals the following patterns:

Table 5.2 Real defence budget authority by mission, FY 1978–1987

Category	FY 78	FY 87	Percentage change
	Billions of FY 87 dollars		
Strategic forces	15.0	21.1	40.7
General-purpose forces	68.0	114.9	69.0
Intelligence and communications	13.0	27.7	113.1
Airlift and sealift	2.6	7.1	173.1
Guard and reserve	11.4	15.7	37.7
Research and development	16.5	27.5	66.7
Central supply and maintenance	19.7	22.7	15.2
Training, medical, etc	39.3	35.5	–9.7
Administration	3.6	6.6	83.3
Support of other nations	0.5	0.7	40.0
Total budget authority	189.6	279.5	47.3

Source: Budget of the United States Government, FY 1980 and FY 1989.

Table 5.3 Active military personnel and forces, FY 1978–1987

Service or force category	FY 78	FY 87	Percentage change
Military personnel (in thousands)			
Army	771	777	0.7
Navy	526	582	10.7
Marine Corps	191	199	4.2
Air Force	572	609	6.5
Total	2060	2167	5.2
Strategic forces			
Intercontinental ballistic missiles			
Minuteman	1000	973	–2.7
Titan II, Peacekeeper	54	27	–50.0
Polaris, Poseidon, Trident	656	640	–2.4
Strategic bomber squadrons	25	23	–8.0
General-purpose forces			
Land forces			
Army divisions	16	18	12.5
Marine divisions	3	3	0.0
Tactical air forces			
Air Force wings	26	25.5	–3.1
Navy attack wings	12	14	16.7
Marine Corps wings	3	3	0.0
Naval forces			
Attack and multipurpose carriers	13	14	7.7
Nuclear attack submarines	70	97	38.6
Other warships	166	217*	30.7
Amphibious assault ships	64	61	–4.7
Airlift and sealift			
C–5A airlift squadrons	4	4	0.0
Other airlift squadrons	13	13	0.0
Sealift fleet	48	61	27.0

Note: *Includes three reactivated battleships not present in the FY 1978 force.

Source: Budget of the United States Government, FY 1980 and FY 1989

- The level of the strategic forces declined slightly. The combined number of Minuteman and Peacekeeper (MX) missiles was constant, but the phaseout of Titan II missiles and two bomber squadrons slightly reduced the number of Air Force strategic systems. The reduction in submarine-based missiles is temporary; the higher level is projected to be restored in FY 1989.
- The Army added two light divisions but did not experience a significant change in total personnel. Light divisions are best suited for rapid deployment in low-intensity conflicts; they would be much less effective in a European conflict.
- Only the Navy experienced a substantial increase in forces, even though it was considerably superior to the Soviet Navy at the beginning of the defence buildup.
- Air Force tactical air wings and airlift squadrons were about constant, despite a sharp increase in real outlays for those forces.

In no case was the increase in personnel or force units as large as the increase in real defence spending. With the exception of naval general-purpose forces, the substantial increase in real defence spending had very little effect on the level of US military forces.

Weapons Modernization

The second dimension of military capability is the number and quality of modern weapons. The sharp increase in real spending for procurement and R&D did not lead to a proportionate increase in the number of major weapons purchased, because the average real unit price of weapons also increased. Table 5.4 displays the number and real unit price of major weapons purchased in 1981–87 relative to those purchased in 1974–80. Although there was a substantial increase in the procurement of some types of weapons – the most important of which are helicopters, theatre nuclear missiles, tanks and other combat vehicles, and noncombat ships – the procurement of other types of weapons increased only slightly or declined.

The average real price of most types of weapons, moreover, increased sharply. At the level of aggregation shown, of course, the change in average real price reflects both a change in the mix of weapons purchased within each category and a change in the average real price of each weapon. Most of the increase in the average real price of air transport aircraft, for example, reflects purchases of the very expensive C–5B intercontinental airlifter and smaller purchases of the less expensive C–130

Table 5.4 *Major weapons purchased and average real unit price: 1981–1987 relative to 1974–1980 (percentage change)*

Weapon category	Number purchased	Real unit price
Fixed-wing aircraft		
Combat	8	48
Airlift	18	627
Rotary aircraft	79	126
Missiles		
Strategic and theatre nuclear	162	−25
Tactical	−21	166
Ships		
Combat	0	46
Noncombat	333	−74
Tanks and other combat vehicles		
Heavy	99	50
Light	−44	77
Other	131	51

Source: Congressional Budget Office, September 1987.

intratheatre cargo plane. Similarly, the decline in the average real price of strategic and theatre nuclear missiles largely reflects the relative increase in purchases of the less expensive theatre missiles. One study, however, indicates that the real prices of a sample of major weapons increased by 9 to 64 per cent from 1981 to 1985. The increase in the real price of most major weapons seems to have declined somewhat since 1983, but the real price of weapons first purchased after 1980 (such as the C–5B and the MX) increased sharply.[5]

For several years the Department of Defense claimed that an increased procurement rate would reduce real unit prices; the available data are more consistent with the conventional view that real unit prices may decline as a function of the cumulative number of weapons purchased but are likely to increase as a function of the annual production rate.

As noted earlier, US weapons expenditures (for procurement, R&D, military construction and defence-related activities by other agencies)

Table 5.5 US and Soviet production of selected weapons, 1978–1987

Weapon category	US	Soviet
Tanks	7600	25 300
Other armoured vehicles	10 800	46 000
Artillery, mortars, and rocket launchers	3200	27 300
Tactical aircraft	3600	7700
Surface warships	87	83
Attack submarines	33	65

Source: Secretary of Defense, *Annual Report to Congress*, FY 1989.

increased sharply from FY 1978 to FY 1987 – to a level that slightly exceeded the Soviet Union's estimated weapons expenditures in FY 1987.[6] During the same period, however, the Soviets produced far more weapons in every major category other than surface warships. Table 5.5 compares the two countries' production of selected weapons during the buildup years.

The difference between those production levels is striking and disturbing, but the implications for US policy are less clear. The Department of Defense maintains that the quality of most US weapons is superior to that of Soviet weapons. That may be true, but the quality of some Soviet weapons is impressive. The new FST-1 Soviet tank, for example, is reportedly 'virtually impervious to weapons currently in NATO's arsenal, and the new tank carries a new 135–mm gun with shells that can pierce the West's toughest tank armor.'[7] DoD also asserts that it would be risky to reduce the current US weapons production levels. That may also be true, but the available data suggest that the rapid increase in US real expenditures for weapons procurement and R&D did not increase the number and quality of US weapons relative to those of our main potential adversary.

Moreover, the comparative weapons production data should lead us to inquire whether the United States has made the correct tradeoff between quantity and quality, whether it has been producing the right types of weapons, and whether it has been relatively inefficient at producing weapons (and if so, why). Before approving a renewed increase in real defence spending, Congress should ask DoD to address those questions.

Military Personnel

The most dramatic improvement in US military capability was in the quality of enlisted personnel. Today more than 90 per cent of Army recruits are high-school graduates, compared with 70 to 75 per cent during the draft era.[8] Less than 10 per cent of Army recruits are now drawn from Category IV (the lowest acceptable rating on the Armed Forces Qualification Test), compared with about 50 per cent in 1980. The reenlistment rates for the total military force are now more than 50 per cent after the first term of service and more than 80 per cent after the second term and subsequent terms, compared with 39 per cent and 71 per cent in 1980. About 50 per cent of the enlisted personnel now have more than four years of service, compared with 42 per cent in 1980.

Those substantial improvements in the qualifications and experience of military personnel have enabled the military to use more complex weapons and have permitted a reduction in real outlays for training and related expenses. The improvements were a consequence of substantial increases in both real military compensation and pride in service. Moreover, they were achieved during a period in which the absolute size of the US teenage population declined and real outlays for military personnel increased much less sharply than any other major component of defence outlays. The Reagan administration deserves credit for strengthening the nation's commitment to a volunteer professional military.

Readiness and Sustainability

There does not appear to have been a substantial increase in the readiness and sustainability of US forces during the defence buildup.[9] Such indicators as training days per battalion, flying hours per crew, steaming days per ship, and years of schooling did not change very much. Equipment and supplies on hand was reported to have increased for the Navy and Marine Corps air forces, remained fairly stable for the Marine Corps land forces, and declined for the Army and the Air Force. DoD reported that the percentage of 'mission capable' equipment was only 'steady or slightly increasing'. As a percentage of the war reserve requirements, the stock of munitions increased substantially, but the stock of secondary items declined slightly after 1980 for all services other than the Air Force.

A General Evaluation of Military Capability

The most difficult dimension of military capability to evaluate, even for those with access to classified data, is the quality of weapons. A large share of the increase in real defence spending since 1978 was in outlays for procurement and R&D, so such indicators as force size, the number of weapons purchased and readiness may understate the overall increase in US military capability during the buildup period. Ultimately, military capability can be evaluated only during a war, and, fortunately, we have not had a critical test of whether the quality of modern US weapons has increased in proportion to their average real cost. On the basis of the available data, one can only conclude, as did the Congressional Budget Office, that 'despite widespread improvements, most of the aggregate indicators have not increased markedly, with a few exceptions like personnel quality'.[10]

SOME IMPORTANT RELATED CONSIDERATIONS

Was the Buildup Affordable?

The answer is an unambiguous 'yes'. As a share of GNP, US defence spending is now lower than it was in any year from 1951 to 1972.

The United States can clearly afford to spend more for defence, even a great deal more, if doing so is essential to its national security. However, the United States cannot afford to keep spending the amount that Americans now spend for all purposes. In 1987 the United States spent about 3.5 per cent more than it produced, borrowing the difference from foreigners. That would not have been a problem if domestic private investment had been unusually high. In that case, the investment would have yielded a stream of returns sufficient to pay the interest on the increased foreign debt. For the past several years, however, domestic private investment has been weak, and the United States has increasingly borrowed abroad in order to finance unusually high private consumption and government purchases. The need to reduce the growth of either private consumption or government purchases relative to the growth of output will be a central political issue for some time. It is also a central feature of the economic context in which decisions about the defence budget should be based.

To What Extent Did the Buildup Resolve the Perceived National Security Problems at the Beginning of the Period?

The answer is 'not very much'. Several examples provide a basis for that conclusion.

A decade ago there was serious concern that the increased number and accuracy of Soviet strategic warheads had increased the vulnerability of the US land-based strategic forces. Most of the US strategic systems deployed since then have not reduced that vulnerability. The MX missiles now deployed in Minuteman silos, unfortunately, should probably be considered destabilizing, in that they increase the payoff (in terms of US warheads destroyed) of a Soviet first strike. If some or all of the MX missiles were deployed in rail garrisons, their vulnerability would be reduced only if the United States had sufficient strategic warning time (probably around two hours) to move them on to the general rail network.

For reasons that have yet to be explained, DoD recently proposed a large reduction in development funding for the road-mobile Midgetman, the only potential land-based missile system that would be relatively invulnerable. The B1–B bomber, the new Stealth bomber, and an advanced air–launched cruise missile would increase the possibility of penetrating the Soviet Union's extensive air defence system, but they would not reduce the vulnerability of the US bomber force to a Soviet first strike. (Each of those systems is both late and substantially over budget.) Only the new Trident submarine and the D–5 missile make a significant contribution to a stable strategic deterrence, but the small number of submarines deployed would be increasingly vulnerable to an improved Soviet antisubmarine warfare capability.

For many years the Soviets have maintained conventional forces in central Europe that are larger than the combined NATO forces.[11] The major changes in the structure of US conventional forces during the recent defence buildup did not significantly alter the balance. The two additional Army divisions are US-based light divisions designed for low-intensity conflict. The number of Air Force tactical air wings is now lower than it was in 1978 and is scheduled to be reduced further. Although the US Navy was superior to the Soviet navy prior to the defence buildup, it was the only service that experienced a substantial increase in conventional forces during the buildup – and the military value of these additional forces in a European conflict is not obvious.

The balance was altered slightly by the United States' improved tactical weapons and increased ability to move forces to Europe, the latter a consequence of increased airlift and sealift and the pre-positioning of heavy equipment for US-based divisions committed to the continent's defence. In general, however, the buildup did little to alleviate the long-standing concern about the force balance in Europe.

An increased ability to respond to outbreaks of low-intensity conflict in regions other than Europe was probably the most significant change in US military capability during the buildup period – an improvement provided by the two additional Army light divisions, the additional Navy forces, and the increased airlift and sealift. During the same period, however, both the American public and the Department of Defense expressed an increasing reluctance to commit US forces to regional conflicts that do not directly threaten vital US interests. Secretaries of State Alexander Haig and George Shultz both chafed at DoD's reluctance. Nevertheless, Secretary Caspar Weinberger's 1985 statement on defence strategy was probably correct – military commitments should be made in response to only those conflicts that involve our most important national security concerns and cannot be sustained in the absence of popular support. One wonders, however, why Weinberger promoted the increase in US military forces to respond to low-intensity conflicts.

In summary, the defence buildup did not do much to resolve the perceived national security concerns that were the basis for the initial consensus for the buildup. The nature of the buildup appears to have been determined more by longstanding 'service requirements' than by a change in national security objectives or military commitments.

Was the Buildup Worthwhile?

The answer is 'maybe.' Political and military conditions have improved markedly in several respects since 1980. The recently ratified INF (intermediate-range nuclear forces) treaty will eliminate all US and Soviet intermediate-range nuclear missiles from Europe, and the START (Strategic Arms Reduction Talks) treaty being negotiated promises to reduce US and Soviet strategic nuclear forces by about 50 per cent. Both of those measures go far beyond the 'nuclear freeze' proposal by leftist critics of US defence policy. Moreover, no additional nations have been drawn into the Soviet orbit, and the Soviets have begun a withdrawal from Afghanistan. Something important may be happening in the Soviet Union as a result of the Gorbachev initiatives, and there may soon be a basis for a new European arrangement in the interest of both blocs. No one in the West anticipated such favourable developments at the beginning of the buildup period.

It is plausible to assert that the US defence buildup was one of the causes of those developments. The case would be stronger if it were more clear that the substantial increase in real defence spending led to a corresponding increase in military capability. A sustained increase in real defence spending of 3 to 5 per cent annually plus a coherent defence programme consistent with that funding, however, might have brought about the same developments at a much lower cost. The increase in real spending by itself may have contributed to those developments, because the Soviets may have as much difficulty evaluating the capability of US military forces as we do. Our current challenge is to channel US defence spending into more-demonstrable military capability and to focus that capability on our most important national security interests.

THE NEAR-TERM DEFENCE BUDGET
AND PROGRAMME

Real defence outlays are now projected to decline by about 3 per cent through FY 1989, and Secretary Frank Carlucci recently instructed the services to prepare a defence programme based on a 2 per cent increase in real budget authority in each subsequent year. Thus, after a few years real defence outlays will be about as high as they were in FY 1987.

Given a roughly constant real defence budget, however, US military force levels are projected to decline.[12] Military personnel are to be reduced by 35000 by FY 1989. The personnel in two Army divisions will be reduced, and the Army will be smaller than it was in FY 1978. Midgetman development will remain at a minimal level, and four B-52G squadrons will be reassigned to the conventional forces. About 450 helicopters will be eliminated from the force structure. The procurement of two sets of division equipment for pre-positioning in Europe has already been slowed. One Navy tactical air wing and 16 frigates will be deactivated, and the planned procurement of the A-6F carrier-based fighter bomber has been cancelled. Air Force active and reserve tactical forces will be reduced by three wings in FY 1990.

Thus, the levels of at least three important elements of the nation's military forces will be lower in FY 1990 than they were in FY 1978: strategic missiles and bombers, Army personnel and Air Force tactical air wings. The force reductions since FY 1987 are primarily the result of the bow wave of procurement spending approved in prior years. As observed at the beginning of this chapter, a real defence budget about 60 per cent higher than that of FY 1978 will soon support a military force that is smaller and more vulnerable in some dimensions than it was at the beginning of the buildup.

Moreover, the Department of Defense has yet to prepare a Five Year Defense Program (FYDP) consistent with the new Carlucci budget guidance. According to the latest FYDP, DoD's plans are based on cumulative budget authority for FY 1989–92 that is about $282 billion higher than that of the Carlucci guidance and $362 billion higher than a path of constant real budget authority.[13] If current procurement plans are not substantially revised, US military forces will undergo a larger reduction than has been scheduled to date.

The next several years are likely to be a period of bloodletting in the Pentagon that has not been observed for two decades, even if real budget authority continues to increase at the 2 per cent rate consistent with the Carlucci guidance. According to an anonymous DoD budget official,

The administration of the Pentagon has collapsed. Not only are we cheating the public by signing them up for things that we can't afford, but we're hurting the military because there's going to be a readiness bloodbath. We would be worse off in 1992 than in 1979 and still be spending $260 billion a year.[14]

The critical choice will be whether to maintain the weapons procurement plan or the level and readiness of US forces. Secretary Carlucci has chosen to maintain most elements of the procurement plan at the expense of small reductions in the military forces. The next administration should undertake a major review of national security objectives and the defence programme before deciding whether to continue on that path.

LESSONS OF THE DEFENCE BUILDUP

As noted earlier, the sharp increase in real defence spending during the Reagan administration was approved without a review of national security objectives and before the preparation of a defence plan consistent with the increased real budget authority. The broad consensus for a buildup permitted DoD to transform a window of vulnerability into a window of opportunity for defence spending. Accelerating the buildup was an understandable and possibly correct initial response to the concerns and the sense of urgency that prevailed in 1981. Secretary Weinberger, however, never resolved the growing disparity between defence plans and approved funding levels. That problem was recognized as early as 1982, when it was the focus of a briefing by then defence logistics chief Lawrence J. Korb to the Defense Resources Board. Moreover, an internal study by programme analyst Franklin Spinney concluded that the planned defence buildup was underfinanced by as much as 30 per cent.

A January 1983 report by the conservative Heritage Foundation described an 'internal cancer' at DoD, citing increasing modernization and readiness costs and unrealistic budget projections. The report concluded, 'We see no sign that Department of Defense planning is more realistic for the future.'[15] That assessment proved to be correct. At no time did Secretary Weinberger force the services to develop a defence programme consistent with the first-year budgets approved by Congress.

Asked recently whether defence programming should have precluded a plans–reality mismatch, former Navy Secretary John Lehman responded, 'No, it should not have been done differently. It would have been highly irresponsible to plan for the Congress's stupidity'.[16] Lehman was apparently referring to the failure of Congress to approve budgets as high as those on which defence plans were based. Many of the actions of

Congress are indeed stupid, but Lehman's position is wrong; defence plans should be based on approved budgets, not budget approval on defence plans. In failing to recognize that principle, DoD was irresponsible. At any rate, Weinberger and Lehman were ultimately unable to convince Congress that the continued increase in real defence spending necessary to fund the defence programme planned for the late 1980s would be worth the cost.

The first lesson of the buildup period is that Congress will not sustain an increase in real defence budget authority in the absence of a war. Before the buildup real defence budget authority had never increased in peacetime for more than three years; thereafter it increased for six years (from FY 1980 to FY 1985). DoD received more funding than it had reason to expect. It only recently started to base defence plans on approved budgets.

A second lesson of the buildup is that national security objectives must ultimately conform to what the nation is prepared to support. Lehman was half-right in asserting that

> we have to stop living beyond our means and playing as if we can be the world's policeman as we used to do during the Marshall Plan days. If we are not willing to pay for it, then [we should] stop pretending that we can do it. If you are going to cut defense, then you have to cut commitments.[17]

Our national security objectives and military forces have been remarkably stable, except during the Korean and Vietnam wars, for about 40 years. Although the Soviet Union has maintained a formidable military establishment and has continued to improve its military technology, however, other conditions have changed dramatically. At the time the United States organized NATO and made a commitment to defend Europe, the economies of the West European nations were in shambles, the stability of their political systems was tenuous, and US strategic forces were much stronger than Soviet strategic forces. Our European allies now have a combined economic output about twice as high as that of the Warsaw Pact, and the United States has lost its strategic superiority.

Likewise, at the time the United States committed forces to northeast Asia, the economies of Japan and Korea were in a shambles, and China was the main adversary in the region. Japan now has the second-largest economy in the world, South Korea's rapidly growing economy is about five times as large as that of North Korea, and China is no longer considered an adversary.

Our national security commitments and military forces, however, have not reflected those dramatic changes. NATO defence strategy, for example, is still based on the credibility of an increasingly suicidal US strategic response to a Soviet invasion.[18] As a share of GNP, US defence spending is about twice as high as that of our NATO allies and about six times as high as that of Japan.[19] In effect, our substantial expenditure to defend Europe and other regions is one of our major exports, but it is one for which we are not compensated. A major review of our national security commitments is clearly overdue.

But Lehman was only half-right. There are still substantial opportunities for the United States to increase military capability or reduce costs by redesigning forces to make them more efficient for specific missions. The vulnerability of land-based strategic missiles, for example, could probably be reduced most efficiently by a mobile basing mode. There is a good case for a force of large attack carriers for use in low-intensity conflicts in regions where the United States does not have established land bases; it is much less clear that such a force (the investment cost of which is now about $18 billion per carrier task force) should also be designed to operate within range of Soviet land-based air forces. There is no reason to regard a review of US military and security commitments and the redesign of US forces as mutually exclusive means of achieving a better match between defence plans and approved budgets. Both are important.

A third lesson of the buildup is that a major reorganization of the Department of Defense may be in order. DoD is now the third-largest command economy in the world. No command economy works very well, and Americans are not especially efficient at managing a command economy. One approach that should be considered is to improve the buyer–seller system within DoD. Most of the defence budget, for example, could be allocated directly to the unified and specified commands, which would maintain their own organizations for testing and evaluation. The four services would then compete to provide forces, weapons and supplies to the commands.

Two changes would be needed to make such a system effective. The 'Key West agreement', in effect a cartel to divide missions among the services, should be terminated. Doing so would permit the Army to provide strategic missiles and fixed-wing tactical aircraft, the Marine Corps to provide forces to the major regional commands, and the Air Force to compete for the sea-control mission. The promotion system for higher-grade officers should also be changed in order to reward superior performance among officers in the joint commands and to protect them when the priorities of those commands conflict with the interests of their respective services. The Department of Defense Reorganization Act of 1986 was a step in that direction, but its immediate effects are likely to be quite limited.[20]

A major reorganization of DoD along the lines suggested deserves a careful review, but such a review should not be delayed. The current system of planning and organizing US military forces does not serve the United States very well.

In February 1986 the first report of the President's Blue Ribbon Commission on Defense Management, chaired by David Packard, concluded,

> Today, there is no rational system whereby the Executive Branch and Congress reach coherent and enduring agreement on national security strategy, the forces to carry it out, and the funding that should be provided – in light of the overall economy and competing claims on national resources. The absence of such a system contributes substantially to the instability and uncertainty that plague our defense program. These cause imbalances in our military forces and capabilities, and increase the costs of procuring military equipment.[21]

Unfortunately, that is still the case.

According to the Constitution, the single most important role of the federal government is to 'provide for the common defense.' The large increase in real defence spending that began in 1979 did not contribute much towards the achievement of that goal. We now need to identify the commitments that are essential to our common defence and to develop sufficiently effective and efficient forces to meet those commitments.

NOTES

1. Estimates of the change in real spending over a long period are dependent on the general price index used to deflate the nominal spending series. For example, on the basis of the GNP implicit price deflator, in 1987 real defence spending was 66.6 per cent higher than in 1978 and 19.7 per cent higher than in 1968. In contrast, on the basis of the GNP fixed-weight deflator, real defence spending was 64.1 per cent higher than in 1978 and 36.9 per cent higher than in 1968. Thus, those two deflators provide roughly similar estimates of the change in real defence spending since 1978 but quite different estimates of the change since 1968.
2. *Budget of the United States Government*, FY 1989, Washington, DC: Government Printing Office, 1988.
3. The real outlays displayed in Figure 5.1 are adjusted by the GNP fixed-weight deflator.
4. Budget authority is the amount appropriated by Congress for each fiscal year. Defence outlays, funded in part through prior budget authority, increased more rapidly than defence budget authority. The distribution of defence spending by mission is published on a budget-authority basis only.
5. Estimates of the changes in the real unit prices of selected weapons are from Congressional Budget Office, 'Defense spending: what has been accomplished?,' staff working paper, April 1985.
6. Estimates of the comparative weapons expenditures of the United States and the Soviet Union are from the Secretary of Defense's *Annual Report to Congress*, FY 1989.
7. 'A tank in shining armor,' *Newsweek*, 11 April 1988.
8. Changes in personnel quality are from *Annual Report* and 'Defense Spending'.

9. 'Defense Spending.'
10. Ibid.
11. Total defence expenditures by NATO, however, are estimated to have been larger than the defence expenditures by the Warsaw Pact in most years, and the spending gap has increased Since 1980. See *Statistical Abstract of the United States,* Washington, DC: Government Printing Office, 1988, p. 318.
12. *Budget,* FY 1989.
13. David C. Morrison, 'And now, the guillotine,' *National Journal,* 27 February 1988.
14. Ibid.
15. Ibid.
16. Ibid.
17. David C. Morrison, 'Cut the other guy', *National Journal,* 12 March, 1988.
18. For an evaluation of the current US options for the defence of Europe, see Christopher Layne, 'After the INF Treaty: a new direction for America's European policy', Cato Institute, *Policy Analysis,* No. 103, 21 April 1988.
19. Robert Hale, Congressional Budget Office, statement to the Senate Budget Committee, 1 March 1988.
20. David Isenberg 'Missing the point: why the reforms of the Joint Chiefs of Staff won't improve U.S. defense policy,' Cato Institute, *Policy Analysis,* No. 100, 29 February 1988.
21. President's Blue Ribbon Commission on Defense Management, *An Interim Report to the President,* 28 February 1986.

6. The District of Columbia: America's worst government?*

Washington the Capital is a symbol of democracy and America. Washington the city is a symbol of almost everything that sincere and thoughtful men know is wrong with democracy and America. Washington the Capital is the hope of world freedom. Washington the city is overcrowded, badly housed, expensive, crime-ridden, intolerant, with inadequate transportation, schools, and health facilities. It staggers under a dilapidated and hopeless governmental organization, and its problems are rapidly getting worse.

(Alden Stevens)

Although written in 1941, those words are disturbingly descriptive of the Washington of 1991. Washington the capital is still the marble mecca of democracy. And in some ways it has improved over the past half century. Washington the city is now more cosmopolitan, more tolerant, and air-conditioned. Commercial development has greatly increased the property tax base. The District of Columbia, which provides the services of both a city and a state government, now has substantial home rule. The government of the nation's capital, however, is probably the worst in the nation – maybe not as bad as the city government of Detroit but clearly worse than the government of any state. District expenditures per resident, excluding the cost of special federal services in Washington, are about twice the national average of state and local expenditures. Despite the high level of District spending, the performance of students in the public schools is lower than in any state, and the murder rate, infant mortality rate and several other measures of social pathology are higher than in any state. A local satirical revue recently described the District Building (Washington's city hall) as 'the nation's first work-free drug zone'. Such are the record and the reputation of the District of Columbia that Mayor Dixon recently inherited.

Sharon Pratt Dixon brings to her new position a record of personal integrity, good management and an overwhelming election victory. That will not be enough. One should remember that Mayor Marion Barry first

* Reprinted by permission from the Cato Institute. First published as Cato *Policy Analysis*, No. 165, 18 November 1991.

came to office with a reputation for high energy and political entrepreneurship. Honesty, good management and politics-as-usual will not be sufficient to resolve the major problems of the District of Columbia. This analysis summarizes the major dimensions of the cost of District government, social conditions in Washington and the radical changes that may be necessary to improve those conditions.

COMPARATIVE GOVERNMENT SPENDING AND SOCIAL CONDITIONS

The magnitude and characteristics of the problems of the District government are best illustrated by comparing government expenditures and various measures of social conditions in Washington with those elsewhere in the nation. Most of the comparative data are for 1987 or 1988, the latest years for which they are available, and most of the data are from the *Statistical Abstract of the United States*, a government publication that is available in almost every library. Any concerned resident could have made the same comparisons, but the public has paid very little attention to the lessons to be gleaned from these data.

General Economic and Demographic Conditions

General economic and demographic conditions in Washington, with one exception, compare favourably with those in the rest of the nation; the one exception is the unusually high poverty rate (Table 6.1).

The problems of Washington are apparent. What may be less apparent is that most of the general economic and demographic conditions are better than the national average. Average personal income per resident is 30 per cent higher than the national average, and higher than in all but two states. The average salary of those who work in Washington is nearly 40 per cent higher than the national average, and higher than in any state. The percentage of Washington residents who are employed is also unusually high.

The most striking condition in Washington is the combination of a high average income and an unusually high poverty rate. The only states with higher poverty rates are those on the lower Mississippi, where average incomes are the lowest in the nation. The variance of (pretax and pretransfer) income in Washington is higher than in any state and is the primary explanation of the unusually high political demand for transfers and social services. The other client groups for government services, however, are either about the same or a lower percentage than elsewhere. The

Table 6.1 General economic and demographic conditions, 1988

	Nation	District	Percentage difference[a]
Personal income per resident	$16 489	$21 389	+30
Average salary	$21 871	$30 254	+38
Employment rate	62.3%	66.5%	+7
Client groups (percentage of residents)			
Poor (1979)	12.4	18.6	+50
Unemployed	2.7	2.8	+1
Age 17 and under	26.0	22.3	−14
Age 65 and over	12.4	12.4	0

Note: [a] Calculated from unrounded totals.

Source: Statistical Abstract of the United States, 1990, pp. 23, 399, 408, 437, 458.

unemployed are a lower percentage of the labour force but about the same percentage of the resident population. The percentage of Washington residents age 17 or younger is lower than in any state. The percentage aged 65 and over is the same as the national average. And Washington's high population density (not shown) should make it possible to economize on police and highway services.

In summary, Washington's general economic and demographic conditions, even the high poverty rate, are *not* a sufficient explanation of the combination of unusually high District expenditures and unusually poor social conditions.

District Expenditures, Employment and Earnings

Expenditures
Expenditures by the District are *much* higher than are needed to provide good government services. District expenditures per resident are about *twice* the national average of state and local governments; they are higher than in any state except Alaska (Table 6.2). Moreover, direct expenditures by the District do not include the cost of those government services that some of us value most highly – specifically, the District's contribution to Metro and the federal expenditures to maintain and police the parks, the museums; and the zoo – costs that residents of other major cities bear directly.

Table 6.2 State and local expenditures per resident, 1987

	Nation ($)	District ($)	Percentage difference
Direct general expenditures	2685	5163	+92
Capital outlay	404	886	+119
Total	3089	6049	+96

Source: Statistical Abstract of the United States, 1990, p. 281.

Employment
Employment by the District government is much higher than average. Average earnings, however, may be insufficient to attract a quality workforce.

Government employment in the District is about one for each eleven residents, nearly 80 per cent higher than the average state and local government employment rate, and higher than the rate in any state (Table 6.3). Again, the District total does not include the many federal workers who provide local government services in Washington. The District government is *hugely* overstaffed, by far more than the 2000 positions that candidate Dixon pledged to cut or the 6000 positions that the Rivlin Commission (a special commission of private citizens that reviewed the District budget) recommended be cut. A level of District government employment equal to the average state and local government employment per resident, even though few states are models of efficiency, would permit a reduction of 25 000 positions.

Table 6.3 State and local government employment and earnings, 1987

	Nation	District	Percentage difference
Employees per 10 000 residents	496	888	+79
Average monthly earnings	$2090	$2706	+29

Source: Statistical Abstract of the United States, 1990, p. 303.

Earnings

Average earnings of District employees are nearly 30 per cent higher than the national average of state and local employees, higher than in any state except Alaska. District employee earnings, however, are not significantly out of line with other earnings in Washington. Nationwide, earnings of state and local government employees are about 15 per cent higher than average earnings; the earnings of District government employees are about 7 per cent higher than average earnings in Washington. Indeed, there may be a case for *increasing* the average earnings of District employees if necessary to recruit and maintain a higher-quality workforce.

Public Education

District expenditures for primary and secondary schools are reasonable, but student performance is lower than in any state (Table 6.4).

Table 6.4 Public education, 1987–1990

	Nation	District	Percentage difference[a]
Share of current budget (1987)	34.7%	17.7%	−49
Cost per resident	$931	$913	−2
Primary and secondary schools			
Costs, employment, and earnings			
Cost per student (1988)	$4509	$5827	+29
Employees per 100 students (1987)	11.5	13.3	+16
Average teacher salary (1989)	$29 000	$37 500	+29
Student performance			
High school graduation rate (1989)	75%	55%	−27
SAT score (1990)	900	717	−20
Public higher education, costs and			
employment			
Public cost per student (1988)	$4092	$9326	+127
Employees per 100 students (1987)	19.2	18.2	−5

Note: [a] Calculated from unrounded totals.

Source: Statistical Abstract of the United States, 1990, pp. 139, 144, 154, 159, 302.

Expenditures for the University of the District of Columbia are extra-ordinarily high and have little apparent return.

Expenditures for education are the largest share of the District budget, as is the case in the rest of the nation. The education share of the current budget, however, is unusually low for two reasons: the relatively low public school enrolment in the District and the very high expenditures for other services.

Costs per student in the District's primary and secondary schools are nearly 30 per cent higher than the national average. That may seem reasonable, given the high salaries necessary to recruit government employees in Washington. One is chastened, however, to recognize that the average cost per student in District schools is about 50 per cent higher than the cost at Archbishop Carroll High School and about *three* times that at the Catholic elementary schools in the Washington area.

The more serious problem is the *very low* performance of District students; by several measures it is lower than in any state. Only 55 per cent of District ninth graders in 1985, for example, graduated from District high schools in 1989 – a percentage that is much lower than the national average. (That may understate the relative graduation rate in the District, however, because it does not include those students who graduate later from other school systems.) The scholastic aptitude test (SAT) score of District students hoping to enter college is 20 per cent lower than the national average, and lower than in any state in which students take that exam. (The average score probably overstates the average performance of District students, because only the best 20 per cent of District students take the exam.)

District support of public higher education is limited to the University of the District of Columbia, where public expenditures per student are *more than twice* the national average. That university should now be recognized as a failure. It has been plagued by scandal, incompetence and pervasive mediocrity since its inception and now risks losing its accreditation – a bad investment for both the District and the students. The recent offer of a teaching position in criminal justice to the former mayor was only its latest offence.

Courts, Police and Corrections

District expenditures per resident for courts, police and corrections are *more than four times* the national average. Despite those very high expenditures, the reported crime rates in the District are higher than in any state and most major cities (Table 6.5).

Expenditures for courts, police and corrections are the second largest component of the District budget, a share that is more than twice the national average. Expenditures per resident are more than four times the national average, much higher than in any state. Most of the higher expenditures reflect a much larger number of public safety employees. The numbers of police and corrections employees per resident are each several times the national average. And a roughly equal number of federal and Metro police, not included in the District data, also serve in Washington. The total number of police in Washington is nearly six times the national average per resident.

Table 6.5 Courts, police and corrections, 1987 and 1988

	Nation	District	Percentage difference[a]
Costs and employment (1987)			
Share of current budget	7.9%	17.4%	+121
Expenditure per resident	$211	$900	+327
Employment per 10000 residents			
Police	27.2	74.1	+172
Corrections	16.5	59.6	+261
Reported crime per 100000 residents (1988)			
All violent crimes	637	1922	+202
Murder	8.4	59.5	+608
Property crimes	5027	7993	+59

Note: [a] Calculated from unrounded totals.

Source: Statistical Abstract of the United States, 1990, pp. 171, 181.

Crime rates in the nation's capital, however, are a national scandal; they are higher for each type of crime than in any state. The rate of violent crime is more than three times the national average, even though it is less than in eleven other major cities. The murder rate in 1988 was more than seven times the national average, the highest in any major city, and it increased in 1989 and 1990. The rate of property crime is nearly 60 per cent higher than the national average, although it is about average for the major cities. The combination of very high expenditures for public safety and unusually high crime rates is the single most perplexing problem facing the District government.

A Special Analysis of Police and Corrections

Many readers will correctly observe that it is not strictly appropriate to compare government expenditures and social conditions in Washington with the average for the states. Washington is a major city, and major cities face special conditions that may increase expenditures or cause unusual social problems. The available data, unfortunately, do not permit a direct comparison of Washington with other major cities. The costs of those District services usually financed from a state budget are not separately identified. Many city governments do not finance education and public welfare. And data on most economic, demographic and social conditions are not available by city.

Fortunately, statistical analysis of the data available for each state and the District provides a way to sort out the issue. This chapter summarizes that type of analysis for only police and corrections services. Such analyses are complex and never fully definitive, but, at least conceptually, they could also be applied to other state and local government services.

The primary questions of interest are the following: how much do District expenditures, police employment, crime rates and the like (the data presented Table 6.5) differ from those of the rest of the nation, *given* the conditions that explain the systematic variation of those 'dependent' variables among the states? This analysis uses a sample of the 48 continental states plus the District. The full set of statistical results is described in the appendix.

Most of the variation in expenditures per resident for police and corrections and in the number of police and corrections employees per 10 000 residents appears to be explained by five conditions: federal revenues per resident, personal income per resident, the violent crime rate, the property crime rate and population density. In turn, most of the variation in crime rates appears to be explained by three conditions: the percentage of the population that resides in metropolitan areas, the percentage of the population that is poor and population density. (One of the most disturbing results of this analysis is that increases in police services, within the observed range. do *not* appear to reduce crime rates.) Most of those conditions suggest that both District expenditures for police services and crime rates in Washington should be expected to be higher than the national average. The more disturbing conclusion is that each of those variables is higher than in other, 'normal' large cities that have the same conditions (Table 6.6).

Table 6.6 Comparison of a 'normal' large city and the District

	'Normal' city	District	Percentage difference
Costs and employment (1987)			
Expenditures per resident	$601	$898	+49
Employment per 10 000 residents			
Police	53.7	74.1	+38
Corrections	40.1	59.6	+49
Reported crimes per 100 000 residents (1988)			
All violent crimes	876	1922	+119
Murder	12.5	59.5	+376
Property crimes	4336	7993	+84

Source: See Appendix.

The top line of Table 6.6 indicates that the District spends about 49 per cent more per resident for police and corrections than would be expected in a jurisdiction with the same federal revenues, personal income per resident, crime rates and population density. For comparison, the fourth line indicates that the rate of violent crime is about 119 per cent higher than would be expected in another jurisdiction that is also 100 per cent metropolitan and has the same poverty rate and population density. A comparison of Table 6.6 with Table 6.5 indicates that some of the differences between the District and national average conditions are explained by the economic and demographic conditions specific to the District. Even under those conditions, however, expenditures per resident and crime rates in the District are still substantially higher than the expected levels, and the difference is statistically significant in all cases. District officials should not be held responsible for the differences summarized in Table 6.5. Elimination of the differences summarized in Table 6.6, however, would be a reasonable goal.

Public Welfare

District expenditures per resident for public welfare are *much higher* than the national average, even though the average benefits per recipient are not unusual (Table 6.7). That is the result of a large recipient population and an unusually large welfare staff.

Table 6.7 Public welfare, 1987 and 1988

	Nation	District	Percentage difference[a]
Costs and employment (1987)			
Share of current budget	12.3%	17.4%	+42
Expenditure per resident	$329	$899	+173
Employment per 10 000 residents	17.1	32.2	+89
Recipients and benefits (1988)			
Welfare			
Recipients per 100 residents	6.1	10.5	+72
Average monthly benefits	$374	$347	−7
Unemployment			
Insured unemployment per 100 residents	0.8	1.2	+44
Average weekly benefits	$145	$188	+30

Note: [a] Calculated from unrounded totals.

Source: Statistical Abstract of the United States, 1990, pp. 281, 302, 362, 267, 368, 399.

Expenditures for welfare are the third largest component of the District budget, a much higher share than the average of state and local budgets. Expenditures per resident are more than 2.7 times the national average, and public welfare employment per resident is nearly twice the national average.

The finding that surprised me is that average benefits per recipient are not unusual. Average welfare benefits are slightly lower than the national average, despite the high cost of living in Washington. Average unemployment benefits are 30 per cent higher than the national average, but that percentage difference is not quite as high as the percentage difference in average salaries.

The more perplexing issue is why the recipient populations are so large. The population of welfare recipients, for example, is 72 per cent greater than the national average, compared with a poverty rate (in 1979) that was 50 per cent above the average. And the population of the insured unemployed is 44 per cent above the national average, although the number of unemployed per resident is about the same as the national average. Those differences may be due either to a different composition of the recipient populations or to more relaxed eligibility criteria. The data, by themselves, do *not* indicate that Washington is unusually generous to either welfare recipients or the unemployed. There is more reason to question the large size of the District's welfare staff.

Public Medical Care

District expenditures per resident for public medical care are more than twice the national average, but average health conditions are much worse (Table 6.8).

Expenditures for public health and hospitals are the fourth largest component of the District budget, a slightly higher share than the average for state and local budgets. Expenditures per resident are more than twice the national average, and the number of District medical care employees per resident is nearly 2.5 times the national average. There are many able professionals in the District medical care system, some of whom work beyond the call of duty, but anyone dependent on that system would testify that it was substantially overstaffed with low-quality support employees.

Across the nation, the average health status of the population generally increases with average income, the share of employment that is low risk, and the share of the population age 18 to 64. On that basis, the average health status of Washingtonians should be among the highest in the nation, whatever the level of public expenditures for medical care. Unfortunately, that is not the case. The number of infant deaths per 1000 live births is nearly twice the national average, higher than in any state.

Table 6.8 Public medical care, 1987

	Nation	District	Percentage difference
Costs and employment			
Share of current budget	8.7%	9.4%	+8
Expenditure per resident	$234	$486	+108
Employment per 10 000 residents	53.6	133.7	+149
Vital statistics			
Infant deaths per 1000 births	10.1	19.3	+91
Total deaths per 1000 residents	8.7	11.9	+37
Expected life at birth (1980)	73.9	69.2	−6

Source: Statistical Abstract of the United States, 1990, pp. 73, 76, 78, 281, 302.

Total deaths per 1000 residents are nearly 40 per cent higher than the national average, and higher than in any state, despite the small share of the population in the most vulnerable age groups. And, as of the 1980 census, the expected life of District residents was nearly five years shorter than the national average, and shorter than in any state. The combination of very high public expenditures for medical care and unusually poor health is probably the second most challenging problem facing the District government.

Highways and Other Services

Highway construction and maintenance are the one service for which District expenditures are relatively low (Table 6.9). District expenditures per resident for all other services not previously addressed, however, are unusually high.

Expenditure per resident for highways is slightly less than the national average, but even that level of expenditure is surprisingly high. District road mileage per resident is one-ninth the national average; the weather is generally clement; and the District's record of repairing road damage is notoriously bad.

District expenditure per resident for the wide range of other government services not previously discussed is more than twice the national average. Most of the services that I use and value as a District resident are in that group, and the quality of those services seems adequate, but I have no explanation of why the expenditure for them is so high. The two activities that the District seems to pursue with any zeal are enforcement of parking regulations and assessment of residential real estate.

Table 6.9 Highways and other services, 1987

	Nation	District	Percentage difference
Highways			
Share of current budget	8.0%	3.6%	−55
Expenditure per resident	$214	$187	−13
All other services			
Share of current budget	28.5%	34.5%	+21
Expenditure per resident	$765	$1786	+133

Source: Statistical Abstract of the United States, 1990, p. 281.

After so much data mongering, the mind wanders . . . Journalists will have to complete the record with their stories of local saints and sinners.

A RADICAL AGENDA FOR THE DISTRICT

Mayor Dixon promised Washington a District government that is clean, competent, tough-minded and caring. She deserves our best wishes. There is reason for hope, with the cooperation of the District Council, that her promise can be realized. And that would change the District's record of scandal and corruption. The mayor's approach, however, will not be sufficient to change the District's record of very high expenditures and very poor government services.

This section summarizes a 'radical' agenda for the District – suggestions for changes in the way the District is organized and operates that offer some hope of alleviating the most serious problems in Washington. These changes may not be 'realistic', in that they stem from a view of the problems that differs fundamentally from the conventional perspective. Given the magnitude of the District's problems, however, these changes deserve serious consideration. In the end, what proves to be realistic will depend on perceptions of what works.

Self-deception and Shibboleths

One of the major barriers to acknowledging and addressing the problems of Washington is the pattern of self-deception and shibboleths that characterizes local political discussion. The necessary first step towards substantial reform is to recognize the self-deception and to reject the shibboleths.

The major self-deception, as is often the case, is about money – the illusion that a substantial increase in District revenues either is possible or would resolve the major problems. The favourite illusion is that someone else will pay the bills, either through an increased federal grant or a commuter tax. Federal revenues are now nearly 40 per cent of total District revenues, excluding the direct federal cost of several local services in Washington. Neither Congress nor the Bush administration has expressed much willingness to make a further increase in the federal grant. Nonresidents already pay a substantial part of District revenues as commuter and tourist customers and nonresident owners of District corporations and property. The District does not have the authority to levy a commuter tax, and Congress has expressed no willingness to authorize such a tax.

District officials should also recognize the limits on local tax revenues. Despite the large share of District revenues that comes from the federal government, local taxes consume a larger share of personal income than they do in all but two states. More important, District individual, corporate and sales tax rates are substantially higher than in Maryland and Virginia. The population of Washington has declined 20 per cent in the past 20 years, and higher local tax rates would increase the loss of those residents who contribute most to Washington and thus might not increase long-term tax revenues.

The perception that higher revenues would alleviate the major problems of Washington is also an illusion. The District spends nearly twice the national per resident average of state and local governments without providing a single high-quality government service. In the absence of major changes in the organization and operation of the District, there is no reason or evidence that more money would make much difference.

The major local shibboleths involve the political status of the District, specifically the commitment to full home rule and statehood. Those objectives have no relevance to any major problem in Washington. The largest employer and property owner in any jurisdiction has substantial political influence. The federal government generally interferes too much with state and local governments, but there is no case that the relative federal influence on the District is too great. As long as federal revenues are nearly 40 per cent of total District revenues, the federal government will and should exercise substantial influence on the activities of the District.

The case for District statehood is even less relevant; statehood would provide several opportunities for District politicians to advance their careers but would provide no significant benefits for District residents. There is a good general case that every citizen should have representation in Congress; that could be achieved easily by reincorporating the District into Maryland. The fact that statehood advocates do not endorse that option suggests that they have some other more parochial objective.

General Organization, Employment and Revenue Reforms

Many District officials have aspirations that the District become a state. They should take that idea seriously. The major organizational change that should be considered is to restructure the District as a state, rather than as a unitary city-state. There are very few economies of scale in government services – certainly not in primary and secondary education, most police services, street maintenance and most other local services. Individual communities in Washington could be granted the authority to form separate cities, to select the local services that each will provide and to set their own property tax rates. The District could retain responsibility for higher education, courts and corrections, public health and welfare, highways and whatever local services the new cities do not provide and would retain all taxes other than the property tax. The District also could provide grants to the poorer cities to increase the revenues available for local services. The structure of cities in the District and the division of services between each city and the District should not be implemented by a master plan but should be permitted to evolve on the basis of some common rules. The primary benefits of that type of structure are that it permits increased diversity in the level, character and quality of local services and induces greater efficiency. As the capital of the world's major federal nation, the District should take the idea of federalism seriously.

In many cases, Washington would be better served by a District that was a financier of public services, rather than both the financier and the provider. There is a good case for government financing of a limited range of services; there is no good case for the same government's organizing and supplying those services. Many services now provided by the District could be better supplied under contract with private organizations or other governments or through vouchers for services to specific individuals. Moreover, the authority to contract for services, in whole or in part, would increase the incentive for District agencies to improve their performance.

The District is now hugely overstaffed – a condition that reflects, in part, a perspective that District employment is an instrument of political favouritism, job creation and welfare policy. A rejection of that perspective is requisite to important changes in employment practices. The important changes would be to increase the salary and qualifications of higher-level managers, to substantially reduce the number of middle managers and to tighten the quality standards for District employees. Another valuable change would be to eliminate all residency requirements for non-political positions, greatly increasing the pool from which District employees are selected. For those few workers subject to emergency recall, there is a basis for setting a time limit from residence to work station, but that need not preclude residence in a nearby suburb. The District will never provide high-quality services until District employment is considered a contract to supply specific services, rather than a sinecure.

The District should consider two changes in its revenue base but *not* try to increase total revenues. Over time, the base for the property tax could be gradually shifted from buildings to land by attributing future increases in assessments to the general price of land in the site area rather than to the value of the building on a specific site. That would increase the efficiency of land use and eliminate the current disincentive to improve buildings. If the property tax base were shifted to new cities in the District, of course, those cities should have this option.

The second change would be to collect congestion fees on all vehicles entering or leaving the District during peak hours. Simple technology is now available to do that without tollbooths. Expected congestion could be reduced to any desired level and the use of Metro increased. The revenues from those fees should be divided equally between the District and the jurisdiction in which the vehicle is registered, thereby reducing the opposition of adjacent governments to the fees.

The best use the District could make of additional revenues from the recommended changes would be to reduce those tax rates that are higher than in adjacent jurisdictions. The two proposed revenue measures would substantially increase the incentives to live, shop and invest in Washington and would reduce the dependence of the District on federal employment and revenues.

Education

Washington has a relatively small population of families who care about education but cannot afford a private school. That is both an effect and a cause of a poor public school system. The parents and students who choose not to participate in the District system are those on whom better schools are most dependent. That situation has led to a progressive decline in the performance of the District schools with no prospect for recovery.

Only a radical change in the organization of local schools has any potential for improving their record. There are ample reasons to maintain a high level of District spending per student; both average incomes and average salaries in Washington are unusually high. The District, however, should phase out of the business of organizing and managing the local schools.

The most promising reform has two essential characteristics: *parental choice* and *school-based management*. Full parental choice would permit every Washington family to send their children to any public or private school in the area, subject only to a District-specified core curriculum and a nondiscrimination standard. An amount of money equal to a share of the average District spending per student at each grade level, maybe in the second prior year, would be transferred to any private school selected.

Full school-based management would permit each school to set its own tuition, teacher credentials and salaries, and all other standards affecting the curriculum, pupil–teacher ratios, textbooks and the like. The reform should probably be phased in, one year at a time beginning with kindergarten, both to permit a gradual adjustment of the public schools and the expansion of other schools and to avoid a windfall to those families who now send their children to private schools. Those who are most concerned about education should recognize that this reform would *increase* local political support for school financing, both because current resident families would have greater options and because more families who value education would choose to live in Washington. Over time, this reform would improve, education, change the composition of Washington's population and probably reduce crime. The District must now make a choice between managing a poor school system and financing better education.

The University of the District of Columbia (UDC) should be recognized as a failure and be subject to the public equivalent of bankruptcy and reorganization. There are a dozen good colleges and universities in the Washington area and no apparent reason to maintain an unusually expensive and low-quality District university. A scholarship to any resident high-school graduate in an amount less than the average District spending per student at UDC would be more than sufficient to pay tuition at the other universities. One wonders whose interests are served by maintaining the pretence of higher education at UDC, surely not those of the students or the Washington community.

Courts, Police and Corrections

The District and the federal government spend an extraordinary amount for courts, police and corrections in Washington without providing much public safety. The rate of violent crime in Washington is several times the national average and many times that in other nations. The sad fact is that America's capital is one of the most dangerous cities in the world. The high crime rate may be due primarily to cultural attitudes and social conditions, but that is not a very helpful observation in the short run. The immediate challenge is to make much more effective use of the large number of police already employed in Washington.

Many readers of these comments will recognize that the magnitude of this problem overwhelms my understanding of the feasible measures that might be most effective. For that reason, I offer the following suggestion as a concerned and moderately informed resident of Washington, not as an expert on police and crime.

The first step towards improved police effectiveness is to change the priorities for the use of police. The District, like most governments, has passed more laws than can be feasibly enforced; for that reason, all police forces must set priorities among the many laws they are charged to enforce. The highest priority use of police should be to protect people against crimes against which it is difficult to protect or insure oneself. The highest priority should be to reduce the extraordinarily high rate of violent crimes, even at the cost of less enforcement of laws against property crimes or other crimes, such as drug use and prostitution, that are offensive but not directly threatening.

The second step is to change police tactics to reduce crime rates, even at the cost of lower arrest rates. For Washington, that requires a higher *visible* presence of police in areas of high violent crime and the substitution of civilian personnel for most police in desk jobs. That tactic has been most effective in Charleston, South Carolina; was recently adopted in New York City; and was strongly endorsed by the police experts on the Rivlin Commission.

The District also spends an extraordinary amount on corrections. The major opportunities for economy in this area appear to include speeding up court procedures, reducing the use of incarceration for nonviolent crimes, and contracting with nearby governments or private prisons.

Welfare, Medical Care and Other Services

The District's unusually high spending for public welfare and medical care, along with many of Washington's social problems, is primarily due to one condition: about 60 per cent of recent births in Washington are to unmarried women, nearly 2.5 times the national average. Moreover, most of those births are to adult women; only 17 per cent are to teenage mothers, some of whom are married. Nevertheless, births to teenagers are about 35 per cent above the national average. Unmarried women and their children are now the dominant family type of a substantial part of the Washington population. And the government, in effect, has become the marriage partner of last resort. Many of Washington's depressing social problems – from high infant mortality to low school performance to high welfare case loads and a high crime rate – derive primarily from that condition. It is unclear, however, whether that condition would be responsive to changes in social policy.

District welfare payments per recipient and the standards for welfare eligibility are not unusual; Washington is *not* a welfare magnet. The problem is that unusual conditions demand unusual policy responses, and no such responses have been tried. The most difficult policy challenge is to discipline irresponsible behaviour by adults without penalizing innocent children. None of the alternatives is easy, but none should be precluded for that reason. The federal welfare legislation of 1988 already requires that an unmarried teenage mother (with special exceptions) live with her mother to be eligible for welfare, but teenage mothers are a small part of the District's welfare population.

One option is much more rigorous child support enforcement, recognizing that fathers may be difficult to locate or may not have much apparent income. A second option is to eliminate the increase in welfare payments per mother with any future increase in the number of dependent children, an option that is less desirable because it would penalize dependent children if it were not effective in limiting their number. A District government that is not willing to consider such options must accept responsibility for a large underclass that is costly to others and dangerous primarily to its own members. The high cost and poor performance of other District services such as medical care, housing and social services derive from the same cause and are not addressed further.

CONCLUSION

The government of the District of Columbia may or may not be America's worst. That issue is provocative but not important. The sad fact is that the District government does not bring credit to the nation's capital, does not use its huge resources effectively and continues to face a distressing array of social problems. Mayor Dixon may be effective in reducing the corruption and the more conspicuous waste that mushroomed during the administration of her predecessor, and she deserves our support. The major problems of the District will remain unresolved, however, unless the new mayor and District Council acknowledge them and are willing to consider radical changes that offer some promise of a government that is worthy of the nation's capital.

STATISTICAL APPENDIX 6A

This appendix presents the results from six linear regressions that are the basis for the special analysis of police and corrections summarized earlier (see Tables 6A.1 and 6A.2).

Policy analysis

Table 6A.1 Expenditure and employment regressions

	Dependent variables		
Independent variables	*PCE*	*POL*	*COR*
CON	−104.211	6.978	2.561
	(38.857)	(3.715)	(4.167)
DCD	296.758	20.402	19.479
	(83.035)	(8.370)	(9.389)
FRR	0.111	0.006	0.003
	(0.038)	(0.004)	(0.004)
PIR	0.013	0.001	0.000
	(0.002)	(0.000)	(0.000)
VCR	0.138	0.013	0.012
	(0.026)	(0.003)	(0.003)
PCR	0.006	0.000	0.000
	(0.005)	(0.000)	(0.000)
LDN	−15.357	−1.433	−0.305
	(4.766)	(0.480)	(0.539)
$\bar{R}^2$	0.943	0.886	0.841
SER	28.044	2.827	3.171

Table 6A.2 Crime-rate regressions

	Dependent variables		
Independent variables	*VCR*	*MDR*	*PCR*
CON	−457.024	−8.329	2304.377
	(142.229)	(1.673)	(780.997)
DCD	1046.265	46.964	3656.544
	(194.858)	(2.292)	(1069.993)
POV	29.662	0.720	71.822
	(7.455)	(0.088)	(40.937)
MET	10.981	0.134	59.621
	(1.623)	(0.019)	(8.910)
LDN	−34.501	−0.0650	−573.046
	(25.435)	(0.299)	(139.665)
$\bar{R}^2$	0.747	0.946	0.543
SER	163.5	1.924	898.091

Definition of Variables

PCE = expenditures per resident for police and corrections (1987)
POL = police per 10 000 residents (1987)
COR = corrections employees per 10 000 residents (1987)
VCR = violent crimes per 100 000 residents (1988)
MDR = murders per 100 000 residents (1988)
PCR = property crimes per 100 000 residents (1988)
CON = constant
DCD = 1 for DC, 0 for all states
FRR = federal revenues per resident (1987)
PIR = personal income per resident (1987)
MET = percentage of residents in metropolitan areas (1987)
POV = percentage of residents below poverty line (1979)
LDN = population per square mile (1988), natural logarithm.

All data are from the *Statistical Abstract of the United States* 1990.

Notes on Interpreting the Regressions

For each regression, the top number in each row presents the effect of a one-unit increase of the specific independent variable on the dependent variable. For example, a $1 increase in federal revenues per resident appears to increase state and local spending per resident for police and corrections by about 11 cents. Similarly, a 1 percentage point increase in the share of a state's population that lives in metropolitan areas appears to increase the violent crime rate by about 11 crimes per 100 000 residents. The numbers in parentheses are the standard errors of each coefficient. $\bar{R}^2$ is the share of the variance of each dependent variable that is explained by the combination of the independent variables. SER is the standard error of the regression, measured in the units of the dependent variable.

The interpretation of the expenditure and employment regression is rather straightforward. The demand for police services is a positive function of federal revenues, personal income, and crime rates and a negative function of population density. The crime rate regressions are more disturbing. The level of crime appears to be primarily dependent on the poverty rate, the degree of metropolitanization and population density, and does not appear to decline in response to a larger number of police. Indeed, adding the POL variable (police per 10 000 residents) to the crime rate regressions yields a positive coefficient at high levels of statistical significance. Although other studies have found a similar effect, I cannot accept the conclusion that additional police increase crime. For that reason, I have reported only those crime rate regressions that do not include the police expenditure and employment variables.

The results of the regressions are interesting and suggestive but not definitive. Much more analysis would be necessary for a thorough understanding of these relations. For this chapter, the primary purpose of the analysis was to estimate the DCD coefficients that measure how much police expenditures, police and corrections employment and crime rates differ in the District, given the conditions that explain those variables across the nation. For that limited purpose, this limited analysis should be sufficient.

7. Economists and drug policy*

INTRODUCTION

For most economists, surely for this one, the illegal drug market is like a distant country with a language and culture that we do not understand and about which the data range from poor to nonexistent. For this reason, an economist who addresses drug policy risks being an innocent abroad.

What do economists have to say about drug policy? Specifically, what do we have to say that might convince political officials to change current drug policies? This chapter addresses these questions, based primarily on data available to the general public and the developing literature on this issue by other economists. My primary incentives for addressing these issues are that the Cato Institute has been a leading advocate for reconsidering drug policy and that I live near the centre of a city with the nation's highest murder rate. My only advantages in addressing this issue are my own graduate-school studies of the markets for cigarettes and alcoholic beverages and my developing scepticism about the case for 'wars', whether in some distant desert or in the inner city. This chapter, thus, is a record of my own odyssey through the available data and economic literature in a continuing attempt to sort out my own views on drug policy.

THE PUBLIC RECORD ON DRUGS

In a nationally televised address in September 1989, President George Bush stated that 'All of us agree that the gravest domestic threat facing our nation today is drugs'.[1] Let us first look at the generally available data that might have led President Bush and many others to this conclusion. Most of these data are summarized in the annual *Statistical Abstract of the United States: 1990.*

* Reprinted by permission from *Carnegie-Rochester Conference Series on Public Policy*, No. 36, 1992, pp. 223–48, North-Holland.

Drug Use

The most comprehensive data on drug use are collected every several years by the *National Household Survey of Drug Abuse*.[2] Table 7.1 summarizes the data from the 1988 household survey. This table excludes the available data on the nonmedicinal use of a variety of other legal and illegal drugs (inhalants, hallucinogens, analgesics, stimulants, sedatives and tranquillizers) for which use rates are similar to those for cocaine. Other data from the survey (not shown) indicate that the weekly use rate is about 56 per cent of the monthly use rate for marijuana and about 28 per cent for cocaine. Other sources estimate that the total number of current heroin users is about 0.5 million.[3]

The most obvious lesson from this table is that only a small share of the population is a current user of any illegal drug. Many commentators, including President Bush, have repeated the estimate that 23 million Americans are current drug users. The number of drug users, however, is not additive across types of drugs. Most users of the hard drugs, for

Table 7.1 Drug use by type of drug and age group, 1988

Use rate Type of drug	Age group (percentage of group)							
	12–17		18–25		Over 25		Total[1] (millions)	
	Ever	Current	Ever	Current	Ever	Current	Ever	Current[2]
Alcohol	50.2	25.2	90.3	65.3	88.6	54.8	172.5	108.4
Cigarettes	42.3	11.8	75.0	35.2	76.6	29.8	152.5	58.5
Marijuana	17.4	6.4	56.4	15.5	30.7	3.9	67.6	12.0
Cocaine	3.4	1.1	19.7	4.5	9.9	0.9	21.8	3.0
Heroin	0.6	na	0.4	na	1.1	na	1.9	na

Notes:
1. Assumes drug-use rate in nonhousehold population is the same as in the household population.
2. Current use is defined as those who have used a specific drug at least once in the prior month.
na: Not available.

Source: US National Institute on Drug Abuse, *National Household Survey of Drug Abuse,* 1988; data summarized are from US Bureau of the Census, *Statistical Abstract of the United States: 1990*, p. 122.

example, also use marijuana, and many drug users use combinations of drugs, such as stimulants and opiates, with opposite pharmacological characteristics. The total number of current drug users, thus, is only somewhat higher than the number of marijuana users, about 6 per cent of the total population.

A more interesting lesson from these data is the revealed pattern of addiction rates. The concept of addiction is subject to a range of interpretations and measures. For my purpose, the addiction rate is best measured by the percentage of those who have ever used a specific drug who are current users. Table 7.2 presents estimates of the addiction rate by type of drug and age group, based on the same data presented in Table 7.1, excluding heroin for lack of data on the current-use rate. The revealed addiction rates presented in this table display several patterns. First, in general, the addiction rate *declines* as a function of the potency of a drug, a pattern that economists may find reasonable but that is quite contrary to popular perceptions. Second, the addiction rate for legal drugs peaks in the 18–25 age group. Third, the addiction rate for illegal drugs peaks in the 12–17 age group.

The primary problem of interpreting Table 7.1 and Table 7.2 is that the pattern of drug use by age group reflects both an age effect and a cohort effect. Those now over 25, for example, were young teenagers in years in which social attitudes and the illegal drug market were quite different from current conditions. Those who are now young teenagers will have a quite different ever-used record when they are over age 25. These two effects, however, can be separated by statistical analysis of the household survey data. For this purpose, I have used the following test equation:

$$LCU = C + bYAD + cADD + dCGD + eALD + fLEU$$

Table 7.2 Addiction rate by type of drug and age group, 1988

	Age group (%)		
Type of drug	12–17	18–25	Over 25
Alcohol	50.2	72.3	61.9
Cigarettes	27.9	46.9	37.4
Marijuana	36.8	27.5	12.7
Cocaine	32.4	22.8	9.1

where:

    LCU is the natural log of the current-use percentage,
    C is the constant,
    YAD is a dummy variable for the 18–25 age group,
    ADD is a dummy variable for the over–25 age group,
    CGD is a dummy variable for cigarettes, specific to the two older
             age groups,
    ALD is a dummy variable for alcohol, specific to the two older age
             groups, and
    LEU is the natural log of the ever-used percentage.

The results of this regression, based on a sample of all of the drugs included in the 1988 household survey except heroin, are summarized in Table 7.3.

Table 7.3 Regression results

Variables	Coefficient	Standard error
C	−1.840	0.148
YAD	−0.577	0.130
ADD	−1.004	0.130
CGD	0.683	0.243
ALD	1.114	0.248
LEU	1.248	0.062

Notes: $N = 29$; $R^2 = 0.974$; $SER = 0.273$.

For the most part, these regression results are consistent with the patterns revealed in Table 7.2. The strongest effect on the current-use rate is the ever-used rate, with an elasticity significantly larger than unity. The constant and the several dummy variables each measure the effect on the current-use rate relative to the ever-used rate; in effect, the constant is the dummy variable for the 12–17 age group. The coefficients for the age-group dummies indicate that the addiction rate is lowest among the 12–17 age group, highest among the 18–25 age group and somewhat lower among the over-25 age group. The coefficients on the drug-type dummies indicate that the addiction rate is somewhat higher for cigarettes and alcohol than for the set of illegal drugs; it is not clear whether this effect is specific to these types of drugs or whether it is a consequence of the legal status of these drugs for most people in the two older age groups.

These relations should also be helpful in forecasting future drug use under present drug policies. The ever-used rate for the group now of ages 12–17 is lower than for the same age group a decade ago for almost every drug. This implies that current drug use among the older groups would probably continue to decline slowly under present drug policies.

Drug Arrests

A substantial amount of police resources are used to control the distribution and use of both legal and illegal drugs. Table 7.4 summarizes the arrest rates for alcohol and illegal drugs from the Federal Bureau of Investigation (FBI) crime reports for 1988.

The first lesson from this table is that even legal drugs involve a substantial amount of enforcement activity (the summary arrest data do not include any arrests for violation of the tobacco laws). This implies that regulation of other drugs by a system of social controls similar to that for alcohol would involve substantial continued enforcement expenditures. (A large share of the current expenditures to control illegal drugs, however, is for enforcement activities in other countries or at the US border, and legalization would nearly eliminate these activities.) A second lesson is that the arrest rates per current user are roughly the same for alcohol, marijuana and drugs other than cocaine and heroin. The arrest rates per current user of cocaine and heroin, however, are many times that for the other drugs, roughly ten times as high for distribution violations and five times as high for use or possession violations.

It is important to recognize that the laws bearing on alcohol and illegal drugs differ in two major ways. The importation, manufacture and sale of alcoholic beverages is legal subject to specific restrictions, and the distribution arrests are for violations of these restrictions. For illegal drugs, the importation, manufacture and sale is illegal except for narrowly restricted medical use. For alcohol, the abuse violations are for specific types of offensive or threatening public behaviour. For illegal drugs, the abuse violations are for mere possession.

Health Effects of Drug Use

Most of the legal and illegal drugs have significant health effects. Table 7.5 summarizes the available data on the number of annual medical treatments, emergencies and deaths attributable to specific drugs for various years in the late 1980s.

The first lesson from this table is that use of the major legal drugs is a major cause of health problems and deaths. About 350 000 people are clients of alcoholism treatment centres, about 0.3 of 1 per cent of current

Policy analysis

Table 7.4 Arrests for distribution or use of drugs, 1988

	Rate per 100000	
Type of drug	Residents	Current users[1]
Alcohol		
Distribution	260	454
Drunkenness	321	559
Driving while intoxicated	685	1194
Total	1266	2207
Marijuana		
Distribution	25	520
Possession	130	2665
Total	155	3185
Cocaine or heroin		
Distribution	75	5253
Possession	154	10794
Total	229	16047
Other drugs		
Distribution	24	817
Possession	42	1462
Total	66	2279

Note:
1. Estimates of current users based on 1988 *National Household Survey*. Estimates of arrest rates for cocaine or heroin and for other drugs assume current-use rates are additive within these groups; for these groups, the estimated arrest rates are biased downwards.

Source: US Federal Bureau of Investigation, *Crime in the United States*; data summarized are from the US Bureau of the Census, *Statistical Abstract of the United States: 1990*, pp. 177, 178.

alcohol users. About 600000 deaths per year may be attributable to the direct and indirect effects of alcohol and cigarette consumption, nearly 30 per cent of deaths from all causes. (I do not necessarily endorse these estimates; they are difficult to reconcile with the detailed data on mortality, which report about 26000 deaths due to chronic liver disease and 141000 deaths due to lung cancer in 1988. The total number of deaths due to alcohol and cigarettes, however, must be at least several hundred thousand.)

The more important lesson from this table is that illegal drugs cause substantial health problems but remarkably few deaths. About 260 000 people are clients of drug-abuse treatment centres, nearly 2 percent of the current drug users. About 160 000 emergency-room episodes per year are attributable to some drug, about 1 per cent of the current drug users. A total of 6756 deaths were reported as drug induced or drug related in 1988, 21 per cent of which were apparent suicides. For comparison, the number of accidental deaths due to drugs is only somewhat larger than the number of accidents due to drowning or fires. Only a few deaths are

Table 7.5 Health effects of drug use 1987 or 1988 (thousands of people per year)

Types of drug	Treatment[1]	Emergencies[2]	Deaths[3]
Alcohol	351	46.6	229
Cigarettes	na	na	390
Drugs			
Marijuana	na	10.7	0.3
Cocaine	na	62.1	3.3
Heroin	na	20.6	2.5
Other	na	121.5	10.4
Total	264	160.0	6.8

Notes:
na: Not available.

1. Number of clients served by alcoholic and drug-abuse treatment centres, 1987. Source: US National Institute on Drug Abuse and US National Institute on Alcohol Abuse and Alcoholism, *National Drug and Alcoholism Treatment Unit Survey: Main Findings 1987*; data summarized are from US Bureau of the Census, *Statistical Abstract of the United States: 1990*, p. 122.
2. Number of emergency-room episodes in 1988 in which a specific drug is mentioned as a cause of the emergency. The number of alcohol-related episodes include only those episodes for which alcohol is used in combination with one or more other drugs. The total number of drug 'mentions' is much higher than the number of drug episodes, because 46 per cent of the episodes involve more than one drug. Source: US National Institute on Drug Abuse, *Drug Abuse Warning Network (DAWN) Annual Data 1988*, Series 1, No. 8.
3. Source of the number of deaths due to alcohol: US Department of Health and Human Services, *Fifth Special Report to the US Congress on Alcoholism and Health*. Source of the number of deaths due to smoking: US Public Health Service, 'Reducing the health consequences of smoking: 25 years of progress', 1989. Number of deaths due to drugs is from the DAWN report (referenced above). Number of deaths due to a specific drug includes those in which more than one drug is mentioned as a cause of death. The total number of drug-death 'mentions' is much higher than the number of drug deaths, because 77 per cent of drug-related deaths involve the use of more than one drug.

attributed to marijuana use only. The attribution of deaths to any specific drug is necessarily imprecise because of the prevailing pattern of multiple drug use. The use of drugs that are now illegal clearly causes substantial health problems, but it is difficult to understand the basis for a conclusion that it represents 'the gravest domestic threat to our nation today'.

THE CONTRIBUTION OF ECONOMISTS TO UNDERSTANDING DRUGS

Economists have made a substantial contribution to understanding drug use and drug policy, despite the paucity of personal experience and relevant data. The general skills that economists bring to this issue are the same as have proved valuable to understand other issues – a theory of rational behaviour, understanding of markets, sophisticated empirical techniques and a distinctive approach to the analysis of public policy. This section reviews the major contributions by economists to understanding the most important questions that bear on the choice of drug policy.

A Theory of Rational Addiction

Several Years ago, Becker and Murphy (1988) developed a characteristically elegant model of rational addiction. This model incorporates the effects of both 'reinforcement' and 'tolerance' on current consumption. Reinforcement implies that higher past consumption increases the demand for current consumption, but tolerance implies that the utility from current consumption is a negative function of prior consumption. The model is developed from the following function:

$$U(t) = u[c(t), S(t), y(t)],$$

where $U(t)$ is utility at time t, $c(t)$ is the current consumption of an addictive good, $S(t)$ is the stock of 'addictive capital' that depends on past consumption, and $y(t)$ is the current consumption of a nonaddictive good. The authors then demonstrate that revealed consumption behaviour in a steady state (where $c = \delta S$) will reflect a net reinforcement effect only if

$$(\sigma + 2\delta)\, U_{cs} > -U_{ss},$$

where σ is the individual's rate of time preference, and δ is the rate of depreciation on the stock of addictive capital. For such addictive goods, the past, current and expected future consumption are complements.

From this simple model, the authors derive a rich set of behavioural hypotheses:

- Addictive behaviour is more likely for those who have a high rate of time preference, such as young people and the poor.
- Addictive behaviour is more likely for those goods for which the rate of depreciation of the stock of addictive capital is higher.
- Some people never consume addictive goods.
- Some people return to a zero consumption level after some prior consumption of addictive goods.
- Some consumers of addictive goods go on a consumption 'binge' until they reach a higher steady state.
- The long-run (absolute) price elasticity of demand is higher than the short-run elasticity.
- The long-run price elasticity is higher for those with a stronger addiction.
- The ratio of the long-run to short-run price elasticity is higher for those with a stronger addiction.

This is an impressive theoretical development, and the behavioural hypotheses are consistent with the observed consumption behaviour in the markets for a number of legal drugs.[4] The important issue is whether this model describes the consumption behaviour for those drugs that are now illegal.

The Price Elasticity of Demand for Illegal Drugs

For several reasons, there are no conventional studies of the demand functions for illegal drugs. The available price data are limited and usually do not control for drug potency. In addition, there are no direct measures of consumption.

As far as I know, there are only two careful studies of the price elasticity of demand for illegal drugs, one for marijuana and one for heroin, both using unconventional techniques.

Nisbet and Vakil (1972) report estimates of the price elasticity for marijuana from −1.0 to −1.5 based on a mailed confidential 'what if?' survey of students at the University of California (Los Angeles). These estimates seem consistent with the Becker–Murphy hypotheses, but they are not based on revealed behaviour and do not merit additional comment.

The only careful study of the price elasticity of demand for illegal drugs based on revealed behaviour is that by Silverman, Spruill and Levine (1975). This study examines the effects on monthly variations in property crime in Detroit of the variations in the street price of heroin, controlled for trend, seasonal conditions, law-enforcement activities and the potency of the heroin sold. The test equations reflect an assumption that increases in the expenditure for heroin increase the incentive to augment other income by property crime. The estimated price elasticities for heroin, based on the sample of all property crimes, are reported in Table 7.6.

Table 7.6 Estimated price elasticity of demand for heroin

	Current price	÷	Average price
	2		1
Heroin potency (%)			
2.5	−0.380		−0.241
10.0	−0.355		−0.215

These results are strongly inconsistent with several of the Becker–Murphy hypotheses. The long-run price elasticity is *lower* than the short-run elasticity, suggesting that past and current consumption are substitutes. Second, the price elasticity for those who purchased the more potent heroin is somewhat lower than for those who used the less potent heroin.[5] In addition, some supplementary calculations indicate that the price elasticities were much lower in the poor neighbourhoods of Detroit than in the more affluent neighbourhoods. These several estimates suggest that the (absolute) elasticity of demand by casual users is quite high but that the long-run price elasticity by regular users is much lower, more consistent with the conventional wisdom. The Becker–Murphy model may not have much relevance to goods, like heroin, for which the addiction rate is quite low.

The Effects on Drug Consumption of Drug Legalization

These quite precise, but indirect, estimates of the price elasticity of the demand for heroin are the best available. For several reasons, however, these estimates are of little value for estimating the effects on drug consumption of drug legalization:

- Theory and the available evidence are not sufficient to determine the *form* of the demand function over a substantial price range. This is not important for small price changes but is very important for large price changes. For example, given a price elasticity of −0.24 within the observed price range, a 90 per cent reduction in the retail price would lead to a 74 per cent increase in per capita consumption if the demand function is logarithmic but only a 22 per cent increase in per capita consumption if the demand function is linear.

- The retail price of legal drugs is quite uncertain and would be strongly dependent on tax and regulatory policies. The potential reduction in the retail price, however, is huge. For cocaine and heroin of uncertain quality that now sells on the street for $10, the cost of production is five to ten cents.[6] (I do not know of similar estimates for marijuana.) As with alcohol, both the legal retail price of drugs and the remaining illegal market would depend on the level of product-specific taxes and regulations on legal distribution.
- Most important, legalization of drugs would increase the demand for drugs at any price. Current users of illegal drugs face two types of costs in addition to the street price. First, the costs of purchase include search costs and the risks of assault and arrest. Second, the costs of use include the risks of drugs of uncertain potency, adulterants and of some use techniques Drug legalization would eliminate most of these two types of costs. Moreover, legal cocaine and heroin would probably include known antidotes that substantially reduce the toxicity of these drugs.

In summary, legalization would both reduce the price of drugs and shift the demand function for drugs. Economists are now able to offer only crude estimates of the price effects and no evidence of the demand-shift effects.

Three other types of evidence also bear on this issue: the level of alcohol consumption before, during, and after 'the noble experiment' with the national prohibition of alcohol, the available record on drug use prior to the prohibition of hard drugs beginning in 1914 and of marijuana beginning in 1937, and the experience with alternative policies in other nations.

The classic study by Warburton (1932) provides the best estimates of the effects of prohibition on the consumption of alcoholic beverages. Table 7.6 presents the Warburton estimates of consumption during prohibition and the public data for comparable periods before and after prohibition. Miron and Zwiebel (1991) have recently reaffirmed Warburton's estimates of the effect of prohibition on the total consumption of alcohol, based on a different functional form and a longer sample period. Apparent consumption of each alcoholic beverage declined in the early years of prohibition, most sharply for beer. Although expenditures to enforce the Volstead Act increased sharply during the 1920s, apparent consumption of spirits and wine was higher at the end of the decade than prior to prohibition. During the late 1920s, the real price of each beverage was about 2.5 times the price prior to World War I. As of 1940, when real per capita income had recovered to the 1929 level, the level of spirits and wine consumption was about the same as during the late years of prohibition, and beer consumption was about the same as prior to prohibition. After the early years, the primary effects of prohibition on alcohol consumption, thus, appear to have been a reduction in the consumption of beer. Several related statistics also bear on the effects of the prohibition of alcohol: the death rate from chronic liver disease roughly doubled from the 1920s to 1970 and has since declined by about one-third. The death rate from alcohol poisoning, however, increased sharply during prohibition and declined sharply after the end of prohibition. From this experience with alcohol prohibition, Miron and Zwiebel speculate that the legalization of drugs would not lead to a substantial increase in drug consumption. The primary reason to qualify the relevance of this experience is that the end of alcohol prohibition reduced the real retail price by about 60 per cent, whereas drug legalization might reduce the retail price by more that 90 per cent.

The other US experience that may provide some guidance to the probable effects of drug legalization was the use of drugs prior to the imposition of national controls beginning in 1914.[7] In the late nineteenth century, opium, morphine and cocaine were legal and widely available without prescription. Parke-Davis sold cocaine for a variety of beverage, smoking and medicinal uses beginning in 1885. Heroin was the brand name of a cough suppressant sold by Bayer beginning in 1898. After an accumulation of medical warnings, however, the use of opiates peaked in the 1890s at about twice the estimated present rate, and the use of cocaine peaked about 1905. After passage of the Pure Food and Drug Act in

Table 7.7 Consumption of alcoholic beverages, 1911–1941 (annual gallons per capita)

Years	Spirits	Wine	Beer
1911–14	1.71	0.59	20.53
1921–22	1.07	0.51	1.49
1927–30	1.88	0.98	6.27
1939–41	1.73	1.06	19.67

Source: Clark Warburton, *The Economic Results of Prohibition*, New York: Columbia University Press, 1932. Later data from industry publications.

1906, which required that the presence of specific drugs be identified on the label of patent medicines, the use of these drugs declined by one-third to one-half long before their use was prohibited. Although popular magazines increasingly warned their readers against the use of patent medicines including these drugs, there was no organized drug prohibition movement and no press reports of a 'drug crisis'. The major lesson from this experience is that drug use peaked at rates about twice the estimated present rate and subsequently declined in response to more broadly available information about the effects of drug use.

The current record of drug policies and drug use in the Netherlands and Great Britain may provide an even better guide to the effects of relaxing drug-use controls in the United States. For nearly two decades, the Netherlands has had the most relaxed drug laws of any industrial country, generally treating drug use as a public-health problem rather than as a police problem.[8] Drug users are provided with clean needles, counselling, and treatment but are not subject to prosecution for use or for possession of small amounts of any drug. Criminal prosecution is focused on major suppliers. Many coffee houses sell marijuana and are not subject to police interference unless they sell wholesale quantities or to those under age 16, or unless they advertise more than by a marijuana-leaf decal on their windows. Current-use rates among Dutch teenagers are slightly higher than in the United States for alcohol and tobacco but are a fraction of the US rates for other drugs, and marijuana use appears to be declining; these data overstate the current use rates among the native Dutch, because a substantial share of drug users are foreigners. In a population of 15 million, there are less than 100 drug-related deaths a year. And the murder rate in Amsterdam is about one-tenth that in Washington, DC. Drug policies in the Netherlands are broadly supported, and the results of these policies so impressed the American ambassador that he recommended careful study of this experience.

British policies affecting cocaine and heroin addicts are similar to those in the Netherlands, despite the tightening of official policies in the late 1960s and the strident rhetoric of British politicians.[9] Legal cocaine and heroin are not available for recreational use, but British physicians may prescribe these drugs to their addict-patients. Local governments are experimenting with different treatment practices. Such policies, however, do not apply to marijuana, smoked opium or a range of other drugs. The British are broadly perceived to have rejected the 'decriminalization option' in 1968, but this is misleading. A comparison of arrest records, for example, indicates that the number of drug arrests per capita in the United States is ten times the British rate; excluding marijuana, for which British policies are similar to American policies, the US arrest rate is 35 times the British rate. The British courts have progressively increased the proportion of those arrested for drug-use offences who are subject to probation and treatment rather than incarceration. Current-use rates in Britain are lower than in the United States and appear to have declined since the mid-1980s. The *de facto* British policy of 'harm reduction' does not appear to have led to a significant increase in drug use or health problems, and the costs of social control are much lower than in the United States.

My rough judgement, based on these several types of evidence, is that drug legalization might double the present rates of drug use but that any estimate of this effect is subject to large error.

Other Conditions Affecting Drug Use

As the above section illustrates, economists have been able to make only indirect inferences about the effects of drug price on drug consumption. The available information however, permits a much better understanding of the other conditions that affect drug use. Gill and Michaels (1991) have recently completed an analysis of the 1984 *National Longitudinal Survey of Youth*, using a probit analysis to estimate the effects of a variety of personal and economic conditions on the probability that a person has used one or more illegal drugs in the prior year. Their general conclusion is that personal characteristics, rather than economic variables, are the primary determinants of drug use. For example, drug use appears to be most strongly related to alcohol abuse, frequency of going to bars, a record of prior illegal activities or income from illegal sources, and dissatisfaction with one's job. Drug use appears to decline with the education of the respondent but to increase with the education of parents. Drug use is higher among single people, males, urban residents, Westerners and (for hard drugs) whites. Given these personal characteristics, there appears to be no significant effect of the respondent's wage rate or income from other legal sources. This study is not a sufficient basis for concluding that the income elasticity of the demand for drugs is negligible, because it addresses only whether the respondents used some illegal drug in the prior year rather than the amount consumed. The most encouraging conclusion is that most regular drug use is limited to a small part of the population, most of whom have other personal problems.

The Effects of Drug Use on Productivity

One of the perceptions that affects drug policy is that drug use reduces productivity and, in turn, wage rates and earnings. The only apparent basis for this perception is the observation that many drug users have low wages. The correct inference, however, may be the opposite of the common perception: the personal characteristics associated with low wages may be the same that lead to drug use. As part of the study of drug use summarized in the above section, Gill and Michaels (1990) also estimated the wage differences between drug users and nondrug users by techniques that control for both the personal characteristics that affect wages and those that affect drug use. They estimate that drug use (at least once in the prior year) appears to *increase* wages about 7 per cent and that hard drug use may increase wages as much as 20 per cent. This finding may be surprising, but it is quite consistent with a similar study by Berger and Leigh (1988) that concludes that alcohol consumption up through two drinks a day also appears to increase wages. These studies are not sufficient to resolve the economic concern about drug use because they do not address the possible effects of drug use on employment, but they suggest that moderate alcohol and drug use is not a major economic problem.

Drug Enforcement and Crime

It is not clear that the rapid increase in drug enforcement activities in the 1980s reduced drug use. Both the price and the potency of marijuana increased sharply. The price of both cocaine and heroin declined substantially, and the average potency of both drugs increased.

There is more evidence, however, that increased drug enforcement increases property crime. This relation operates through two effects: the effect of drug price and the effect of a diversion of police resources. Consider the following simple model:

$$C = aA^{-b} P^c$$

$$A = dL^e S^{-f}$$

$$P = gL^h S^i$$

where C is the total property crime rate, A is the probability of arrest for a property crime, P is the price of drugs, L is the total number of police per capita, and S is the share of police resources allocated to enforcing the drug laws. Solving this model for the property crime rate yields

$$C = (ad^{-b}g^c) \, L^{-be + ch} \, S^{bf + ci}$$

The study of property crime in Detroit by Silverman, Spruill and Levine (1975) provides estimates of the first equation, where $b = 0.42$ and

$c = 0.29$. A recent study of property crime in Florida by Benson and Rasmussen (1991) provides estimates of the second equation, where $e = 0.45$ and $f = 0.34$. (These estimates do not reflect the additional effects on property crime of the reduction in conviction rates and effective penalties resulting from the crowding of courts and jails by drug-law offenders or of the reduced reporting of property crime resulting from a reduced clearance rate.) I know of no estimates of the third equation, but for this purpose it is useful to examine the effects of h and i over the range from 0.3 to 0.7. Combining these estimates yields the following relations between C, L and S:

$$h = i = 0.3 \quad C = \propto L^{-0.10} S^{0.23}$$

$$h = i = 0.7 \quad C = \propto L^{-0.01} S^{0.34}$$

These equations suggest that the property crime rate is a weak (negative or positive) function of the number of police and a stronger positive function of the share of police resources allocated to drug enforcement. Moreover, these conclusions are stronger the more effective is police activity in increasing the price of drugs. Some part of the high property crime rates in our major cities must be attributed to enforcement of the drug laws.

There are no similar studies of the relation between drug enforcement and violent crime. The selective evidence available, however, should not be dismissed.[10] One study estimates that about 10 per cent of assaults in 1980 were drug related. For the entire United States, nearly 8 per cent of recent murders were drug related. Officials in Miami, Washington and New York City estimate that 30–40 per cent of recent murders in these cities were drug related. It is also important to observe that most of these drug-related assaults and murders are attributed to disputes over contracts or territory in the illegal market, not to the psychopharmacological effects of drug use. The victims of most of these assaults and murders were participants in the illegal drug market, although there have been some well-publicized deaths of third parties and police. A final piece of evidence may be the most convincing: the murder rate and the rate of assault with firearms increased substantially during the national prohibition of alcohol and then declined continuously for a decade after the end of prohibition.

Drug Enforcement and Health

Economists do not have a comparative advantage in evaluating the health effects of drug enforcement and drug use. A number of economists, including Reuter (1990), have reviewed these effects, but the basic studies are by pharmacologists and physicians. Economic theory, however, is useful to explain some of the health effects of drug enforcement. Since the probability of arrest is a positive function of the volume of drugs shipped and the number of transactions, one should expect drug enforcement to increase the potency of each drug and to shift consumption to the more potent drugs. One should also expect the 'quality' of drugs (in terms of the variance of potency and the risk of dangerous adulterants) to decline in response to increased enforcement of the street markets, because such enforcement reduces the potential for a sustained relation between buyers and sellers. Drug use, in turn, should be expected to decline in response to both increased potency and lower quality. The available evidence is roughly consistent with these expected effects. Marijuana use peaked in about 1979 in association with the sharp increase in potency. Cocaine use peaked about 1985, shortly after the introduction of crack in the street markets. Heroin has largely replaced the use of opium and morphine.

Drug enforcement may also have led to more dangerous use techniques. Closing the 'head shops' has probably reduced the use of water pipes in favour of smoking the now increasingly potent marijuana. Sniffing cocaine appears to have been largely replaced by smoking crack. Many of the deaths (from AIDS and hepatitis) associated with the use of injected drugs such as heroin appear to be the result of dirty needles.

A careful review of the available studies indicates that many of the adverse health effects of current drug use, maybe most of these effects, are due to the side-effects of prohibition of these drugs – overdose, adulterants, more risky use techniques and a reluctance to seek early medical treatment.[11] Most of the drugs that are now illegal present some risk even in a controlled setting, but the risks appear to be much lower. In Canada, for example, cocaine is routinely applied in nasal surgery in doses that are about the same as in recreational use. A survey of surgeons revealed that this use of cocaine led to five deaths and 34 severe reactions following 108 032 applications of cocaine.[12] Even at this rate, however, a once-a-week cocaine user faces a probability of death that is roughly double that for nonusers. There are ample reasons to discourage the use of such drugs. The important issue is whether such drugs should be illegal.

SORTING OUT THE ISSUES ABOUT DRUG POLICY

Economists who address drug policy characteristically ask the following three questions:

- What are the effects of a specific drug policy on drug users and suppliers?
- What are the effects on third parties?
- What would be the benefits and costs to each group of a change in drug policy?

Most of the current debate on drug policy concerns marginal issues about more or less enforcement, more or less education and treatment. These are important issues but ones about which I have no special understanding or interest. This section addresses the more important structural issue about whether the prohibition of specific drugs is superior or inferior to a system of social controls, more like that for alcohol and tobacco, where drugs are legal; drug sales are subject to an excise tax; drug sales and some types of uses are regulated; there are penalties for those types of drug use that harm or threaten third parties; and private institutions establish their own rules affecting drug use by customers, employees or members.[13] My judgement is that the available data and studies are not sufficient to make good quantitative estimates of the benefits and costs of these two major alternative systems for the social control of drugs, but there is a reasonable basis for estimating the *direction* of most of the effects of drug legalization and, in some cases, the rough magnitude of these effects.

Economic Effects on Drug Users and Suppliers

The legalization of drugs would have two substantial effects on the market for drugs: the price of legal drugs (including an excise tax) would probably be 10 per cent or less of the street price of illegal drugs. The demand for drugs at any price would increase in response to lower search costs and risks of purchasing legal drugs and the lower health risks per unit of legal drugs consumed. Figure 7.1 illustrates these two effects. The price elasticity of illegal drug use is based on the study by Silverman, Spruill and Levine (1975) discussed above. For this example, the legalization of drugs is assumed to reduce the price per representative unit from $10 to $1 and to shift the demand function from *di* to *eg*. Given these two assumptions, the consumption of legal drugs would be twice the consumption of illegal drugs.

In the illegal market, total expenditures are illustrated by the rectangle *ackj* and the net benefits to users by the triangle *cdk*. In the legal market, total expenditures are illustrated by the rectangle *abfh* and the net benefits to users by the triangle *bef*. Given these assumptions, thus, legalization would reduce the total expenditure for drugs by 80 per cent and would increase the net benefits to users (the difference between the triangles *bef* and *cdk*) by about 300 per cent.

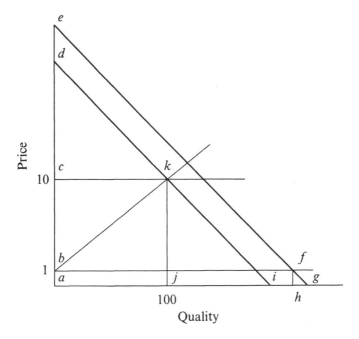

Figure 7.1 Economic effects of drug legalization on users and suppliers

The economic effects of drug legalization on the suppliers of illegal drugs are more difficult to estimate, because there are no estimates of the supply function of illegal drugs. If the effective supply function is represented by the line from *c* through *k*, all suppliers would be at the margin, there is no rent in the illegal market, and the legalization of drugs would not reduce the net benefits to the illegal suppliers. The vicious turf wars in the illegal market, however, suggest that there is substantial rent in this market. For this reason, the supply function of illegal drugs is probably better represented by the line from *b* through *k*. In this case, legalization would reduce the rent to the suppliers of illegal drugs by the triangle *bck*, an amount about 45 per cent of the total expenditures for illegal drugs, and increase the combined net benefits to users and the suppliers of illegal drugs by about 130 per cent.

A reasonable estimate of the total expenditures for illegal drugs would permit estimation of the magnitude of the effects of legalization on the net benefits to users and the loss of rents to the illegal suppliers. The most recent estimate, by the White House Office of National Drug Control Policy, is that Americans spent $40.4 billion on illegal drugs in 1990.[14]

This estimate is far lower than previous estimates but still seems too high; total expenditures for alcohol and tobacco, for example, are now about $50 billion. The $40 billion estimate would imply about one million full-time-equivalent workers in the illegal drug market, about one worker per 15 current users of any drug. On the basis of this recent estimate, legalization would increase the annual net benefits to drug users by about $74 billion and reduce the rents to the suppliers of illegal drugs by about $18 billion, and expenditures for legal drugs would be about $8 billion.

All of these estimates, of course, are substantially speculative. The major lessons from this analysis, however, are not dependent on the range of uncertainty about these estimates. The first lesson is that drug legalization would lead to very large net benefits to drug users. The second lesson is that drug prohibition probably leads to large rents to the suppliers of illegal drugs.

Safety and Health Effects on Drug Users and Suppliers

One clear effect of drug legalization is that it would nearly eliminate the many assaults and murders in the illegal drug market. For 1988 the FBI attributed 1023 murders to illegal drugs, but this is surely an underestimate because the motive for nearly 27 per cent of murders was unknown;[15] a more reasonable estimate is that about 1400 murders were directly attributable to the conditions of the illegal drug market.

Estimating the effects of drug legalization on the health of drug users is more complex and involves estimates of the following three effects:

- the increase in consumption;
- the reduction in the health risks per unit of consumption from using quality-controlled legal drugs of a known potency (possibly including an antidote that reduces drug toxicity), from the change in use techniques and from the probable shift to less potent drugs; and
- the change in the use of other risky substances, such as alcohol and tobacco.

Each of these effects is uncertain but is subject to reasonable bounds.

As explained earlier, my judgement is that drug legalization would roughly double the consumption of drugs. A large body of evidence suggests that many, perhaps most, drug-related health problems and deaths are due to unexpectedly high drug potency, risky adulterants in illegal drugs, and to more risky injection techniques. The Canadian record of cocaine use in nasal surgery, for example, would explain only about one-half of the recent US deaths attributable to the use of illegal cocaine. A large share of heroin-related deaths, plus more than 3500 AIDS deaths a year, are attributable to the use of dirty needles. The experience following the end of alcohol prohibition, in turn, suggests that drug legalization would shift drug use to the less potent drugs. The combination of these offsetting effects suggests that drug legalization may either increase or reduce the total number of health problems and deaths due to drug use, but in any case the net effect would probably be small. There are no available estimates of the third effect. Although a substantial share of drug-related health problems and deaths are attributable to the use of drugs in combination with alcohol, it is not clear whether drugs and alcohol are substitutes or complements. If drugs and alcohol are substitutes at the margin, as is the case for most products, drug legalization would reduce the consumption of alcohol and the health problem and deaths attributable to alcohol, probably by a small amount.

In summary, the popular perception that drug legalization would lead to a large increase in health problems and demands on the medical system by drug users appears to be without merit. The potential net effects appear to be small and may be negative.

Major Effects of Drug Legalization on Third Parties

For most of us (those who are not drug users or suppliers), most of the effects of drug legalization would be beneficial. One can be quite confident about the direction and relative magnitude of the following effects:

- The threats to foreign nations (most importantly Mexico, Colombia, Peru and Bolivia) from illegal drug suppliers would be nearly eliminated.
- US drug control expenditures (now more than $10 billion a year), the crowding of courts and jails, the corruption of police and officials and the arbitrary use of police power would be substantially reduced. A system of social controls on legal drugs similar to that for alcohol, however, may still cost several billions a year.
- Assaults and murders incident to the illegal drug market and to drug-induced robberies would be substantially reduced.
- Property crime would decline, possibly by a substantial amount.
- The transmission of AIDS to the sexual partners of drug users would be substantially reduced.
- The excise taxes on legal drugs would generate tax revenue, probably about $4 billion a year.

There are several potential adverse effects of drug legalization on third parties that merit more attention. The progressive socialization of medical insurance has created a new type of externality: all of us pay some part of the medical costs of the publicly insured and the uninsured. As a consequence, all of us have a stake, in addition to normal human caring, in the number of people with serious drug-related health problems. As explained in the above section, however, it is not clear that legalization would increase the number of drug users with health problems, and the potential effects appear to be small in any case.

A more serious potential problem is that different drugs have different psychopharmacological effects. Heroin is an opiate that substantially reduces all active behaviour and may increase welfare dependency. Cocaine is a stimulant that can increase aggressive behaviour The available evidence suggests that both of the effects are very small at current rates of drug use. The magnitude of these effects is probably proportional to drug consumption and might double with drug legalization.

The most serious potential problem is that drug use (as well as alcohol and tobacco use) during pregnancy can affect the health of the baby and may affect its future learning ability. A recent survey suggests that about 11 per cent of babies born in major metropolitan areas are exposed to some illegal drug, primarily cocaine, during pregnancy. Nearly one-third of these babies have some health problem, usually low birth-weight, at birth. The risk of low birth-weight due to cocaine exposure during pregnancy appears to be roughly equal to that resulting from moderate to high consumption of alcohol and tobacco. The research on the longer-term effects of drug exposure during pregnancy is still quite inconclusive.[16] Drug legalization would probably increase this problem; penalizing the mother is not a sufficient policy response because sanctions discourage early medical examinations, warnings and care.

In summary, the legalization of drugs, as with alcohol and tobacco, would reduce some problems and increase others. There is a reasonable basis for informed people to disagree on the balance of the benefits and costs of drug legalization, especially if the substantial benefits to drug users are not considered relevant. Most economists who have studied drug issues appear to favour the legalization of at least some drugs, reflecting our scepticism about corner solutions. One should also recognize, however, that politicians make a living by transforming virtues into requirements and sins into crimes, and they often regard the policy views of economists as quite bizarre.

NOTES

1. Address by the President on National Drug Policy, 5 September 1989.
2. This survey is subject to three types of error – sampling bias, sampling error and reporting bias – but the potential magnitude of these errors is probably not large. About 3 per cent of the US population are in institutions or are homeless and are not covered by the survey; most of this group, however, are in institutions (old-age homes, hospitals, prisons and military quarters) where access to illegal drugs is severely restricted. The *Household Survey* is based on a sample of nearly 9000, so the sampling error is quite small except for those drugs for which reported use is small. The survey results are now based on written confidential responses; drug use is probably under-reported and this bias may have varied over time, but the magnitude of this bias is probably small. A more serious problem is the substantial nonreporting share of those sampled. There has been no effort to resample this group, so there is no basis for confidence that those reporting are a representative sample of the total number sampled. These results, however, are quite consistent with other types of samples where there is an independent confirmation of drug use based on urine samples.
3. President's Commission on Organized Crime (1986).
4. The consumption of alcohol, however, does not appear consistent with these hypotheses. The study by Cook and Tauchen (1982) found that the long-run effect of increases in state liquor taxes on cirrhosis mortality was slightly lower than the first-year effect, and the effect on cirrhosis mortality was lower than on liquor consumption. A mathematical I appendix to this study explains the conditions for which the long-run effect would be about double the short-run effect, but the empirical results on cirrhosis mortality are not this hypothesis.
5. Both of these results are consistent with those from the study of alcohol consumption by Cook and Tauchen (1982).
6. Lord (1990) estimates that the price paid to the Medellin cartel for a kilogram of cocaine is about 0.8 per cent of the street price. Kaplan (1975) reports that the morphine equivalent of heroin available through legal medical channels sells for about 0.7 per cent of the street price of heroin.
7. For an efficient summary of the US experience with drugs prior to prohibition, see the article by Musto (1987).
8. See Ruter (1990) and Trebach and Zeese (1990) for summaries of the Dutch experience.
9. See Mandel (1990) and Trebach (1987) for summaries of the British experience.
10. For an efficient summary of this evidence, see the study by Ostrowski (1989).
11. Ostrowski (1989) estimates that as much as 80 per cent of the adverse health effects of illegal drugs may be due to these characteristics. This estimate, however, is that by a careful lawyer, not a medical specialist.
12. The book by Alexander (1990) summarizes this record.
13. For an efficient summary of the case for drug legalization subject to these types of social controls, see Nadelmann (1989).
14. This estimate was reported in the *Washington Post* on 21 June 1991.
15. US Bureau of the Census (1990), p. 173.
16. For an efficient summary of this evidence, see the article by Gieringer (1990).

REFERENCES

Alexander, B. (1990), *Peaceful Measures: Canada's Way Out of the War on Drugs*, Toronto: University of Toronto Press.
Becker, G. and K. Murphy (1988), 'A theory of rational addiction', *Journal of Political Economy*, **96**, 675–700.

Benson, B. and D. Rasmussen (1991), 'The relationship between illicit drug enforcement policy and property crimes', *Contemporary Policy Issues*, **IX** (4), 106–15.

Berger, M. and P. Leigh (1988), 'The effect of alcohol use on wages', *Applied Economics*, **20**, 1343–51.

Cook, P. and G. Tauchen (1982), 'The effect of liquor taxes on heavy drinking', *Bell Journal of Economics*, **13**, 379–90.

Gieringer, D. (1990), 'How many crack babies', *The Drug Policy Newsletter*, March/April, 4.

Gill, A. and R. Michaels (1990), 'Drug use and earnings: accounting for the self-selection of users', Working Paper 11–90, California State University, Fullerton.

Gill, A. and R. Michaels (1991), 'The determinants of illegal drug use', *Contemporary Policy Issues*, **IX** (3), 93–105.

Kaplan, J. (1975), 'A primer on heroin', *Stanford Law Review*, **27**, 801–26.

Lord, N. (1990), 'Violence in drug trafficking: an optimal strategy for dealers', in Arnold Trebach and Kevin Zeese (eds), *The Great Issues of Drug Policy*, Washington, DC: Drug Policy Foundation, 318–25.

Mandel, J. (1990), 'Pussy cats and lions: British vs. U.S. drug problems', in Arnold Trebach and Kevin Zeese (eds), *The Great Issues of Drug Policy*, Washington, DC: Drug Policy Foundation, 179–86.

Miron, J. J. Zweibel (1991), 'Alcohol consumption during prohibition', *American Economic Review*, **81**, 242–7.

Musto, D.F. (1987), 'The History of legislative controls over opium, cocaine, and their derivatives', in Ronald Hamowy (ed.), *Dealing with Drugs*, Lexington, MA: Lexington Books pp. 37–71.

Nadelman, E.A. (1989), 'Drug prohibition in the United States: costs, consequences, and alternatives', *Science*, **245**, 939–46.

Nisbet, C. and F. Vakil (1972), 'Some estimates of the price and expenditure elasticities for marijuana among U.C.L.A. students', *Review of Economics and Statistics*, **54**, 473–5.

Ostrowski, J. (1989), 'Thinking about drug legalization', Cato Institute, *Policy Analysis*, No. 121, Washington, DC.

President's Commission on Organized Crime (1986), *America's Habit: Drug Abuse, Drug Trafficking, and Organized Crime*, Washington, DC.

Reuter, P. (1990), 'On the consequences of toughness', Paper presented at a Hoover Institute conference, November.

Ruter, C.F. (1990), 'Basis of Dutch policy', in Arnold Trebach and Kevin Zeese (eds), *The Great Issues in Drug Policy*, Washington, DC: Drug Policy Foundation, 191–4.

Silverman, L., N. Spruill and D. Levine (1975), 'Urban Crime and Heroin Availability', Center for Naval Analysis, Washington, DC: Public Research Institute Report, 75–81.

Trebach, A. (1987), 'The need for reform of international narcotics laws', in Ronald Hamowy (ed.), *Dealing With Drugs*, San Francisco: Pacific Research Institute, 103–36.

Trebach, A. and K. Zeese (eds) (1990), 'The Dutch do it better', in *Drug Prohibition and the Conscience of Nations*, Washington, DC: Drug Policy Foundation, 45–9.

US Bureau of the Census (1990), *Statistical Abstract of the United States: 1990*, Washington, DC.

US Department of Health and Human Services (1988), *Fifth Special Report to the U.S. Congress on Alcoholism and Health*, Washington, DC.

US Federal Bureau of Investigation (1988), *Crime in the United States*, Washington, DC.

US National Institute on Drug Abuse (1988), *National Household Survey of Drug Abuse*, Washington, DC.

US National Institute on Drug Abuse (1989), *Drug Abuse Warning Network (DAWN) Annual Data 1988*, Series 1, No. 8, Washington, DC.

US National Institute on Drug Abuse and US National Institute on Alcohol Abuse and Alcoholism, *National Drug and Alcoholism Treatment Unit Survey: Main Findings 1987*, Washington, DC.

US Public Health Service (1989), 'Reducing the Health Consequences of Smoking': 25 Years of Progress Surgeon General's Report, Washington, DC.

Warburton, C. (1932), *The Economic Results of Prohibition*, New York: Columbia University Press.

8. Student performance and school district size*

INTRODUCTION

In response to the first postwar 'managerial wave' of public school reform, the number of school districts in the United States declined sharply – from 108 579 in 1942 to 14 741 in 1987. The average number of enrolled students per school district was 3345 in 1987, slightly lower than during the peak enrolment year of 1975 but many times the average enrolment per district at the beginning of this period.

This chapter summarizes the evidence of the relation between student performance on standardized tests and school district size – controlling for school expenditures per student and student, family, and community characteristics. A number of studies conducted by other economists are summarized. And the major focus is on a consultant report that I prepared in 1974 (with the support of Mickey Levy, then one of my graduate students) for the Local Government Reform Task Force reporting to Ronald Reagan, then governor of the State of California.[1]

The major result of these studies is that there appears to be either no economies or significant diseconomies of scale over a large range of students per school district.

THEORIES OF OPTIMAL SCHOOL DISTRICT SIZE

The general economic theory of optimal scale, as applied to school districts, can be summarized as follows.

The major potential economies of scale arise from spreading the cost of a given level of school services among more students and from any positive geographic externalities.

* Reprinted by permission from *Florida Policy Review*, **6** (1), Summer 1990, 1–5. This paper was drawn from a larger study (with Mickey Levy) on 'Cities and Schools: a case for Community Government in California', University of California (Berkeley), Graduate School of Public Policy Working Paper No. 14, June 1974.

The major potential diseconomies of scale arise from managerial inefficiency, the lower value of crowded services, and the higher variance of preferences for school services. And, the optimal size of a school district involves a balancing of the marginal economies and diseconomies of scale.

A quite different theory of optimal school district size, however, had developed in the education literature and merits understanding. This theory is summarized as follows:

- educators determine a desirable range of courses and student services that each school district should provide;
- educators then determine the maximum desirable number of students per teacher, per counsellor, and so on; and
- the optimal school district size, thus, is based on the arithmetic product of the above two determinations.

An increase in the desired number of courses and services, for example, would increase the optimal size of the school district, and a reduction in the student/professional ratio would reduce the optimal size.

This line of reasoning had a powerful effect on both educators and legislators. In 1959, James Conant (the former president of Harvard) recommended a minimum school district of 2000 students.[2] In 1958, the American Association of School Administrators had recommended a minimum school district of 10 000–15 000 students.[3] The differences in these recommendations were primarily attributable to differences in the range of courses and services that were to be offered directly by the school district. The following statement from a 1961 study guide prepared jointly by the California State Committee on School District Organization and the State Committee on Education efficiently summarizes the views of education officials on this issue:

Studies have shown that it is not likely that a district having fewer than twelve to fifteen hundred pupils in grades 1 through 12 can provide even minimum desirable services at a reasonable cost. For such districts a number of services would undoubtedly have to be provided through the county superintendent of schools office. In an area where continued rapid growth is expected for a number of years, a unified school district which initially would have 2,000 plus pupils could be reasonably satisfactory This statement, however, does not mean that a district should be organized for each area which has the minimum number of pupils. One having ten thousand or more students would be adequate in size and able to provide needed services at a reasonable cost. Other things being equal, optimum in terms of size is probably one having from ten thousand to forty or fifty thousand students.[4]

Policy analysis

Table 8.1 The size distribution of Florida school districts, 1988

Size	Number of districts	Average enrolment (K–12)
Less than 1000	1	835
1000–4999	23	2911
5000–9999	9	7185
10 000–19 999	12	13 726
20 000–49 999	13	30 567
50 000–99 999	5	78 372
More than 100 000	4	158 635
Total	67	

Source: Florida Statistical Abstract, 1989.

These views were widely shared by education officials and were substantially incorporated in state education codes. For example, the California State Board of Education grants greater local authority to unified school districts of 1500 or more students, and the State of Florida has long had only one school district per county regardless of size (see Table 8.1 for the size distribution of Florida school districts). As far as I can determine, however, there was no study available at that time that indicated that school districts larger than the minimum recommended size were superior on a student performance basis. The collective views of educators merits attention, but they are not a sufficient guide to good policy.

Most importantly, the approach leading to these recommendations accounts for only one of the conditions affecting the optimal size of a school district – the spreading of the cost of a given set of services over a larger number of students. The above quotation from the California study guide concludes with a statement that 'Districts may, of course, be too large as well as too small for satisfactory operation', but there was no further consideration of the potential diseconomies of scale.

My own review of this issue does not contest the value of the historical consolidation of many small school districts. At the level of very small school districts, the economies of spreading the cost of a given set of services probably dominate the several types of diseconomies. The early stage of the school district consolidation movement probably reduced per student costs or, more likely, increased the range of courses and services. The early school consolidation movement, interestingly, was strongly supported by taxpayer associations and by chambers of commerce. Two conditions, however, are now very different. The long process of consolidation of school districts has now almost run its course. And a growing body of formal research that addresses the economies of scale of school districts is now available. It is now appropriate to question whether the state education codes bearing on school district organization are appropriate to contemporary conditions.

EMPIRICAL STUDIES BY OTHER SCHOLARS

Over the past 30 years, a growing body of research has addressed the effects of school size or school district size. This section addresses the major studies of this issue by other scholars.

Several of the early general studies of state or local government expenditure functions also addressed the relation of public school expenditures to the population served. The studies by Harvey Brazer,[5] by Werner Hirsch,[6] and by Thomas Borcherding and Robert Deacon[7] – using different methodologies and data sources – each found no significant economies of scale in the provision of public school services. The primary limitation of these early studies is that they did not directly address the effects on student performance of the size of schools or school districts.

The more relevant later studies directly estimated the relation of student performance on various types of standardized tests to school size or school district size – controlling for the characteristics of the students, the schools and the community – and each using the ordinary-least-squares estimation method. A 1967 study by Jesse Burkhead, Thomas Fox and John Holland estimated this relation separately for high schools in Chicago, Atlanta, and several smaller communities.[8] A 1986 study by M.C. Alkin, C.S. Benson and R.H. Gustafson estimated this relation for school districts in California.[9] Both of these studies found no significant relation of student performance to the size of school or school district.

Two studies by Herbert Kiesling, based on individual student data from New York State, were the most thorough of this round of studies. Kiesling's 1967 study of the relation of student performance to school district size concluded that 'when all districts in the ... sample are considered, together, there are few student populations where the relationships of size and performance is not negative at advanced levels of statistical significance'.[10] His 1968 study of the relation between student performance and size of the high school found a consistent negative effect of high-school size over a range of schools from fewer than 200 students to more than 4000 students.[11] Kiesling also found strong effects of student IQ and a significant effect of spending per student only among the larger school districts.

In a review of this round of studies, Thomas James and Henry Levin conclude that

> all of the studies that have tried to relate school or school district size to education outcomes have found either no relationship or a negative one between school enrollments and the level of educational output. These answers are not necessarily the final ones, for each of these studies acknowledges a number of methodological shortcomings that would qualify its conclusions. Yet, what cannot be dismissed in the consistency of these conclusions – that while diseconomies of scale, appear, economies of scale do not – despite differences in the techniques of analysis, samples of schools, measures of educational outcomes, and so on.[12]

The most recent similar study only strengthens these conclusions. In their 1987 study based on New Jersey data, Herbert J. Walberg and William J. Fowler, Jr. conclude that

> The results contradict the hypothesis sometimes put forward that large districts are more efficient. ... These striking trends confirm other recent studies of district size and suggest that the policy of district consolidation undertaken by states in this century may have hurt rather than helped learning since they suggest diseconomies rather than economies of scale.[13] Our public school authorities, however, appear to have been immune to the accumulation of this evidence over a 30-year period. School district consolidation continued throughout the 1980s, albeit only at a slower rate.

THE NISKANEN–LEVY STUDY

The primary study on which Mickey Levy and I modelled our own research was the superior study of school district size by Herbert Kiesling. One major advantage of the Kiesling study was his access to individual student data, which he aggregated by socioeconomic groups within each district. The most serious qualification of his study is that his ordinary-least-squares estimates of the effects of IQ and expenditures per student may be biased. Students' performance in basic subjects, IQ scores and expenditures per student are probably jointly determined by family background and community characteristics. In this case, Kiesling's estimation procedure may overestimate the effect of IQ and underestimate the effect of expenditures on student performance, but there is no similar reason to question his estimate of the negative effect of school district size.

Our own study of the relation of student performance to school district size was conducted for two reasons – to base the estimates on data specific to the largest California unified school districts and to correct for the major potential methodological weakness of the Kiesling study. Our major disadvantage was the lack of access to individual student performance scores and student characteristics. Kiesling's estimates, thus, were probably more efficient than ours but were possibly biased, and they were clearly less relevant to the California experience.

Our basic sample included 144 of the 146 largest unified school districts in California, all districts with average daily attendance of 2000 or more students in the school year 1970–71. One district was deleted for lack of complete data. The basic sample also excluded the large Los Angeles unified school district; this district of 600 00 students was nearly six times the the size of the next largest district, and we did not want this one observation to dominate the estimated effect of district size. Additional estimates (not presented here) based on the expanded sample including the Los Angeles district were essentially identical to those from our basic sample, so this concern was not merited. The basic sample included districts including 46 per cent of the total public school students in California and 70 per cent of those in unified districts. The expanded sample included 60 per cent of the total students and 91 per cent of those unified districts.

Table 8.2 presents the basic structural equation for each of our tests and the definition of each variable. The formulation followed that by Kiesling, although we used a different transformation of several variables. (In addition, Kiesling included the percentage growth in the number of students per district, but this variable was not generally significant. We also included this variable in our initial estimates with the same result, so this variable was deleted from our basic estimates.)

The specific form of our dependent variable, $S/(S^*-S)$, is the ratio of correct answers to incorrect answers on each test. This form was based on a belief that test scores are probably not a linear measure of student achievement and, if so, this form should reduce the change in the variance of the residuals over different levels of the variable.

We also recognized the possibility that student performance on cognitive tests, the measured level of IQ, and school expenditures per student may be jointly determined. Both student performance and IQ, for example, may be jointly determined by school characteristics and family background. And parents of high-potential children may be willing to spend more for schooling, given any community tax base. In these cases, both IQ and expenditures per student should be considered as 'endogenous' variables, and the ordinary-least-squares estimates of these variables would be biased.

Table 8.2 Test equation and definition of variables

Test equation

$$S/(S^* - S) = a + bI + cX + d \ln N + u$$

Endogenous variables

$S/(S^* - S)$, where

S is the median test score on each test

$S^*$is the number of questions on each test

I is the median IQ for each grade

X is the current expenditures per student in each district

Instrumental variables

N is the average daily attendance, grades 1–12

P is the index of family poverty

M is the percentage of minority (Black, Hispanic and Native American) students

A is the assessed value per student

For this reason, we used a two-stage least-squares estimation procedure, the one unique methodological distinction of our study. The first stage 'reduced form' equations express IQ and expenditures per student in terms of the full set of instrumental variables, reflecting family and community characteristics and the school district size. The estimated level of IQ and expenditures per student from these equations are then used as independent variables in the estimates of the structural equations. These estimates, thus, will reflect only those effects on student performance of poverty, minority status and community wealth that operate through the effects of IQ and expenditure per student. All of the data are from the *California State Testing Program, 1970–1971*,[14] with the exception of the expenditure data, which are from the *California School Districts Financial Analysis, 1970–1971*.[15]

Student performance equations were estimated from both reading and mathematics skill at both the sixth and twelfth grade levels. The IQ variable in each test is specific to each grade. All other variables are common to the district.

Several contentious issues should be addressed before reporting our results. We do not contend that student performance on cognitive tests captures all of the attributes of school outputs. And different school districts place different emphasis on the skills measured by these tests. Other conditions – such as the range of courses offered, the pleasantness of the school environment, student understanding of their colleagues and community, and so on – are surely important. We share the view, however, expressed previously by Joe Kershaw and Roland McKean, that

> despite ... qualifications, we take the position that achievement in basic subjects is the most widely accepted and the most important dimension of school output. Learning in these subjects, is a necessary part of the foundation for accomplishing the things that most people, individually or as nations, seem to want. We think, therefore, that scholastic performance is an appropriate measure of output to use in comparing education policy.[16]

We also do not contend that our results apply to unified school districts with fewer than 2000 students or to elementary or high school districts. There may still be value to consolidating the smallest school districts or the elementary and high school districts in a common area, but we do not address these issues. Our sample includes a high proportion of public school students in California and most of those for which there has been a special concern. Any conclusion from our estimates should be specific to the sample from which they are made.

Table 8.3 presents the two-stage estimates of the structural equations from the basic sample. The major conclusions from these tests are the following:

1. Median student IQ makes a positive and highly significant contribution to student performance on all tests. The effect of IQ on student performance, however, appears to be significantly larger at the sixth grade level than at the twelfth grade.
2. Current expenditures per student make a significant positive contribution to both reading and mathematics performance at the sixth grade level. There appears to be no significant effect of school district spending per student at the twelfth grade level.
3. School district size has a consistently *negative* effect on student performance that is highly significant on three of the four tests.
4. The explained variance of median student performance is slightly higher for reading tests than for mathematics and is slightly higher at the sixth grade than at the twelfth grade.

These conclusions are almost wholly consistent with those from Kiesling's study of New York State data. More importantly, they confirm the general conclusion from a number studies that have found either no relationship or a negative one between student enrollments and the level of educational output.

Table 8.3 Student performance in relation to IQ, spending and size

	Constant	*I*	*X*	*N*	*R²*
Sixth grade					
Reading	−14.38	0.18	0.52E–3	−0.11	0.90
	(−20.65)	(26.92)	(1.94)	(−3.73)	
Mathematics	−13.43	0.17	0.75E–3	−0.04	0.85
	(−16.01)	(20.30)	(2.34)	(−1.05)	
Twelfth grade					
Reading	−2.16	0.03	0.51E–6	−0.17	0.81
	(−12.34)	(17.98)	(0.85E–2)	(−2.46)	
Mathematics	−2.42	0.03	0.19E–4	−0.18	0.78
	(−11.07)	(15.53)	(0.25)	(−2.11)	

Notes: Sample size is 144. Numbers in parentheses are '*t*' statistics.

The conclusion that student performance in large school districts is lower than in smaller districts is sufficiently important and significant to merit more detailed examination of the underlying reasons for this relation. We were able to examine some of these phenomena. Using only data from the *California State Testing Program* and our basic sample of 144 of the largest school districts, we tested the relation of school district size to a number of district characteristics not included in our test equation. We found, for example, that staff turnover has a significant negative relation to school district size. We also found that median teachers' salaries have a significant positive relation to district size, not because the salary scales are substantially different, but just because of the lower turnover of teachers. Large school districts, apparently in response to higher median teachers' salaries, have larger average class sizes. In general, thus, larger school districts appear to have older teachers, higher teachers' salaries and larger classes – and these conditions may explain much of the lower relative performance of their students for a given expenditure level. We were surprised by two of our findings: neither the number of nonteaching personnel per student nor the rate of pupil mobility appears to be significantly related to school district size. A closer examination of these phenomena, however, is necessary to provide a guide for more detailed school management policy.

IMPLICATIONS FOR EDUCATION POLICY

What to do? The sustained consolidation of school district appears to have contributed to the long decline in student performance (from 1963 to 1979 on the Scholastic Aptitude Test) but was only a small part of the problem. In most cases, however, I suggest that breaking up existing school districts is *not* the best policy response.

The school district is the lowest unit in the American public school system that is both a financing and administrative unit. At present, school districts not only determine the local school budget and tax rates but they establish teacher salary schedules, the authority of school principals and a wide variety of input standards, subject to the increasing financing and control from the state board of education.

My preferred option is to transform the school district into only a financing district, relieving it of all administrative roles except, possibly, for establishing a core curriculum and enforcing nondiscrimination guidelines. Parents would be allowed to send their children to any school in the district that has available space. Moreover, parents would be allowed to send their children to any public school in another district, subject only to the approval of the school attended, with a financial transfer to the district of attendance equal to the lower of the school budget per student in the district of residence and the district of attendance. (As a personal aside, the 1974 Niskanen–Levy study was apparently the first to propose a parental choice plan involving schools in other districts.)

The necessary other side of this proposal is to give the local school principal almost full authority to determine the teacher salary schedule, hire and fire teachers, set class sizes and other input standards, and expel disruptive students. Parents and school professionals should be allowed to establish new schools that are eligible for the district funding, and existing schools that fail to attract sufficient students, of course, must be allowed to fail.

In summary, I am encouraged by the parental choice plans now developing in the public schools in more than 20 states, but I am worried that this will soon be regarded as another school reform failure unless it is paired with a substantial decentralization of administrative authority to the individual public school. At present, until the constitutional issues affecting a more general voucher system (in which church-related schools could participate) are resolved, the combination of parental choice and local school empowerment is probably the most promising next step in American education.

Policy analysis

NOTES

1. William A. Niskanen and Mickey Levy, 'Cities and schools: a case for community government in California', University of California (Berkeley), Graduate School of Public Policy Working Paper No. 14, June 1974.
2. James Conant, *The American High School Today*, New York: McGraw-Hill Book Company, 1959.
3. American Association of School Administrators Commission on School District Organization, *School District Organization*, Washington, DC, 1958.
4. California State Department of Education (Combined Committee on School District Organization), *Problems of School District Organization in California*, Sacramento, California, 1961.
5. Harvey Brazer, *City Expenditures in the United States*, New York: National Bureau of Economic Research, 1959.
6. Werner Hirsch, 'Expenditure implications of metropolitan growth and consolidation', *Review of Economics and Statistics*, 41 August 1959, 232–41.
7. Thomas Borcherding and Robert Deacon, 'The demand for the services of non-federal governments: an econometric approach to collective choice', *American Economics Review*, December 1972, LXII, 5, 891–901.
8. Jesse Burkhead, Thomas Fox and John Holland, *Input and Output in Large-City High Schools*, Syracuse University Press, 1967.
9. M.C. Alkin, C.S. Benson and R.H. Gustafson, 'Economy of scale in the production of selected educational outcomes', A paper prepared for the American Educational Research Association Meetings, Chicago, February 1968, unpublished.
10. Herbert Kiesling, 'Measuring a local government service: a study of school districts in New York State', *Review of Economics and Statistics*, 49, August 1967, 366–70.
11. Herbert Kiesling, 'High School Size and Cost Factors', Final Report for the US Office of Education, Bureau of Research Project 6–1590, US Department of Health, Education and Welfare, 1968.
12. H. Thomas James and Henry M. Levin, 'Financing community schools', in *Community Control of Schools*, Washington, DC: Brookings Institution, 1973, 250–74.
13. Herbert J. Walberg and William J. Fowler Jr. 'Expenditure and size efficiencies of public school districts', *Educational Researcher*, October 1987, 5–13.
14. California State Department of Education (Office of Program Evaluation), *Report on the California State Testing Program, 1970–71: Profiles of School Performance*, Sacramento, California, 1971.
15. California Agency for Research in Education, *California School Districts Financial Analysis, 1970–71*, No. 2, December 1971.
16. Joseph A. Kershaw and Roland McKean, *System Analysis and Education*, Santa Monica, CA: RAND Corporation, RM–2473–FF, 1959.

9. Land prices substantially underestimate the value of environmental quality*

Because the value of fixed assets is equivalent to the discounted present value of their future expected outputs, differences in the price of fixed assets – particularly of land – have been used as measures of the benefits and costs associated with public policies that affect the productivity of fixed assets.[1] Lacking prices for environmental amenities, economists have used differences in land prices as surrogates for the worth of environmental amenities. The general argument for employing land prices in the environmental field runs along the following lines: by evaluating the relationship between differences in environmental parameters and their resulting capitalization in land prices, the dollar consequences of these differences in environmental parameters can be measured, with differences in land prices reasonably indicating consumers' willingness-to-pay for differences in environmental conditions.

A rich theoretical literature has developed, primarily in the pages of the *Review of Economics and Statistics*, which is focused on the conditions that must be met before one can properly use differences in land prices as surrogates for the worth of environmental amenities (Anderson and Crocker 1972; Freeman 1971, 1974a, 1974b, 1975; Lind 1973, 1975; Polinsky and Shavell 1975; and Small 1975). This theoretical literature was largely spawned by the early empirical studies that attempted to measure the benefits of clean air by using differences in land prices (Ridker and Henning 1967; Anderson and Crocker 1971; and Zerbe 1969), and was highly critical of the theoretical foundations upon which these empirical studies were based. The theoreticians correctly pointed out, among other things, that the regression equations that had been used in empirical work could be used to predict differences in land prices within an urban

* Coauthored with Steve H. Hanke. Reprinted by permission from *Review of Economics and Statistics*, **59** (3), August 1977, 375–7.
   We are grateful for the computational assistance of Richard W. Wahl and for the comments of A. Myrick Freeman and an anonymous referee.

area, *ceteris paribus*, but that these equations should not be used to pre-dict changes in aggregate land prices when the quality of air over an entire urban area is altered.

We do not wish to pursue issues that have been raised with regard to the conditions that must be met before the use of differences in land prices can be properly employed as surrogates for the worth of environ-mental amenities. Rather, we turn to a fundamental oversight in the existing literature. We argue that this oversight will result in a significant underestimate of the value of environmental quality, regardless of which formulation of the land-value approach for measuring the value of improvements in environmental quality is employed.

The literature on the land-value approach has assumed that the bene-fits of a public project or policy are equivalent to the difference in the market price of the land affected by the project or the policy. In other words, the discounted present value of the flow of net revenue and ser-vices that the private owners of land receive from a project or a policy is the *only* value that has been considered. But this measure underestimates the total difference in the productivity of land resulting from a policy change. Local governments also have an equity interest in land because the price of land is a base for property taxes. Differences in land prices are an adequate proxy for project benefits only if the capitalized value of the changes in local property tax flows are also included as a benefit from a public project or policy change. To assess properly the differences in the productivity of land, differences in both the private and the public value of land must be determined and summed. Because the public value of land is not incorporated into existing models and empirical studies, bene-fits from projects and programmes that increase the productivity of land have been consistently and substantially underestimated.

The following simple model illustrates the relation between differences in the total value of land and differences in the market prices. Let

$$P = (R - tP) / i,$$ (9.1)

where P is the market price of land, R is the annual rental value of land in the absence of property taxes, t is the effective property tax rate on the market price of land, and i is the real opportunity cost of capital to pri-vate owners. This equation assumes that the property tax, is fully capitalized in the market price of land, that is, there is no shifting of the property tax on land. The value of the local government's equity in land is

$$G = tP / i,$$ (9.2)

where, for this formulation, the real opportunity cost of capital to the government is assumed to be the same as to the private owner. The total value of land, therefore, is

$$V = P + G = R / i = P\left(1 + \frac{t}{i}\right). \tag{9.3}$$

From a policy or benefit–cost perspective, what we are interested in is the difference in total property value associated with policy change. This is given by

$$\Delta V = \Delta P\left(1 + \frac{t}{i}\right). \tag{9.4}$$

From (9.4), we only need to obtain the effective tax rate, t, and the marginal borrowing rate for the local taxing jurisdiction, i, to appropriately incorporate the government's value of land into the estimated difference in total land value. These data and the difference in the market price of land, ΔP, combine to yield the total change in land value associated with a proposed policy change. The magnitude of the percentage error in the value of differences in environmental conditions that would occur if estimates were based upon current formulations is indicated by the ratio t/i.

The error resulting from the exclusion of the government's equity in land is illustrated by using equation (9.4) to readjust the difference in land-value figures for the major studies that have related air quality parameters to land prices. The studies under review show a significant positive relationship between air quality and residential land prices. The magnitudes of the estimated relationships are misleading, however, because the governmental claim on a portion of the difference in the value of land was not included. Table 9.1 shows that the error in these studies was significant, since the difference in land values was underestimated by *60 per cent to 99 per cent*. It is important to note that these errors would have occurred with any of the existing formulations of the land-value approach, if used at the sites and times mentioned, since the government's equity in land has not been included in either the empirical investigations or the theoretical formulations.

The traditional land-value approach that is commonly used in benefit–cost studies understates the real change in the value of land because the government's equity in land is not included. Policies that are based upon these studies will, therefore, be inefficient. For example,

Table 9.1 Error estimates in air pollution – land value studies

Location of Study	Median annual tax rate	Median assessment ratio	Median effective tax rate	Moody bond rating 1960–1961	Average long-term yields 1960–1961	Rate of inflation	Real rate of interest	Percentage of error
			t		i^{*g}	r^h	$i = i^* - r$	(t / i)
	(%)	(%)	(%)		(%)	(%)	(%)	(%)
St. Louis, Missouri[a]	4.99c	34.6c	1.70	AA	3.49	1.3	2.19	78
Washington, DC[a]	2.70c	44.1c	1.19	AAA[e]	3.27	1.3	1.19	60
Kansas City, Kansas[a]	14.32c	13.8c	2.17	AA	3.49	1.3	2.19	99
Greater Metropolitan Toronto[b]	5.14d	32.3d	1.66	A[f]	3.72	1.3	2.42	69
Toronto, Ontario[b]	6.0d	32.3d	1.94	AA[f]	3.49	1.3	2.19	89
Hamilton, Ontario[b]	5.9d	34.7d	2.05	A[f]	3.72	1.3	2.42	85

Notes:
a. Anderson and Crocker (1971) and Ridker and Henning (1967).
b. Zerbe (1969).
c. *1967 Census of Governments*, Washington, DC: US Government Printing Office. p. 151.
d. *Report of the Ontario Committee on Taxation*. Vol II, Toronto: Queens Printer, Province of Ontario, 1967.
e. Note that Washington, DC has no general obligation bonds and can borrow from the federal government.
f. Payable in US dollars.
g. *Moody's Municipal and Government Manual*.
h. Average rate of change in the consumer price index 1960–61.

the willingness-to-pay for environmental amenities will be underestimated (see Table 9.1), resulting in goals for optimal levels of environmental quality that are too low and public investments in pollution control that are too small.

The policy mistakes stemming from errors in estimating changes in land values are more direct and substantial than in other areas where the government has an equity interest in assets. The government, for example, has a roughly 50 per cent interest in US corporations because of its claim on corporate incomes through income taxes. As a rule, however, the government has left the management of corporate assets to the private sector. This is not the case with land. Public policies and management directly and significantly alter land values. Hence, the proper evaluation of the private and the public components of land values are particularly important when public policies are based upon land-value studies.

NOTE

1. For examples of empirical work, see Anderson and Crocker (1971) on air quality, the Commission on the Third London Airport (1970) on noise levels, David (1968) on water quality, Ridker and Henning (1967) on air quality, Struyk (1971) on flood control, and Zerbe (1969) on air quality.

REFERENCES

Anderson, R.J., Jr. and T.D. Crocker (1971), 'Air pollution and residential property values', *Urban Studies*, **8**, October, 171–80.

Anderson, R.J., Jr. and T.D. Crocker (1972), 'Air pollution and property values; a reply', *Review of Economics and Statistics*, **54**, November, 470–73.

Commission on the Third London Airport (1970), *Papers and Proceedings*, **VII**, parts 1 and 2, London: HMSO.

David, E.L. (1968), 'Lake shore property values: a guide to public investment in recreation', *Water Resources Research*, **4** August, 692–707.

Freeman, A.M. III (1971), 'Air pollution and property values: a methodological comment', **53**, November, 415–16.

Freeman, A.M. III (1974a), 'Air pollution and property values: a further comment', *Review of Economics and Statistics*, **56**, November, 554–6.

Freeman, A.M. III (1974b), 'On estimating air pollution control benefits from land value studies', *Journal of Environmental Economics and Management*, **1**, May 74–83.

Freeman, A.M. III (1975), 'Spatial equilibrium, the theory of rents, and the measurement of benefits from public programs: a comment', *Quarterly Journal of Economics*, **89**, August, 470–73.

Lind R.C. (1973), 'Spatial equilibrium, the theory of rents, and the measurement of benefits from public programs', *Quarterly Journal of Economics*, **87**, May, 188–207.

Lind, R.C. (1975), 'Spatial equilibrium, the theory of rent, and the measurement of benefits from public programs: reply', *Quarterly Journal of Economics*, **89**, August, 474–6.

Polinsky, A.M. and S. Shavell (1975), 'The air pollution and property value debate', *Review of Economics and Statistics*, **57**, February, 100–104.

Ridker, R.B. and J.A. Henning (1967), 'The determinants of residual property value with special reference to air pollution', *Review of Economics and Statistics*, **49**, May, 246–57.

Small, K. (1975), 'Air pollution and property values: a further comment', *Review of Economics and Statistics*, **57**, February, 105–7.

Struyk, R.J. (1971), 'Flood risk and agricultural land values', *Water Resources Research*, **7**, August, 184–93.

Zerbe, R.O., Jr. (1969), *The Economics of Air Pollution: A Cost–Benefit Approach*, Toronto: Ontario Department of Public Health, July.

10. Fiscal effects on US economic growth*

Most empirical studies of the fiscal effects on economic growth are of two types. One set, the focus of most applied public finance, estimates the partial effects of changes in specific government expenditures or tax provisions, based on the data from one country (for example, see Aschauer 1990; Jorgenson and Yun 1990). The other set, the focus of several recent studies, estimates the effects of changes in highly aggregated fiscal conditions, based on cross-country data (for example, see Barro 1989; Barth and Bradley 1987; Grier and Tullock 1987; Kormendi and Meguire 1985; Landau 1983).

These two types of studies are subject to different limitations. The microstudies invite concern about whether the estimated effects may be partly due to omitted variables. The aggregated studies invite concern that the effects of different types of government spending and receipts may be quite different; in addition, there is reason to question whether the estimates based on cross-country data sets reflect the effects of fiscal conditions in any one country. Both types of studies, in addition, have characteristically assumed that changes (or differences) in fiscal conditions are exogenous.

Some of the results of these studies are also inconsistent. For example, Aschauer (1990) finds a strong positive effect of public capital on US output, but Barth and Bradley (1987), in a study based on a cross-country data set, find no significant effect of government investment. Some of the studies based on cross-country data sets find a negative effect of various measures of government consumption expenditures on economic growth; others find no significant effects.

This chapter summarizes the results from a study of data somewhat intermediate between the above two types. The data set comprises annual US observations for the period 1950–89. Economic growth is measured in three dimensions: real GNP per working-age adult, output per hour

* Reprinted by permission from Benjamin Zycher and Lewis C. Soloman (eds), *Economic Policy, Financial Markets, and Economic Growth*, Boulder, CO: Westview Press, 1993, pp. 235–46.

worked in the business sector, and hours worked in the business sector per working-age adult. Combined government sector (federal, state and local) expenditures are aggregated in three groups – defence expenditures, other government purchases of goods and services, and transfer payments plus net subsidies – without any a priori identification of these expenditures as consumption or investment expenditures. Government revenues are aggregated in only two groups: total tax revenues and the net deficit. The test equations do *not* control for the level of private saving and invest-ment, because these conditions are clearly endogenous to changes in fiscal conditions. In this sense, the test equations are reduced-form equa-tions in a larger model in which the effects of fiscal conditions operate, in part, through the level of private saving and investment. The effects on each of the three dimensions of economic growth are estimated simulta-neously by the iterative three-stage least-squares technique.

The advantages and limitations of this approach are also obvious. One advantage is that there is no clear a priori basis for separating govern-ment expenditures into investment (or property rights-enhancing) expenditures and consumption expenditures. A second advantage is that this study, to my knowledge the only one of its type, recognizes that eco-nomic growth and the fiscal variables are jointly determined. Another advantage is that the study is based only on US data, at least reducing the omitted variables problem specific to cross-country tests. The major limi-tation, of course, is that the government expenditures and revenue variables are still highly aggregated, both by type and across the three levels of US government.

SOME (MINIMAL) THEORY

Robert Barro (1990) has recently developed a characteristically elegant model of the effects of government spending on economic growth that is an adequate basis for selecting the test equations and interpreting the results presented in this chapter. Barro's model, like most other recently developed growth models, assumes constant returns to scale in producing total output. In his model, however, the production function exhibits con-stant returns to scale in the combination of private capital and the level of government investment services, but diminishing returns to each com-ponent separately.

$$y = \phi(k,g) = k \cdot \phi(g/k), \qquad (10.1)$$

where y is output per worker, k is the private capital stock per worker, and g is the level of government investment services per worker. There are two reasons government investment services are imperfect substitutes for private capital. Some government services, such as defence and the maintenance of law and order, are not efficiently excludable. And for some government services, user fees are not efficient because the services either are nonrival in consumption or have positive external effects.

In the simple case where governments produce only investment services and finance these services entirely by a flat tax rate,

$$g = t = \tau \cdot y = \tau \cdot k \cdot \phi(g/k) \qquad (10.2)$$

For this case, the rate of growth of consumption expenditure per worker is

$$y = i/c = 1 / \sigma[(1-\tau) \cdot \phi(g/k) \cdot (1-\eta) - \rho], \qquad (10.3$$

where σ is the (constant) marginal utility of consumption, η is the elasticity of y with respect to g, and ρ is the (constant) rate of time preference of the representative worker. Further, if the production function is Cobb–Douglas, η is also constant. For this case, there is a unique optimum level of g that maximizes both the growth rate and the utility of the representative worker. At lower levels of g, the positive marginal effect of g is higher than the negative marginal effect of τ, the opposite is the case at higher levels. Because private saving is a function of $(1 - \tau)$, k is endogenous (in a closed economy) and the private saving rate peaks at a level of g lower than the optimum; in the region near the optimal level of g, thus, the partial effect of g on private saving is negative.

In the more complex (and realistic) case, governments supply both investment and consumption services. For this case,

$$t = (\tau g + \tau h) \cdot y, \qquad (10.4)$$

$$y = 1/\varepsilon \cdot [(1 - \tau g - \tau h) \cdot \phi(y/k) \cdot (1 - \eta) - \rho], \qquad (10.5)$$

where the new term τg is g/y, τh is h/y, and h is the level of government consumption services.. In this case, the rate of economic growth and the optimum level of government investment services are both a negative function of the level of government consumption expenditures, and the combination of private and government decisions does not maximize the utility of the representative worker.

For this chapter, this model implies that the test equations should express the several dimensions of economic growth as a logarithmic function of the level of real government expenditures and the combined *after*-tax rate; the parameters σ, η and ρ are each assumed to be constant.

For test purposes, there are several problems with this formulation. First, there is no a priori basis for identifying the type and amount of government expenditures that provide investment services or consumption services (to either the population or a self-serving government). Second, governments finance part of their expenditures by borrowing. For this reason, the test equations summarized in the next section include each of the major types of government expenditures and test for the effects of both taxes and borrowing.

TEST RESULTS

Structure of the Test Equations

As in any time-series analysis, the appropriate form of the test equation depends on whether the variables are stable in the level or in the first or some higher-order difference of these variables. For this reason, each of the test variables was subject to the augmented Dickey–Fuller unit root test. The results of these tests indicate that none of the dependent variables is trend stable but that the first difference of each of these variables (with a trend) is stable. The first statistical implication of these tests is that each of the test equations should be expressed in first difference form with a trend term. The second implication is that the standard error of forecast of the *level* of these variables is unbounded. The important economic implication of these tests is that shocks to each of the dependent variables are permanent. A shock that reduces productivity in one year, for example, reduces the level of productivity in each subsequent year; in other words, there is no evidence that productivity growth will return to its prior trend. This is the primary reason economic forecasts for more than one period ahead are subject to such large errors.

Sample and Test Variables

The samples for each of these tests are annual observations for the period 1950 to 1989. The economic and fiscal data are based on the July 1992 revision, but the population data for 1981–89 are subject to revision based on the 1990 census. All of the economic and fiscal data are from the 1988 and 1992 issues of the *Economic Report of the President* and the July 1992 *Survey of Current Business*. The data on oil prices and net imports were provided by the American Petroleum Institute.

Each test equation includes the same list of independent variables. The dependent and common independent variables are described below:

Dependent variables

D(LRGNP) first difference, natural log of real GNP per working-age adult

D(LPROD) first difference, natural log of output per hour in the business sector

D(LHOUR) first difference, natural log of hours worked in the business sector per working-age adult

Independent variables

C   constant

YEAR   50–89

D(UER)   first difference, civilian unemployment rate

D(NDEPY) first difference, real defence expenditures as a percentage of (prior year) real GNP

D(LROGE) first difference, natural log of real other government purchases of goods and services per working-age adult

D(LRTRP) first difference, natural log of real transfer payments and net subsidies per working-age adult

D(LOMTR) first difference, natural log of (1 – TAX/GNP), where TAX is the total government tax receipts

D(LOMDR) first difference, natural log of (1 – DEF/GNP), where DEF is the net total government deficit

D(OIEPY) first difference, domestic price of oil times the level of (prior year) net oil imports as a percentage of GNP.

Some minor additional explanation is necessary. The number of working-age adults is the population age 20 to 64. Real national security expenditures are based on a price index of my construction, splicing the implicit price deflator for total federal purchases of goods and services to 1971 to the implicit price deflator for defence expenditures since 1972. Some experimentation indicated that the marginal effects of defence expenditures are more significant in the linear form than in the logarithmic form. Real other government purchases of goods and services are the total real purchases of goods and services minus (my estimate of) real national defence expenditures. Real transfer payments and net subsidies are based on the implicit price deflator for personal consumption expenditures. Among the independent variables, C, YEAR, D(NDEPY), D(LROGE) and D(OIEPY) are exogenous. Variables D(UER), D(LRTRP), D(LOMTR) and D(LOMDR) are treated as endogenous.

Instrumental variables used in the system estimates include the included exogenous variables, one-period-lagged values of both the dependent variables and the included endogenous variables, and several excluded exogenous variables that specifically affect D(UER) and

D(LRTRP). The several additional instrumental variables are the next-year armed forces overseas share of the working-age population, the first and second lagged ratios of the corporate (Aaa) bond rate to the commercial paper rate, the population age 65 and over as a share of the working-age population, and the relative price of consumer goods. (More information on all variables and data sources is available from the author on request.)

The Estimation Procedure

The three test equations were estimated by the iterative three-stage least-squares procedure. This procedure yields more efficient estimates than from two-stage estimates of the separate equations if there is any correlation among the residuals of the several equations. Estimates from this procedure are asymptotic full-information maximum likelihood estimates.

Test Results

Table 10.1 presents the systems estimates of the fiscal effects on real GNP, productivity and hours worked. (The numbers in parentheses are the standard errors of each coefficient.) This table also presents two other columns, where D(LRBDP) is the first difference of the log of real (gross) business domestic product and D(LRNBP) is the first difference of the log of real nonbusiness product (the sum of government payrolls and output originating in nonprofit institutions, households and abroad). The coefficients in these columns (but not the standard errors) can be calculated from the estimates in the other columns. Given that real business sector output is the product of productivity and hours worked in the business sector, the coefficients in the second column are the sum of the coefficients in each row of the third and fourth columns. In addition, as real GNP is the sum of real business domestic product and real nonbusiness product, the coefficients in each row of the first column are the weighted sum of the coefficients in the second and fifth columns, where the weights are the respective shares of business and nonbusiness product in real GNP. At the sample means, real business domestic product was 0.831 of real GNP, and real nonbusiness product was 0.169 of real GNP. The coefficients of the fifth column, thus, are calculated by solving for the effects on real nonbusiness product from the coefficients in the first and second columns. This procedure provides estimates of the fiscal effects on all of the components of real GNP without solving a more complicated five-equation model with interequation coefficient restrictions. The primary disadvantage of this procedure is that it does not

Policy analysis

Table 10.1 System estimates of the fiscal effects on economic growth

Independent variables	Dependent variables				
	D(LRGNP)	D(LRBDP)	D(LPROD)	D(LHOUR)	D(LRNBP)
C	0.03789 (0.0092	0.0359	0.0503 (0.0140)	−0.0144 (0.0083)	0.0477
Year	−0.0003 (0.0001)	−0.0003	−0.0005 (0.0002)	0.0002 (0.0001)	−0.0005
D(UER)	−0.0060 (0.0032)	−0.0076	0.0086 (0.0048)	−0.0162 (0.0029)	0.0019
D(NDEPY)	0.0162 (0.0025)	0.0127	0.0139 (0.0038)	−0.0012 (0.0022)	0.0332
D(LROGE)	0.2647) (0.0526)	0.2698	0.2235 (0.0805)	0.0463 (0.0476)	0.2396
D(LRTRP)	0.0623 (0.0351)	0.0614	0.1173 (0.0537)	−0.0559 (0.0318)	0.0667
D(LOMTR)	1.1286 (0.3055)	1.0622	0.4778 (0.4673)	0.5844 (0.2763)	1.455
D(LOMDR)	1.7636 (0.2722)	1.9514	1.4727 (0.4164)	0.4787 (0.2462)	0.8396
D(OIEPY)	−0.0031 (0.0050)	−0.0154	−0.0211 (0.0077)	0.0057 (0.0045)	0.0574
R^2	0.9985		0.9977	0.9803	
SER	0.0077		0.0117	0.0069	
DW	2.0004		1.8461	2.1554	

Note: Standard errors in parentheses.

provide estimates of the standard errors of the coefficients in the second and fifth columns.

At this stage, it is useful to discuss the effects of each of the independent variables on the several dimensions of economic growth based on the estimated coefficients presented in Table 10.1.

The first and second rows present estimates of the annual exogenous increases in the several dimensions of economic growth. The primary lesson from these estimates is that the 'natural rate' of increase of real GNP, productivity, and hours worked has changed substantially over the postwar years. Table 10.2 summarizes the estimates of these natural rates over this period. The exogenous contributions to productivity growth are declining, but the exogenous decline in hours worked per member of the working-age population was reversed in the late 1960s.

The third row presents the effects of an increase of one percentage point in the civilian unemployment rate. Such an increase reduces real GNP by 0.6 per cent, with a somewhat larger effect on the business sector. An increase of one percentage point in the unemployment rate increases productivity in the business sector by 0.9 per cent but reduces hours worked by 1.6 per cent.

The fourth row presents the effects of changes in real defence expenditures. An increase in defence expenditures by 1 per cent, of GNP, for example, appears to increase real GNP by about 1.6 per cent primarily by increasing productivity in the business sector and expenditures in the non-business sector. This result, however, should be interpreted with caution, because defence expenditures are valued at cost – not at market value. The effect of defence expenditures on real GNP should be considered a benefit, of course, only if these expenditures are worth at least what they cost.

The fifth row in Table 10.1 presents the elasticities of the dependent variables with respect to the real level of other government purchases of goods and services – most of which are for education, physical infrastructure, police, fire protection, and the like. A 10 per cent increase in real expenditures for these services increases real GNP by about 2.6 per cent, primarily by increasing productivity in the business sector – suggesting that the services financed by most of these expenditures are complementary to inputs in the business sector.

Table 10.2 Exogenous annual changes in economic conditions (in percentages)

Variables	1949	1969	1989
RGNP/Population	2.3	1.6	1.0
Productivity	2.6	1.5	0.5
Hours/Population	–0.4	0.1	0.5

The sixth row presents the elasticities of the dependent variables with respect to real transfer payments and net subsidies. A 10 per cent increase in real transfer payments increases real GNP by about 0.6 per cent, the net effect of an increase in productivity and a reduction in hours worked in the business sector.

The seventh row presents the elasticities of the dependent variables with respect to the *after*-tax rate. The proportional effect of a change in the average tax rate, in turn, is $-b(1 - TR)^{-1}$ where b is the estimated elasticity on the after-tax rate and TR is the ratio of total tax receipts to GNP. An increase in the average tax rate has a large significant negative effect on both real GNP and business sector output and, interestingly, an even larger negative effect on expenditures by the nonbusiness sector. The elasticity of real GNP with respect to the after-tax rate b can also be used to estimate the revenue-maximizing tax rate (t^*), where $t^* = 1/(1 + b)$. The estimate of b indicates that the revenue-maximizing average tax rate in the United States is about 47 per cent.

The eighth row of Table 10.1 presents the elasticities of the dependent variables with respect to the *after*-deficit rate. The proportional effect of a change in the deficit rate, in turn, is $-b(1 - DR)^{-1}$, where b is the estimated elasticity on the after-deficit rate and DR is the ratio of the net total deficit to GNP. An increase in the deficit has a large significant negative effect on real GNP, reflecting significant negative effects on both productivity and hours worked in the business sector. The effect of deficits on expenditures by the nonbusiness sector appears to be smaller than the effect of taxes.

The ninth row presents estimates of the effects on each of the dependent variables of changes in expenditures for oil imports. An increase in expenditures for oil imports by 1 per cent of GNP reduces productivity in the business sector by about 2.2 per cent but appears to increase hours worked and expenditures in the nonbusiness sector. The net effect on real GNP is not significant.

In summary, the sign, level and significance of most of the estimates from these tests are satisfactory, and the statistical characteristics of the three test equations are quite satisfactory.

Further Implications of the System Estimates

The partial effects of a $1 billion increase in any of the fiscal variables depends on the form of the variable. For this test, real defence expenditures are expressed as a percentage of real GNP in the prior year. The partial effects of a $1 billion increase in defence expenditures, thus, is

$$\frac{\partial Y}{\partial X} = b[\, Y/\text{RGNP}(-1)],$$

where b is the estimated coefficient, Y is the level of the economic variable, and RGNP (-1) is the level of real GNP per member of the working-age population in the prior year. This is the only fiscal variable for which the partial effects are independent of the level of the variable.

The estimates of the other fiscal variables are expressed in terms of constant elasticities. The partial effects, for example, of a \$1 billion increase in these fiscal variables, however, are a function of both the level of the economic variable and the level of the fiscal variable. Specifically,

$$\partial Y/\partial X = b(Y/X), \qquad \frac{\partial Y}{\partial T} = -b[\, Y/(Y - T)],$$

where b is the estimated elasticity, Y is the level of the economic variable, X is the level of the expenditure variable, and T is the level of tax receipts or the deficit.

Table 10.3 presents the partial effects of an additional \$1 billion of each of the fiscal variables, given the level of the economic and fiscal variables in 1989. An increase in defence expenditures appears to increase GNP by about the same as the negative effects of the taxes or deficit necessary to finance these additional expenditures. At the margin of current conditions, additional defence expenditures are not a good investment in terms of the marketed output of the business sector. One cannot judge whether the United States underinvests in national security without estimating the security value of the additional expenditures. The above estimates are not sufficient for making that judgement

Some increase in other government expenditures, however, may be worth the additional taxes or deficit. At the margin of current conditions, the positive effects on GNP of additional expenditures of this type appear to be somewhat higher than the negative effects of the additional taxes or deficit. This result is consistent with but more general than the conclusion of Aschauer and others that the United States underinvests in physical infrastructure.

An increase in transfer payments, however, appears to be a bad economic investment. The increase in GNP is much smaller than the negative effects of taxes or the deficit. The value of additional transfer payments, such as additional defence expenditures, must be judged on other grounds

Additional taxes and borrowing have roughly similar negative effects on GNP. The most important implication of these estimates is that gov-

*Table 10.3 Partial effects of the fiscal variables in 1989
          (in billions of dollars)*

	Total	Business	Other
Defence	1.6	1.3	0.3
Domestic	2.1	1.8	0.3
Transfers	0.5	0.4	0.1
Taxes	−1.6	−1.3	−0.3
Deficit	−1.8	−1.7	−0.1

ernment spending for any programme should be constrained to a level for which the marginal value of additional spending is equal to 1.6 times the incremental budget cost if financed by taxes or 1.8 times the additional cost if financed by borrowing. The effects of taxes on the business sector are somewhat lower and on the nonbusiness sector are somewhat higher than the corresponding effects of government borrowing.

In summary, the aggregate fiscal package of US governments does not appear to maximize economic growth. At the margin of current conditions, defence expenditures and transfer payments appear to be consumption expenditures, which may be valuable on other grounds but reduce economic growth. The United States, however, appears to under-invest in other government expenditures. A fiscal strategy that reduced national security expenditures and transfer payments, increased other government expenditures, and reduced taxes and the deficit would almost surely increase US economic growth.

An Omitted Variable

One other variable was included in prior versions of these tests: the number of lawyers in active practice. There is reason to believe that the increase in the number of lawyers in active practice reflects conditions that reduce US economic growth, particularly the increase in litigation, lobbying, regulation and other forms of rent-seeking and rent-defending activity. Stephen Magee (1991), for example, estimates that the average lawyer reduces US GNP by $1 million, based on a cross-country study of economic growth that included, as one variable, the number of lawyers as a percentage of white-collar workers. For this reason, I included the following variable in some prior tests:

$$\text{LOMLS} = \log(1 - L/N),$$

where L is the number of lawyers in active practice and N is the working-age population. This variable is not measured very accurately; only ten consistent observations at different intervals on the number of lawyers in active practice are available in the postwar years, and the other data points were estimated by exponential smoothing around the available observations. The results of these tests were striking but not conclusive. As of 1989, the conditions that led to the employment of the marginal lawyer appeared to reduce GNP by $2.5 million(!), with an even larger proportional effect on business sector productivity; moreover, in prior tests based on the levels of the dependent variables, this variable was quite significant. In the first difference form of the test equations, however, the significance of this variable was reduced, and deletion of this variable did not much change the estimates of the fiscal variables. This is an important issue and a striking estimate, however, and merits further research.

NEXT STEPS

This chapter is the first report of a larger study. One part of this continued research will be to refine the estimates of the policy effects on US economic growth. More attention to separating the effects of peacetime and wartime national security expenditures is merited. It may be useful to divide the large aggregate of other government purchases of goods and services into education expenditures and an 'other expenditures' variable. The effects of transfer payments may be better measured in the (1 – transfer rate) form, consistent with the treatment of the tax and deficit rates, for which the marginal effects are increasing. The tax variable should be expressed in terms of the effective average marginal rates, rather than average rates, but I do not know whether there is an adequate time series on average marginal tax rates. I am compelled to find an adequate index of the level of regulation and litigation activity. Suggestions are welcome.

The other part of this research will use the data base to estimate jointly the demand functions for government services, the tax and deficit function, and real GNP. From some prior estimates, some further refinement of the variables in these functions is probably necessary. This study, to my knowledge, will be the first to estimate jointly the several fiscal functions and the effects of fiscal conditions on real GNP.

REFERENCES

American Petroleum Institute (1990), Washington, DC.

Aschauer, D.A. (1990), 'Is government spending stimulative?', *Contemporary Policy Issues*, **8**, 30–46.

Barro, R.J. (1989) 'Economic growth in a cross section of countries', NBER, Working Paper 3120.

Barro, R.J. (1990), 'Government spending in a simple model of economic growth', *Journal of Political Economy*, **98** (supplement), S103–S125.

Barth, J. and M.D. Bradley (1987), 'The impact of government spending on economic activity', Unpublished manuscript, George Washington University.

Grier, K.B. and G. Tullock (1987), 'An empirical analysis of cross-national economic growth, 1950–1980', Unpublished manuscript, California Institute of Technology.

Jorgenson, D.W. and K.Y. Yun (1990), 'Tax reform and U.S. economic growth', *Journal of Political Economy*, **98** (supplement), S151–S193.

Kormendi, R.C. and P.G. Meguire (1985), 'Macroeconomic determinants of growth: cross-country evidence', *Journal of Monetary Economics*, **16**, 141–63.

Landau, D.L. (1983), 'Government expenditure and economic growth: a cross-country study', *Southern Economic Journal*, **49**, 783–92.

Magee, S.P. (1991), 'The negative effect of lawyers on the U.S. economy', *International Economic Insights*', January/February 34–5.

United States (1988, 1992), *Economic Report of the President Transmitted to the Congress*, Washington, DC: US Government Printing Office.

United States (1992), *Survey of Current Business*, Washington, DC: Department of Commerce, July.

11. Political guidance on monetary policy*

This chapter focuses on a narrow but important topic: the nature of political guidance to the Federal Reserve on monetary policy. The Constitution authorizes Congress 'to coin Money [and] regulate the Value thereof'. As a rule, however, Congress has delegated this authority to the Federal Reserve, either without guidance or, more recently, with sufficiently confused, redundant, or contradictory guidance to permit the Fed to chart its own course. We could do worse. The performance of the Federal Reserve has usually been better than that of most other central banks.

I believe we can also do better – much better – and shall summarize a proposal for a new monetary rule along with a process for approving, implementing and monitoring this rule.

SELECTING A MONETARY POLICY RULE

First, I shall focus on the choice of a monetary rule. There are only three viable monetary rules. One is to maintain a path of the price of some specific commodity such as gold or some broader price index. Second is to maintain a path of some monetary aggregate such as the monetary base or a measure of the money supply. And third is to maintain a path of some measure of total demand in the economy such as nominal GNP or domestic final sales.

Any one of these rules would be better than guidance based on interest rates or exchange rates, or on any real variable such as the growth of output or the level of the unemployment rate. Some comments are in order, however, concerning the reasons for choosing one or the other of these three rules.

* Reprinted by permission from the *Cato Journal*, **12** (1), Spring/Summer 1992, 281–6, Cato Institute.

A Price Rule

Wayne Angell and others have performed a valuable service by reviving the case for a price rule that is based on gold or some broader commodity index. The primary problem with a price rule is that the price of commodities depends on both demand and supply conditions, and a price rule can lead to considerable instability in other markets. The long experience with the several types of gold standards, for example, included several short periods of inflation caused by major gold discoveries, long periods of deflation, frequent recessions and the Great Depression. The primary value of the gold standard was to prevent cumulative inflation over a much longer period of time. As best we can measure, for example, the US price level in 1939 was about the same as in 1789. A price rule based on a broader set of commodities, however, would have the same general types of problems, although the variability of conditions in other markets would probably be smaller than one based on a commodity such as gold. In the modern world, for example, a price rule would require the Fed to deflate the general economy in response to an oil shock. I believe that we can do much better than that.

A Monetary Aggregate Rule

For about 20 years, most monetary economists promoted a rule to stabilize the path of some monetary aggregate such as M2. The case for this rule was based on a belief that there was a roughly stable relation between the level of the money supply, however measured, and the level of some measure of total demand in the economy. In other words, the objective of the monetarists was to stabilize the path of total demand, and they believed that a stable path of some measure of the money supply would best serve this objective. In response to this advice, the Fed has set targets for several monetary aggregates since 1970, and Congress has reviewed and approved these targets since 1975.

For most of the postwar years until the end of 1981, the relation between total demand and money appeared to be roughly stable. There was a reasonable case that the increasing inflation and occasional recessions were primarily due to the Fed's failure – with rare exception – to stay within the approved target ranges for the money supply.

Since the end of 1981, however, the relation between total demand in the United States and each of the monetary aggregates has changed sharply. Specifically, total demand has continuously declined relative to the level of the money supply. The reasons for this continued decline in the velocity of money are not too clear, but it was probably due to the effect of the decline in market interest rates, the increase in interest rates on bank deposits permitted by deregulation, and, I think importantly, the substantial increase in the value of other financial assets.

Moreover, the accumulating econometric evidence indicates that the relationship between *changes* in total demand and *changes* in the money supply is roughly stable, but the relationship between the *levels* of these conditions is not stable. In technical terms, this relationship appears to be difference-stable but not trend-stable.[1] The most important implication of these findings is that a stable growth of the money supply will not lead to a stable growth of total demand. For this reason, the primary policy rule promoted by what I call the 'high church monetarists' does not appear to be the best rule.

A Target Path of Total Demand

Another alternative is for Congress to approve a target path of total demand in the American economy.[2] This is best measured, I suggest, by what the Department of Commerce defines as 'final sales to domestic purchasers'. It would also be valuable to exclude purchases by the Federal Commodity Credit Corporation from this aggregate. These purchases, although they are measured as final sales, are actually increases in government inventories of farm products and are unusually volatile. The primary reason for selecting this variable rather than nominal GNP is that the demand for money in the United States appears more closely related to total purchases by Americans than to the dollar level of total output by Americans.

It is important to recognize that a demand rule is consistent with any desired price-level path, including a stable price level. (For this chapter, I shall avoid the issues that bear on the choice of the desired price-level path.) My primary point is that a demand rule is superior to a price rule, whatever is the desired price-level path, because of the different response to changes in supply conditions. A central bank following a demand rule would not respond to either positive or negative supply shocks; such shocks would lead to a one-time change in the combination of price and output changes in that year but would not lead to a long-term change in the inflation rate. A central bank following a price rule, however, would increase the monetary base in response to a positive supply shock and would tighten the base in response to a negative shock, thereby increasing the variance of output. Both rules are consistent with any desired price-level path. The primary case for a demand rule is that it reduces the variance of output.

In summary, a demand rule is superior to a price rule because it does not lead to adverse monetary policy in response to unexpected – either favourable or unfavourable – changes in supply conditions. Similarly, a demand rule is superior to a money rule because it accommodates unexpected changes in the demand for money. For these reasons, I suggest that implementation of a demand rule is the most appropriate next step for US monetary policy.

ESTABLISHING AND MONITORING A DEMAND RULE

How might a demand rule be approved, implemented and monitored? The beginning of this process would be much like the current process. In February of each year, the administration would propose a target path of nominal domestic final sales for a several-year period as part of its projections in the budget and in the economic report. This proposed target path would reflect the combined effect of the administration's forecast of real final sales plus a recommended price-level path, reflecting how fast the administration proposes to reduce inflation. The Joint Economic Committee (JEC) would then review the proposed target path, in addition to those targets that may be proposed by the Fed, the Congressional Budget Office and private economists. There need be no review or approval of the target ranges for any of the monetary aggregates, as is currently the case. This procedure would focus the attention of Congress on a value issue (the desired price path), not on the technical issues affecting the choice of the path of some monetary aggregate.

At this stage some change in procedure may be desirable. My preference would be to have the JEC approve a bill that would formally instruct the Fed to follow a specific target path of nominal domestic final sales, a bill that would then have to be approved by both houses of Congress and the president. Some formal legislative authority by the JEC, I believe, would also contribute to reviving this once important committee. My only reservation about this process is that Congress, as a body, has usually had an inflationary bias. But the central role of the JEC and a potential presidential veto, I think, probably should be enough to discipline this bias.

Once the target path for final sales is selected, the Fed would set an instrumental target for the monetary base, which is the sum of currency plus bank reserves, to implement the approved target path of nominal domestic final sales. This instrumental target would be selected based on the historical relation between the change in nominal final sales, which is what Congress has approved, and the change in the monetary base, which is what the Fed can control.

At this stage, there may be some opportunity to use current data from forward-looking auction markets, such as the several first suggested by Manuel Johnson (1988), to determine whether there is a likely change in the relation between changes in final demand and the monetary base. I am intrigued by this suggestion, but I am not yet convinced that one can improve on the type of adaptive rule suggested by Bennett McCallum (1984) that is based on the historical data on demand and the base, even though both series are subject to frequent revision. In any case, it is important to use data on commodity prices, interest rates and exchange rates only as clues to setting the base target, rather than the current and quite dangerous practice of using the federal funds rate as an instrumental target.

There is no reason for an external review of this instrumental target for the monetary base. Most importantly, as often as once a quarter, the Fed would compare the actual final sales in the previous quarter with the approved target and would then change the target for the monetary base for the current quarter in order to return to the approved target path. This process, over time, should be designed to minimize the variance of actual final sales relative to the approved target, even though the process may increase the variance of changes in the monetary base. Over time, the path of nominal GNP will roughly track the path of nominal domestic final sales but with a somewhat higher variance due to changes in inventory accumulation and exports that are less affected by US monetary policy. This process would not lead to a stability of all macro conditions, but minimizing the variance around an approved target path of nominal domestic final sales is probably the most that can be expected of monetary policy.

The third step in this process would be for the administration and Congress to monitor the Fed's performance, maybe as often as once a quarter. This review should focus on the reasons why actual final sales may have differed from the target path in the previous quarter. An increasing difference between the actual and the target final sales over a period as long as two quarters should automatically trigger such a review. There is ample reason to criticize the Fed for an accumulating difference between the actual final sales path and the approved target path. But as long as the Fed maintains a roughly stable level of final sales relative to this path, both the administration and Congress should refrain from criticizing the Fed because of a concern about a wide range of other conditions.

CONCLUSIONS

In summary, we now expect the Fed to do too much. As a consequence, the Fed does not perform its most important function very well. At various times, our political system pressures the Fed to sustain the recovery, to reduce inflation, to reduce interest rates, to reduce the unemployment rate, to strengthen or weaken the dollar, to finance the government debt, or whatever.

One of the most important lessons of political economy is that a government must have at least as many policy instruments as it has goals. The Fed has only one policy instrument, specifically the level of the monetary base. It is important to focus this instrument on the single, most-important, achievable goal of monetary policy. That goal, I suggest, is a stable path of nominal domestic final sales. At the same time, it is important to recognize that we need to put our fiscal and regulatory house in order if we are to achieve our other economic goals.

NOTES

1. This characteristic of the velocity of money was first identified by Gould and Nelson (1974), who used annual data, and confirmed by Haraf (1986), who used quarterly data.
2. The case for a demand rule was first made in the early 1980s by Hall (1981), McCallum (1984) and Gordon (1985).

REFERENCES

Gordon, Robert J. (1985), 'The conduct of domestic monetary policy', in Albert Ando et al. (eds), *Monetary Policy in Our Times*, Cambridge, MA: MIT Press, 45–81.
Gould, John and Charles Nelson (1974), 'The stochastic structure of the velocity of money', *American Economic Review*, **64**, June, 405–18.
Hall, Robert (1981), 'Lowering inflation and stimulating economic growth', in *Politics and the Oval Office: Toward Presidential Governance*, San Francisco: Institute for Contemporary Studies, pp 207–27.
Haraf, William S. (1986), 'Monetary velocity and monetary rules', *Cato Journal*, **6**, Fall, 641–62.
Johnson, Manuel H. (1988), 'Current perspectives on monetary policy', *Cato Journal*, **8**, Fall, 253–60.
McCallum, Bennett T. (1984), 'Monetarist rules in the light of recent experiences', *American Economic Review*, **74**, May, 388–91.

12. Economists and politicians*

THE ROLE OF THE POLICY ADVISER

Why do politicians hire advisers? The first step towards answering this question is a recognition that the focus of political choices is among alternative laws, regulations, administrative orders and other formal statements of policy, but, in many cases, the primary concern is with the effects of these choices. Political officials rely on policy advisers, among others, to supply information that bears on the effects of these political choices.

Policy advisers are expected to provide five types of information, the first four types requiring a progressive increase in skills.

First, what are the objective conditions in some areas of concern to politicians? For example, what is the distribution of the unemployment rate among groups and over time? Developing such descriptive statistics requires some measurement skills, but is not dependent on any specific behavioural theory relating this condition to others.

Second, what explains the differences in some objective condition? And a related question: how will these conditions change if there is no change in policy? For example, what explains the differences in the unemployment rate among groups and over time? The responses to this type of question are most likely to reflect the specific training of the policy adviser; an economist, for example, is likely to respond to this type of question differently from a sociologist. And, what will happen to the unemployment rate if there is no change in policy? A response to this type of question requires some understanding of the dynamics of the objective condition and will affect whether the politician is likely to initiate or support a change in policy. The political reaction to a specific unemployment rate, for example, depends on whether this rate is likely to increase or decline without a change in policy.

Third, what are the effects of a change in some specific policy on the objective conditions of concern to the politician? For example, what

*   Reprinted by permission from *Journal of Policy Analysis and Management*, **5** (2), 1986, 234–44.
    The article was based on a speech delivered to the Pacific Regional Meeting of the Mont Pelerin Society, Sydney, Australia, 21 August 1985.

would be the effects of increasing the rate of growth of the money supply on the unemployment rate? A response to this type of question requires an understanding of the relationship between the growth rate in the money supply (a policy instrument) and the unemployment rate (the condition of concern). The focus on policy instruments often distinguishes the work of policy advisers from other researchers concerned with the same subject.

Fourth, what other potential policy changes would be superior, in some dimension of concern to the politician, to the specific policy changes proposed by others? For example, would a restructuring of unemployment insurance have a larger long-term effect on the unemployment rate than an increase in the growth of the money supply? One of the most important responsibilities of a policy adviser is to broaden the policy alternatives in order to prevent his or her specific client from being faced by an all-or-nothing choice posed by others. The formulation of such alternative policy choices affecting the same set of conditions requires the highest skill of a policy adviser. In general, such alternatives must be introduced early in the process in order to prevent the pressure of time from limiting the choice to the policy changes proposed by others.

Fifth, what are the views of other experts on the subject on the first four types of questions? For example, what are the views of other experts on the causes of changes in the unemployment rate or on the effectiveness of alternative policies to reduce this rate? Politicians may respect their own adviser and yet act against his or her advice if there is reason to expect substantial opposition from politicians served by other advisers. Policy advisers best serve their specific clients by accurately representing the views of other experts, because opposition is more damaging to the politician if it is unexpected.

Any policy adviser, whatever his or her speciality, provides one or more of the five types of information described above. The observation that governments hire a large number of policy advisers and that politicians spend some time reading or listening to the information they provide suggests that, on net, this information is valued by the politicians. A politician will value advice on a specific issue, however, only when each of two conditions exists. First, the politician must be primarily concerned about the objective conditions that are affected by the choice of policies. Second, the relation between a change in policies and the change in the objective conditions must not be self-evident to the politician, based on his or her own convictions or the information available from other sources.

Policy advisers, however, should recognize that there are several conditions for which the value of policy advice to politicians may be zero or even negative. The interests of politicians – in terms of reelection, promotion or personal convictions – may be more closely identified with support or opposition to specific policies, rather than with the effects of these policies on the objective conditions affecting the population. Politicians are likely to be rewarded if their actions are perceived to benefit their constituencies, whether or not they, in fact, do so. A concern about effects is likely to be relatively less important when the effects of a policy are uncertain, diffused or deferred, especially when elections are close at hand. The choice of policies may be self-evident to politicians based on some criterion not perceived by the policy adviser or on information from other sources. Politicians in these situations may prefer no information to some information, if the effects of the information are to question their personal judgement or to reduce support from others for their favoured policies.

Politicians share a pervasive concern that such information will leak. Some leaks are accidents. Many leaks are the consequences of someone trading favours with others in the government or with journalists. In the US, the Freedom of Information Act permits anyone to have access to many government documents if they know such documents exist. Some leaks are clearly motivated by an attempt to undermine others in the government, and there is some risk that a politician's own policy adviser may try to appeal to a larger group. In such cases, politicians often prefer not to be informed if the information questions their own judgement or if the process of becoming informed risks the distribution of this information to others.

THE GROWING ROLE OF THE ECONOMIC ADVISER

Over the past several decades, economists have become the most influential and pervasive group of policy advisers. Maybe this should have been anticipated. Some part of the increased demand for economic advisers is surely attributable to the increasing role of government in the economy; that is, there are now more economic policy issues. This condition, however, does not explain the increasing role of economists as advisers on defence, law, medical care and a wide range of policy issues that are not directly perceived to be primarily economic. An explanation for this broader role of the economist as policy adviser may be found in the usefulness of economic skills in providing the types of information valued by the politicians (especially the second, third and fourth types of information described above).

Economists have long believed that they could make a special contribution as policy advisers, although a more general recognition of these skills was slow to develop. Adam Smith described economics as 'the science of the legislator'.[1] As Frank Knight described them, the characteristic activities for which economics 'furnish[es] guidance are those of the citizen and statesman, not those of the individual as a *wirtschaftender Mensch*'.[2] A recent book by Rutledge Vining defines economics as the analysis of economic policy, relegating the rest of what most of us consider economics to the science of management and administration or to a special branch of psychology.[3] I am not one to quibble about definitions. My own role as a policy adviser has drawn on the many different contributions of economists – from linear programming to the analysis of political behaviour.

What are the characteristics of economics that have led economists from Adam Smith to date to believe they could make a special contribution as policy advisers? The distinctive assumption of economic theory (one that is not directly testable) is that individual behaviour is purposive in pursuit of the individual's own interests. The characteristic activities of economists are the formulation and testing of hypotheses about social behaviour based on this assumption. These 'models' of social behaviour are the basis for providing the second and third types of information of interest to politicians – the probable change in some objective condition if there is no change in policy or if some specific policy is changed. During the 1950s and 1960s, economists also developed both a normative theory of the state (welfare economics) and the rudiments of a positive theory of the state (public choice). Welfare economics provided a useful framework for what the state ought to do, based on the provision of 'public' goods and the correction of market failures. The developing field of public choice has provided a useful balance by demonstrating that the processes of government decision making lead to numerous types of government failure. Both of these developments have affected the general intellectual environment in which government operates. For the most part, however, policy advisers accept the authority of the government in their own area of responsibility. The case for a fundamental change in the role of government must be made outside the government and operate through the incentives of politicians.

The number and distribution of economists in the US government suggest the nature and breadth of their current role. Only a few economists serve in the most senior political positions. One member of the Senate is an economist, and several economists have served in the House of Representatives in recent years. One member of the cabinet is an economist, and a dozen or so economists serve as subcabinet political officials. Many of the senior staff advisers to these political officials, however, are economists. The federal government now employs about

6000 economists. Ten departments, the Federal Reserve and the Congressional Budget Office each employ more than 100 economists. The senior economists among this group form an informal network for the exchange of information, the resolution of technical issues and occasionally the resolution of interagency disputes.

The Council of Economic Advisers (CEA) is the most visible and distinctive group of economists in the government. The Council was established in the executive office of the president by the Employment Act of 1946. The Full Employment and Balanced Growth Act of 1978 later added some reporting requirements concerning the progress towards goals concerning unemployment, inflation and investment. The three members of the Council are nominated by the president and confirmed by the Senate; one of these members is appointed as chairman by the president. Members of the Council are usually selected from a university appointment, have some prior experience that demonstrates their political credentials, and serve for about two years. The Council staff now includes twelve senior economists, eight junior economists, and a small permanent statistical office. Most of the senior economists are on leave from a university appointment for a period of one to two years. The junior economists, who serve for one year, are often graduate students who have not yet completed their dissertations. The structure and size of the Council have changed little over its history of nearly 40 years. The only public reports of the Council are its Annual Report (published with the Economic Report of the President) and the monthly Economic Indicators, a compilation of current and recent statistics on economic conditions, plus occasional testimony and speeches by the members.

The Council is sometimes described as economic advisers to the president, but this is somewhat misleading. Presidents have a habit of choosing their own advisers, whatever the formal structure of government. Only a few of the Council chairmen have had a close relation with the president, but the effectiveness of the Council has not proved to be dependent on this relation. A chairman's contact with the president is usually limited to periodic briefings on the economy and as an informal member of the cabinet. Most of the work of the Council is presented to the several forums responsible for the presidential policy review and to *ad hoc* working groups on specific issues. During President Ronald Reagan's first term, for example, the policy review was primarily conducted by nine cabinet councils, subcommittees of the cabinet responsible for specific policy areas. As a rule, the chairman or some member of the CEA would participate in each of the cabinet councils, with the exception of those addressing national security and some foreign policy issues. The CEA role in these reviews, however, is not established by law, and each new group of members must earn the right to participate. During President Reagan's second term, reviews have been conducted by only three cabinet councils, and the CEA is formally represented on only one of these councils. The chairman of the CEA, by tradition, is also a member of the 'troika', an informal group chaired by the secretary of the Treasury and including the budget director and one or two other members of the cabinet. The most important feature of the presidential review process and the CEA role in it is that everything is subject to 'the pleasure of the President'. The law establishes the CEA in the executive office of the president, but no law requires that anyone pay attention to their views. A similar Council for Environmental Quality, for example, is also established in the executive office, but has been effectively defunct for some years.

The external relations of the CEA involve both requests for information and the dissemination of information, often coupled in an exchange with the same party. For the Council to be effective, it must maintain a network of contacts, often with other economists around the government, as a means of gathering technical information and determining the status of proposals initiated in the agencies and in Congress. Early warning of emerging issues is very important to provide time for analysis before the often-brief presidential review. It is also important to sort out issues of fact and analysis before they reach the political level. Contact with scholars at universities and research organizations is important as a source of empirical research and policy analysis. Lobbyists often provide valuable technical information, and members of the press, often the best-informed people in Washington on rapidly developing events, provide timely information.

The most awkward feature of these external relations is that maintaining a source often requires an exchange of information. The CEA's relation with other government economists is collegial, not hierarchical. Employees of other agencies, members of Congress, lobbyists and the press have their own agenda. On occasion, the CEA is requested to disseminate information in speeches, congressional testimony and press contacts. Although testimony and, occasionally, speeches are subject to clearance, there is no way to protect oneself against a selective quotation, a careless reporter or a careless headline writer. Chairmen of the CEA have reacted to the potential problems involving the dissemination of information in various ways. Arthur Burns was reluctant to testify before congressional committees. Martin Feldstein solicited public appearances and cultivated the press.

The policy focus of the CEA analysis has changed substantially over its history. As with many government agencies, the CEA has survived a change in its initial mission. The views that led to establishing the CEA in

1946 were shaped by a memory of the 1930s, a concern that the end of war production would lead to a severe recession, a planner's perspective on the importance of government planning, and a cautious enthusiasm for the new Keynesian science of macroeconomics. This perspective survived the sceptical conservatism of the Eisenhower administration and shaped the role of the CEA until the late 1960s. As described in a recent paper by Dennis Mueller,

> Theoretical and empirical work discussed how fiscal, monetary, and trade policies could be coordinated to control unemployment, inflation, and balance of payments. A kind of macro-Walrasian counting of policy goals and instruments was popular, and could be achieved if government could be free to vary all of the instruments potentially at its command.[4]

A sometimes arrogant confidence that economics had solved the major macroeconomic problems began to erode in the late 1960s, even though the US had experienced eight years without a recession. An unsuccessful war and rising inflation reduced the general confidence in the government. Moreover, there were major changes in the economics profession. Milton Friedman summarized the monetarist perspective on macroeconomics in his presidential address to the American Economic Association in 1967. And the developing evidence convinced many economists that monetary policy had a stronger effect on total demand than did fiscal policy. For the CEA, this was an awkward development because the Federal Reserve was (and is) stubbornly independent, formally responsible to Congress, not to the president. In January of 1970, the Federal Reserve adopted a money growth target for the first time. The influence of the Keynesian perspective had already peaked when President Richard Nixon announced that 'We are all Keynesians now'.

Other changes in the economy, the government and the economics profession also shaped the role of the CEA. An increasing share of economic policy issues subject to presidential review were microeconomic in focus, and the number of economists trained to address these issues had increased rapidly. A microeconomist was first appointed as a member of the CEA in 1968. The US economy was also becoming more dependent on international conditions. The trade share of gross national product (GNP) doubled between 1960 and 1980, and issues concerning international trade and finance became more important to the administration. The first international specialist was appointed as a member of the CEA in 1972.

The composition of the CEA during the Reagan administration reflects the substantial shift in the role of the Council. Of the five members who served during the first term, three were microeconomists and two were monetary economists. A monetary economist was first appointed as chairman in 1985. The Council staff reflects an increasing diversity of specialists – including subject specialists in agriculture, energy, health, housing, law, labour trade and transportation.

The Council has survived the end of the Keynesian revolution, which had guided its role since 1946, by responding to the changing demands for economic analysis and making use of the increasing range of skills within the economics profession. Some of this change probably reflects the economic policies of the Reagan administration. For the most part, however, I expect that the composition and role of the CEA in the next administration of either party will be more like the current Council than like the Council under prior administrations.

The Council has also survived a recent institutional crisis created by the public activities of Martin Feldstein. Although Feldstein, a first-rate economist, sincerely believed that his speeches and press contacts supported administration policy, they were widely perceived to be critical and embarrassing to the administration. As a consequence, Feldstein was ridiculed by senior administration officials and progressively excluded from the inner circles. The activities of the two other members and the Council staff, however, were not significantly affected. After Feldstein resigned in July 1984, there was serious consideration about abolishing the Council or downgrading its role. The major lesson of this episode is that a policy adviser must sacrifice any external role that conflicts with his or her internal role. Members of the CEA, and other senior policy advisers, should be selected on the basis of three criteria: professionalism, loyalty to the fundamental goals of the government in their area of responsibility and an ability to operate in a political environment. A passion for anonymity may be necessary to meet this third criterion. The press may interpret reduced public visibility of the CEA as a downgrading of its internal role, but lower visibility may be necessary to preserve an effective voice within the administration.

THE EFFECTIVENESS OF POLICY ADVISERS

The effectiveness of policy advisers, like that of the politicians they serve, is measured by their ability to affect the choice of policies. The degree and extent of effectiveness, in turn, depends on the political efficacy of groups that they serve and on the size, degree of consensus and the effective decision rules of these groups.

Two types of groups should be distinguished within the government. Most proposed changes in policy originate in subcommittees of Congress or in the bureaux and agencies that are responsible for implementing these policies. The objective of these groups is to propose a change in policy that maximizes their interests, subject to the constraints imposed by the necessity of gaining approval from other groups in the political system. Policy advisers to such groups often have the dominant influence on the design of proposed changes in policies for which each group is responsible, but, of course, they have no special influence on other policies.

The proposed changes to policy, in turn, are reviewed by groups with broader authority – the full committees, each house of Congress, the cabinet departments, and the presidential budget and policy review staffs. In many cases, this review is limited to determining whether the specific change in policy proposed by the smaller group serves the interests of the larger group. The special challenge of the review group is to determine whether some other feasible change in policy is superior, in terms of the interests of the review group, to either the current or the proposed change in policy. Policy advisers to the review groups are often influential in affecting these decisions. They typically have less influence on a specific policy than those advisers who serve the proposing group, but they have an opportunity to affect a broader range of decisions.

A simple example illustrates the role of the two groups of advisers. Assume that the current budget for some activity is $100 million. A change in conditions leads the agency providing the service to believe that the review group would.approve a larger budget. Policy advisers to the agency design a proposed budget of $120 million. The first task of the policy advisers to the review group is to provide information that bears on whether the proposed change serves the interests of the review group. Some other budget, however, say $110 million, may be preferable to the review group. If the review group does not have the authority or the skill to formulate an alternative to the initial proposal, the agency will have the dominant influence on the approved policy change. For this example, the budget would be $10 million higher than preferred by the review group and perhaps only slightly better from their perspective than the current policy.

Actual decision processes in the government, of course, are more complicated than suggested by this example. Some competition exists among the proposing groups. There are multiple levels and parallel channels of review. The example, however, is sufficient to illustrate the power of the group that sets the agenda for a subsequent decision. If the interests of the proposing group are served by a higher budget, more regulation, and so on, than preferred by those with the authority for final approval, government activities will be at higher levels than preferred by a majority of the politicians. (The relation between the interests of the legislative majority and the interests of the population is a separate but similar story.) Policy advisers are part of this problem and can be part of the solution as well, depending on the authority and incentives of those they serve.

The effectiveness of policy advisers depends on their ability to influence the 'marginal vote' required for approval of some proposed change in policy. This first depends on their ability to influence the specific politicians that they serve. In turn, the power of a specific politician depends on the size of the decision group, the degree of consensus and the effective decision rules in that group. The vote of one legislator, for example, is more likely to affect the group decision in a subcommittee than on the floor of the house. The position of one member of the cabinet is more likely to affect the decision of a cabinet council than of the whole cabinet. In any group, one vote is important only when the probable votes of others are closely divided relative to the decision rule of that group. There is little payoff to investing in making a case on a specific proposal for which there is substantial consensus either for or against, except to use the opportunity to try to influence future votes on a similar issue.

My sense is that policy advisers, for better or for worse, are more influential – powerful if you will – than is generally perceived. Of course, individual policy advisers are not likely to have much influence for the same reason that individual politicians are rarely in a position to cast a deciding vote. Senior policy advisers, however, or, for that matter, leading journalists, clearly have more influence than the average member of Congress because they are in a position to shape how those with direct political authority think about issues. In the specific case of the CEA, the chairman and occasionally the members have earned the right to participate in cabinet committees in exchange for providing information and analysis. In the US, the cabinet itself is only an advisory body, but the president rarely acts in opposition to a substantial consensus of the cabinet. My own experience includes many cases where my colleagues or I were able to reverse, shape or defer a decision by a temporary majority of the cabinet when the views of some of the majority were not well informed or strongly held. A policy adviser with strong views about what government ought to do (or not do) must learn to live with frustration. But such frustration is not unique to policy advisers. Many politicians also have strong views about what government ought to do. The source of frustration in both cases is that power is widely diffused in democratic governments. Frustration is the price one pays for knowing that someone who holds a contrary view is probably also frustrated.

On net, have policy adviser been defenders of the values of a free society? The answer must be no. For the most part, politicians employ the policy advisers who serve their interests. The world's most oppressive regimes are served by many of the brightest minds in these nations. A large, occasionally influential group of policy advisers is clearly neither necessary nor sufficient to defend a free order.

There are some patterns, however, of how policy advisers use their occasional influence. The most consistent pattern is the defence of views that are widely shared in their own profession. This is particularly the case for such groups as the CEA, most of whose members expect to return to a university. A near consensus among American economists on the recent proposals for an 'industrial policy', for example, was sufficient to defer, at least temporarily, approval of such proposals. A similar consensus among economists on the merits of free trade has been important to define 'the high ground' on trade issues, and the CEA has been the most consistent defender of free trade within the US government. This has not proved to be sufficient to defend free trade against the consequences of a strong dollar, but it has been sufficient to place a burden of argument on the protectionists. A politician who states, 'I'm in favour of free trade, but . . .' is already on the defensive. A growing consensus among economists on the various forms of economic regulation has contributed to the substantial recent deregulation of transportation, energy and financial institutions.

If the profession is divided, however, policy advisers usually serve the current interests of the politicians. One important example is the issue of price controls. Until the Reagan administration, the CEA had an intermittent record of supporting some form of price controls or guidance as a means to restrain inflation. The most striking irony is that the Nixon price controls were designed, supported, and administered by Chicago economists, who had every reason to know better. One other example is the issue of the government debt. The extraordinary confusion in the economics profession about the effects of the government debt has contributed to a climate that permitted a conservative president to nearly double the federal debt in four years.

A division of the professionals on a given issue increases the range of policy choices available to politicians. This can have both good and bad effects, depending on the convictions of the politicians. On some economic issues, I believe, President Reagan's convictions are better than those of many economists. This has permitted a greater focus on the structure of the tax code and on the role of a monetary policy than if most economists had maintained a Keynesian perspective. A substantial division among the professionals, however, would also increase the flexibility of another president with different convictions.

In summary, policy advisers are likely to be defenders of the values of a free society only if these values, and policy views consistent with these values, are widely shared in their profession. The politicians they serve are likely to be defenders of these values only if they are widely shared in the population and the structure of the political system restricts the opportunities for personal gain at the expense of others. There is no alternative to the sometimes discouraging task of promoting the values of a free society and to the demanding intellectual task of designing a constitution that reflects these values.

NOTES

1. Adam Smith, *The Wealth of Nations*, Oxford: Clarendon Press, 1976, pp. 19, 428.
2. Frank Knight, '"What is truth" in economics', in *On the History and Method of Economics*, Chicago: University of Chicago Press, 1956, pp. 151–78.
3. Rutledge Vining, *On Appraising the Performance of an Economic System*, Oxford: Cambridge University Press, 1984, p. xiv.
4. Dennis Mueller, 'The "Virginia School" and public choice', Lecture at George Mason University, April 1985, p. 7.

13. Reaganomics*

'Reaganomics' was the most serious attempt to change the course of US economic policy of any administration since the New Deal. 'Only by reducing the growth of government', said Ronald Reagan, 'can we increase the growth of the economy'. Reagan's 1981 Program for Economic Recovery had four major policy objectives: (1) to reduce the growth of government spending, (2) to reduce the marginal tax rates on income from both labour and capital, (3) to reduce regulation, and (4) to reduce inflation by controlling the growth of the money supply. These major policy changes, in turn, were expected to increase saving and investment, increase economic growth, balance the budget, restore healthy financial markets and reduce inflation and interest rates.

Any evaluation of the Reagan economic programme should thus address two general questions: how much of the proposed policy changes were approved and how much of the expected economic effects were realized? Reaganomics continues to be a controversial issue. For those who do not view Reaganomics through an ideological lens, however, one's evaluation of this major change in economic policy will depend on the balance of the realized economic effects.

President Reagan delivered on each of his four major policy objectives, although not to the extent that he and his supporters had hoped. The annual increase in real (inflation-adjusted) federal spending declined from 4.0 per cent during the Carter administration to 2.5 per cent during the Reagan administration, despite a record peacetime increase in real defence spending. This part of Reagan's fiscal record, however, reflected only a moderation, not a reversal, of prior fiscal trends. Reagan made no significant changes to the major transfer payment programmes (such as Social Security and Medicare), and he proposed no substantial reductions in other domestic programmes after his first budget.

Moreover, the growth of defence spending during his first term was higher than Reagan had proposed during the 1980 campaign, and since economic growth was somewhat slower than expected, Reagan did not

* Reprinted by permission from David Henderson (ed.), *The Fortune Encyclopedia of Economics*, New York: Warner Books Inc., 1993, pp. 290–93.

achieve a significant reduction in federal spending as a percentage of national output. Federal spending was 22.9 per cent of gross domestic product (GDP) in fiscal 1981, increased somewhat during the middle years of his administration, and declined to 22.1 per cent of GDP in fiscal 1989. This part of the Reagan record was probably the greatest disappointment to his supporters.

The changes to the federal tax code were much more substantial. The top marginal tax rate on individual income was reduced from 70 per cent to 28 per cent. The corporate income tax rate was reduced from 48 per cent to 34 per cent. The individual tax brackets were indexed for inflation. And most of the poor were exempted from the individual income tax. These measures were somewhat offset by several tax increases. An increase in Social Security tax rates legislated in 1977 but scheduled for the eighties was accelerated slightly. Some excise tax rates were increased, and some deductions were reduced or eliminated.

More important, there was a major reversal in the tax treatment of business income. A complex package of investment incentives was approved in 1981 only to be gradually reduced in each subsequent year 1985. And in 1986 the base for the taxation of business income was substantially broadened, reducing the tax bias among types of investment but increasing the average effective tax rate on new investment. It is not clear whether this measure was a net improvement in the tax code. Overall, the combination of lower tax rates and a broader tax base for both individuals and business reduced the federal revenue share of GDP from 20.2 per cent in fiscal 1981 to 19.2 per cent in fiscal 1989.

The reduction in economic regulation that started in the Carter administration continued, but at a slower rate. Reagan eased or eliminated price controls on oil and natural gas, cable TV, long-distance telephone service, interstate bus service and ocean shipping. Banks were allowed to invest in a somewhat broader set of assets, and the scope of the antitrust laws was reduced. The major exception to this pattern was a substantial increase in import barriers. The Reagan administration did not propose changes in the legislation affecting health, safety and the environment, but it reduced the number of new regulations under the existing laws. Deregulation was clearly the lowest priority among the major elements of the Reagan economic programme.

Monetary policy was somewhat erratic but, on net, quite successful. Reagan endorsed the reduction in money growth initiated by the Federal Reserve in late 1979, a policy that led to both the severe 1982 recession and a large reduction in inflation and interest rates. The administration reversed its position on one dimension of monetary policy: during the first term, the administration did not intervene in the markets for foreign exchange but, beginning in 1985, occasionally intervened with the objective of reducing and then stabilizing the foreign-exchange value of the dollar.

Most of the effects of these policies were favourable, even if somewhat disappointing compared to what the administration predicted. Economic growth increased from a 2.8 per cent annual rate in the Carter adminis-tration, but this is misleading because the growth of the working-age population was much slower in the Reagan years. Real GDP per working-age adult, which had increased at only a 0.8 annual rate during the Carter administration, increased at a 1.8 per cent rate during the Reagan admin-istration. The increase in productivity growth was even higher: output per hour in the business sector, which had been roughly constant in the Carter years, increased at a 1.4 per cent rate in the Reagan years. Productivity in the manufacturing sector increased at a 3.8 per cent annual rate, a record for peacetime.

Most other economic conditions also improved. The unemployment rate declined from 7.0 per cent in 1980 to 5.4 per cent in 1988. The infla-tion rate declined from 10.4 per cent in 1980 to 4.2 per cent in 1988. The combination of conditions proved that there is no long-run tradeoff between the unemployment rate and the inflation rate. Other conditions were more mixed. The rate of new business formation increased sharply, but the rate of bank failures was the highest since the thirties. Real inter-est rates increased sharply, but inflation-adjusted prices of common stocks more than doubled.

The US economy experienced substantial turbulence during the Reagan years despite favourable general economic conditions. This was the 'creative destruction' that is characteristic of a healthy economy. At the end of the Reagan administration, the US economy had experienced the longest peacetime expansion ever. The 'stagflation' and 'malaise' that plagued the US economy from 1973 through 1980 were transformed by the Reagan economic programme into a sustained period of higher growth and lower inflation.

In retrospect the major achievements of Reaganomics were the sharp reductions in marginal tax rates and in inflation. Moreover, these chances were achieved at a much lower cost than was previously expected. Despite the large decline in marginal tax rates, for example, the federal revenue share of GDP declined only slightly. Similarly, the large reduction in the inflation rate was achieved without any long-term effect on the unem-ployment rate. One reason for these achievements was the broad bipartisan support for these measures beginning in the later years of the Carter administration. Reagan's first tax proposal, for example, had pre-viously been endorsed by the Democratic Congress beginning in 1978, and the general structure of the Tax Reform Act of 1986 was first proposed by two junior Democratic members of Congress in 1982. Similarly, the 'monetarist experiment' to control inflation was initiated in October 1979, following Jimmy Carter's appointment of Paul Volcker as chairman of the Federal Reserve Board. The bipartisan support of these policies permitted Reagan to implement more radical changes than in other areas of economic policy.

Reagan failed to achieve some of the initial goals of his initial programme. The federal budget was substantially reallocated – from discretionary domestic spending to defence, entitlements and interest payments – but the federal budget share of national output declined only slightly. Both the administration and Congress were responsible for this outcome. Reagan supported the large increase in defence spending and was unwilling to reform the basic entitlement programmes, and Congress was unwilling to make further cuts in the discretionary domestic programmes. Similarly, neither the administration nor Congress was willing to sustain the momentum for deregulation or to reform the regulation of health, safety and the environment.

Reagan left three major adverse legacies at the end of his second term. First, the privately held federal debt increased from 22.3 per cent of GDP to 38.1 per cent and, despite the record peacetime expansion, the federal deficit in Reagan's last budget was still 2.9 per cent of GDP. Second, the failure to address the savings and loan problem early led to an additional debt of about $125 billion. Third, the administration added more trade barriers than any administration since Herbert Hoover. The share of US imports subject to some form of trade restraint increased from 12 per cent in 1980 to 23 per cent in 1988.

There was more than enough blame to go around for each of these problems. Reagan resisted tax increases, and Congress resisted cuts in domestic spending. The administration was slow to acknowledge the savings and loan problem, and Congress urged forbearance on closing the failing banks. Reagan's rhetoric strongly supported free trade, but pressure from threatened industries and Congress led to a substantial increase in new trade restraints. The future of Reaganomics will depend largely on how each of these three adverse legacies is resolved. Restraints on spending and regulation would sustain Reaganomics. But increased taxes and a reregulation of domestic and foreign trade would limit Reaganomics to an interesting but temporary experiment in economic policy.

The Reagan economic programme led to a substantial improvement in economic conditions, but there was no 'Reagan revolution'. No major federal programme (other than revenue sharing) and no agencies were abolished. The political process continues to generate demands for new or expanded programmes, but American voters continue to resist higher taxes to pay for these programmes. A broader popular consensus on the appropriate roles of the federal government, one or more constitutional amendments, and a new generation of political leaders may be necessary to resolve this inherent conflict in contemporary American politics.

REFERENCES

Lindsey, Lawrence B. (1990), *The Growth Experiment: How the New Tax Policy Is Transforming the U.S. Economy*, New York: Basic Books.

Niskanen, William A. (1988), *Reaganomics: An Insider's Account of the Policies and the People*, New York: Oxford University Press.

14. Economic Regulation*

One of the four 'key elements' of Ronald Reagan's programme of economic recovery was 'a far-reaching programme of regulatory relief'. Despite that initial commitment, the Reagan administration made few proposals for new deregulatory legislation, and it did not manage the deregulation that had been previously approved especially well. My remarks here summarize the reasons for this outcome and focus on the traditional subjects of economic regulation – leaving others to address the interesting issues involving the regulation of financial institutions; health, safety and the environment; antitrust; and trade.[1]

POLICIES AND PEOPLE

The initial and continuing focus of the Reagan regulatory programme was relief, not reform. In his December 1980 'economic Dunkirk' memo, David Stockman summarized the rationale for this approach:

> A dramatic, substantial *recission* of the regulatory burden is needed for the short term cash flow it will provide to business firms and [for] the long term signal that it will provide to corporate investment planners. A major 'regulatory ventilation' will do as much to boost business confidence as tax or fiscal measures.[2]

Most of this regulatory relief was to be accomplished by administrative rulings rather than by new legislation.

The new administration moved quickly to implement this approach during its first month in office. A Task Force on Regulatory Relief, chaired by Vice-President George Bush, was established to provide general policy guidance. A large number of pending regulations were suspended for sixty days to permit review by the new administration, and the remaining price controls on oil and Jimmy Carter's voluntary price and wage controls were terminated. The regulatory review was centralized under the Office of Information and Regulatory Affairs (OIRA), which

---

* Reprinted by permission from Martin Feldstein (ed.), *American Economic Policy in the 1980s*, Chicago, University of Chicago Press, 1994, pp. 441–6.

was part of the Office of Management and Budget (OMB). The most important of these initial measures was a new executive order that instructed the executive agencies, to the extent permitted by law, to use the maximum net benefit criterion to choose among regulatory options. This executive order also established a special procedure for major regulations and authorized the OIRA to review all proposed rules prior to their publication in the *Federal Register*.

Most of the new appointees to regulatory positions had a strong commitment to deregulation. Two economists who had designed the initial regulatory agenda were soon appointed to key positions – Murray Weidenbaum as chairman of the Council of Economic Advisers (CEA) and James Miller as head of the OIRA. The most important other initial appointments included William Baxter as assistant attorney general for antitrust and Mark Fowler as chairman of the Federal Communications Commission (FCC). Many of the subsequent appointments also reaffirmed this commitment. I and Tom Moore each served four years as the microeconomic member of the CEA. Miller's successors as head of the OIRA were Chris DeMuth, Douglas Ginsburg and Wendy Gramm. Miller later served as chairman of the Federal Trade Commission and Ginsburg as assistant attorney general for antitrust. The later appointment of Heather Gradison as chairman of the Interstate Commerce Commission proved important to forestall pressures to regulate railroads and trucking. For the most part, the disappointing re-regulatory record of the Reagan administration cannot be blamed on a lack of skills or commitment on the part of those with the most direct responsibility.

THE RECORD OF ECONOMIC REGULATION

A brief review of major developments in economic regulation illustrates the patterns of the Reagan record.

Agriculture

Two early reviews of agricultural marketing orders were aborted without substantial change. In 1979, a consumer group had innocently asked the Department of Agriculture to review the federal milk marketing orders. In April 1981, however, the department denied this request on the basis of estimates that a more efficient distribution of milk production would increase the federal budget costs of supporting milk prices. A major review of the broader set of marketing orders led to a preliminary 1982 decision to eliminate the restrictions on entry and to increase substantially the limits on the rules of fresh products. A storm of protest from

California citrus growers, however, led the administration to modify the final 1983 guidelines, which phased out the entry restrictions on two small crops and only slightly increased the sales limits on the major crops. Congress locked up this decision by one of the first of many new 'muzzling laws' that prohibited any further expenditure of funds to study this issue.

Communications

The major changes in the regulation of communications were the result of forceful early initiatives by two individuals, Mark Fowler and Bill Baxter. In 1981, the FCC deregulated most radio broadcasting restrictions, implemented a simplified system for renewing radio licences, and induced Congress to extend the licence period for both radio and television stations and to authorize a lottery system for the award of new licences. The later record, however, was mixed. A 1983 initiative to relax the 'financial interest and syndication rules', which restrict the right of television networks to develop original programming and to syndicate reruns, was stopped by 'the California mafia' in the White House responding to pressures from Hollywood. In 1984, Congress approved the full deregulation of cable rates but did not approve any new entry into the monopoly cable markets. After the sharp subsequent increase in cable rates, Congress may soon compound this error by reregulating cable rates, again without permitting new entry. And the major missed opportunity was the failure to change the system for allocating the electronic frequency spectrum, a system that corresponds roughly to the way the Soviets run their economy. As a consequence, some new technologies have been delayed even though large parts of the spectrum are underutilized.

The major change in communications regulation was the result of Baxter's January 1982 resolution of the long-standing antitrust case against AT&T. Under the threat of a court decision imposing a divestiture plan, Baxter and AT&T worked out a plan, effective in 1984, that allowed AT&T (formerly the American Telephone and Telegraph Company) to maintain its long-distance services, its unregulated communications services and its manufacturing company but required it to divest its 22 local operating companies. As expected, this decision led to a substantial reduction in long-distance rates and a substantial increase in the (state-regulated) local rates. This decision was not broadly popular, and Congress considered more than a dozen bills to stop or limit the increase in subscriber charges. After a considerable amount of populist posturing, Congress forced the FCC to delay the access charge ruling but did not reverse this basic change in the structure of the telecommunications service industry.

Energy

After the important early decision to terminate the price controls on oil, the administration's later record on energy regulation was disappointing. A simple bill to deregulate the wellhead prices of natural gas was approved by the cabinet council in 1982 but was deferred by the White House as part of a general strategy of avoiding any more controversial issues prior to the election. A more complicated 1983 proposal by the Department of Energy received no support in Congress. The reaction by both the White House and Congress was based on a broadly shared but incorrect expectation that decontrol of natural gas would have increased retail gas prices.[3] In the end, the Federal Energy Regulatory Commission effectively decontrolled gas prices by setting price caps that, until this summer, were above market prices. And, in 1988, Congress quietly terminated the Fuel Use Act, which had restricted the use of oil and natural gas in new power plants. The administration also equivocated on other energy issues. For example, the required corporate average fuel economy on new cars was administratively reduced by one mile per gallon, but the administration would not propose the termination of this absurd law; Congress is now considering a large proportionate increase in the required fuel economy – a measure that, not incidentally, would be biased against Japanese cars.

Labour

The Department of Labor made several administrative changes in the regulations affecting work under federal construction contracts and on work at home but would not propose a change in the laws athorizing these regulations. The only major legislative proposal was to authorize a lower minimum wage for teenage summer employment, a proposal that was strongly rejected by Congress.

Transportation

The Reagan administration and Congress made only small changes to extend or complement the major transportation deregulation measures instituted during the Carter administration. In 1982, the administration concluded an agreement with the major European nations to permit greater flexibility in the fares on transatlantic flights. Also in 1982, Congress approved the full deregulation of intercity bus travel – a measure that provoked little controversy because there never was a basis for regulating that industry and the demand for bus services had slowly declined in response to rising income and airline deregulation. And, in 1984, Congress approved the Shipping Act to enable ocean shipping companies to offer lower rates and better services than permitted by the shipping conferences. The administration's proposal to terminate the Interstate Commerce Commission on its centennial in 1987, however, fell on deaf ears, and the ICC still maintains considerable authority that could be used to regulate trucking and the railroads.

The major missed opportunity was the failure to reform, expand or privatize the airports and airways systems in response to the large increase in commercial flights induced by airline deregulation. For example, the number of air traffic controllers is now about the same as before the 1981 strike, and the system for allocating landing slots at congested airports has yet to be rationalized as no new major airport has been built for fifteen years. In late 1985, after several years of pressure from the OIRA and the CEA, the Department of Transportation approved the resale of landing slots at the four most crowded airports, but this action was later challenged by Congress. In 1988, the department even overruled an increase in landing fees on light aircraft using Logan Airport. And the administration showed no interest in several proposals to subcontract or privatize parts of the airports and airways systems. The failure to follow airline deregulation with complementary changes in the airports and airways system is the primary reason for the increased airport congestion and airline delays and the background rumbles, primarily from business travellers, for some reregulation.

PATTERNS AND LESSONS

The major pattern of the Reagan record on economic regulation was the attempt to rely primarily on administrative deregulation and the reluctance to propose changes in legislation that would extend or lock in prior deregulation. The primary reason for this pattern is that regulatory relief was clearly the lowest priority of the four key elements of the Reagan economic programme. This should not be surprising. The other key elements were more ambitious and promised clearer benefits. Deregulation usually leads to diffused benefits and concentrated costs. Some types of deregulation were checked by campaign commitments that Reagan had made to the construction, trucking and maritime unions and by business interests, especially in California, to which the administration was responsive.

The major lesson from this record is that the potential for administrative deregulation is quite limited. The able people who led the OIRA probably pushed the White House regulatory review process as much as possible, given the limited change in regulatory legislation. Their aggressive actions to review, modify or delay regulatory proposals initiated by the executive agencies, however, were ultimately checked by both Congress and the courts. On several occasions, Congress threatened to constrain the authority of the OIRA or to eliminate its funding, a controversy that has not yet been resolved. (For example, the position of the head of the OIRA has not been filled for over a year, and Congress is again bargaining with the administration over measures that would reduce the authority of the OIRA.) A more explicit construct was the application of a 'hard look' doctrine by the federal court of appeals for the District of Columbia to proposals for both regulation and deregulation. The primary effect of this doctrine is to require a more explicit rationale, based on the criteria in the regulatory legislation, for regulatory changes of any kind. This role of the courts, a position generally endorsed by the Reagan administration, increases the importance of changing the regulatory legislation if the momentum for deregulation is to be revived.

Another lesson is that budget policy sometimes got in the way of good regulatory policy. This was first apparent when David Stockman agreed to the egregious sugar programme in exchange for a few votes on the fiscal year 1982 budget. US budget accounting conventions are also a problem. Since user fees are treated as an offsetting receipt, for example, both the deposit insurance funds and the airports and airways fund showed negative net outlays for most of the Reagan years, despite a rapid increase in liabilities and investment backlogs. The objective of any budget director to limit measured budget outlays was part of the reason why the administration was slow to address both the deposit insurance disaster and the increased airline delays, The major current threat of mandated benefits of several kinds, in turn, is primarily a consequence of the perception that it is difficult to expand the welfare state through the federal fisc. We still need a system that forces a review of the costs of proposed and recurring federal actions of all kinds.

For all these problems, the Reagan regulatory record was probably better than average. The total costs of regulation, as measured by several indirect indices, increased at a slower rate than at any time since the 1950s. For those of us who were directly involved, however, this record was very disappointing. Some mistakes and, more important, the missed opportunities failed to sustain the momentum for deregulation initiated in the 1970s and set the stage for what portends to be a regulatory explosion in the 1990s.

NOTES

1. For obvious reasons, most of this summary is taken from Niskanen (1988, pp. 115–54).
2. The 'economic Dunkirk' memo is reproduced in Greider (1982, pp. 137–59).
3. For my own analysis of the effects of controls on the wellhead prices of natural gas, see Niskanen (1986).

REFERENCES

Greider, William (1982), *The Education of David Stockman and Other Americans*, New York: Dutton.

Niskanen, William A. (1986), 'Natural gas price controls: an alternative view', *Regulation*, 10, November/December, 46–50.

Niskanen, William, A. (1988), *Reaganomics: An Insider's Account of the Policies and the People*, New York: Oxford University Press.

15. US trade policy

US trade policy turned sharply protectionist during the Reagan years. Moreover, *all* of the new trade restraints imposed were initiated or approved by the administration, despite a general endorsement of free trade in its public rhetoric. The cost of trade protection to American consumers was about $65 billion in 1986, an increase of nearly 100 per cent since 1980. About one-quarter of the products imported by the United States are now subject to trade restraints, an increase from about one-eighth in 1980. Since no major trade legislation was enacted until the Omnibus Trade Act of 1988, this deterioration in US trade policy was implemented largely without any major changes in trade law. The Reagan administration must bear the primary responsibility for this record. This chapter addresses the following questions: what happened to US trade policy and why, and where do we go from here?

ADMINISTRATION MEASURES

Only a brief summary of the major trade cases during the past eight years is needed to convey the scope and nature of the administration's import policies.

Automobiles

Following a campaign pledge that 'one way or another ... the deluge of [Japanese] cars must be slowed while our industry gets back on its feet', and the introduction of a Senate bill that would sharply limit the import of Japanese cars, the Reagan administration pressured the government of Japan to impose a 'voluntary export restraint' (VER) on car exports to the United States. The agreement limited exports to 1.68 million cars through March 1982. To counter congressional pressure for a 'domestic content' bill, the Japanese maintained this limit for two more years, then

* Reprinted by permission from *Regulation*, No. 3, 1988, 34–42, American Enterprise Institute.

increased it to 1.85 million cars in the fourth year. Although the Reagan administration did not ask the Japanese to renew the export agreement in 1985, the government of Japan, for its own reasons, has maintained an annual limit of 2.3 million cars since that time.

The gains accruing to the two nations under this agreement have been predictable, if lopsided. For Japan, the agreement increased prices and profits of Japanese auto firms, increased their relative sales of higher-value cars, increased their production in the United States and increased the control of the Ministry of International Trade and Industry (MITI) over their auto industry (see Denzau 1988). The US auto industry got higher prices, profits and employment and American consumers bore the cost – about $5.8 billion in 1984, or about $105 000 per job saved in the domestic industry. (These estimates of consumer losses, and those for the industries below except steel, were made by Gary Hufbauer, Diane Berliner and Kimberly Elliot, 1986.)

The VER with Japan was entirely 'extralegal' in that it was not authorized under US law or under the General Agreement on Tariffs and Trade (GATT). It nevertheless set an unfortunate precedent for the administration's response to most other major trade cases.

Textiles and Apparel

As a candidate, Ronald Reagan also pledged to 'relate' the growth of imports of textiles and apparel to the growth of domestic sales. In response to this pledge the administration decided in 1981 to renew the MultiFiber Agreement (MFA) in a form that would meet this goal. (The MFA, an outgrowth of the 'short-term' cotton agreement of 1961, is a complex system of quotas set by the industrial countries on textile and apparel imports from developing countries.) The continued growth of imports led the administration to broaden the products covered by these quotas and to change the country-of-origin rules.

For the exporting countries the effects of these measures were similar to those of the auto quotas: increased prices, profits and government control of their textile and apparel industries. The United States got increased prices and profits and a slower decline in employment in the domestic firms. The cost to American consumers was about $27 billion, or about $42 000 per job saved in the domestic industry.

For three decades the United States has been the prime mover in establishing a worldwide cartel for textiles and apparel sales, the only commodity group (other than agriculture) that is exempt from the normal GATT rules. The primary effect of the Reagan measures was to increase the scope and cost of this cartel.

Steel

In response to a 1982 petition by the steel industry for antidumping penalties and countervailing duties against imports of carbon steel from European firms, the administration arranged for VERs for steel. Under the agreements, steel imports from Europe were limited to 5.5 per cent of the US market, and a similar limit was placed on pipe and tube imports. Negotiations were initiated to achieve similar limits from other countries. The quotas established under the agreement were independent of the amount by which a country's or a firm's products were determined to have been dumped or subsidized; an 'unfair trade' case was thus transformed into a general limit on European steel exports to the United States, irrespective of the extent to which individual firms had been charged with unfair trade practices.

In response to a 1983 'escape clause' petition from the speciality-steel industry, the administration imposed a set of tariffs and quotas on imports of selective speciality-steel products. Total steel imports, however, continued to increase, primarily from countries not included in these agreements. When another such petition was filed by the steel industry in 1984 and a bill was introduced to limit all steel imports, the administration decided to seek VERs from all major steel-exporting countries. It sought to limit total imports of finished steel to 18.5 per cent of the US market as well as to limit imports of semifinished steel. Strong US demand and a delay in negotiating and implementing these VERs, however, reduced their short-term effects; between 1984 and 1986, total steel imports declined from a peak of 26.4 per cent of the US market to 23 per cent.

Together these measures effectively created a worldwide cartel of steel exporters to the United States, increasing the prices and profits of firms receiving quotas and increasing government control of these firms. The US steel industry experienced higher prices and profits and a slower decline in employment. The annual cost to American consumers was about $6.5 billion, or about $75 000 per job saved in the domestic industry! Since steel is a major input to other products, these measures also reduced the international competitiveness of other American industries.

Semiconductors

In 1986 the semiconductor industry petitioned to impose antidumping duties on imports of general-purpose memory chips from Japan. The price of Japanese chips was *higher* in the United States than in Japan, but was lower than the cost of Japanese production as estimated by the US

Department of Commerce. As in the 1982 steel case, the administration chose to negotiate a broad agreement with the exporting country, rather than to impose the duties authorized by law. Under pressure from the US government, the Japanese government agreed to set a floor price on memory chips sold in the United States equal to the 'fair market value' (as determined by the Commerce Department), to set a similar floor price on sales in third countries, and to promote an increase in the sales of US chips in Japan. In the absence of this agreement the United States would have no authority to impose the latter two conditions. In 1987 the administration determined that Japan had not met the second and third provisions of this agreement (although it would not reveal the data on which it based this determination). It then imposed 100 per cent tariffs on $300 million worth of other Japanese imports. In fact, the government of Japan had already ordered a substantial reduction of chip production to reduce the large inventory being sold in third countries; it also had implemented several measures to promote the sale of foreign chips in Japan. Although the administration later determined that Japan had ceased 'dumping' in third countries, it maintained the punitive tariffs on a reduced set of products to induce Japan to increase the US share of its chip market.

In effect, the semiconductor agreement created a two-country memory-chip cartel. Combined with steady demand growth, the agreement led to a sharp increase in the price of memory chips in both Japan and the United States, from $2.50 in early 1986 to $5.50 in March 1988. Since chips are a major input in the production of computers, the agreement will reduce the international competitiveness of the much larger computer industries in both countries.

Other Cases

There was no consistent pattern in the administration's handling of other trade cases. On the one hand, the administration established (in 1981) a system of quotas on sugar imports to maintain the domestic sugar price; these quotas were progressively tightened and later extended to the import of food products containing even minimum amounts of sugar. As of 1984, the domestic price of sugar was about four times the world price – the highest effective tariff on any legal product – at a cost to American consumers of about $1 billion. The administration also set a high temporary tariff on large motorcycles (in 1983) to protect about 2000 jobs in one company; it requested (in 1986) VERs on imports of machine tools from four countries, after rejecting two prior petitions for restraints under different sections of US law; and, during the sensitive early negotiations on the US–Canada free-trade agreement in 1986, the administration imposed substantial tariffs on imports of cedar shingles and softwood lumber from Canada.

On the other hand, the administration rejected or removed trade restraints on three products. The administration rejected petitions (in 1981 and 1985) to continue or reimpose quotas on footwear. It rejected a petition (in 1984) to limit copper imports because of the adverse effects on the much larger copper products industry. And it convinced Congress (in 1986) to delete the 'manufacturing clause' in copyright law that required most books and magazines to be printed and bound in the United States in order to receive US copyright protection (a provision that dated from 1891). The footwear and printing industries are the only industries for which trade restraints are now substantially lower than in 1980.

EXPORT MEASURES

The administration's export policies are best described as inconsistent. The administration removed the embargo on grain sales to the Soviet Union but imposed an embargo on the sale of US equipment and US-licenced equipment made in Europe for the natural gas pipeline from the Soviet Union to Europe. After a protest from European governments, this embargo was removed. For foreign policy reasons the administration imposed selective embargoes on trade with Poland, Libya, Nicaragua, Syria and, in response to strong congressional pressure, South Africa. Several times the administration proposed reducing funding for the Export–Import Bank while simultaneously agreeing to increase subsidies on agricultural exports. The administration did not ask Congress to remove the bans on exporting logs or Alaskan oil, or the requirement that 50 per cent of all government-financed agricultural exports be carried on American ships. American firms still lack clear guidelines on the export of defence-related technology that are consistent with the rules affecting sales by other Western nations. For many years the federal government has promoted the export of some products and restricted the export of others, with little apparent rationale. For the most part, this is still the case.

At the same time, however, the administration stepped up pressure on other governments to open their markets to US goods. The general tactic was to threaten limits on their exports to the United States in order to induce them to reduce their limits on US sales in their markets. The Reagan administration initiated ten such cases during its first term and

22 such cases after September 1985, when trade policy became markedly more aggressive. These measures had some success. Japan reduced or eliminated tariffs on aluminium products, cigarettes and leather products, and substituted high tariffs for very restrictive quotas on beef and citrus. Korea reduced its barriers on US movies and television programming. Taiwan opened its market to beer, wine and cigarettes. Europe reduced restraints on imports of corn and citrus. And so on.

But this tactic, by its nature, risked imposing substantial costs on the United States, both in terms of higher US trade barriers and an erosion of our bargaining leverage on more important issues. For example, in response to a loss of corn sales to Spain and Portugal upon their joining the common market, the administration threatened to impose a 200 per cent tariff on imports of selected alcoholic beverages and agricultural products from Europe. The escalation of this dispute was only narrowly averted. Threats of steep US duties on European spaghetti and fancy pasta sold in gourmet groceries became even more tangled, with the European Community retaliating against US walnuts and lemons, the US delaying concessions on semifinished steel and Europe imposing duties on US fertilizer, paper products and beef tallow. One might hope that America's limited leverage with major allies would be focused on more important issues, such as our shared defence burden. Threatening to impose costs on both US consumers and foreign producers in order to increase the benefits to US producers, generally over trivial issues, may turn out to be a game of Russian roulette.

CONGRESSIONAL MEASURES

Congress also bears substantial responsibility for the deterioration in US trade policy during the Reagan years. Although little trade legislation was approved until 1988, a large number of trade bills were introduced, and a few were passed by one or both houses. Heading off these bills became the administration's primary internal rationale for its own protectionist actions.

During Reagan's first term, Congress was stepping up pressure for protectionist trade legislation, but its signals were still mixed. Congress overrode a veto to extend the manufacturing clause of the copyright law, but subsequently allowed this provision to expire. Twice the House approved a bill that would have required domestic production of up to 90 per cent of the value of all cars sold in the United States, but on both occasions the bill died in the Senate. A more general Trade and Tariff Act was approved in 1984, after an extraordinary effort by William Brock (the

US Trade Representative in the first term) to delete most of the small protectionist provisions. This act strengthened the authority to retaliate against unfair trade practices, broadened the definition of injury in escape clause cases, and included a small number of minor protectionist provisions; on the other hand, it reduced tariffs on about 100 products, extended the Generalized System of Preferences on imports from the developing nations, and provided authority for bilateral negotiations for free-trade agreements with specific nations.

Trade policy turned more aggressive in the second term. In 1985 the House passed a bill to tighten the quotas on textile and apparel imports and the Senate passed a similar bill, adding protection for the copper and footwear industries that had been denied relief by the president; this bill, however, was subsequently vetoed. In 1986 both houses began to develop comprehensive trade bills, focusing on trade authority and rules rather than on specific products. The general thrust of these bills was to broaden the conditions that would be defined as unfair trade practices, restrict the presidential authority to deny trade relief, and (for a few goods and services) to require a 'reciprocal treatment' of US sales in foreign markets and foreign sales in the US market. Two years of deliberations on this legislation culminated in the Omnibus Trade Act of 1988, the 1000-page trade bill passed by large margins in both houses. The president's response to this legislation was remarkable. He first vetoed the bill, objecting primarily to a provision requiring early notice of plant closings and substantial layoffs. When Congress responded by passing a separate plant closing bill, the president endorsed the trade bill and chose not to veto the plant closing bill.

Only a few provisions of the Omnibus Trade Act are likely to be trade-expanding: the president is granted special authority to negotiate the new GATT round; the rules affecting US business practices in other countries are made more realistic; tariffs are reduced or eliminated on many products for which there is no US source; and the 'windful profits' tax on US oil is repealed. These provisions came at a very high price, however.

The primary problem with the act is that it represents a unilateral US declaration of the rules of trade. It reverses 40 years of US leadership towards a set of trade rules to which all parties agreed. In effect, the United States has told the rest of the world, 'Play by our rules or we will not buy your products'; in the name of reducing unfair trade by other countries, the United States changed the rules of trade by an unfair process. One should not be surprised by strong foreign opposition to this act or by the prospect of other countries applying unilateral rules to the United States.

INTERNATIONAL AGREEMENTS

One creative instrument of trade policy initiated during the Reagan years was the bilateral free-trade agreement with selected countries. A free-trade agreement with Israel was approved in 1985, for example, and a broad agreement with Canada, our largest trading partner, has recently been approved. A 'framework agreement' with Mexico, our third largest trading partner, will provide guidance for future trade negotiations. Such agreements have been considered with other countries.

Bilateral free-trade agreements promise to increase the benefits of trade to each participating country. In addition they expand the dollar-bloc free-trade area, which can provide leverage – perhaps our only substantial leverage – to achieve a desirable outcome from the new round of GATT negotiations. The United States entered these negotiations in 1986 with an ambitious agenda to broaden GATT rules to agriculture, services and investment. The prospects for this round, however, are not encouraging. The Europeans have strongly resisted the elimination of trade-related agricultural subsidies and are more concerned about completing the integration of the European Economic Community. And most countries have been provoked by the more aggressive US trade policy of recent years. In the absence of creative leadership, the world trading system may well devolve into regional trading blocs with higher barriers to trade among blocs – a sad outcome for an administration that was once committed to 'improvements and extensions of international trade rules'.

THE POLITICAL ECONOMY OF TRADE POLICY

What explains the substantial change in US trade policy during the Reagan years?

First, when the Reagan administration came to office, it had no strong, consistent convictions on trade policy. Indeed, the president and other key officials never resolved the tension between their public pro-market rhetoric and their private pro-business sympathies. The initial statement of the Reagan economic programme barely acknowledged the international dimensions of economic policy. One paragraph described how the proposed policies were expected to improve international conditions, but there was no mention of the principles that would guide our economic relations with other nations. Increased spending for defence and business investment was a major objective of the initial programme, but there was no recognition that these measures would have a substantial effect on the real exchange rate and the trade balance.

Fortunately the administration developed a more comprehensive statement of US trade policy in mid-1981. The primary theme of this statement was 'free trade, consistent with mutually accepted trading relations'. It committed the administration to five specific trade policy objectives which, given the economic conditions anticipated in 1981, would have been a satisfactory and sufficient framework for trade policy. Unfortunately these conditions did not prevail.

Second, adverse economic conditions in the early 1980s – the long recession and the rapid increase in the exchange rate and trade deficit – led to strong pressure from business, unions and Congress for selective trade restraints. This pressure, in combination with some 1980 campaign commitments and controversy within the administration, led to numerous breaches in the announced trade policy.

Third, even after the economy rebounded, the increasing disparity between the announced trade policy and the developing trade record was resolved by changing the official trade policy, rather than by correcting the record. In 1985 a draft speech prepared for the president that would have renewed his commitment to free trade was revised, under the auspices of White House Chief of Staff Donald T. Regan, to conclude that 'if trade is not fair for all, then trade is "free" in name only'. The major element of Reagan's new Trade Policy Action Plan was the initiation of a series of actions against 'unfair' trade practices by other governments, including practices not covered by existing GATT rules. This unilateral definition of fair trade was a major change from the announced trade policy of the first term and set the stage for the broader US definition of fair trade in the trade bills being developed by Congress. This change in policy was roughly coincident with the appointment of Clayton Yeutter as the new US Trade Representative and with Secretary of the Treasury James A. Baker III's Plaza Agreement for coordinated action to devalue the dollar, which signalled a more interventionist policy on a range of international economic issues.

Finally, trade policy became a major focus of the special interest demands for government benefits. While the total demand for such benefits may be roughly constant, several major changes in economic policy during the Reagan years – specifically the substantial reduction in real spending on discretionary programmes, continued economic deregulation, and broadening of the tax base in the Tax Reform Act of 1986 – reduced the special benefits distributed by other means. The large budget deficit continues to constrain the potential to distribute special benefits through the budget and tax code. This is likely to create continuing demands for special benefits through trade policy (as well as through new types of economic regulation such as mandated benefits).

While the administration rationalized its major protectionist actions and, ultimately, the shift in its announced trade policy as necessary to head off even more aggressive measures by Congress, the outcome of this strategic retreat was not satisfactory. For the first time since World War II the United States added more trade restraints than it removed. Although US pressure led to some reduction in trade-distorting practices, it also consumed political capital that continues to be important in GATT and other international forums. And the Omnibus Trade Act of 1988 ended a half-century of US leadership towards a more open world trading system based on mutually accepted rules of trade.

THE PROSPECTS FOR US TRADE POLICY

Where do we go from here? For the next several years US trade policy is likely to be increasingly aggressive – despite a sustained economic recovery, a declining trade deficit, and a sharply lower foreign-exchange value of the dollar. Both presidential nominees, George Bush and Michael Dukakis, endorsed the Omnibus Trade Act while generally supporting free trade. Congress is in an ugly mood, both about foreign trade practices and foreign investment in the United States. The Omnibus Trade Act, best described as 'procedural protectionism', invites an increasing number of petitions for trade restraint and requires more administration investigations of foreign trade practices. Since the president and the US trade representative still retain a measure of discretion in implementing trade measures, US trade policy will continue to be dependent on how the new administration uses this discretion. My own judgement is that the prospects for the new GATT round are not encouraging, unless the United States develops an effective strategy to break the logjam on agricultural issues.

We now need to develop a longer-term strategy to preserve and extend free trade. Supporters of free trade have been too defensive for too long – opposing or trying to limit new trade restraints, but rarely proposing reductions in trade restraints. This is a no-win strategy. When we win, it is a draw; when we lose, the scope and level of trade restraints are increased. What is needed is an *offensive* strategy to *reduce* trade restraints, both in the United States and abroad, with the hope of shaping the perceptions that will affect US trade policy well into the next century.

What might be the elements of such a strategy? The following general approaches should be considered.

First, and most important, we need to regain the moral and economic high ground for free trade. The fundamental moral case for free trade, both within nations and between nations, is based on the principle of consent. The most important role of government is to secure the rights of individuals to make consensual arrangements of any kind that do not affect the rights of others, including arrangements across national borders. The economic case for free trade is that it increases the combined income of the affected nations and, except in rare conditions, also increases the income of each nation. This perspective on international trade is now more threatened than at any time in the postwar years.

Many supporters of free trade, unfortunately, became too involved in the narrow politics of current issues to recognize the power of ideas in shaping legislation. During the past decade, however, three of the more important changes in US economic policy were the result of a convergence of élite opinion across parties and without any significant popular pressure. These changes were the substantial reduction of domestic economic regulation, the Gramm–Rudman–Hollings deficit reduction process, and the Tax Reform Act of 1986. We need to reassert the moral and economic case for free trade so that, at some point in the future, free trade will be similarly recognized as an idea whose time has come.

Second, we need to support measures, both in the United States and abroad, that reduce the US trade deficit. A trade deficit is of no particular concern when domestic investment is unusually high. The current US trade deficit, however, is the result of conditions that are neither sustainable nor desirable: the unusually low level of US saving net of government borrowing. In effect, the US trade deficit is providing the net inflow of goods and services to permit an unsustainable level of private consumption and government spending. There is no prospect for changing the direction of US trade policy until these conditions are changed.

The primary responsibility for reducing the US trade deficit, of course, must rest with the United States. The several types of measures that should be considered include reducing the remaining biases in our tax system against private saving, reducing the growth of government spending for both services and transfer payments, and, only if politically necessary, increasing taxes to reduce the growth of private consumption.

It is important to recognize that measures by other governments to increase their private consumption, defence spending or domestic investment would also reduce the US trade deficit. As a rule, and in contrast with many US government officials, I am most reluctant to pressure other governments to change their domestic policies. In the case of defence spending, however, the current US share of our common defence is disproportionate. The United States now spends about 6.5 per cent of GNP for defence – about twice the share by our NATO allies and about five times the share by Japan. Our disproportionate share of the burden of providing the common defence is, in effect, one of our largest exports – but one for which we are not compensated. For various reasons the United States is likely to reduce its overseas military forces during the next decade, forcing the governments of Europe and Japan to reassess their own contribution to the regional defence against the continuing Soviet threat. An increase in defence spending by Europe and Japan that matches the reduction of US defence spending would reduce the US trade deficit by more than the amount of the shift in the defence burden. This is a complex issue but one that cannot be avoided by pretending it does not exist.

Third, we need to force the political pressures for US trade restraints through the formal processes authorized by US trade law and the GATT. Many of the US trade restraints implemented since 1980 have been extralegal 'voluntary' export restraints under which other governments have agreed to avoid a formal action under US trade law. My own judgement is that the acquiescence of other governments, particularly Japan, to these restraints has been most shortsighted because it induced the United States to impose other such measures. The scope of US trade restraints, I believe, would have been narrower if other governments had resisted US pressure for such extralegal restraints.

Fourth, we need to broaden the use of bilateral free-trade agreements. Bilateral agreements serve two objectives: they broaden the dollar bloc of free-trade agreements in the absence of a more general agreement under GATT; and they put substantial pressure on the Europeans (who have expressed considerable concern about being left out of such agreements) to broaden and strengthen GATT in the current negotiations.

My views on this issue were reinforced by hearing the French agriculture minister's proposal (in the Chirac government) for cartelizing the world's major cereal exporters. The current European position on agricultural trade threatens to undermine any prospect for success of the GATT round unless the United States presents a credible threat of walking out of these negotiations. The GATT may increasingly become an instrument of *managed* trade, unless the United States presents a credible alternative framework for world trade – even if that alternative is less desirable than some conceivable multilateral arrangement. The US bilateral initiatives should not be regarded as a threat to GATT but as part of a strategy to achieve a successful negotiation of a broader multilateral arrangement.

Finally, at some stage, we need to make the case for *reducing* the scope of trade law. My suggestions are the following:

- Exclude dumping, on either a price or cost basis as a basis for duties. The dumping code, which is especially vulnerable to abuse under flexible exchange rates, penalizes foreign firms for practices that are regularly used by domestic firms. And accountants at the Commerce Department have amply demonstrated their creativity in identifying dumping under a wide range of conditions.
- Restrict countervailing duties to the amount of the *net* subsidy by foreign governments (subsidy minus the incremental cost of meeting specific domestic regulations). For example, a small German subsidy to steel mills offsets the requirement to use German coal. This is effectively a subsidy to German coal, not to German steel, and should not be a basis for a countervailing duty against German steel. Likewise, many governments subsidize firms that locate in specific regions. Such regional development subsidies typically offset the higher costs of operating in these regions, do not reduce the net cost of production, and should not be a basis for a countervailing duty. A net subsidy criterion would apply a countervailing duty only when the subsidy reduces the price at which the good or service could be sold on the world market.
- Restrict or eliminate the Section 301 authority for trade restraints. This section of US trade law has been used to authorize retaliation on the basis of foreign practices that are wholly consistent with GATT and it has been subject to considerable abuse.

Such changes would channel pressures for trade restraints primarily through two existing sections of US trade law, sections 201 and 232. Section 201 authorizes trade restraints when an increase in imports has been the major cause of injury to a domestic industry. This provision has the advantage of permitting the president to consider the interests of consumers and other industries in determining whether to approve or modify a recommended trade restraint, and requires compensation of the exporting country. Section 232 authorizes trade restraints when an increase in imports would threaten the industrial base necessary for national security. Even Adam Smith acknowledged that 'defence is more important than opulence'.

The process and criteria for approving trade restraints under these two sections of US trade law are wholly consistent with GATT, and these sections have not been subject to substantial abuse.

In summary, we can develop a long-term strategy to preserve and extend free trade. This will require intelligence, a sense of realism, a commitment to principle and considerable patience. Alternatively, we can simply respond to political pressures for new trade restraints and allow the world trading system to continue to deteriorate. The future of US trade policy and of the world trading system depends on the outcome of this choice.

REFERENCES

Denzau, Arthur T. (1988), 'The Japanese automobile cartel', *Regulation*, No. 1, 11–16.

Hufbauer, Gary, Diane Berliner and Kimberly Elliot (1986), *Trade Protection in the United States: 31 Case Studies*, Washington, DC Institute for International Economics.

Richman, Sheldon (1988), 'The Reagan record on trade: rhetoric vs. reality', *Policy Analysis*, No. 107, Washington, DC: Cato Institute.

Volokh, Eugene (1988), 'The semiconductor industry and foreign competition', *Policy Analysis*, No. 99, Washington, DC: Cato Institute.

16. The determinants of US capital imports*

For most of the period after World War I, the United States was a net exporter of capital. In every year since 1982, however, the United States has been a large net importer of capital. What explains this substantial change in net US foreign investment? Is there reason to be concerned about this condition? What, if anything, should be done about it? This chapter addresses the evidence that bears on the first of these questions and the arguments that bear on the other two questions.

A BRIEF HISTORY OF NET US FOREIGN INVESTMENT

The large net import of capital by the United States beginning in the 1980s represents a major change from the immediate prior decades, but it is not a new condition. For about 300 years, from the first English settlements in Virginia and Massachusetts until World War I, foreigners invested more in the area that became the United States than Americans invested in other countries. This permitted the capital stock in the United States to grow more rapidly than could have been financed from our own saving, a condition that was an important contribution to the growth of output and real wages in the United States. This process accelerated in the nineteenth century with British investment in railroads, German investment in chemical plants, and so on. For the most part, American officials welcomed this net import of capital despite occasional populist complaints about the foreign ownership of domestic firms. As of World War I, the United States was the largest economy in the world but was also a large net debtor to the rest of the world.

For most of the next 70 years, for several reasons, the United States was a net exporter of capital. The two world wars destroyed much of the

* Reprinted by permission from *Annals of the American Academy of Political and Social Science*, **516**, July 1991, 36–49, Sage Publications.

physical capital of the other participating nations. In addition, the depression of the 1930s was more severe in the United States than in most other nations. As a consequence, the rate of return on investment in Europe and Asia was higher than in the United States for several decades after each war. A net export of capital by the United States was an appropriate response to the conditions of this period but should not be regarded as a natural long-run outcome. There is no inherent reason, for example, for a net flow of private capital from rich to poor nations. Most nations are poor, in part because their institutional conditions limit the risk-adjusted after-tax rate of return on private investment. Most foreign investment is among the developed countries. After the capital stock of Europe and Japan was rebuilt following the devastation of World War II, it was not obvious whether the United States would continue to be a net exporter of capital.

As we now know, the United States again became a large net importer of capital in the 1980s. Some basic accounting is a necessary foundation to understand this condition. Net foreign investment by the United States, the difference between exports and – broadly defined – imports, is equal to savings by Americans minus investment in the United States. Net foreign investment thus is positive if the export of goods and services is larger than total imports and is negative if imports exceed exports. A failure to understand this relation between the balance of trade and the balance of saving and investment has been a source of much misguided policy, reflected by measures to promote exports or restrict imports without changing the balance of saving and investment. Gross saving by Americans, in turn, is equal to the sum of household saving and gross business saving minus the combined deficit of the federal, state and local governments. If we save more than is invested at home, exports will be greater than imports, and we invest the difference abroad. Similarly, if domestic investment is higher than total saving by Americans, imports will be greater than exports, and we borrow abroad to finance the difference. Changes in net foreign investment are thus a function of conditions that change the level of saving relative to the level of domestic investment.

Figure 16.1 illustrates these relations during the years since World War II, with gross saving, domestic investment and net foreign investment each expressed as a percentage of gross national product (GNP).[1] Two main patterns are apparent. First, gross saving was slightly higher than domestic investment in most years until the 1980s, yielding a small positive net foreign investment. The gross saving rate, however, declined sharply in the 1980s, yielding a large negative net foreign investment. Second, saving and domestic investment were strongly correlated through about 1973. Investment increased relative to saving in high-growth years and declined

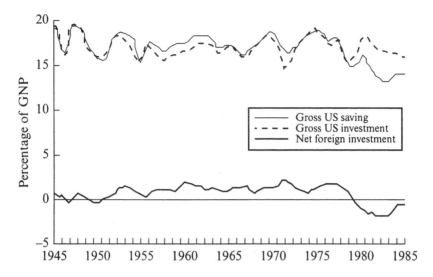

Figure 16.1 Net foreign investment equals saving by Americans minus investment in the United States

relative to saving in recessions. As a consequence, net foreign investment was usually low or negative in high-growth years and largest in recession years. Since about 1973, however, the relation between saving and domestic investment has been much weaker. A later section of this chapter summarizes a statistical analysis of these patterns to identify those conditions that led to the large net import of capital beginning in the 1980s.

Another simple accounting rule is helpful to identify whether a change in net US foreign investment was due primarily to changes in domestic or foreign conditions: net foreign investment by the United States is equal to new US investment abroad minus new foreign investment in the United States. Figure 16.2 illustrates these relations for the period since 1960, again with each variable expressed as a percentage of GNP.[2] Again, several patterns are apparent (1) capital flows in both directions – as a percentage of US GNP – increased slowly until the early 1980s without any clear relation to US economic conditions; (2) the sharp decline in net foreign investment from 1982 to 1985 reflected a sharp decline in US investment abroad with no significant change in foreign investment in the United States; and (3) the continued large negative net foreign investment from 1985 to 1989 reflected the net effect of a recovery of US investment abroad and a large increase in foreign investment in the United States. Any explanation of the large net US import of capital in the 1980s should also be consistent with these patterns.

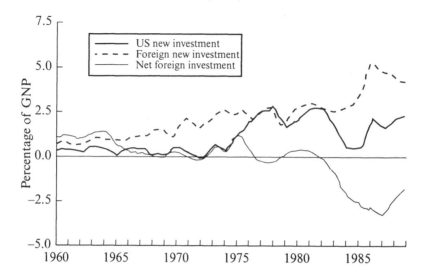

Figure 16.2 Net foreign investment equals US investment abroad minus foreign investment in the United States

In summary, the long record of net US foreign investment includes three distinct periods: a large cumulative net import of capital until World War I, a large cumulative net export of capital from World War I until 1982, and a large continuous net import of capital since 1982 that will probably continue for some years.

POSSIBLE EXPLANATIONS OF THE LARGE NET IMPORT OF CAPITAL IN THE 1980s

The large increase in the net US import of capital since 1982 provoked both economists and policy officials to offer several explanations of this development. These explanations are usefully aggregated in four groups: US economic conditions, US government fiscal policies, foreign economic conditions and foreign economic policies.

US Economic Conditions

The patterns illustrated by Figure 16.1 indicate that net US foreign investment has usually declined during years of high US economic growth, reflecting the higher cyclicality of domestic investment relative to saving.

Although this pattern continued in the 1980s, it is an insufficient explanation of the large net import of capital because the average rate of increase of US real GNP in the 1980s was lower than in any prior decade since World War II.

Economists have recently refined our understanding of the relation between changes in domestic demand and net capital flows by pointing out that this relation depends on the degree of substitutability between domestic and foreign goods and services.[3] Specifically, an increase in substitutability increases the effect of an increase in domestic growth on the net now of capital. There are several conditions that suggest that the substitutability of domestic and foreign goods may have been higher in the 1980s. The increase in oil prices beginning in 1974 clearly increased the relative competitiveness of foreign automobiles in the US market. The increase in the quality of electronic products from Asian countries had the same effect. An estimate of the magnitude of this effect is presented in the next section.

US Government Fiscal Policies

The most broadly shared explanation of the large net inflow of capital in the 1980s is the roughly coincident large federal budget deficit. This is a plausible explanation for two reasons. First, the accounting rule discussed previously indicates that an increase in the combined government sector deficit, given the levels of private saving and domestic investment, reduces net foreign investment by an equal amount. Second, of course, both the net inflow of capital and the federal deficit were unusually high in the 1980s.

My own prior views on this relation have been equivocal for several reasons.[4] First, the evidence for the chain of effects that purportedly links net foreign investment to the government deficit is surprisingly weak. The standard explanation of this relation is that government deficits increase the real, inflation-adjusted interest rate, an increase in the real interest rate increases the real foreign exchange rate, and the increase in the real exchange rate reduces the broad trade balance and net foreign investment. Each of these purported links is plausible. The relation between government deficits and real interest rates, however, has been surprisingly difficult to estimate by even the most refined econometric techniques. In turn, although the relation between the real interest rate and the real exchange rate has been moderately strong, the relation between the real exchange rate and the balance of trade and capital flows has been weaker and more variable than expected. Second, the direct relation between net foreign investment and the government deficit, either over time or across countries, is surprisingly weak.[5] The large federal budget deficit of the 1980s, however, is still the most plausible explanation of the large net import of capital, so it is important to test this relation in a more complex model that also controls for the other related conditions.

Several economists, myself included, have also suggested a more specific fiscal explanation of the changes in net foreign investment in the 1980s. This explanation is in terms of the substantial changes in the US tax treatment of domestic business investment.[6] The Economic Recovery Tax Act of 1981, for example, substantially reduced the effective tax rate on new domestic business investment. In turn, the reduction in this tax rate should have been expected to increase the real interest rate and the real exchange rate. The Tax Reform Act of 1986, the major features of which were first proposed in late 1984, substantially increased the effective tax rate on new domestic business investment. This act, in turn, should have been expected to reduce the real interest rate and the real exchange rate. In fact, the patterns of the *ex post* real interest rate and the real exchange rate in the 1980s, as illustrated by Figure 16.3, are quite consistent with this explanation.[7] For this chapter, however, the more important question is whether the changes in net foreign investment were significantly related to these two major changes in the effective tax rates on new domestic business investment.

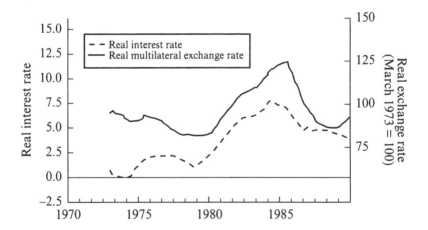

Figure 16.3 The US real interest rate and real exchange rate

Foreign Economic Conditions

Slow economic growth in the other major industrial nations might also explain the net flow of capital to the United States. The rate of growth of real GNP in the 1980s slowed in most other nations, especially in Europe, but this is an insufficient explanation because the US growth rate also declined. Although the average US growth rate (2.6 per cent) was higher than in the European Community (1.5 per cent), it was lower than in Canada (3 per cent), Japan (4.3 per cent) and the industrial countries taken together (2.9 per cent). Annual variations in the growth rates in other nations, however, may have contributed to the annual variations in the net US foreign investment.

Foreign economic policies

Several changes in economic policies in other nations may also have contributed to the net flow of capital to the United States. Early in the decade the Treasury Department attributed the strengthening dollar to a flight of capital in search of a 'safe haven'. This was a plausible explanation, especially after the suspension of debt service by several governments, the 1982 nationalization of the banks in France and Mexico, and political instability in some other countries. In addition, there was clearly a considerable flight of private capital from some countries, primarily from Latin America.

A more important policy change may have been the Yen–Dollar Agreement of May 1984, in which the government of Japan agreed to eliminate all remaining controls on the import and export of capital. Ironically, the origin of this agreement was pressure on the Reagan administration by American industrialists to induce Japan to implement some measure that would strengthen the foreign exchange value of the yen. The immediate effect of the agreement, as predicted by the Council of Economic Advisers, was to strengthen the dollar, because most of the remaining controls were on the export of capital. This agreement, followed by substantial Japanese investment in the United States, may have contributed to the large net US import of capital in the second half of the decade.

Sorting out the effects of these two developments requires a comparison of the patterns of US real interest rates and the real exchange rate and a comparison of the patterns of US investment abroad and foreign investment in the United States.

SORTING OUT THE EVIDENCE

My first task is to estimate how much of the variation in net US foreign investment can be explained by US macroeconomic conditions and the combined US government sector budget deficit. This test can then identify whether any other domestic or foreign conditions and policies specific to the 1980s may also have contributed to the large net US import of capital in this decade.

The Model

For this purpose, I have used the following simple model:

$$NFI^* = a - b\ PCRY - c\ GD + u \tag{16.1}$$

$$NFI - FNI_{-1} = d\ (NFI^* - FNI_{-1}) + v \tag{16.2}$$

$$NFI = ad - bd\ PCRY + cd\ GD + (1 - d)\ NFI_{-1} + (du + v) \tag{16.3}$$

Definition of variables

NFI^* = equilibrium value of NFI (not directly observable)
NFI = net foreign investment as a percentage of GNP
$PCRY$ = percentage change in real GNP
GD = combined government sector deficit as a percentage of GNP.

Equation (16.1) expresses the equilibrium level of net foreign investment as a negative linear function of the percentage change in real GNP and the level of the combined government sector deficit. Equation (16.2) expresses the change in the level of net foreign investment as a positive linear function of the difference between the equilibrium level of net foreign investment and the actual level in the prior year; the coefficient d, thus, is the rate by which the actual level of net foreign investment adjusts to the equilibrium level in one year. Substituting equation (16.1) into equation (16.2) and solving for NFI yields equation (16.3), which is the test equation. Estimates of the coefficients of equation (16.1), in turn, can be derived by dividing the first three estimated coefficients in equation (16.3) by the estimate of the coefficient d. Equation (16.3) thus provides an estimate of how much macroeconomic conditions and the government budget deficit affect net foreign investment in the same year.

Equation (16.1) provides an estimate of how much these conditions affect the long-run equilibrium level of net foreign investment.

Empirical Tests

Table 16.1 presents ordinary least-squares estimates of equation (16.3) for three sample periods: 1953–73, 1974–89 and 1953–89. The total sample was divided to test whether the coefficients were stable over the period of the full sample. The sample was divided at 1973 because the first general floating of exchange rates, which removed the primary reason for controls on capital flows, and the first oil shock were in that year. For each sample, the first line presents the estimated coefficients, the numbers in

Table 16.1 Estimates of the conditions that affect net foreign investment

Sample	Short-run coefficients				
	Constant	PCRY 1	PCRY 2	GD	NFI_{-1}
1953–73	0.529	−0.075		−0.266	0.660
	(0.158)	(0.039)		(0.081)	(0.189)
	[3.341]	[−1.914]		[−3.299]	[3.497]
	$\bar{R}^2 = 0.411$ SER = 0.327 DW = 1.960				
1974–89	0.515		−0.177	−0.201	0.755
	(0.309)		(0.061)	(0.108)	(0.101)
	[1.670]		[−2.918]	[−1.859]	[7.482]
	$\bar{R}^2 = 0.866$ SER = 0.562 DW = 1.965				
1953–89	0.522	−0.081	−0.174	−0.228	0.732
	(0.154)	(0.039)	(0.041)	(0.060)	(0.070)
	[3.399]	[−2.099]	[−4.306]	[−3.820]	[10.511]
	$\bar{R}^2 = 0.884$ SER = 0.423 DW = 2.238				

	Long-run coefficients				
	Constant	PCRY 1	PCRY 2	GD	Adjustment rate
	1.952	−0.304	−0.651	−0.851	0.268

Source: Author's estimates.

parentheses are the standard errors of the coefficients, and the bracketed numbers are the *t* ratios of the coefficients. $\bar{R}^2$ is the share of the annual variation in each sample that is explained by these conditions. SER is the standard error of the regression equation, measured as a percentage of GNP. DW is the Durbin–Watson statistic, a measure that is about 2.0 if there is no serial correlation of the error terms. The bottom row of this table presents estimates of the coefficients of equation (16.1) and equation (16.2) based on the full sample estimates of equation (16.3).

The major conclusions from these tests are the following:

1. Three conditions explain nearly 90 per cent of the annual variation in net foreign investment: the percentage changes in real GNP, the level of the government deficit and the level of net foreign investment in the prior year.
2. The relative effects of these conditions were quite stable over the total sample, with one exception. The negative effect of domestic economic growth on net foreign investment was significantly higher in the period after 1973, suggesting that the substitutability of domestic and foreign goods was much higher in this period.
3. A 1 per cent increase in the growth of real GNP since 1973 reduces net foreign investment by about 0.17 of 1 per cent of GNP in the same year and by about 0.65 of 1 per cent of GNP in the long run.
4. An increase in the combined government sector deficit by $100 billion reduces net foreign investment by about $23 billion in the same year and by about $85 billion in the long run.
5. The observed level of net foreign investment adjusts to the long-run equilibrium level at an annual rate of about 0.27.

In summary, the pattern of net foreign investment in the 1980s was different from the prior patterns for two primary reasons. First, increases in real GNP had a larger negative effect on changes in net foreign investment than in the years up through 1973. Second, the most important condition that led to the large net import of capital, consistent with the standard explanation, was the large sustained government budget deficit. Nearly one-quarter of the budget deficit appears to be financed abroad, directly or indirectly, in the same year, and most of the deficit appears to be financed abroad in the long run.[8] The standard explanation of the so-called twin deficits appears to be correct. The primary remaining puzzle concerns the process that leads the government deficit to reduce net foreign investment, given the apparent lack of a strong effect of the deficit on interest rates and foreign exchange rates.

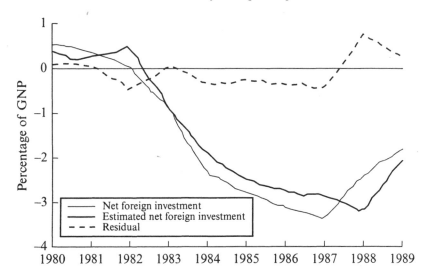

Figure 16.4 Actual and estimated net investment in the 1980s

Evidence Bearing on the Other Possible Explanations

The simplest way to identify whether other conditions may have also contributed to the large net US import of capital in the 1980s is to examine
the pattern of the error terms from the estimates of equation (16.3), as
displayed in Figure 16.4. These error terms (plotted in the line 'residual')
are nearly random and display no strong pattern that appears consistent
with the timing of the other conditions and policies that may have
affected net foreign investment. In other words, these other conditions
and policies do not appear to have had a substantial effect on the large
net US import of capital in the 1980s, except to the extent that they may
have affected the rate of change of US real GNP or the US government
sector budget deficit.[9] Nevertheless, it is valuable to evaluate these other
conditions and policies with other types of evidence.

Changes in the Tax Treatment of US Domestic Investment

Changes in US tax laws in 1981, 1982, and 1986 substantially changed
the effective tax rates on new investment in the United States. The combined effect of the 1981 and 1982 laws reduced the average effective tax

rate on new corporate investment by about 3 per cent, and the Tax Reform Act of 1986 increased this rate by about 5 per cent.[10] The patterns of real interest and exchange rates displayed in Figure 16.3 are roughly consistent with the direction of changes in these tax rates, since real interest rates are a negative function of the effective tax rate on new investment. These tax rate changes, however, are not sufficient to explain the magnitude of the change in the real interest and exchange rates; several studies, for example, suggest that only one-tenth to one-quarter of the increase in the real exchange rate from 1980 to 1985 was a result of the reduction in tax rates.[11]

Other types of evidence bearing on this explanation are also mixed. The pattern of new US investment abroad – to which the special tax incentives for domestic investment did not apply – is consistent with this tax explanation. As Figure 16.2 indicates, US investment abroad declined sharply when the tax incentives for domestic investment increased and increased sharply when these incentives were reduced. The pattern of foreign new investment in the United States, which was eligible for the tax incentives, is not consistent with this explanation, however. As Figure 16.2 also indicates, foreign new investment in the United States was roughly stable when the tax incentives increased, and it increased sharply when these incentives were reduced.

In summary, the changes in the effective tax rates on new domestic investment are a partial explanation of the changes in real interest and exchange rates and the changes in US new investment abroad. These tax rate changes, however, do not explain the patterns of foreign new investment in the United States or the net balance of foreign investment.

Foreign Economic Conditions

A closer examination of Figure 16.4 suggests that there may have been some effects of changes in economic growth abroad on net US foreign investment. In the years from 1983 to 1987, net foreign investment was slightly lower than the level estimated by equation (16.3) and, during these years, economic growth in Europe was lower than in the United States. Conversely, in 1988 and 1989, net foreign investment was somewhat higher than estimated by equation (16.3), probably in response to increased relative economic growth abroad. For the United States, however, the effects of these changes in foreign economic conditions are small, and they are an insufficient explanation for the large continued net US import of capital since 1982.

Foreign Economic Policies

The safe-haven explanation of the change in net foreign investment in the early 1980s is plausible but is not consistent with several types of evidence. If this effect had been the primary explanation of the change in net foreign investment, US real interest rates would have declined and foreign new investment in the United States would have increased. Figures (16.3) and (16.2), however, indicate that the US real interest rate increased sharply in the early 1980s and foreign new investment in the United States was roughly stable, In the second half of the 1980s, the improvement of foreign economic conditions and policies was paired with a decline in the US real interest rate and a large increase in new foreign investment in the United States. In summary, the changes in US real interest rates and in new foreign investment in the United States in the 1980s appear to be inconsistent in direction with the changes in foreign economic policies.

In one case, however, a change in the economic policy of a foreign government appears to have affected the source and level of new foreign investment in the United States. Specifically, the relaxation of controls on capital exports by the government of Japan following the Yen–Dollar Agreement of May 1984 was followed by a substantial increase in Japanese investment in the United States. During the late 1980s, however, new investment abroad also increased substantially, and the balance of foreign investment does not appear to have been affected by the conditions that led to the increase in Japanese investment in the United States, given US macroeconomic conditions and the level of the combined government sector budget deficit.

IS THE LARGE NET IMPORT OF CAPITAL A POLICY PROBLEM?

Should Americans be concerned about the large net import of capital since 1982? A casual reading of the press or of quotes by members of Congress would suggest that this is a major problem. An increase in the trade deficit is regularly described as 'disturbing'. Foreign direct investment, especially by the Japanese, is usually described as the sale of 'our' firms and resources. Congress has responded to these perceptions with both mercantilist legislation and a special process to review foreign direct investment. On the other hand, most of our governors and mayors appear to welcome foreign investment as a stimulus to local economic development. For example, more state governments now have offices in Tokyo than in Washington. Our political system seems to be divided on this issue.

Policy analysis

Let me try to sort this issue out. The primary basis for concern about the net import of capital is the concern about any debt; as a group, Americans are now accumulating a large net debt to foreigners that, at some time in the future, will have to be serviced by increased domestic output or reduced consumption. The primary basis for welcoming the net import of capital is that it permits domestic investment to be higher than saving by Americans; if our capital markets had been closed to foreigners in the 1980s, for example, real interest rates would have been even higher, domestic investment would have been reduced to the level of domestic saving, and the rate of economic growth would have been lower.

These perspectives may seem inconsistent, but both are correct. As with any increase in debt, one should evaluate a net import of capital by addressing how the proceeds are used. A loan to finance an increase in consumption, for example, must be financed by a subsequent reduction in consumption. A loan to finance an increase in investment, however, permits an increase in future consumption if the return on the investment is higher than the service charges on the loan. Another glance at Figure 16.1 should be sufficient to sort this issue out. The large net import of capital was the result of an unusually low level of saving by Americans, not an unusually high level of domestic investment. In effect, we borrowed abroad to finance an increased level of private and public consumption, and we will have to reduce the growth of our future consumption to service this debt.

In summary, the large net US import of capital since 1982, by itself, is not a problem but is the result of a problem. The proper focus of policy is the low rate of private saving and the large government deficit. Solving that problem will require reducing the growth of either private consumption or government consumption, and that will be the primary fiscal policy issue of the 1990s.

NOTES

1. The measure of gross saving in Figure 16.1 includes the statistical discrepancy.
2. The measure of additions to the US investment abroad in Figure 16.2 includes the statistical discrepancy and the small differences between the national income account measure of net foreign investment and the balance-of-payment account measure of the current-account balance.
3. A. Lans Bovenberg, 'The effects of capital income taxation on international competitiveness and trade flows', *American Economic Review*, **79**, December 1989, 1045–64.
4. William A. Niskanen, *Reaganomics: An Insider's Account of the Policies and the People*, New York: Oxford University Press, 1988, pp. 252–54; idem, 'The uneasy relation between the budget and trade deficits', in James A. Dorn and William A. Niskanen (eds), *Dollars, Deficits, and Trade*, Boston: Kluwer Academic, 1989, pp. 305–16.

5. See Niskanen, 'Uneasy relation', for a summary of this evidence.
6. Council of Economic Advisers, *Economic Report of the President*, Washington, DC: Government Printing Office, 1985, pp. 33–6; Hans-Werner Sinn, 'Why taxes matter: Reagan's accelerated cost recovery system and the U.S. trade deficit', *Economic Policy*, 1 November 1985, 240–50; Lawrence H. Summers, *Tax Policy and International Competitiveness*, National Bureau of Economic Research Working Paper No. 2007, August 1986; Bovenberg, 'Effects of capital income taxation'.
7. The measure of the real interest rate in Figure 16.3 is the yield on US Treasury securities with a ten-year maturity minus the inflation rate on the fixed-weight GNP deflator. The real exchange rate is the multilateral trade-weighted value of the US dollar adjusted for changes in consumer prices.
8. The substantial proportion of the US government budget deficit financed abroad, in turn, is probably the best explanation why the deficit does not have much affect on domestic interest rates.
9. The tax preferences on domestic business investment in the 1980 tax law, for example, appear to have contributed to the unusually strong rate of investment and real GNP growth in 1983 and 1984. See Michael J. Boskin, *The Impact of the 1981–1982 Investment Incentives on Business Fixed Investment*, Washington, DC: National Chamber Foundation, 1985.
10. Niskanen, *Reaganomics*, p. 104.
11. Bovenberg, 'Effects of capital income taxation', p. 1060.

17. Welfare and the culture of poverty*

At the dawn of the American welfare state, in his 1935 State of the Union message, President Franklin D. Roosevelt (1938, pp. 19–20) proposed social security, unemployment insurance, and (what was then called) aid to dependent children to help the deserving poor, but he added an ominous warning:

> The lessons of history, confirmed by evidence immediately before me, show conclusively that continued dependence on relief induces a spiritual and moral disintegration fundamentally destructive to the national fiber. To dole out relief in this way is to administer a narcotic, a subtle destroyer of the human spirit. It is inimical to the dictates of sound policy. It is a violation of the traditions of America.

More than 60 years later, it should be clear that the narcotic of 'continued dependence on relief' is less subtle and more destructive than Roosevelt feared.

SUMMARY

Welfare is both a consequence and a cause of several conditions best described as social pathologies. These conditions include dependency, poverty, out-of-wedlock births, nonemployment, abortion and violent crime.[1] The basic hypothesis of this study is that welfare dependency and the other pathologies are jointly determined and are derivative of a common set of other conditions.

Differences in the levels of these conditions among the states provide a basis for estimating the specific effects of welfare benefits, the relations among the social pathologies, and the extent to which the pathologies are based on a common set of root causes.

Analysis of the state data for 1992 yields the following estimates of the effects of an increase in Aid to Families with Dependent Children

* Reprinted by permission from the *Cato Journal*, **16** (1), Spring/Summer 1996, 1–15, Cato Institute.

(AFDC) benefits by 1 per cent of the average personal income in the state: the number of AFDC recipients would increase by about 3 per cent; the number of people in poverty would increase by about 0.8 per cent; the number of births to single mothers would increase by about 2.1 per cent; the number of adults who are not employed would increase by about 0.5 per cent; the number of abortions would increase by about 1.2 per cent; and the violent crime rate would increase by about 1.1 per cent.

The social pathologies associated with the current welfare system no longer seem acceptable, not so much because of their fiscal costs but because of their malign effects. An important question addressed in this study is the extent to which these pathologies are dependent on conditions that could be changed by government policy.

SOCIAL PATHOLOGIES

For this study, the six conditions are described as social pathologies, not because they are necessarily illegal or immoral in an individual case but because the level of these conditions is broadly considered as undesirable. There is less consensus, however, about the relative undesirability of these conditions. An increase in welfare dependency, for example, may be considered desirable if it reduces one or more of the other conditions. As it turns out, however, an increase in AFDC benefits increases *all* of the six pathologies that are the focus of this study.

Welfare Dependency

In 1992, 5.4 per cent of the national population were dependent on cash benefits from AFDC, with a range from 2.0 per cent in Idaho to 10.8 per cent in the District of Columbia. This programme is jointly financed by the federal and state governments and is administered by the states subject to numerous federal guidelines. All AFDC recipients are also eligible for food stamps and medicaid, and many also receive benefits from special food programmes, utility assistance and housing assistance.

An additional 2.6 per cent of the population receive cash benefits from other federal and state programmes, for a total of 8 per cent who are dependent on cash benefits. A broader 9.9 per cent of the population receive food stamps, and 11.9 per cent are covered by medicaid. A more complex study would be necessary to estimate the causes and consequences of the broader set of means-tested programmes. For this study, the level of welfare dependency is defined as the percentage of the population that receive cash benefits from the AFDC programme.

Poverty

A total of 14.5 per cent of the population have money income below the official poverty line, with a range from 7.6 per cent in Delaware to 24.5 per cent in Mississippi. The national poverty rate is now about the same as when the War on Poverty was instituted 30 years ago, despite the expenditure of over $5 trillion (at 1993 prices) for means-tested public assistance programmes in the intervening years and a 75 per cent increase in average real income. More means-tested benefits may or may not have contributed to the incidence of poverty but they have clearly not reduced it.

Any definition of poverty, of course, is somewhat arbitrary, depending on what types of income are included. The government estimates national poverty rates for 15 different aggregations of income, taxes and transfers, with a range from 10.4 per cent based on all after-tax income and transfers to a high of 22.6 per cent based only on pretax money income. For this study, the level of poverty is defined as the percentage of the population with pretax money income and cash transfers below the official poverty line, the only such data available by state.

Out-of-wedlock Births

Out-of-wedlock births are the most rapidly increasing social pathology. On a national basis (in 1991), 29.2 per cent of births were to single mothers, with a range from 14.3 per cent in Utah to 65.9 per cent in the District of Columbia. Since 1960, the illegitimacy rate has increased from 2.3 per cent to 22 per cent for whites and from 21.4 per cent to 6.8 per cent for blacks. A substantial part of the current generation of inner city young people has grown up without a father, a contributor to the increase in violent crime and the decline in school performance as well as to some of the pathologies addressed in this study.[2]

Nonemployment

The percentage of the adult population that is not employed has been declining for many years and, compared to many other nations, is unusually low. For lack of a better word, I shall define this condition with the inelegant word nonemployment, because the word unemployment has usually been used to describe those not working but seeking work. Formally, the nonemployment rate is the percentage of the civilian noninstitutional population age 16 and over that is not employed. On a national basis the nonemployment rate is 38.6 per cent with a range from 31.1 per cent in Nebraska to 51.7 per cent in West Virginia.

Abortion

Abortion is the most contentious issue in contemporary American politics, primarily because the polar positions have dominated the debate. The 'pro-choice' advocates consider any restriction on abortion as a violation of a woman's rights. The 'pro-life' advocates consider any abortion as murder. No study of the causes and consequences of abortion would reconcile these positions. Most Americans, however, appear to favour legal and social rules that would make abortion legal, safe and rare. For the most part, abortion is legal and safe but it is not rare. On a national basis there are 379 abortions per 1000 live births (somewhat lower than the prior peak of 436 in 1983), with a range from 74 in Wyoming to 1104 in the District of Columbia. For the broad group of Americans who regard most abortions as undesirable but not a crime, abortion is appropriately described as a pathology and an understanding of the conditions that explain the large variation in abortion rates can be valuable to aid their judgement on this contentious issue.

Violent Crime

Violent crime may be the most serious social pathology in the United States. The reported violent crime rate has increased substantially for several decades and is much higher than in other nations. And the number of violent crimes estimated from victimization surveys is much higher than the number reported to and by the police. On a national basis, there were 758 reported violent crimes. per 100000 residents, with a range from 83 in North Dakota to 2833 in the District of Columbia.

ROOT CAUSES OF THE CULTURE OF POVERTY

One objective of this study is to identify the extent to which the six social pathologies are the consequence of a common set of root causes. The conditions examined included the level of welfare benefits in each state, a measure of general economic conditions, the racial and ethnic composition, and several social and cultural indicators.

Welfare Benefits

The one variable that best reflects the welfare policy in a state is the level of AFDC benefits per recipient household. State governments also set eligibility standards subject to federal guidelines, but differences in these standards are not easily measurable. For this study, welfare benefits are defined as the annual AFDC benefits per recipient household as a percentage for the pre-tax personal income per capita in the state. On a national basis such benefits are 23 per cent of personal income per capita, with a range from 10.4 per cent in Mississippi to 40.8 per cent in Alaska.

Total welfare benefits per recipient household, one should recognize, are much higher than the direct cash benefits from AFDC. The total benefits for those households from AFDC, food stamps and medicaid only range from 50 to 100 per cent of personal income per capita. And the total benefits for those AFDC recipients who also receive housing assistance, utility assistance and specialized food programmes range from 90 to 125 per cent of personal income per capita.[3] These estimates of total benefits provide a better sense of why welfare has become a trap for so many women. For reasons that are not clear, however, the several measures of social pathology that are the focus of this study are more closely related to the narrow cash benefits from AFDC than to the broader measures of total welfare benefits, maybe because many AFDC recipients value cash benefits more than noncash benefits or are not eligible for the broader set of benefits.

Economic Conditions

General economic conditions in a state are represented by the pretax personal income per capita. On a national basis average personal income is $20 105, with a range from $14 082 in Mississippi to $27 909 in the District of Columbia.

Race and Ethnicity

The racial and ethnic composition in a state is represented by the percentage black and the percentage Hispanic. Blacks are 12.4 per cent of the national population, with a range from 0.3 per cent in Montana to 65.0 per cent in the District of Columbia. Hispanics are 9.5 per cent of the national population, with a range from 0.4 per cent in West Virginia to 38.2 per cent in New Mexico. These two groups are combined in a percentage minority measure when preliminary tests indicate that their effects are not statistically different.

Social and Cultural Indicators

Social and cultural conditions in a state are represented by four indicators: church membership, educational level, percentage metropolitan and average temperature. The distinctive attribute of each of these indicators is that they reflect individual choices of whether to join a church, continue education and where to live.

Church membership is measured as the sum of the percentage of the resident population who are Christian adherents (1990) plus the percentage who are Jews. By this measure 55 per cent of the national population are church members, with a range from 32.6 per cent in Alaska to 80 per cent in Utah.

The educational level in a state is measured as the percentage of the resident population age 25 and over with a high school or higher education (1990). On a national basis 75.2 per cent are educated at this level, with a range from 64.3 per cent in Mississippi to 86.6 per cent in Alaska.

The metropolitan population is measured as the percentage of the population resident in metropolitan areas. On a national basis 79.7 per cent of the population are residents in a metropolitan area, with a range from 24 per cent in Montana to 100 per cent in the District of Columbia.

The average daily low temperature measure used in this study is roughly proportional to the distance from North Dakota. This variable, which is significant only in the welfare dependency regression, reflects some combination of the tighter welfare eligibility standards in the southern states and the social and cultural differences among regions that are correlated with temperature. Whatever the balance of these effects, including this measure is important to increase the precision by which the effects of other conditions is estimated.

METHODOLOGY

The patterns of pathology are estimated by least-squares regression techniques.[4] For each of the six pathologies, two types of relations are estimated. The first relation includes one or more other jointly determined pathologies and a subset of the root causes; this relation is estimated by a weighted two-stage (TS) regression where the whole set of root causes is used as instrumental variables. The first relation provides estimates of the relation among the several pathologies and the partial effects of specific root causes *given* the level of the other included pathologies. The second relation includes only a set of root causes; the relation is estimated by a weighted least-squares (LS) regression. The second relation provides estimates of the *total* effect of specific root causes that operate both directly on the specific pathology and indirectly through their effect on other related pathologies. All variables in both relations are weighted by the resident population of each state. This increases the relative effects of conditions in the largest states and makes the estimates correspond more closely to the effects of national conditions. Only those variables that are statistically significant at a 95 per cent level or more are included in either of the relations; as it turns out, most of the included variable are significant at a much higher level.

PATTERNS OF SOCIAL PATHOLOGY

The patterns of social pathology are summarized in Tables 17.1–3. First, some general advice on reading these tables. The top tier of coefficients in each table are estimates of the percentage change in the focus pathology from a 1 per cent increase in some other condition. For example, in. Table 17.1, a 1 per cent increase in the poverty population in a state increases welfare dependency (the number of AFDC recipients) by about 0.6 per cent. The lower tier of coefficients (except for temperature) are estimates of the percentage change in the focus pathology from a 1 *percentage point* increase in some other condition. For example, in Table 17.1, a 1 percentage point increase in the population living in a metropolitan area increases the AFDC population by about 1.3 per cent The coefficients on the temperature variable are estimates of the effect of a 1 *degree* (Fahrenheit) increase in the average daily low temperature. The numbers in parentheses are the standard errors. If the estimate of the coefficient is unbiased, there is a 95 per cent probability that the true (unknown) level of the coefficient is within two standard errors of the estimate. The $\bar{R}^2$ is the percentage of the weighted and unweighted variance of the focus pathology among the states that is explained by each relation.

Welfare Dependency

The patterns of welfare dependency summarized by the first two columns of Table 17.1 support the following conclusions:

1. Welfare dependency is strongly related to poverty. Specifically, a 1 per cent increase in the poverty population in a state increases the population of AFDC recipients by about 0.6 per cent.
2. An increase in AFDC benefits by 1 per cent of personal income, about $17 a month in 1992, would increase the dependent population in a state by about 2.2 per cent given the number of the poor and by about 3.0 per cent including the effect on poverty. Some part of this increase may be induced immigration from other states, so the proportionate effects of a uniform national increase may not be as high.

Table 17.1 Welfare and poverty

	Welfare dependency		Poverty	
	TS	LS	TS	LS
Effect of a 1 per cent increase				
Dependency			0.27 (0.06)	
Poverty	0.63 (0.17)			
Income		−1.04 (0.29)	−0.72 (0.17)	−0.81 (0.18)
Effect of a 1 percentage point increase				
Benefits	2.18 (0.23)	2.96 (0.26)		0.75 (0.21)
Church	−0.69 (0.15)		0.41 (0.12)	0.36 (0.15)
Education	−3.92 (0.88)	−4.25 (0.87)		−1.76 (0.68)
Metropolitian	1.05 (0.17)	1.31 (0.31)	−0.40 (0.18)	
Minority		0.70 (0.31)	1.38 (0.14)	1.14 (0.15)
Temperature	−2.11 (0.36)	−2.15 (0.50)		
$\bar{R}^2$				
Weighted	0.99	0.99	0.99	0.99
Unweighted	0.39	0.21	0.64	0.67

3. Economic conditions and the minority population affect welfare dependency only through their effects on the poverty rate. A 1 per cent increase in average personal income reduces dependency by about 1.0 per cent. A 1 percentage point increase in the minority population increases the dependent population by about 0.7 per cent.
4. Given the number of the poor, welfare dependency declines with an increase in church membership. A 1 percentage point increase in church membership reduces the dependent population by about 0.7 per cent. A

1 percentage point increase in the population completing high school reduces the dependent population by about 4 per cent. And a 1 degree (Fahrenheit) increase in average temperature is associated with a 2.1 per cent decrease in the dependent population. This temperature effect probably reflects the tighter welfare eligibility standards in the southern states.
5. Urbanization increases dependency. A 1 percentage point increase in the population residing in metropolitan areas increases the dependent population by about 1.3 per cent.

Most of these findings are expected, in direction if not in magnitude. Welfare dependency is primarily determined by the level of welfare benefits and the conditions that affect the poverty rate. One important finding is that an increase in the minority population does not increase dependency except to the extent that it increases the poverty rate. In other words, poor minorities are no more likely to be dependent on welfare than are poor whites. One puzzling finding is the positive effect of urbanization on dependency, given that urbanization (as also shown on Table 17.1) has a negative effect on the poverty rate; the urban poor are apparently more likely to be dependent on welfare than are the rural poor.

Poverty

The patterns of poverty summarized by the last two columns of Table 17.1 support the following conclusions:

1. Poverty is also related to dependency. A 1 per cent increase in the dependent population increases the poor population in a state by about 0.3 per cent. An increase in AFDC benefits by 1 per cent of average personal income increases the number of poor residents of a state by nearly 0.8 per cent.
2. Poverty declines with an increase in average income and education. A 1 per cent increase in average personal income reduces the poor population in a state by about 0.8 per cent. A 1 percentage point increase in the population with high school or higher education reduces the poor population by about 1.8 per cent.
3. The size of the poor population in a state is strongly related to the size of the black and Hispanic population. A 1 percentage point increase in the percent minority increases the poor population by about 1.1 per cent.
4. For reasons that are not obvious, a 1 percentage point increase in church membership appears to increase poverty by about 0.4 per cent.[5]

Again, most of these findings are expected. Poverty is primarily determined by the level of AFDC benefits, general economic conditions, education and the percentage minority. The major puzzle is the positive effect of church membership on poverty, compared to its negative effect on welfare dependency.

Out-of-wedlock Births

The patterns of out-of-wedlock births summarized by the first two columns on Table 17.2 support the following conclusions:

1. Out-of-wedlock births are strongly related to welfare dependency. A 1 per cent increase in the welfare dependent population in a state increases the number of births to single mothers by about 0.5 per cent.
2. Illegitimacy is also related to nonemployment. A 1 per cent increase in the nonemployed population increases the births to single mothers by about 0.9 per cent.
3. The level of welfare benefits, in turn, indirectly increases illegitimacy through the effects on the size of the dependent population and on the number of the nonemployed. An increase in AFDC benefits by 1 per cent of average income increases the number of births to single mothers by about 2.1 per cent.
4. Out-of-wedlock births decline with an increase in church membership. A 1 percentage point increase in church membership reduces the number of illegitimate births by about 0.4 per cent.
5. In this case, the effects of the two large minority groups are very different. A 1 percentage point increase in the black population increases the number of illegitimate births by about 2.3 per cent. In contrast, a 1 percentage point increase in the Hispanic population reduces the number of illegitimate births by about 0.5 per cent.

Nonemployment

The patterns of nonemployment summarized by the last two columns of Table 17.2 support the following conclusions:

1. Welfare dependency reduces employment. A 1 per cent increase in the dependent population increases the number who are not employed by about 0.1 per cent.
2. An increase in welfare benefits reduces employment by increasing the number of welfare dependents. An increase in AFDC benefits by

Policy analysis

Table 17.2 Out-of-wedlock births and nonemployment

	Out-of-wedlock births		Nonemployment	
	TS	LS	TS	LS
Effect of a 1 per cent increase				
Dependency	0.52		0.13	
	(0.11)		(0.04)	
Nonemployment	0.93			
	(0.40)			
Effect of a 1 percentage point increase				
Benefits		2.11		0.49
		(0.23)		
Church	−0.42	−0.36		(0.12)
	(0.19)	(0.17)		
Education			−1.36	−2.00
			(0.30)	(0.34)
Metropolitan			0.44	0.49
			(0.11)	(0.10)
Black	0.88	2.27		
	(0.36)	(0.36)		
Hispanic	−0.68	−0.48	−0.39	−0.44
	(0.19)	(0.17)	(0.10)	(0.10)
$\bar{R}^2$				
Weighted	0.95	0.95	0.93	0.93
Unweighted	0.46	0.44	−0.51	−0.41

1 per cent of average income increases the number who are not employed by about 0.5.
3. Education has a strong effect on employment. A 1 percentage point increase in the population with high school or higher education reduces the number who are not employed by about 2 per cent.
4. Employment is also related to the relative size of the metropolitan and Hispanic populations. A 1 percentage point increase in the metropolitan population increases the number who are not employed by about 0.5 per cent. A 1 percentage point increase in the Hispanic population reduces the number who are not employed by about 0.4 per cent.

Abortion

The patterns of abortion summarized by the first two columns of Table 17.3 support the following conclusions:

1. Abortion is strongly related to nonemployment. A 1 per cent increase in the adult population not working increases the number of abortions by about 1.7 per cent.
2. An increase in AFDC benefits by 1 per cent of average income would indirectly increase the number of abortions by about 1.2 per cent by increasing the nonworking population.
3. A 1 per cent increase in average income increases the number of abortions by about 1 per cent.
4. Education, like income, contributes to abortion. A 1 percentage point increase in the population with education at the high school level or higher, for a given number of nonemployed, increases the number of abortions by about 3.6 per cent.
5. The effects of the two large minority groups are somewhat different. A 1 percentage point increase in the black population increases the number of abortions by about 1.8 per cent, whereas a 1 percentage point increase in the Hispanic population increases abortions by about 0.8 per cent.

The pattern of abortions is *not* consistent with the usual patterns of the culture of poverty. The number of abortions increases with nonemployment and the percentage minority, but it also increases with education and income. Maybe the most surprising finding is another blank space: the number of abortions appears to be independent of church membership.

Violent Crime

The patterns of violent crime summarized by the last two columns of Table 17.3 support the following conclusions:[7]

1. The level of violent crime is strongly related to welfare dependency. A 1 per cent increase in the welfare dependent population increases the violent crime rate by about 0.6 per cent.
2. An increase in welfare benefits indirectly increases the violent crime rate by increasing the number of welfare dependents. An increase in AFDC benefits by 1 per cent of average income increases the violent crime rate by about 1.1 per cent.

Table 17.3 Abortion and violent crime

	Abortion		Violent crime	
	TS	LS	TS	LS
Effect of a 1 per cent increase				
Dependency			0.61 (0.16)	
Nonemployment	1.65 (0.34)			
Income	1.03 (0.22)	1.42 (0.16)	−1.33 (0.64)	
Effect of a 1 percentage point increase				
Benefits		1.22 (0.24)		1.12 (0.46)
Education	3.61 (0.99)			
Metropolitan			0.83 (0.37)	1.25 (0.37)
Minority			1.27 (0.43)	
Black	1.77 (0.41)	1.76 (0.32)		3.83 (0.66)
Hispanic	1.21 (0.16)	0.82 (0.15)		1.91 (0.37)
$\bar{R}^2$				
Weighted	0.99	0.99	0.99	0.99
Unweighted	0.44	0.56	0.59	0.64

3. The level of violent crime is also related to the composition of the population, reflecting both a direct effect and an indirect effect operating through the level of the welfare dependent population.[8] A 1 percentage point increase in the metropolitan population increases the violent crime rate by about 1.3 per cent.

    A 1 percentage point increase in the black population increases the violent crime rate by about 3.8 per cent, and a 1 percentage point increase in the Hispanic population increases the violent crime rate by about 1.9 per cent.

PATTERNS ACROSS PATHOLOGIES

A comparison of the effects of the eight root causes across the six pathologies is useful to identify the conditions that most consistently contribute to or defend against these pathologies.

The level of AFDC benefits relative to the average personal income in each state is the one condition that increases each of the six focus pathologies, with effects ranging from a weak effect on nonemployment to disturbingly strong effects on welfare dependency and illegitimacy.

The next most consistent correlate of these conditions is the percentage of the population that is black, a root cause for five of the pathologies other than nonemployment. The percentage Hispanic contributes to welfare dependency, poverty, abortion and violent crime but reduces illegitimacy and nonemployment.

The most consistent defences against these pathologies are education and higher average income. A higher percentage of the population with high school or higher education reduces dependency, poverty and nonemployment. Higher average income reduces dependency, poverty and violent crime. Both higher education and income, however, increase abortion.

The effects of the other conditions examined are more mixed. Church membership reduces welfare dependency and illegitimacy but appears to increase poverty. A higher percentage of the population of a state that is resident in metropolitan areas increases dependency, nonemployment and violent crime but reduces poverty. The contrary effects of church membership and the metropolitan population on welfare dependency and poverty are probably the most puzzling results of this study.

THE GOOD SAMARITAN'S DILEMMA

For the most part, the political support for welfare reflects a generous motive to help those who are poor, single and with children. Welfare would provoke little controversy and benefits would probably be higher if these conditions were substantially accidental or temporary – the result, for example, of the death, disability or temporary unemployment of the major contributor to a family's income. That is why welfare was first promoted as a widow's allowance. That is why President Bill Clinton supports welfare as a safety net but not as a way of life. The moral dilemma, of course, is that welfare, like most forms of social insurance, increases the number of people with the insured condition. This study, for example, estimates that an increase in AFDC benefits per household by 1 per cent of average income would increase the number of welfare dependents by about 3.0 per cent and the number of births to single mothers by about 2.1 per cent.

There is no obvious resolution of this age-old dilemma, and I claim no special moral insight. The patterns of pathology associated with the current welfare system, however, no longer seem acceptable, not so much because of their fiscal cost but because of their malign effects. The welfare legislation that Congress recently approved will give the state governments a greater incentive and opportunity to experiment with different approaches to welfare. The effects of this major welfare reform are difficult to predict, because state governments will have more flexibility to set benefit rates and eligibility conditions and there are many types of exemptions from the remaining federal mandates. The most important change is probably the substitution of lump-sum payments to the states for the current system of matching grants; this will increase the marginal cost to state taxpayers from the current 20 to 50 per cent of AFDC benefits to 100 per cent.

This study suggests that the state governments may be best advised to focus welfare on the innocent – widows, the genetically or accidently disabled and children – and to set firm time limits on the welfare eligibility of others. Education and a strong general economic climate appear to be the most effective policy-responsive conditions to reduce the remaining pathologies. A blind compassion may be admirable but a knowledgeable compassion is twice blessed.

NOTES

1. The sample for this study is the average level of these six conditions in the 50 states plus the District of Columbia. All data are from the *Statistical Abstract of the United States* and are for 1992 unless specially noted.
2. My earlier study of 'Crime, police, and root causes' (Niskanen 1994) estimated that a 1 percentage point increase in the births to single mothers increased the violent crime rate by about 1.7 per cent. For the effect of illegitimacy on school performance, see Card (1981) and Hill and O'Neill (1994).
3. For an analysis of the total level of welfare benefits by state, see Tanner, Moore and Hartman (1995).
4. For statistical reasons, the dependent variables in each of these regressions (other than for violent crime) are of the form $\log[P/(100 - P)]$ where P is the percentage of the residents of each state that are subject to the specific pathology. The coefficients presented in Tables 17.1–3, thus, are transformations of the direct regression results at the sample means. The direct regression results are available from the author on request.
5. The substitution of the nonemployment rate for the church membership rate (not shown) yields a strong positive effect of nonemployment on poverty with only slightly weaker statistical results.

6. The substitution of the dependency rate for both the nonemployment rate and the education rate (not shown) yields a strong positive effect of the dependency rate on abortion with only slightly weaker statistical results.
7. This regression also includes the number of police per 10 000 residents (now shown) as a jointly determined control variable.
8. The substitution of the divorce rate for both average income and the metropolitan percentage (not shown) yields a strong positive effect of divorce on violent crime with only slightly weaker statistical results.

REFERENCES

Card, J.J. (1981), 'Long-term consequences for children of teenage parents', *Demography*, **18**, 137–56.
Hill, A.M. and J. O'Neill (1994), 'Family endowments and the achievement of young people with special reference to the underclass', *Journal of Human Resources*, Fall, 1090–91.
Niskanen, W.A. (1994), 'Crime, police, and root causes', *Cato Policy Analysis*, No. 218, Washington, DC: Cato Institute.
Roosevelt, F.D. (1938), *The Public Papers and Addresses of Franklin D. Roosevelt*, Vol. 4, *The Court Disapproves: 1935*, New York: Random House.
Tanner, M., S. Moore and D. Hartman (1995), 'The work vs. welfare trade-off', *Cato Policy Analysis*, No. 240, Washington, DC: Cato Institute.

PART II

Public Choice

18. The president is not our leader*

Any weekday morning in any metropolitan area, thousands of cars leave their many separate origins, mix with trucks and buses, and make their way to their many separate destinations. The driver of each car determines when to start, what route to take, and the tactical management of the car in traffic. The cars have been produced by many different companies in a number of different countries over a decade or so. The highways have been constructed by other companies, financed by a number of governments, over routes developed many years ago. The highways are maintained and patrolled by units from a number of local and state governments. Several radio announcers periodically broadcast weather and traffic conditions to augment the information on which the many individual decisions are based.

At the busiest intersection in the central city, where the traffic is too complex to manage by programmed signals, a traffic policeman performs his duties. Most of the time, he does his job so well that he is nearly invisible; drivers accept his necessary role, follow his signals, and are only vaguely aware of him as they pass. On occasion, some traffic policeman will perform his duties with such style and grace that drivers notice and appreciate his skills. Some reporter may even take his picture and write an article about him and his family. His style, however, is ancillary to his duties; it is a nice personal touch, but not essential. On occasion, some traffic policeman will not perform his duties very well. At such times, for a very short period, congestion will increase and there may be an accident. In a slightly longer period, traffic will flow around this intersection. If this problem develops again in the evening rush, the traffic policeman will probably be replaced and reassigned to some less important duty such as the vice squad. The traffic policemen who regularly man this position perform a valuable, limited function that is widely, if somewhat vaguely, appreciated by the local community.

As a rule, the urban traffic 'system' works very well. Most drivers arrive at their expected destination within a few minutes of their expected time. Some accidents occur, but most do not substantially reduce traffic

* Reprinted by permission from *Reason*, January 1979, pp. 33 and 36, Reason Foundation.

flow, and a pattern of accidents usually induces some corrective action. The cars, highways and traffic-management technology are continuously maintained and improved. Over time, traffic volume and average speed continue to increase and the accident rate continues to decline. Every driver has some complaints, usually about the behaviour of other drivers, but there are few obvious changes in the urban traffic system on which there would be a consensus.

HEADING UP TRAFFIC

Who directs or heads the urban traffic system? 'Nobody' is the simple answer. No one person directs any combination of the many functions involved in maintaining the flow of urban traffic. The many people involved do not derive the authority for their own actions from any one person. 'Everybody' is the more complex answer. Every person makes his or her own decisions to serve his or her own interests – subject to the available technology, the legal system and the necessary interactions forced by the inherent limitations of space and time.

The traffic policeman at the busiest intersection probably has a more important role in the urban traffic system than any other one person, but he affects only a small part of the total traffic. No one would seriously contend that he is the 'leader' of the urban traffic system. No one has ever even imagined that he is the leader of the urban community. No one, except maybe his children, would ever expect the traffic policeman to provide moral leadership. The urban community has every reason to expect the traffic policeman to do his limited job well, without burdening him with expectations about a role that is inconsistent with the nature of the urban traffic system and is beyond the capability of mere mortals.

The president of the United States is a traffic policeman. He directs the flow of traffic through the Oval Office, the busiest intersection of the federal government. This is an important, limited role. The president has a more important role than that of the urban traffic policeman because some very dangerous cargoes move through his intersection. Selection of the president is more important because it is more difficult to replace the incumbent for poor performance.

Some presidents, such as Calvin Coolidge, perform their role so well that they are almost invisible; other politicians and officials accept his necessary role, follow his signals, and are only vaguely aware of him as they pass. Some presidents, such as John F. Kennedy, perform their role with such style that academics and Sunday supplement writers fail to notice whether his performance is satisfactory. Some presidents, such as

Richard Nixon, do not perform their duties very well. For a short period, some important decisions will be delayed and some mistakes will be made on other important decisions. In the slightly longer period, more of the political traffic will flow around the Oval Office. If this problem persists, the incumbent president is replaced and reassigned to write his memoirs.

The president as a traffic policeman is a very different role from the president as the head of the federal government, the leader of the nation, and a moral example to the world. The president as a traffic policeman, however, is both more realistic and less dangerous than the contemporary image of this role. The urban traffic system is a better model of the federal government than the hierarchy suggested by the organization charts. The political traffic system involves thousands of people choosing their own routes towards their private ends. Most of this traffic flows over routes that do not pass through the president's intersection. The many politicians and officials derive the authority for their decisions, not from the president, but from the Constitution and legislation. Most of the decisions made within the federal political system are not significantly affected by the party or the personality of the president. Most decisions would be unchanged if a signature machine, following programmed rules, were substituted for a person as the president. In complex conditions, a good president, like a good traffic policeman, can make better decisions than can be programmed, but a bad president can make worse decisions. A president has about the same relative influence as a university president. No one has any illusions that a university president actually runs a university.

Where did the contemporary image of the president as a director, leader and moral teacher arise? The president is not even the head of the federal government; his only constitutional responsibilities are to be chief executive and commander of the armed forces. Members of Congress and the judiciary do not work for the president. There is no single head, or final arbiter, of the federal government.

The contemporary view that the president is the leader of the nation is even more absurd. Our complex national community is not a hierarchy. The federal government is not the superior institution in the nation, and its chief traffic policeman has no claim to be its leader.

The view that the president should provide moral guidance to the world is the most absurd. The process of selecting politicians does not reinforce moral character, and there is some evidence that this is a sub-ordinate trait of the most successful politicians. The US federal government, in any case, does not have a world mission; this government was established to 'secure the Blessings of Liberty to *ourselves* and *our* Posterity' (my emphasis).

Contemporary political writers have not served us very well. They have assumed, like medieval theologians, that the appearance of order proves the existence of a director. They have confused political science with political biography. The president has a difficult, important, limited role. We should not burden him with expectations that he will perform a role that is beyond human capabilities, a role that is both unnecessary and inconsistent with the character of American institutions. If we maintain these unrealistic expectations, every president will be perceived to be a failure, and some, by trying to do too much, will fail in the important role they could perform.

One gains a better sense of the nature of the federal government and the American community from the great paintings of Pieter Brueghel than from contemporary political writing. 'The Carrying of the Cross' and 'Landscape with the Fall of Icarus' are full of life and a sense of order, but one looks with difficulty to find the central heroic figure.

19. Economic and fiscal effects on the popular vote for the president*

THE CONFUSED POLITICS OF ECONOMICS

One of the central perceptions of social science is that the behaviour of a person in a specific role is strongly determined by the conditions affecting his or her survival in that role. Accordingly, one would expect federal economic and fiscal policy to be influenced by the relation between voting behaviour and economic conditions. This relation, however, is not well understood, and the academic literature has only confused the issue.

The 'party' hypothesis, most favoured by political scientists, states that the vote for the conservative party will increase with improvements in economic conditions, regardless of the party of the incumbent president. Scammon and Wattenberg, for example, write: 'As Democrats see it, Democratic prosperity tends to be counterproductive to what had become the Democratic Issue: middle-class poverty. As middle-class poverty disappeared, so did some of the Democratic appeal' (1970, p. 33). A confirmation of this hypothesis, of course, would have most serious implications for economic policy by a Democratic administration. The theory from which the hypothesis is derived, however, is not clear. If voters believe that economic policy can change economic conditions, why would people vote Republican if the economic policy of a Democratic administration has been unusually successful, and why would they vote for the Democratic candidate if the consequences of Democratic economic policy have been disastrous? One plausible theory that would lead to the party hypothesis is that voters believe that changes in economic conditions are random, that is, independent of economic policy, but that a Democratic administration is more likely to provide relief for whatever poverty, unemployment, or other problem that occurs. Maybe so. Several recent empirical studies of voting behaviour are based on this party hypothesis, but these studies neither develop the theory that would lead to

* Reprinted by permission from Douglas W. Rae and Theodore J. Eismeier (eds), *Public Policy and Public Choice*, Beverly Hills, CA: Sage Publications, 1979, pp. 93–120.

this hypothesis nor do they test this hypothesis against the major competing hypotheses (Arcellus and Meltzer 1975; Meltzer and Vellrath 1975).

The 'incumbency' hypothesis has been most carefully stated by Kramer:

> If the performance of the incumbent party is 'satisfactory' according to some simple standard, the voter votes to retain the incumbent party in office to enable it to continue its present policies; while if the incumbent's performance is not 'satisfactory,' the voter votes against the incumbent, to give the opposition party a chance to govern. (1971; p. 134)

Scammon and Wattenberg, perhaps unknowingly, also endorse the incumbency hypothesis:

> Politically, the Economic Issue tends to be a 'Ping-Pong' issue – that is,, when conditions are bad it is the fault of the people in power (a 'Ping') and works for the people out of power (a 'Pong'). (1970, pp. 282–3)

A confirmation of this hypothesis, at least, suggests that the political incentives of an administration of either party work in the right direction. Several recent studies of the vote for congressional candidates are based on this hypothesis (Kramer 1971; Lepper 1974).

Stigler has recently questioned both the existence and the rationality of any relation of voting behaviour to aggregate economic conditions, stating:

> It is foolish to sell one's stock in a corporation simply because that corporation has had recent reverses, and it is equally foolish to assume that the political fire is always more pleasant than the political frying pan. (1973, p. 165)

Economic conditions and economic policy, of course, are not perfectly correlated. It is, in some sense, unfair to vote against an administration that makes the best of bad circumstances, but it is not necessarily foolish. Stigler may be able to identify and directly evaluate past and prospective economic policy, but it seems implausible to attribute such information and expertise to most voters. Given the cost of acquiring information about economic policy and an understanding of the relation between economic conditions and economic policy, it may be rational for most voters to use a simple decision rule based on economic conditions. In any case, theory should not be judged by its plausibility; 'the proof is in the pudding'. Stigler's hypothesis is that there will be no observed relation between voting behaviour and economic conditions and this can be tested.

The combination of abundant argument and scanty evidence, unfortunately, has not achieved any consensus on the relation between voting behaviour and economic conditions. As a consequence, the administration has an understandable but unfortunate incentive to try everything, an incentive that increases as the election nears. Federal economic and budget analysts have had no counter to the assertions that arise from every quarter that the proposed policy or programme is 'necessary for political reasons'. Our understanding of the relations of economic conditions to economic policies is confused enough, but we do not appear to have the minimal understanding of the politics of economic conditions that is necessary to close a theory of economic policy.

APPROACH

For several years, I have been formulating and testing crude economic models of government organizations, starting with the characteristic production unit, the bureau (Niskanen 1971, 1975). More recently, I have been trying to understand the behaviour of the US presidency in terms of the conditions necessary to achieve and retain that position. This approach avoids speculation about the utility function or the psychohistory of specific presidents. As such, this approach does not address the difference in the behaviour among presidents, a topic that has been the focus of popular and sometimes academic fascination. In contrast, this approach focuses on the common behaviour of different men and 'teams' in the same position. An understanding of the presidency, as distinct from the president, I contend, must be based on an explanation of this common behaviour.

The immediate objective of this chapter is to identify the primary economic and fiscal conditions that affect the popular vote for the president, as a first step towards constructing a model of the behaviour of the presidency. In other words, I am trying to estimate a function that would be the maximand in a model of a vote-maximizing presidency or the reelection constraint in a model, such as suggested by Frey and Lau (1971), with a utility maximand. My own experience in the federal government suggests that a president has a large amount of discretion on economic policy that is consistent with his reelection. A vote-maximizing assumption, however, may still be sufficient to explain a president's behaviour. Popular approval may be an element in a president's utility function as well as in the reelection constraint. And the interests of other groups on which a president is dependent – members of his administration, members of his own party in Congress, and so on – are correlated with the popular vote for the president or the successor candidate of his party. For the time being, however, the choice between these two types of models can be deferred.

The seminal article by Kramer shaped the analysis presented in this chapter, although Kramer's work focused on the vote for Congress. My basic hypothesis, following Kramer, is that the popular vote for the president, among other things, is a referendum on the economic *performance* of the governing party. In effect, this hypothesis assumes that voter expectations about future performance are positively correlated with the recent performance. The popular vote for the candidate of the incumbent party in the next election, thus, should increase with an improvement in economic conditions.

A more specific formulation of the incumbency hypothesis can be developed from a model suggested by Lepper (1974). Consider an individual voter with a utility function of the following form:

$$U = a(Y - tX)^b X^c, \qquad (19.1)$$

in which Y is total real family income, X is total real federal expenditures, and t is the family share of the (present and future) taxes necessary to finance current federal expenditures. The marginal value of after-tax income and of total federal expenditures is assumed to be positive over the whole range of the variables.

Second, assume that the voter uses the following voting rule: vote for the candidate of the incumbent party if

$$\frac{U}{U_{-1}} \geq R \qquad (19.2)$$

and vote for the candidate of the major opposition party if

$$\frac{U}{U_{-1}} < R. \qquad (19.3)$$

The rationale for this voting rule follows. The voter believes that economic conditions are correlated with economic policy. The costs of acquiring information and expertise on economic policy, however, are higher than the benefits to him or her of using a more discriminating voting rule based directly on economic policy. The voter, thus, believes that the best indicator of future economic policy is some set of recent economic conditions. Moreover, the voter faces a binary choice, that is, he or she has the opportunity to vote for or against the candidate of the incumbent party but does not have the opportunity to register his or her degree of approval of the expected economic policies. For these conditions, he or she will vote for the candidate of the incumbent party if the recent changes in his or her utility are equal to or greater than could reasonably have been expected, and the value of R will reflect this threshold. This type of behaviour is best described, I believe, as utility-maximizing behaviour under binary-choice conditions rather than, as has been suggested by Kramer and Lepper, as 'satisficing' behaviour.

All voters are assumed to have the same general form of utility functions and to use the same type of voting rule. Voters differ in terms of their preferences for after-tax income and federal spending, their tax share, their expectations of feasible increases in their utility, and the strength of their party identification. A strong partisan of the incumbent party, for example, will have a lower value of R for any given expectation of economic conditions.

For each voter, then, equations (19.1), (19.2) and (19.3) define a boundary of Y and X values in the election year that are just sufficient to induce him or her to vote for the candidate of the incumbent party. Other terms in these boundary functions include values of Y and X in some prior year, the current and prior tax shares, the voter's preferences, and the value of R. The general forms of these implicit boundary functions for each voter, thus, are represented as follows:

$$v_i(YX : Y_{-1}, X_{-1}, t, t_{-1}, b, c, R). \tag{19.4}$$

These functions will be concave from below in the Y, X plane.[1] Figure 19.1 illustrates a set of boundary functions for a community of five voters.

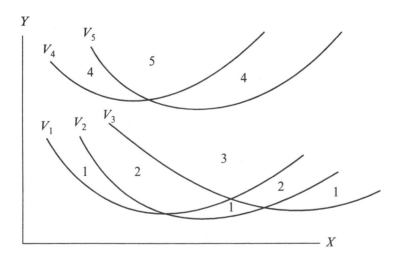

Figure 19.1 Individual voter preferences

Voters 1, 2 and 3, for example, might be partisans of the incumbent party who differ primarily in terms of their preferences and/or tax shares. Voters 4 and 5 demand a higher performance as a condition for voting for the candidate of the incumbent party. The numbers in Figure 19.1 indicate the number of votes a candidate of the incumbent party would receive for different combinations of Y and X. An incumbent party, for example, must generate Y, X combinations above the left section of the V_3 function and the right section of the V_1 function, given majority rule, to be returned to office. The aggregate equal vote functions are the lower bounds of those Y, X combinations that yield an equal number of votes. For a small number of voters with significantly different preferences and/or tax shares, the aggregate equal vote functions are not necessarily continuously concave, but a concave function should be a sufficient approximation for a large number of voters.

Figure 19.2 illustrates the conditions that would generate an observed relation between votes and economic conditions. The V functions are aggregate equal vote functions for different percentages of the popular vote for the candidate of the incumbent party. The F function represents the feasible combinations of Y and X in a given election year. This F function will be convex from below if federal spending has a net stimulative effect at low levels and a net disincentive effect at higher levels; in the absence of these two effects, the F function would be horizontal.

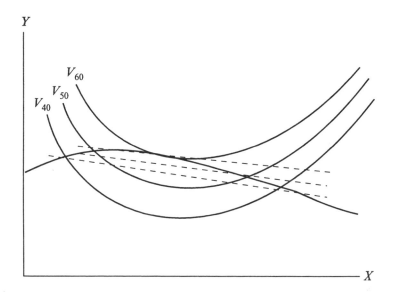

Figure 19.2 Votes and economic conditions

If the V and F functions are stable over elections and incumbent parties always maximize votes, only one combination of V, Y, X would be observed. In the case illustrated, the candidate of the incumbent party would always receive 60 per cent of the popular vote by a Y, X combination at the tangency of the V_{60} and F functions. For such a case, there would be no possibility of observing a relation between votes and economic conditions.

If the V and F functions are stable over elections and incumbent parties do not maximize votes, all of the observable combinations would be along the F function. A linear regression would yield the dashed lines connecting the intersection of the V functions with the F function, rather than the true concave V functions.

If the V functions are stable over elections and the incumbent party does not maximize votes, then shifts in the F function generate observations on the V functions. Only in this case would a single-equation estimate of the V, Y, X relation identify the aggregate relation between votes and economic conditions. For this chapter, no attempt is made to estimate the F function, and the characteristics of the full simultaneous equations system are not defined. It is important to identify other conditions that might shift the V function over elections, however, in order to stabilize this function relative to shifts in the F function. The single-equation estimates presented in the next section, thus, can be interpreted as approximations of the aggregate relation between votes and economic conditions only if the V function is stable relative to the F function *and* the administration either does not try or is not fully successful in achieving a Y, X combination that maximizes votes.

EMPIRICAL ANALYSIS[2]

The Sample

The full sample consists of observations for the 20 presidential election years from 1896 to 1972. The available economic data do not permit expansion of the sample to include elections prior to 1896, and the assumption of stable voting behaviour might be increasingly tenuous. In addition, a restricted set of estimates are made for two pairs of sub-samples. One pair of estimates is made for the ten elections from 1896 to 1932 and for the ten elections from 1936 to 1972 in order to test the stability of voting behaviour over time. Another pair of estimates is made for the ten elections for which the incumbent president was a Republican and for the ten elections in which the incumbent president was a

Democrat in order to test the stability of voting behaviour over parties of the incumbent president; these estimates provide a crude test of the relative strength of the incumbency and party hypotheses.

The Variables

Table 19.1 summarizes the variables included in test equations based on the full sample. Only a few of the independent variables are included in the test equations based on the small subsamples. A more complete description of the basic data is presented in the appendix.

The dependent variable Statistical criteria suggest the use of the logit transformation $\ln(I/1 - I)$ rather than I as the dependent variable. The logit form is unbounded, and the variance of the residuals is expected to be symmetrical and constant. Use of this form of the dependent variable has two other effects. Elections for which I is unusually low or high have a greater effect on the regression results. In addition, for

$$\ln(I/1 - I) = a + bX + \cdots + u$$

$$\varphi I/\varphi X = I(1 - I)b.$$

The differential effect of X on I, thus, is largest for close elections; where $I = (1 - I) = 0.5$, the effect is equal to 0.25 times the coefficient b. As the range of observed values of I is from 0.4 to 0.6, these several effects are not substantial, and the estimated partial derivatives are probably not much different from those from a test equation using I as the dependent variable.[3]

The dependent variable, with the exception of one election year, does not reflect the popular votes for candidates of minor parties. I do not know how to interpret these votes, for example, whether they should be regarded as part of the vote against the candidate of the incumbent party or as a vote against both major parties; my implicit assumption, by omitting these votes, is that they reflect a vote against both major parties. For the 1912 election, however, I included the votes for both William Taft and Theodore Roosevelt as votes for the candidate of the incumbent party (Taft). My treatment of minor party votes, thus, is neither consistent nor entirely satisfactory. One would have to sort out the issues in each election to interpret the preferences revealed by these minor party votes.

The economic variables Economic conditions are represented by five variables – real per capita net national product, the employment rate, the level of consumer prices, the level of real stock prices and the corporate bond rate – the first four of these variables expressed as the percentage change from the prior election year to the current election year. Although

Table 19.1 Test equation variables

Test variable			Basic variables		
Dependent					
$V = \ln\left(\dfrac{I}{1-I}\right)$			I	$=$	fraction of major party popular vote for candidate of the incumbent party
Economic					
DNP	$=$	$(\ln NP - \ln NP_{-4})$	NP	$=$	real per capita net national product
DER	$=$	$[\ln(1-U) - \ln(1-U_{-4})]$	U	$=$	unemployment rate, expressed as a fraction
DCP	$=$	$(\ln CP - \ln CP_{-4})$	CP	$=$	index of consumer prices
DSP	$=$	$(\ln SP - \ln SP_{-4})$	SP	$=$	real stock price index
CBR	$=$	corporate bond rate			
Fiscal					
DFX	$=$	$(\ln FX - \ln FX_{-4})$	FX	$=$	real per capita total federal expenditures
DFR	$=$	$(\ln FR - \ln FR_{-4})$	FR	$=$	real per capita total federal revenues
Political					
LVR	$=$	$\ln\left(\dfrac{I_{-4}}{1-I_{-4}}\right)$	I_{-4}	$=$	fraction of major party popular vote in prior election for candidate of current incumbent party
ID	$=$	1 if incumbent president is candidate, 0 otherwise			
Other					
WD	$=$	1 if election in war year, 0 otherwise			

there is no a priori reason to choose a four-year interval to evaluate the economic performance of the incumbent party, this seemed to be the most obvious simple approach without exploring complex lag relations. One might expect voters to weight recent economic conditions more than earlier conditions, but a prior test using one-year changes produced much weaker results.

Real per capita net national product is the broadest definition of average real output and is the best available approximation of the total real income of the median voter. The coefficient on this variable should be positive.

The *employment* rate, rather than the unemployment rate, is used to reflect an increasing effect at higher levels of unemployment. An increase in the employment rate from 0.88 to 0.94, for example, is a larger proportionate increase than from 0.94 to 0.97, although it represents the same proportionate reduction in the unemployment rate. Although those voters directly affected by unemployment are a small fraction of the electorate, the coefficient on the change in employment rate should be positive if some of the swing voters are unemployed or expect to be unemployed and/or if voters are benevolently concerned about the unemployed. This variable presents a substantial statistical problem, as it is highly correlated with the change in real per capita net national product ($r = 0.9$). For this reason, the estimated coefficients on these variables may be highly unstable in any test equation using both variables, and most of the test equations use only one or the other of these variables.

A change of consumer prices also represents a distributional effect, most strongly affecting those on fixed nominal incomes. Although those voters most strongly affected by a change in consumer prices also represent a small part of the electorate, the coefficient on this variable should be negative if some of those affected are swing voters and/or if other voters are benevolently concerned about their status.

The change of real stock prices is included to reflect two effects – a change in wealth and expectations about future economic conditions. Although a change in wealth may be concentrated among a few voters, stock prices also reflect more general expectations about future real conditions. The coefficient on this variable should be positive.

The corporate bond rate is included as an index of expected inflation. If voters are concerned about expected inflation, the coefficient on this variable should be negative.

The fiscal variables Federal fiscal conditions are represented by two variables – real per capita federal expenditures and real per capita tax revenues – both expressed as percentage changes from the prior election year. The structural relation between the popular vote for the candidate of the incumbent party and federal spending is convex from below: if most voters prefer an increase in federal spending, the popular vote for the candidate of the incumbent party should increase in response to a spending increase within this range. Conversely, if most voters would prefer a reduction in federal spending, the popular vote for the candidate of the incumbent party should decrease in response to an increase in federal spending. The test equations used in this analysis yield an estimate of the average relation between votes and the changes in federal spending in the observed range but do not permit an estimate of the aggregate vote-spending relation over a range in which the sign of the partial effect should change from positive to negative as federal spending increases. Conventional democratic theory suggests that the federal budget would be set at a level equal that maximizes the net benefits to the median voter, in which case the coefficient on the change in federal spending should not be significantly different from zero. My own work suggests that the combination of bureaucratic and legislative processes leads to a budget that is larger than that desired by the median voter, in which case the coefficient on this variable within the observed range should be negative (Niskanen 1975). This analysis provides a crude but important test of the general argument of my theory of bureaucracy and representative government.

If the federal budget was always balanced and/or voters perceived the total opportunity cost of deficits (in displaced investment and future taxes), the vote effect of federal fiscal conditions could be sufficiently represented by the effect of federal spending. The federal budget is never exactly balanced, of course, and voters may not perceive the opportunity cost of deficits. In this case, per capita federal tax revenues may be a better index of the perceived cost of federal activities. The test equations should probably include both the change in federal spending and the change in federal tax revenues, but the correlation of these two variables is too high to include both in the same regression. As a consequence, all of the test equations use only one or the other of these two variables, and the difference in the coefficients can be interpreted as an estimate of the amount of 'debt illusion' by voters.

The political variables Two variables are included to reflect political conditions. The vote ratio in the prior election is intended to reflect any residual net approval of the incumbent party. A coefficient on this variable that is not significantly different from zero suggests that each election is a new event, that is, there is complete depreciation of the prior vote ratio. A positive coefficient would indicate some residual net approval in the current election based on the prior vote ratio.

The incumbent dummy (no pun intended) provides for a crude test of the net advantage accruing to the incumbent as a candidate, as distinct from any advantage that accrues to another candidate of the incumbent party. This advantage probably derives from name recognition, sustained free access to the media, reduced uncertainty about personal behaviour, and so on. The cost of promoting a different candidate suggests that the sign of the coefficient on this dummy should be positive.

The war dummy A war dummy is included to test for voter response to a current war. One popular hypothesis is that voters rally around the flag, in which case the coefficient on this dummy should be positive. My own views are that wars gain a momentum that goes beyond the preferences of the median voter, in which case the coefficient on this dummy should be negative. It is important to recognize that the three presidential elections in war years – 1944, 1952, 1968 – were each in late years of the respective wars, and the findings may not apply to elections in an early year of a war.

Test Procedure

All of the test equations were estimated by ordinary least squares by a manual form of a backward step-wise procedure. The largest set of variables were included, and those for which the coefficients had the wrong sign or were insignificant were stepped-out.

Results from the Full Sample

Table 19.2 summarizes the regression estimates based on the full sample. The results for five pairs of equations are presented; the second equation in each pair differs from the first only in the substitution of *DFR* for *DFX*.

Economic conditions Changes in real per capita net national product have a strong, positive, and significant effect on the popular vote for the candidate of the incumbent party. This effect is consistently stronger and more significant in equations in which federal fiscal changes are represented by *DFR*. From the E10 column of Table 19.2, for example, a 10 per cent increase in real per capita net national product between election years appears to increase the popular vote for the candidate of the incumbent party by about 5.6 per cent of the total vote.

Controlling for *DNP*, the partial effects of changes in the employment rate are negative and insignificant. This result is consistent with Kramer's result that unemployment has no significant effect on the popular vote for Congress. The partial effects of changes in the consumer price level are inconsistent and insignificant; this result is not consistent with Stigler's estimate, based on a reworking of Kramer's data, that inflation has a small negative and significant effect. The apparent absence of distributional effects on the popular vote for the president suggests that a standard benefit–cost model may be sufficient to explain most decisions by the presidency, except when other groups, such as Congress, on which the president is dependent are concerned about these effects.

Deleting *DNP*, the effects of an increase in the employment rate are positive and the effects of an increase in consumer prices are negative. These results are consistent with Lepper's results, which also do not control for

Table 19.2 *Summary of full-sample estimates*

	E1	E2	E3	E4	E5	E6	E7	E8	E9	E10
Variables										
C	0.068	0.009	0.048	0.068	-0.433*	-0.168	-0.006	0.054	0.020	0.077
DNP	2.006*	2.349*			-0.926*	1.652*	0.968*	1.813*	1.511*	2.220*
DER	-0.842	-0.127	1.052	1.447						
DCP	-0.438	0.338	-0.307	-0.194						
DSP			0.328*	0.322*	0.300*	0.189	0.248*	0.135		
CBR					0.063*	0.032				
DFX	-0.316*		-0.077	-0.146	-0.185*		-0.206*		-0.313*	
DFR		-0.645*				-0.416		-0.474*		-0.572*
ID	0.073	0.110	0.201	0.188	0.279*	0.162	0.185*	0.110	0.143	0.077
LVR	0.039	0.155			0.273	0.129				
WD	-0.215	-0.347*	-0.122	-0.158	-0.104	-0.266	-0.166	-0.309*	-0.190	-0.351*
Test statistics										
R^2	0.795	0.873	0.721	0.725	0.854	0.888	0.796	0.881	0.732	0.864
SE	0.173	0.136	1.94	1.92	1.46	0.128	0.160	0.122	0.176	0.126
DW	1.804	2.212	1.639	1.655	2.309	1.961	1.738	1.741	1.885	2.077

Note: *Indicates coefficients with '*t*' of 2 or higher.

247

income changes, on the popular vote for Congress. In columns E3 and E4 of Table 19.2, however, *DER* serves only as a weak proxy for *DNP*. The effects of both *DER* and *DCP* are insignificant, and the significance of other coefficients and the regression are all reduced.

For about a decade, the standard example of the theory of economic policy has been the unemployment–inflation tradeoff. Subsequent analysis suggests that this example has no empirical content: not only has the Phillips curve proved to be unstable but it now appears that there are no partial effects of unemployment and inflation on the primary signals to which politicians respond, given the level of average real output. For whatever reasons, politicians may be compelled to act to reduce unemployment and/or inflation, but there do not appear to be any pressures operating through the popular vote to achieve results. Yet to be explained is why they express concern over these conditions.

An increase in real stock prices has a positive and generally significant effect on the popular vote for the candidate of the incumbent party. The extent to which this reflects a wealth effect and/or expectations of real conditions is not clear. The corporate bond rate has a small, positive, and sometimes significant effect; the sign of this effect is different from that expected, however, it is not clear what it reflects.

Fiscal conditions Changes in real per capita federal spending have a negative and highly significant effect on the popular vote for the candidate of the incumbent party. From column E9 of Table 19.2, for example, a 10 per cent increase in real per capita federal spending between election years appears to reduce the popular vote for the candidate of the incumbent party by about 0.8 per cent of the total vote. Changes in real per capita federal tax revenues has a stronger negative and highly significant effect. From E10, a 10 per cent increase in real per capita federal tax revenues appears to reduce the popular vote for the candidate of the incumbent party by about 1.4 per cent of the total vote. For each pair of test equations, the equation using *DFR* is more significant than that using *DFX* to represent federal fiscal conditions.

These fiscal effects have several interesting implications. Most important, federal budgets appear to have been significantly larger than the vote-maximizing level. An estimate of the *amount* of overspending can be derived by using both the *DNP* coefficient and the *DFX* (or *DFR*) coefficient. From E9, at the margin of 1974 conditions, an $8.86 billion increase in real net national product would be necessary to offset the votes lost by a $10 billion increase in real federal expenditures. This suggests that voters are willing to forgo only $1.14 billion of other uses of national output for federal services which cost $10 billion. From E10, an $11.3 billion increase in real net national product would be necessary to offset the votes lost by a $10 billion increase in real federal tax revenues. This suggests a negative value of $1.3 billion of the services financed by an additional $10 billion of federal tax revenues. Voters appear to be roughly indifferent to an increase in federal spending on revenues only if there is no reduction in the revenues available for other uses, and the marginal value of the aggregate package of federal services appears to be nearly zero. This result is most disturbing but should not be considered conclusive, without support from other forms of evidence. In addition, the significant difference between the *DFX* and *DFR* coefficients suggests that there is considerable 'debt illusion'; voters appear to be substantially more affected by changes in taxes than by changes in the total resource costs of federal services.

Political conditions Any vote advantage accruing to a candidate of the incumbent party who is not the incumbent president, for zero levels of other variables, is indicated by the constant term in each of the test equations. This effect appears to be consistently small and insignificant. An incumbent *party*, thus, does not appear to have any advantage in addition to that deriving from other conditions.

An incumbent *president* running for reelection, in contrast, appears to have a positive and sometimes significant advantage amounting to 3 to 6 per cent of the total vote.

Finally, there appears to be a small positive residual effect of the vote ratio in the prior election, but this effect is insignificant. This suggests that each election is essentially a new event that is determined by conditions since the prior election.

War A war appears to have a negative and marginally significant effect on the popular vote for the candidate of the incumbent party. This conclusion may apply only to those elections held in late years of a war. The magnitude of this effect appears to be 5 to 9 per cent of the total vote.

General All in all, the pattern that emerges is that of quite rational voters who vote for or against the candidate of the incumbent party based on a few objective conditions. Only three or four variables explain 80 to 90 per cent of the variance in the aggregate popular vote. A president is almost assured reelection if a moderate growth of real output can be maintained, if the growth of federal spending is restrained, and a war can be avoided or ended. Another candidate of the incumbent party would do almost as well. This conclusion is consistent with the long periods of one-party dominance of the presidency. Such vote behaviour should produce moderately responsive government as long as a president is concerned about reelection or the future of his party. The evidence suggests, however, that presidents do not maximize votes, and this can lead to nonoptimal levels of some major federal instruments. As long as general

economic conditions are improving and wars avoided, a package of conditions that includes an overly large federal budget is probably sufficient
for reelection. The major changes in the American presidency that are
suggested. by this analysis are to strengthen the incentives for the president to maximize the votes for himself or another candidate of his party
in the next election and to reduce the vote advantage of the incumbent.

Subsample Results

Table 19.3 presents the results based on two pairs of subsamples. The
small number of observations ($n = 10$) in each ot the subsamples requires
use of only the smallest set of variables. The subsample test equations use
only those variables included in column E10 of Table 19.2, and this full-
sample test equation is also presented for comparison.

Time Many people share a perception that voting behaviour has
changed substantially since the first years of the New Deal. According to
this perception, voters now demand better economic performance and
higher federal spending. And the presidency has become more personalized. Only the last of these hypotheses appears consistent with the results
presented in Table 19.3.

The vote effects of changes in real per capita net national product and
in real per capita federal tax revenues are almost identical in the
1896–1932 period and in the 1936–72 period, although the variance of
these effects is somewhat higher in the later period. Voters appear to have
reacted to general economic and fiscal changes in much the same way for
80 years.

The primary difference in vote behaviour between these two periods
appears to be the role of the party and the president. In the early period,
any candidate of the incumbent party appears to have had a significant
advantage equal to about 2 per cent of the total vote, and the president
did not have a significant incremental advantage as a candidate. In this
period, people seemed to be voting for or against the incumbent party
rather than for a specific candidate.

In the later period, a candidate of the incumbent party other than the
president does not seem to have a significant advantage, but the president as a candidate appears to have a significant advantage equal to
about 6 per cent of the total vote. One important effect of this advantage
of the president as a candidate is that it substantially increases a president's discretion on economic and fiscal policies consistent with his
reelection. The presidency appears to have been personalized in the past
40 years. It is plausible to attribute this effect to the increasing role of
radio and television in communicating the president's voice and image;

Table 19.3 Summary of subsample estimates

	Total	1896–1932	1936–1972	Republican	Democratic
Variables					
C	0.077	0.080	0.047	0.105	0.104
	(0.055)	(0.031)	(0.089)	(0.056)	(0.072)
DNP	2.220	2.131	2.190	2.169	2.453
	(0.273)	(0.231)	(0.809)	(0.441)	(0.368)
DFR	−0.572	−0.614	−0.619	−0.590	−0.660
	(0.084)	(0.064)	(0.285)	(0.226)	(0.097)
ID	0.077	—	0.207	—	0.119
	(0.066)		(0.102)		(0.079)
WD	−0.351		−0.327		−0.399
	(0.093)		(0.113)		(0.095)
Test statistics					
R^2	0.864	0.943	0.889	0.784	0.963
SE	0.126	0.097	0.109	0.152	0.082
DW	2.077	2.740	1.158	1.673	3.002
n	20	10	10	10	10

Note: Figures in parentheses are standard errors of the coefficients.

these media probably favour the president, relative to another candidate, because of the president's sustained free access to the media prior to the formal campaign.

It is not possible to test any difference in voter response to wars between these two periods because there were no wars during a presidential election year in the early period.

Party A crude test of the party hypothesis is provided by comparing voter behaviour in the ten elections for which the incumbent president was a Republican with voter behaviour in the ten elections in which the president was a Democrat. The party hypothesis suggests that the effect of increasing real per capita net national product on the popular vote for the candidate of the incumbent party is *negative* if the incumbent president is a Democrat. This test is crude because it is not possible to separate changes in voter behaviour over time from any effects of party. A Republican was president in seven out of the ten election years in the early period, and a Democrat was president in seven out of the ten years in the later period.

The results presented in Table 19.3 are strongly inconsistent with the party hypothesis. Again, the vote effects of changes in real per capita net national product and in real per capita federal tax revenues are almost identical between the two-party subsample test equations, and the effects are somewhat more significant in the Democratic subsample. These results should allay any concern that a Democratic president has a political incentive to promote a recession.

Several minor effects deserve mention: the incumbency effect appears to be specific to the late period rather than to Democratic candidates; the size and significance of the incumbency effect is much lower in the Democratic subsample than in the late period subsample. Again, it is not possible to test any party difference on the vote effect of a war, as there were no wars during election years in which the incumbent president was a Republican.

It may still be worthwhile to make other tests of the relative strength of the incumbency hypothesis and the party hypothesis. These results, however, suggest that the explanatory power of the party hypothesis is as weak as its plausibility.

NOTES

1. For given values of the other variables, the explicit iso-utility relation between Y and X, from equation (19.1) is the following:

$$Y = C(X)^{\frac{-c}{b}} + tX.$$

2. Seymour Neustein aided me with the empirical work for this chapter. Robert Raynsford, Thomas Linn, Robert Berry and Joe Litten contributed to earlier incarnations of this study. Their several contributions are gratefully acknowledged.
3. Lepper (1974) made estimates using both types of dependent variables and found that the estimated partial derivatives are almost identical.

REFERENCES

Arcellus, F. and A.H. Meltzer (1975), 'The effect of aggregate economic variables on congressional elections', *American Political Science Review*, **69**, 1232–9.
Frey, B. and L. Lau (1971), 'Ideology, public approval, and government behaviour', *Public Choice*, **10**, 21–39.
Kramer, G. (1971), 'Short-term fluctuations in U.S. voting behaviour 1896–1964', *American Political Science Review*, **65**, 131–43.
Lepper, S.J. (1974), 'Voting behavior and aggregate policy targets', *Public Choice*, **18**, 67–81.

Meltzer, A.H. and M. Vellrath (1975), 'The effects of economic policies on votes for the presidency: some evidence from recent elections', Paper read at the National Bureau of Economic Research Conference on Economic Analysis of Political Behavior, April.

Niskanen, W.A. (1971), *Bureaucracy and Representative Government*, Chicago: Aldine.

Niskanen, W.A. (1975), 'Bureaucracy and the interests of bureaucrats', Paper read at the National Bureau of Economic Research Conference on Economic Analysis of Political Behavior, April.

Scammon, R.M. and B.J. Wattenberg (1970), *The Real Majority*, New York: Coward McCann.

Stigler, G. (1973), 'General economic conditions and national elections', *American Economic Review*, **63**, 160–71.

APPENDIX 19A   VARIABLES AND DATA SOURCES

I   Popular vote for presidential candidate of incumbent party ÷ total popular vote for presidential candidates of major parties

1892–1896 *Historical Statistics* P–31
1900–1972 *Statistical Abstract* 1974 No. 680

NP   Net national product ÷ (estimated resident population *x* index of consumer prices)

Net national product

1892–1928 Kendrick, John (1961), *Productivity Trends in the U.S.* A–III
1932–1972 *1975 Economic Report of the President* C–14

Estimated resident population

1892–1896 *Historical Statistics* B–31
1900–1972 *Statistical Abstract 1974* No. 2

Consumer prices

1892–1912 *Historical Statistics* L–36
1916–1928 *Historical Statistics* L–41
1932–1972 *1975 Economic Report of the President* C–44

U   Unemployment ÷ total civilian labour force

1892–1896 Lebergott, Stanley (1964), *Manpower in economic Growth*, p. 522
1900–1928 *Historical Statistics* D–47
1932–1972 *1975 Economic Report of the President* C–24

SP   Stock price index ÷ index of consumer prices

Stock prices Standard and Poor's 500 Stock Index

1892–1936 *Historical Statistics* N–215
1940–1972 *1975 Economic Report of the President* C–81

CBR Moody's Aaa coporate bond yield

> 1892–1916 *Historical Statistics* (railroad bond rates)
> 1920–1928 *Historical Statistics*
> 1932–1972 *1975 Economic Report of the President* C–58

FX Total federal expenditures ÷ (estimated resident population x index of consumer prices)

Federal expenditures

1892–1972 *1972 Report of the Secretary of the Treasury*

FR Total federal tax revenues ÷ (estimated resident population ÷ index of consumer prices)

Federal revenues
1892–1972 *1972 Report of the Secretary of the Treasury*

20. The environmental consequences of majority rule*

INTRODUCTION

Our nation has only recently made a collective commitment to improving the quality of our physical environment. The major federal laws designed to improve the quality of the air, water and other physical elements of our 'common wealth' are less than five years old, and it is too early to evaluate the actual consequences of these laws. We can, however, anticipate some of the consequences of these and other environmental laws, based on the observed characteristics of our political decision processes and some of the component models from the developing theory of 'public choice'. The primary purpose of this chapter is to summarize some of the implications of these models for environmental policy.

Any social theory provides both a positive and normative perspective. If majority rule, for example, is an important characteristic of our political process, a model of majority rule decisions should explain some of the actual consequences of environmental law. In addition, if majority rule is considered a criterion for policy, these same models provide a standard against which actual policy can be judged. The environmental (and other) consequences of majority rule depend strongly on other characteristics of our political system – the range of authorized functions and processes, the division of authority within and between governments, the scope of the franchise, the level of political competition, and so on – and the effects of these characteristics will be considered.

In addition, one should recognize that the quality of the environment also depends on other forms of decision processes – the market, the legal system, small-number bargaining and social norms. Indeed, the most important environmental movement in western history – the enclosure movement – was an evolutionary response to market forces that was periodically obstructed by governments acting in response to distributional

---

* First published as University of California (Berkeley) Graduate School of Public Policy Working Paper No. 18, February 1975.

concerns. It is important to understand these other processes and the potential for substitution between the political and other processes, but that must be the basis for other discussions.

Environmental problems, by their nature, concern the allocation of the common wealth. This chapter addresses the consequences of majority rule for the allocation of the common wealth (1) within a single unit of government, (2) within a federal system of governments, and (3) over time. The conceptual models on which these implications are based have been developed by others, and my debt to them is acknowledged.

ALLOCATION WITHIN ONE GOVERNMENT UNIT

A government in which decisions are made by majority rule faces six generic issue-types, defined in terms of the distribution of preferences and the net benefits.[1] Table 20.1 summarizes these issue-types.

A 'majority favours' category should be interpreted as follows: some group consisting of more than one-half of the franchised voters in a specific government favours approval of the issue, given their preferences and the information available. And, similarly, for the other categories. Such groupings do not, by themselves, indicate the strength of the preferences of individual voters for or against each issue. The 'net benefits' column indicates whether the sum of the net benefits over all voters is positive or negative, the net benefits for each voter being the maximum amount (in some common metric, such as dollars) that the voter would be willing to pay to have the issue passed. Only issue-types A, B and C represent 'potential Pareto' changes, in that the net benefits to those who gain are larger than the amount necessary to compensate all those who would lose.

Table 20.1 Generic issue-types

Designator	Preference by each member		Net benefits
	Majority	Minority	
A	Favours	Favours	Positive
B	Favours	Opposes	Positive
C	Opposes	Favours	Positive
D	Favours	Opposes	Negative
E	Opposes	Favours	Negative
F	Opposes	Opposes	Negative

Issue-types A and F are almost trivial: A issues will pass and F issues will fail, given any decision rule. The only interesting implications of these issues involve the scope of the franchise. Some people within the jurisdiction of the specific government may not be franchised, and some people in the jurisdiction of other governments may be affected by the decision of the specific government. The interests of some non voters, such as the children of voters, may be adequately reflected in the preferences of voters, and no additional decision mechanism is necessary to represent their interest. In other cases, voters in one jurisdiction may be dependent on people in other jurisdictions on *other* issues; in such cases there is often an opportunity for small-number bargains that will lead the decisions in one government to reflect the concerns of people in another jurisdiction. If voters in one jurisdiction are not dependent on people outside the jurisdiction and/or bargaining costs are high, some common multi-issue government is necessary to allocate correctly any wealth that is common to several jurisdictions.

The interests of such groups as, say, people in the year 2200, blue whales, trees, and so on present a more complex conceptual problem. This is a trivial problem only if their interests are considered irrelevant (and by whom?); I am prepared to defend a present-focused, anthropocentric criterion for environmental policy, but this view is not uniformly shared. In any case, who speaks for them, and how? At best, the interests of these groups will be reflected in current policy only to the extent that they are shared by the current population, as they have no opportunity to bargain on their own behalf. More on the relations between the present and the future in the last section of this chapter.

In summary, issue-types A and F may be satisfactorily resolved, in terms of the interests of all affected groups, by majority rule (or any other decision rule) when only the voters are affected, when the voters have a strong benevolent relation to affected nonvoters, when voters are dependent on affected nonvoters on other issues and bargaining costs are low, or when there is a common multi-issue government in which all affected groups are represented. Voters in one jurisdiction are most likely to disregard the interests of other affected people for such issues as the use of the seas off some distant small nation whose trade or support in international organizations is not important.

Issue-types B and E, are more interesting. A popular referendum on B issues will usually pass, and a referendum on E issues will usually fail. It is less certain that a group of elected representatives will make the same decisions. In addition to majority rule, four characteristics of our political system sometimes affect the decisions on these issues.

Acquiring information about specific issues and organizing political activity are both costly. Mancur Olson has made a persuasive case that the costs of these activities to producers (including public employees) and polluters are often much lower than the costs to consumers of private and government services and passive users of the common wealth, primarily because such activities are a byproduct of group activity to promote more general producer and factor interests.[2] Since voter turnout and voter perceptions of their interests are partially dependent on such activities, such interest-group politics can even reverse referendum decisions on these issues.

Legislative decisions on these issues are sometimes affected by three other characteristics. First, a majority of legislators elected from equal-voter, single-member districts can be elected by a minority of the popular vote; in the limiting case, only $25 + \varepsilon$ per cent of the popular vote is necessary to elect a majority of legislators from such districts.[3] Empirical evidence suggests that only 40 per cent of the popular vote is necessary to elect a Democratic majority to the House of Representatives and, given the unequal population of the states, a smaller percentage is sufficient to elect a majority of the Senate.[4] This condition can lead to numerous decisions that would not be supported by a majority of all voters, even if every legislator always voted in the interests of a majority of his or her own constituency.

Second, a voter faces a 'package deal' in electing a representative; he or she will support a particular candidate if the *combination* of the issues the candidate promises to support, his or her expected efficacy, and other considerations is superior to that of the other candidate On any one issue, the elected representative may support a position favoured by a minority of his or her constituency. One would expect a legislator to reflect better the preferences of his or her constituency, the greater the perceived relative importance of the issue and the greater the political competition. A recent study, for example, found that municipal expenditures for water pollution abatement were strongly correlated with the plurality of local officials in the most recent election, suggesting that many officials, on this issue, voted for greater expenditures than would be approved by the voters.[5] Several other studies of the popular vote for Congress and the president suggest that most of the variance in votes can be explained by three or four variables reflecting aggregate economic and fiscal conditions and the large advantage of the incumbent.[6] We do not understand well the relation between voter preferences and the behaviour of elected officials but the available evidence suggests that these officials have considerable discretion on most issues.

And third, vote-trading within a legislature can sometimes reverse the decisions on these issues if the majority coalition includes different legislators on different issues. Some members of the minority on B issues, for example, may be in the majority on other issues; if they are more concerned about defeating the B issue than winning another issue, they may make their support of another issue dependent on the defeat of the B issue. A similar process can lead to approval of E issues. Since referenda are very costly or not possible on most issues, we cannot know all the B issues that fail to be approved by legislatures. Our statute books and government budgets, however, include many special interest subsidies, tax exemptions, tariffs and regulations that are clear examples of E issues that have been approved. It is not very helpful, unfortunately, to conclude that referenda are a better process to decide on B and E issues than by legislative vote unless there is some generally accepted way of sorting out issues among these categories before a decision is made.

My sense is that some of our major environmental laws are E issues. I doubt whether the Environmental Protection Agency (EPA) air quality standards would be supported by a majority of voters in many airsheds. Similarly, I doubt whether the water quality standards would be approved by a majority of voters in many watersheds if all of the tax costs of water pollution abatement in each watershed were borne by local voters. My guess is that these major laws are disequilibrium political outcomes that will be changed, initially by relaxing the administrative standards, in a direction that more clearly serves the interests of the majority.

Issue-types C and D are the most interesting. Referenda on C issues will usually fail, and referenda on D issues will usually pass; neither of these outcomes would be potential Pareto changes. A legislature, however, will often pass C issues and defeat D issues through a vote-trading process.[7] Some members of the minority on a C issue, for example, may be in the majority on a D issue. If they are more concerned about winning the C issue than winning the D issue, they may trade votes in a way that leads to both approval of the C issue and defeat of the D issue.

It is important to recognize that this outcome is possible only if there is a different majority on the two issues and the costs of arranging and enforcing a vote-trade are low. The potential for a 'tyranny of the majority' that so worried our founding fathers is greatest when the majority coalition is the same on many issues and the costs of vote-trading are high. The strong role of functional committees in contemporary legislatures has a number of effects that concerned those giants that created our political institutions. Committee membership is generally by self-selection; this has led to committees with a dominant coalition of advocates that is the same on most issues addressed by each committee. This has reduced the potential for vote-trading within a committee even though the costs of vote-trading within a committee are low. The structure of functional committees, in addition, has substantially increased the costs of vote-trading across committees and functions. On most issues, it is nearly impossible to offer substantial amendments on the floor or to force a bill to a floor vote without committee approval. This has led to a system of 'tyranny by committee majorities' that, in fact, represent select minorities of advocates for programmes in each functional area. This problem, of course, is reinforced by the advocacy role and power of monopoly bureaux in each functional area.[8] A substantial reorganization of the structure of our legislatures and bureaucracies – along the lines suggested by Edward Haefle, myself and others – may be necessary to achieve those outcomes sought by our founding fathers. At best, however. the superiority of representative government on C and D issues is partially offset by the potential for decisions that reflect neither majority preferences nor potential Pareto changes on B and E issues.

A recent environmental law in California illustrates the importance of resolving issue-types C and D in a representative assembly. A bill was submitted that would assert the State's right to easements on coastal land without compensation of the local private or public owners. This bill, almost surely a D issue, failed to pass the legislature on several occasions. The supporters of this proposal then organized an initiative campaign to place the issue on the 1972 ballot. This 'coastal initiative' passed by a significant margin. The coastal commissions established by this law have prohibited or halted almost all major development on this coastal land without compensation, even though the owners had met all local zoning and building code provisions. A constitutional challenge of this law is probable, given the strong language of the US Constitution prohibiting the 'taking' of property without compensation and the even more explicit language of the California Constitution prohibiting the 'taking or damage' of property without compensation. One cannot discern from the popular vote whether this law is a B or D issue. If compensation had been required, however, approval of the initiative would have indicated a B issue that had been incorrectly blocked by the legislature, and defeat would have indicated a D issue that had been correctly blocked by the legislature. Again, it is not very helpful to conclude that C and D issues are better resolved by a legislature than by popular vote unless there is some accepted criterion for sorting out issues among these categories; the provisions for compensation, however, may provide the requisite test.

ALLOCATION WITHIN A FEDERAL SYSTEM

Our nation was designed, in Madison's phrase, as 'a compound republic' a system of concurrent regimes. In Madison's conception,

> The federal and State governments are in fact but different agents and trustees of the people, constituted with different powers and designed for different purposes. ... The general government is not to be charged with the whole power of making and administering laws. Its jurisdiction is limited to certain enumerated objects, which concern all of the members of the republic, but which are not to be attained by the separate provision of any. The subordinate governments, which can extend their care to all those other objects which can be separately provided for, will retain their due authority and activity.[9]

Over the past two centuries, we have progressively drifted away from this conception towards a unitary republic, nowhere more than in environmental law, but we still retain the basic structure of a federal system. What can be said about the difference in the environmental consequences of majority rule in a unitary republic and a federal system?

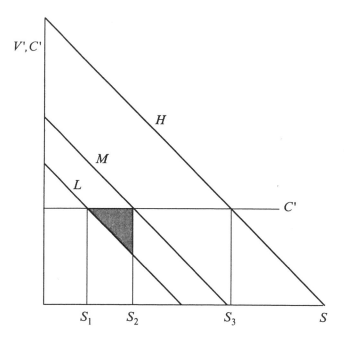

Figure 20.1 Demand differences

First consider the setting of ambient standards. Suppose the population consists of three groups with equal representation in the national government and that each group has a different demand for environmental quality. This condition is illustrated by Figure 20.1. Given a constant per capita marginal cost of achieving a range of ambient standards, the low-demand group would prefer S_1, the median-demand group would prefer S_2 and the high-demand group would prefer S_3. The only common standard that would be approved by a majority of the representatives would be S_2, the level preferred by the median-demand group; (in this case, vote-trading might move the standard towards S_3). If those people with different demands are randomly distributed across the states, roughly the same ambient standard S_2 would also be selected by majority rule in each state. In this case, effective representation and majority rule would lead to the same ambient standard whether selected by the national government or the states.

Next suppose that all of the people with low demands live in the same states, the median-demand group live in other states, and the high-demand group live in the remaining states. In this case, selection of ambient standards in each state would permit each group to select that standard it most prefers. Any national ambient standard above S_1 would cost the low-demand group (who generally have lower incomes) more than it is worth to them. If, for example, the national government selected a common ambient standard of S_2, the low-demand group would lose an amount indicated by the shaded triangle. In general, the loss due to a centralized decision will be a function of the sum of the squared differences between standards that would be set by the low-demand states and the national standard.[10] The high-demand states would select a higher standard S_3, so the common minimum ambient standard would not constrain them.

A similar situation arises even if the demands for environmental quality are uniform, but the costs of meeting the ambient standards differ among the states. This condition is illustrated by Figure 20.2. The population in high-cost states would prefer S_1 and the population in lower-cost states would prefer higher standards. Any national standard above S_1 would cost the population in the high-cost states more than it was worth to them. If, for example, the national government selected a common standard S_2 the population in the high-cost states would lose an amount indicated by the shaded triangle. Again, this amount will be a function of the sum of the squared differences between the standards that would be set in the high-cost states and the national standard. And the states that would select a higher standard are again not affected.

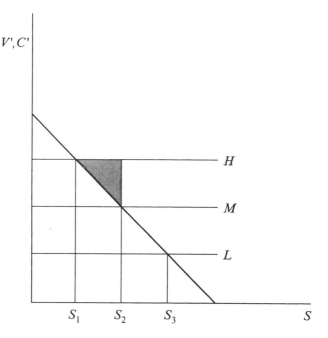

Figure 20.2 Cost differences

In general, national ambient standards will be either redundant or will be seriously discriminatory against the population in those states that would prefer a lower standard. In those cases where two or more states share a common airshed or water body, some small-number bargaining or interstate compact may be valuable, but this does not establish the case for national ambient standards. My sense is that our current national ambient standards do not reflect the preferences of any identifiable majority of the population.

A more complex problem arises when the per capita costs in one state are a function of decisions made for the whole nation. Such problems are most important for decisions on product standards, such as auto emission devices or phosphate controls, and on environmental research.

First consider a case in which the unit costs of some environmental device produced for each of three regional markets is somewhat higher than the unit cost of producing one device for the national market.[11] This small-economies-of-scale case is illustrated by Figure 20.3. Such devices can be produced for a unit cost of $C'(3)$ if one device is produced for each market and at a unit cost of $C'(1)$ if only one device is produced for the

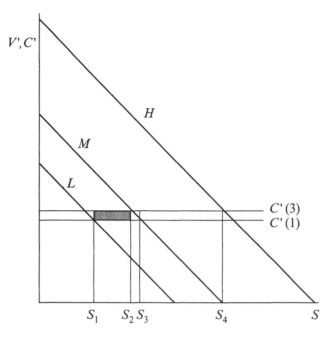

Figure 20.3 Small economies of scale

entire market. A device with a S_3 standard would be selected by majority rule (without vote-trading). This is not an efficient decision if *add-on* devices with higher standards can be purchased at a $C'(3)$ unit cost. The efficient solution is to select devices with an S_1 standard for all cars and to permit those states that prefer higher standards to require the necessary incremental devices. In comparison to the selection of a common S_3 standard, this adds a cost in the median-demand states indicated by the shaded area and a cost in the high-demand states equal to the shaded plus cross-hatched area, but these additional costs are lower than the additional costs in the low-demand states of meeting the S_3 standard. In this case, some vote-trading to offset the loss to the median-demand group is necessary to achieve the efficient solution. Whatever national standard is selected, it is most important to permit states to augment this standard, rejecting the argument of some producers of nationally-distributed products that this would be an unconstitutional restraint on interstate commerce. A common national product standard that is both a minimum and maximum would lead to substantial unnecessary costs to both those who would prefer lower and those who would prefer higher standards. In

such a small-economies-of-scale case, there is no obvious reason for any
national decision on product standards; state standards and a competitive
market for the devices are more likely to achieve the efficient solution
than a national political decision.

Next, consider a case in which the total costs of some environmental
activity, such as research on the effects of some residual, is invariant to
the number of people who value this activity. In this case, the per capita
costs of the activity are inversely proportional to the number of people
financing this activity. This condition is illustrated by Figure 20.4. The
per capita costs to each of three groups of states financing the activity
separately is $C'(3)$, and the per capita cost of a common research activity
financed by the national government is $C'(1)$. A majority rule decision
(without vote-trading) by the national government would lead to an S_1
level of this research activity. (In this case, vote-trading may lead to a
slightly higher level of this activity.) Although some people would prefer
a lower level and others a higher level at the $C'(1)$ cost, all groups prefer
the joint decision to a separate decision on this activity. Such environmental research on problems affecting the whole population is a 'pure
public good' and is one of the few areas of environmental policy, other

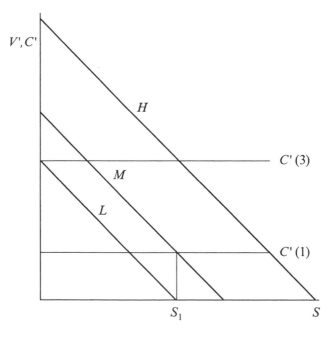

Figure 20.4 Large economies of scale

than facilitation of interstate and international compacts on large-area environmental problems, where national political decisions are clearly superior to the separate decisions of states.

In summary, reflecting on the discussions in the two preceding sections of this chapter the simple models of majority rule decisions do not seem to explain much of the current federal environmental laws and programmes. This suggests either that these simple models are seriously flawed or that the current laws represent a serious departure from the preferences of the majority. I am prepared to accept further analysis and evidence that would lead to either conclusion. For the present, my sense is that most current federal environmental law is best explained by special models of decisions by select minorities and the sociology of élite preferences. Majority rule, of course, is not the only or dominant criterion by which to judge policy; (it is interesting to note that the US Constitution does not specify any decision rule for the routine decisions of Congress). Nevertheless, my sense is that environmental policy that would better reflect majority preferences, in most cases, would also be more consistent with other broadly shared criteria.

ALLOCATION OVER TIME

The future is another dimension of our common wealth. Many private and public decisions we make today affect the character of our common future. The most important of these decisions concern the level and character of investment, including how much of the finite physical resources we save for future use.

The fundamental relation that affects the pattern of consumption of these resources over time is the following: 'The price of finite resources, net of marginal extraction costs, will increase at an annual rate equal to the general rate of return on investment, *gross* of taxes'.[12]

Our present tax structure includes large taxes on capital and the returns on capital. A corporate investment that yields a 10 per cent annual return before taxes, for example, yields about 5 per cent after corporate and property taxes. For an investor with a marginal personal income tax rate of 40 per cent, this investment yields only 3 per cent after all taxes. These taxes drive a large 'wedge' between savings and investment decisions. Most investments that are expected to yield less than a 10 per cent return will not be made, even though savers would be willing to accept any return over 3 per cent.

Among those investments that will not be made include the withholding of a larger amount of finite resources for future use. One direct consequence of our present tax structure is that the current price of these resources is lower and current consumption is higher than would be the case if our tax structure did not bias these savings and investment decisions.

As an illustration of these effects, I have calculated a plausible time path of world oil consumption over the next 100 years, based on a simple model using estimated parameters and probable demand conditions, for rates of return gross of taxes of 10 per cent and 5 per cent.[13] The time paths of world oil consumption per day for these two rates of return are illustrated by Figure 20.5.

The consumption path for a 10 per cent rate of return peaks in about 40 years and oil becomes prohibitively expensive in about 70 years. The consumption path for a 5 per cent rate of return would have lower near-term consumption but would permit a consumption growth for about 90 years and substantial consumption for several more decades. These consumption paths are *not* predictions; there are too many future conditions that will determine the actual path that cannot be now known. They represent, however, a choice that we can make; whatever the economic and technological conditions that will affect the demand and supply of

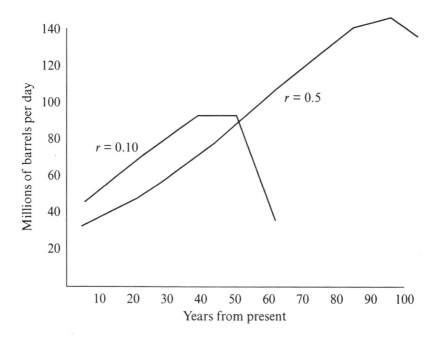

Figure 20.5 Plausible time paths of world oil consumption

oil and other energy sources, we can choose significantly different consumption paths depending on our choice of tax systems.

Our present tax system seems to be the consequence of myopic majority rule. On several major tax choices, we have placed the major tax burden on a minority of the population. Income from earnings is more evenly distributed than income from capital, and we have set much higher tax rates on the income from capital. Consumption is more evenly distributed than income, and we have made income the primary tax base. The major tax changes that would be necessary to reduce the bias against investment and conservation would be to eliminate the corporate income tax and to replace the income tax with a general consumption tax, maybe along the lines of the progressive consumption tax advocated by Nicholas Kaldor and Milton Friedman 30 years ago. For the present, we seem unwilling to even consider such changes because of a concern about the distributional consequences. A continued refusal to face up to the tax effects on our common future, however, may make the welfare state an end-state.

Our population may not be myopic. They may just not recognize the future consequences of actions that seem to be in the interest of the present majority. If this is the case, conservationists have a major educational task. I am less sanguine that a broader conservationist perspective will be translated into near-term policy. We have charged our political officials to look after our common future, but these officials seem to have a shorter time-horizon than the most of us. Some change in our political system is probably necessary to induce them to look beyond the next budget and the next election. As we move into the third century of the grandest experiment in human history, I can think of no more exciting or important challenge.

NOTES

1. This framework is adapted from that suggested by J. Ronnie Davis and Charles W. Meyer, 'Budget Size in a Democracy', *Theory of Public Choice*, Ann Arbor: University of Michigan Press, 1972.
2. Mancur Olson, *The Logic of Collective Action*, Cambridge, MA: Harvard University Press, 1965.
3. James M. Buchanan and Gordon Tullock, *The Calculus of Consent*, Ann Arbor: University of Michigan Press, 1962, Chapter 15.
4. Edward Tufte, 'The relationship between seats and votes in two-party systems', *American Political Science Review*, **67**, June 1973, 540–54.
5. Sharon Oster, 'Municipal expenditures for water pollution abatement', *Water Resources Research*, December 1977.
6. Gerald Kramer, 'Short-term fluctuations in U.S. voting behavior, 1896–1964', *American Political Science Review*, **65**, March 1971, 131–43; William Niskanen, 'Economic and

fiscal effects on the popular vote for president', in Douglas W. Rae and Theodore J. Eismeir (eds), *Public Policy and Public Choice*, Beverly Hills, CA: Sage Publications, 1979, 93–120. (See also Ch. 19 in this book.)
7. Among the best discussions of the vote-trading process are Buchanan and Tullock, *The Calculus of Consent*, Chapter 10, and Edward Haefle, *Representative Government and Environmental Management*, Baltimore: Johns Hopkins University Press, 1973.
8. William Niskanen, *Bureaucracy and Representative Government*, Chicago: Aldine Publishing Company, 1971.
9. *The Federalist Papers*, Modern Library Edition, pp. 304–82 .
10. This 'decentralization theorem', originally developed by Gordon Tullock and Yoram Barzel, is efficiently explained by Wallace Oates, *Fiscal Federalism*, New York: Harcourt Brace Jovanovich, Inc., 1972, pp. 54–63.
11. The general framework for analysing these issues is suggested by James Buchanan, 'Notes on a theory of socialism', *Public Choice*, **VIII**, Spring 1970, 29–43.
12. A more explicit form of this relation is the following:

$$\frac{1}{p}\frac{dp}{dt} = r + \frac{1}{p}\frac{dC}{dt} \ ,$$

where

p =   price of the resource, net of marginal extraction cost
t =   time
r =   general rate-of-return on investment, gross of taxes
C =   marginal extraction costs.

This relation, developed originally by Harold Hotelling, is efficiently explained by Orris C. Herfindahl and Allen V. Kneese, *Economic Theory of Natural Resources*, Columbus, Ohio: Charles Merrill Publishing Co., 1974, Chapter 4.
13. Details of this model are available from the author.

21. Progressive taxation and democratic government: a public choice analysis*

INTRODUCTION

Public choice analysis provides two important types of contributions to understanding and evaluating the tax and transfer systems in contemporary economies. *Positive* public choice analysis addresses such questions as 'What are the characteristics of the tax and transfer system that are likely to be selected by contemporary governments?'. *Normative* public choice addresses such questions as 'What characteristics of a tax and transfer system would commend unanimous consent, given the conditions and preferences of each person affected?' A comparison of the results of these two types of analyses, in turn, provides interesting insights about the direction of desirable changes in the tax and transfer system and about the effects of alternative constitutional rules on the behaviour of governments. This chapter summarizes the major contributions of public choice analysis to these types of questions and illustrates these contributions with some examples that are roughly representative of our contemporary economic and political systems. All of these major contributions and some of the examples were developed by other scholars. My own role is limited to developing the implications of these contributions for the specific issue of the structure of the tax and transfer system and some examples to illustrate these issues.

A POSITIVE ANALYSIS OF TAXES AND TRANSFERS

Contemporary economic and political systems use two types of currencies – money and votes. Since the distributions of money and votes among the population are quite different, one should expect a 'market' to develop in

* Reprinted by permission from Dieter Bös and Bernard Felderer (eds), *The Political Economy of Progressive Taxation*, Berlin: Springer-Verlag, 1989, pp. 1–17.

which some groups use their relative surplus of votes to acquire money and other groups use their relative surplus of money to influence votes.[1] The outcomes of this market, in turn, depend on whether the effective constitution permits such transactions, the decision rules in this market, and the relative distributions of money and votes. This chapter addresses only one side of this market, the use of votes to acquire money. Some other paper will have to summarize the similarly complex process by which groups use money to influence votes. Actual tax and transfer systems, in turn, will reflect the net outcome of these two processes.

A Simple Example of Majority Rule

Consider the following example to illustrate the process of using votes to acquire money:

- A polity consists of five groups, designated as A, B, C, D and E.
- Each group has an equal number of votes.
- The level of income before taxes and transfers of these groups is, respectively, 10, 20, 30, 40 and 50. (This corresponds roughly to the level and distribution of income per worker before taxes and transfers in the United States.)[2]
- Each group votes to maximize its own income after taxes and transfers. (In other words, no group has any net benevolence or malevolence with respect to other groups.)
- Any group may propose a change in taxes and transfers, and any proposal must be approved by a minimum of three of the five groups.
- And, for this example, the level of income before taxes and transfers in each group is given – in other words, is independent of the characteristics of the tax and transfer system.

Table 21.1 illustrates a representative set of outcomes for the conditions specific to this example. This set of outcomes reflects the standard results of this type of analysis. The more important lessons from this type of analysis are the following:

1. The effective coalition on each proposal will be the minimum necessary for approval, and the net gains to each group in the effective coalition will be equal.
2. All transfers will be received by one or more of the lower-income groups, and all taxes will be paid by one or more of the higher-income groups.
3. There is no dominant coalition, however, on taxes and transfers. In other words, some new coalition can gain approval to replace any existing distribution of taxes and transfers.[3]

Table 21.1 The distributional effects of majority rule

	A	B	C	D	E	
			Group			
	A	B	C	D	E	
Before taxes and transfers			Income			Transfer share (%)
	10	20	30	40	50	0.0
After taxes and transfers						
Coalition						
1. ABC	16	26	36	36	36	12.0
2. ADE	20	20	30	40	40	6.7
3. ABC	24	24	34	34	34	14.7
4. CDE	10	20	40	40	40	6.7
5. ABE	13.3	23.3	30	40	43.3	4.0
6. ABC	17.3	27.3	34	34	37.3	13.1
etc.						

4. Moreover, the level and distribution of taxes and transfers differs substantially among the set of viable proposals. Among the limited set of proposals described in Table 21.1, for example, the tax and transfer share of total income varies from 4 per cent to 14.7 per cent, and the amount of transfers to the lowest-income groups varies from 0 to 140 per cent of their income before transfers. (For comparison, it is interesting to note that total transfer payments in the United States are about 13 per cent of net national product, and the poor receive less than one-half of the total transfers.)

5. There is no consistent pattern of marginal tax rates. For this example, marginal tax rates range from zero to 100 per cent but, in some cases, the marginal tax rates on some lower-income groups are higher than on higher-income groups.

   Several obvious extensions of this analysis lead to some additional lessons.

6. An increase in the variance of income before taxes and transfers (or a broadening of the franchise to lower-income groups) increases the maximum level of taxes and transfers.

7. An increase in the share of votes required to approve a tax and transfer proposal reduces the maximum level of taxes and transfers. In the limit, the only transfers that would be approved by a rule of

unanimity would be those that reflect the marginal benevolence of the groups subject to taxes towards some other group.

8. The tax rates on any group are not likely to be higher than that which maximizes revenue from that group. Specifically, $t_i \leq (1 + S_i)^{-1}$, where S_i is the elasticity of supply of taxable income with respect to the income after taxes for group i.[4] The level of both taxes and transfers, thus, declines as function of the magnitude of these supply responses to the tax and transfer system.

9. The extension of this type of analysis to transfers-in-kind is relatively straightforward. Transfer recipients would prefer a transfer of money to a transfer of food, housing, medical care, and so on of equal cost to the groups subject to tax. One or more of the groups subject to tax, however, may prefer a transfer of goods or services to a transfer of money, either because they may be suppliers of that good or service, there may be some marginal external benefit of the consumption of these goods or services by the transfer recipients, or the groups subject to tax may have some paternalistic concern about the mix of consumption spending by the transfer recipients. In this case, the level of taxes and transfer payments will be higher than if only money transfers are considered, and some part of total transfers will be in the form of goods and services.

10. Most important, the tax and transfer system is likely to be stable only if it reflects some marginal benevolence by the groups subject to tax or if some group has the authority to set the voting agenda. A clever agenda-setter, by structuring the sequence of votes and determining when the voting will end, can achieve any outcome within a wide range. The specific tax and transfer system of a democratic government, thus, may depend on the objective of the specific group that has the authority to set the voting agenda.

An Agenda for Future Research

This simple analysis, of course, is not sufficient to explain all of the characteristics of actual tax and transfer systems. We observe, for example, that low-income groups pay some taxes and high-income groups receive some transfers. In addition, many tax rates appear to be lower than the revenue-maximizing rates. Actual tax and transfer systems are much more stable than indicated by this analysis, suggesting that the outcomes of the political process may be shaped by some amount of benevolence or by those who establish the voting agenda. And finally, the level of taxes and transfers has increased substantially over time and differs substantially among nations without any obvious change or difference in the structure of the political system.

In conclusion, a rather simple public choice analysis explains many of the characteristics of tax and transfer systems. Moreover, this analysis contributes to an understanding of the effects of changes in the economy and political system on the level and distribution of taxes and transfers. Much more work, however, needs to be done. The following types of questions deserve more analysis:

- What is the income distribution of voters?
- What are the effects of the various ways by which money is used to influence votes?
- How much does the actual level and distribution of tax and transfers reflect some benevolence?
- Who are the agenda-setters? What are their objectives? What are the effects of the specific rules used by legislatures affecting who is allowed to make a proposal, the sequence of votes, and the termination of voting on a specific issue?
- What explains the rapid growth of taxes and transfers in most countries in this century and the substantial differences that remain?

The first major contributions to economics were made about 200 years ago. The first major contributions to public choice were made in my adult life. There is reason to be pleased about how much public choice has accomplished. One should not be surprised about how much work remains to be done.

A NORMATIVE ANALYSIS OF TAXES AND TRANSFERS

The normative stream of public choice analysis builds on the same foundations as modern welfare economics. Every person is the only judge of his or her welfare. The welfare of individuals are not comparable by any common measure; in other words, the welfare of individuals may not be aggregated in any way to form a 'social welfare function'. And, most important, the consent of all individuals with the relevant rights is the only valid test of a 'social optimum'.

In fact, there are two normative streams of public choice analysis with quite different implications. One stream, which might best be described as 'libertarian', is premised on the consent of all persons to each transaction, assuming that each person knows his or her own conditions. The other stream, which is best described as 'constitutional' or 'contractarian', is premised on the consent of each person to the rules that will determine future transactions, assuming that the persons choosing these rules act as if they do not know their own conditions.

A Libertarian Perspective

Let us first evaluate the implications of the libertarian perspective for three types of goods and services provided by government–private goods, public goods and transfers. The distinctive assumption of the libertarian perspective is that each person has full rights to any property that he or she has acquired legally, including inheritance, even if there may have been a buccaneer somewhere in the family background. The only basis for coercive transfers consistent with this perspective would be to redistribute property that the directly-affected individual has acquired by illegal means.

Private goods

For various reasons, governments provide a range of 'private' goods and services. The appropriate distinction between private goods and public goods is not whether average costs decline with respect to the number of people served but whether there is an efficient means to exclude nonpaying beneficiaries. Indeed, private markets provide many types of goods and services subject to declining average costs if there is some means to charge a sufficient number of beneficiaries to cover total costs.

The pricing rules for private goods supplied by the government are the same as for efficient markets. All people should pay the same price or 'user fee' per unit of these goods provided, regardless of their income. For goods subject to declining average costs, some type of two-part pricing structure is preferable to a uniform price based on average costs. There is reason to question why the government should supply any of such goods, but there is no normative basis for using the tax structure to finance these goods. Although governments do not broadly follow these rules, this is a relatively straightforward analytic issue and need not be further elaborated.

Public goods

The level of public goods provided, by definition, is uniform across the affected population. The normative issue is to select a level of the public good and a distribution of tax shares that would be approved by unanimous consent. This issue, fortunately, was resolved some years ago.[5] The optimum level of public goods is that for which the sum of the marginal values across the population affected is equal to the unit price of the good. For individual demand functions of the form

$$Q = a_i y_i^b \, (s_i P)^{-c},$$

where Q is the common level of the public good, P is the unit price, y_i is the income of group i, and s_i is the share of taxes paid by group i, the optimum income elasticity of the tax share is

$$E(s_i : y_i) = \frac{b}{c}.$$

In other words, the income elasticity of tax shares that would be approved by every person is equal to the ratio of the income elasticity over the (absolute value of the) price elasticity of demand for the public good. The optimum tax structure is progressive if the income elasticity is higher than the price elasticity and is regressive in the opposite case. The optimum tax structure for the financing of public goods, thus, cannot be derived from first principles but must be derived from the revealed demand for these goods.

Table 21.2 provides an example of the optimum financing of public goods, for conditions that are roughly representative of those in the United States. The several available studies of the revealed demand for government services do not provide precise estimates of the relevant elasticities, but they each conclude that the income elasticity appears to be higher than the price elasticity for most such services.[6] For this example, the income elasticity of tax shares is assumed to be equal to 1.5.

For this, example (by design), the structure of average and marginal tax rates is quite similar to the combined structure of income and social security taxes in the United States following the federal Tax Reform Act of 1986. For several reasons, however, one should not conclude that the US tax system is close to optimum. The available studies, for example, indicate that the 'publicness' of most government services is very small. In this case the optimum tax structure would consist of equal payments for each person using these services plus a lower level or progressive taxation to finance the public component of these services. In addition, many government services are financed by other types of taxes or by borrowing, and the overall structure of taxes may not be appropriate to finance the combination of private goods, public goods and transfers provided by the government. The primary lesson of this example is that a progressive income tax may be appropriate to finance the public component of the services supplied by government, depending on the revealed demand for these services.

Table 21.2 The distribution of taxes for public goods

	A	B	C	D	E	Sum
			Group			
			Income			
	10	20	30	40	50	150
Tax share	0.035	0.0990	0.183	0.281	0.393	1.000
Taxes	1.054	2.951	5.477	8.433	11.785	30.691
Average tax rate	0.105	0.149	0.183	0.211	0.236	
Marginal tax rate	0.105	0.193	0.250	0.296	0.335	

Transfers

Given the libertarian perspective, what type and amount of transfers might be preferred by both the donors and recipients? Which of these transfers might best be provided by the government, specifically by the federal government?[7] The first implication of this approach is that the level and characteristics of transfers should be determined entirely by the preferences of the *donors*, as long as the recipients prefer some amount of some type of transfer to no transfer. Recipient preferences for higher income or that reflect malevolence or envy with respect to the donors are irrelevant, because they do not provide a basis for a unanimous consensus on transfers.

Donors may have one or more of three motives for transfers, and each of these motives implies a different type of transfer. Donors may have some amount of pure benevolence with respect to some other people, in which case the optimal type of transfer is a money transfer. Donors may be concerned about some condition specific to some other people – such as their income, health, education or housing – in which case the optimal form of transfer is that which maximizes the specific post-transfer condition of concern, such as a voucher based on earnings or on some measure of the consumption status of the recipient. And third, donors may be uncertain about their own future status, in which case the optimal transfer is a money transfer based on the insured condition, such as unemployment or disability.

In each case, for each donor, the optimal amount of the transfer is that for which the marginal value of the transfer *to the donor* is equal to the marginal value of the other goods and services forgone. The amount of preferred transfers is likely to increase with the income of the donor but may differ among donors of the same income. Such transfers will generally reduce the post-transfer variance of income or some measure of the consumption status within the affected population but will not necessarily be restricted to the poorest individuals.

Some amount of some types of consensual transfers will take place without any government action, especially within families and other small cohesive social units, or where there is an established market for some forms of insurance. The necessary case for government transfers must be based on one or another of the following two conditions:

- numerous potential recipients may be concerned about the condition of the same set of potential recipients, *or*
- there is no potential market for some forms of desired insurance.

The sufficient case for government transfers must be based on both of the following two conditions:

- the benefits to the potential donors must be incremental to the conditions resulting from the combination of recipient behaviour and any nongovernmental transfers including private insurance, *and*
- the incremental benefits to the potential donors must be higher than the transactions costs of an agreement among the donors through governmental processes, where these costs reflect the probability that the amount, nature and recipients of governmental transfers may not be the same as preferred by each donor.

The case for transfers by the federal government must meet each of the above conditions plus one other:

- the benefits to potential donors must be incremental to the conditions resulting from the combination of recipient behaviour, private transfers including insurance, and any transfers by state or local governments.

Federal transfers pose both advantages and disadvantages. Transfers by the federal government greatly reduce the 'free-rider problem' among potential donors, because the costs of emigration from the nation are much higher than from an individual state or local government. At the same time, the transactions costs of federal decisions are likely to be much higher because such decisions require agreement of a larger number of voters with less homogeneous preferences. The greater potential for federal transfers is not a sufficient basis for assuming that any specific transfer or welfare service should be provided by the federal government.

The implications of this perspective for the structure of governmental processes are interesting. Conceptually, all transfer programmes should be decided by referendum or by a separate legislature responsible only for each such programme, in each case for which only donors are allowed to vote. The voting process should be structured to minimize the incentive for 'strategic' voting. And the implicit decision rule, as in private charity organizations, is that all transfers should be approved by a unanimity of the donors (or their representatives) or, in the absence of unanimity, each donor must be allowed to withhold his or her contribution. One must shift to a constitutional perspective to understand the ethical basis for a decision rule on routine legislation that requires less than full unanimity.

It is instructive to compare the implications of this perspective with the current system of transfers and welfare services. This normative perspective is quite consistent with the current types of transfers and the distribution of recipients. We observe a combination of lump-sum money transfers, a substantial amount of conditional transfers of money or specific services, and several forms of social insurance. We also observe that the set of transfers leads to some reduction of the variance of post-transfer conditions, but that a substantial portion of transfers do not go to the pre-transfer poor. There is no clear case that the general character of the current transfer system is inconsistent with the preferences of most potential donors. For the most part, the case for change in the details of this system must be made on narrow technical grounds.

The major differences between the implications of this perspective and the current system concern the amount of transfers. The current system is the result of a political process that is influenced by the preferences of both donors and recipients, as well as by the political agents that structure the alternatives considered. The major results of the actual decision process are that the amount of transfers are larger than are preferred by the current donors and that the nature of the transfers are biased somewhat towards money transfers that are not conditional on the behaviour of the recipient.

The Constitutional Perspective

What are the characteristics of a 'fair' system of taxes and transfers?[8] All too often, contemporary political discussion of taxes and transfers uses a concept of fairness that provides little basis for agreement. A proposed change in taxes or transfers is usually considered fair only when it benefits one's own group or some other group that one favours, whether or not the existing taxes and transfers are fair by any standard. In this context, agreement is possible only if those who would pay higher taxes have some marginal benevolence towards those who would receive higher transfers (or lower taxes), given the existing distribution of income taxes and transfers. Given the existing welfare state, this set of consensual redistributions may be empty. In this context, without such marginal benevolence, any increase in taxes and transfers is a negative-sum game, a form of legalized theft, reducing the total income of the community. The conventional focus on the distributional outcomes of this game, thus, is not a sufficient basis for determining whether these outcomes are the results of a fair game.

This section develops a 'constitutional' or 'contractarian' approach to taxes and transfers. This approach, thus, addresses the rules by which taxes and transfers are determined, rather than the results of a specific application of these rules. The distinctive assumption of this approach is that each person selects the rules affecting later taxes and transfers without knowledge of his or her specific position in the post-constitutional distribution of natural endowments. Given a consensus on these rules, unanimous post-constitutional agreement is neither a necessary nor sufficient basis for judging the fairness of the outcomes. In this sense, this approach is strictly individualistic but not strictly libertarian. The promise of this approach is based on the prospect of a much broader consensus on these rules than on any post-constitutional decisions on policies affecting the distribution of income.

For each application of this approach, each person is assumed to have a general understanding of human behaviour, to know his or her own preferences, to know the post-constitutional distribution of natural endowments, but does not know his or her specific position in that distribution. In this sense, these examples are better characterized by uncertainty rather than ignorance. Two specific assumptions are common to both examples. For each individual, the utility of the outcomes is proportional to the square root of disposable income and leisure, but the general results are common to any utility function with a declining marginal utility of each condition.[9] The distribution of natural endowments is symmetric, with a mean of $30000 (about equal to the current US net national product per worker) in the first example, and a mean of to $15 per hour (equal to $30000 for a 2000-hour work year) in the second example.

Redistribution of unearned income

The first example demonstrates the effects of different distributions of future income, given that all income is 'manna', that is, independent of human effort.[10] Consider the following choice: an individual faces a lottery with a probability of 0.5 that he or she will receive an income of

$12000 or $48000. A certain income of $30000 would maximize utility. For the assumed utility function, however, he or she would prefer any certain income higher than $27000 to this lottery and would be willing to pay the state up to $3000 to provide the tax-transfer programme Table 21.3 summarizes the results of this type of choice for three distributions of natural income.

The first implication of this example is that the level of taxes and transfers increases with the variance of natural income. The first column, for example, could represent the choice of someone selecting social insurance for his or her own generation, and the third column the choice of the same person for the social insurance available to his or her distant grandchildren. This comparison illustrates that the difference between a person's decision on a law or on a constitutional rule is a matter of the degree of uncertainty, not a different type of analysis. A second implication is that the constitutional rule would limit the range of taxes and transfers but may not specify the amount. For the conditions of the second column, for example, taxes may range from $18000 to $21000, and transfers may range from $15000 to $18000, depending on the distribution of the social rent. This rent, which increases with the variance of natural income, could be used to administer the tax and transfer system, finance the protective and productive services of the state, increase transfers or reduce taxes, or could be wasted by the state or in various forms of rent-seeking activities – an allocation that cannot be fully determined at the constitutional stage. In this case, since all income is 'manna', disposable incomes would be equal.

For some, this example may suggest a constitutional basis for a substantial tax on estates. Such an interpretation, however, would be strictly correct only if the level and distribution of the estate is independent of the behaviour of those who inherit the estate. In many cases, of course, people 'earn' their inheritance by behaviour that serves the interests of

Table 21.3 Redistribution of unearned income

	Natural income ($)		
Minimum ($p = 0.5$)	20000	12000	6667
Maximum ($p = 0.5$)	40000	48000	53333
Equivalent income	29142	27000	24428
Minimum transfer	9142	15000	17761
Maximum tax	10858	21000	28905
Maximum rent	858	3000	5572

the person who leaves the estate. One should be cautious about weakening the ties that bind one generation to the next. Nevertheless, an inheritance is closer to 'manna' than is most other forms of wealth, and there may be a constitutional consensus on a higher relative tax rate on income from this source.

Redistribution of earned income
A second example demonstrates the characteristics of the optimal tax and transfer system, given that taxes and transfers affect the hours worked, for a specific distribution of natural wage rates.[11] For this example, the observed wage rate is equal to the natural wage rate; that is, taxes and transfers are assumed to affect hours worked but not the choice of jobs or an individual's investment in his or her skills. An individual faces a lottery with a 0.25 probability of a natural wage rate of $6, $12, $18 or $24 per hour. The sum of taxes and transfers in this case is assumed to be equal. That is, no amount of taxes are necessary to administer the tax and transfer system or any other role of the state. The annual earnings are based on 50 weeks of work per year. Table 21.4 summarizes the characteristics of the tax and transfer system that maximizes expected utility for these conditions.[12]

The most important implication of this example is that the marginal tax rates decline as a function of earnings. This induces those who are most skilled at generating earnings to work more than those who are less skilled and leads to a higher variance of earnings than of the natural wage rate. Average tax rates, of course, increase with earnings, reflecting the redistribution of income from higher-skilled workers. For this example, taxes and transfer payments are 5.4 per cent of total earnings and the variance of disposable income is only slightly less than the variance of natural wage rates.

Table 21.4 Redistribution of earned income

	Natural wage rate			
(p = 0.25 for each rate)	$6	$12	$18	$24
Hours worked per week	27.8	41.5	46.7	49.7
Annual earnings	8347	24900	42016	59584
Annual transfer or				
Taxes (–)	6095	1222	–2473	–4844
Average tax rate (%)	–73.0	–4.9	5.9	8.1
Marginal tax rate (%)	33.3	25.6	17.6	9.4
Annual disposable income	14442	26122	39543	54740

This example assumes that there is only one form of transfer payment, similar to a negative income tax. A superior solution may be to allow the poor to choose one of two forms of transfers, either a negative income tax or an earnings subsidy. Similar calculations for a tax and transfer system that includes an optional earnings subsidy, unfortunately, have not been developed.

Our current tax and transfer system differs from this example in two important ways. One, marginal tax rates are now much higher than the optimal rates for both the lowest- and highest-skilled workers. This reduces the hours worked and earnings of both of these groups. Second, government transfer payments in the United States are now about 13 per cent of net national product, an amount that would be appropriate only if the variance of natural wage rates is much higher than in this example.

Effects of other conditions
For the same distribution of natural wage rates and the same utility function, any change in other conditions would reduce the total amount of transfers relative to this example.[13] Any marginal tax rate on earnings leads people to choose more pleasurable jobs and to invest less in human skills. Any tax on the income from new investment would reduce the size of the complementary stock of physical capital. Any expenditure for the protective and productive services of the state would reduce the transfer share of total output. Any waste of resources by the state or in private rent-seeking activities would have a similar effect. Each of these probable conditions affecting the post-constitutional behaviour of people and governments is realistic to expect at the constitutional stage and would lead to a lower preferred amount of transfers. And finally, the potential to emigrate or, with others, to secede from a state would limit the total amount of coercive transfers from any one individual to the difference between the value of residence in one state and that in the next best alternative, minus the personal costs of moving or of participating in an effective secession. Such rights of emigration and secession, moreover, are likely to be secured by a constitutional consensus, because they are consistent with the principle of maximum compatible liberty.

Although some amount of social insurance may be preferred at the constitutional stage, a realistic consideration of these other conditions may lead to a set of constitutional rules that provides no authority for the redistribution of income. The US Constitution, for example, provides no explicit authority for federal welfare programmes. Article 1, Section 8 describes 18 specific powers of the federal government, without a hint that these powers authorize the redistribution of income or the provision of federal welfare services. The only constitutional authority for the modern welfare state rests on an obscure ruling by the Supreme Court in 1936, in United States v. Butler, that 'the power of Congress to authorize appropriations of public money for public purposes is not limited by direct grants of legislative power found in the Constitution'. Our contemporary national community may share a constitutional consensus for some amount of some types of federal transfers. Our contemporary problem, however, is that there are no effective constitutional limits on the amount or nature of these transfers.

CONCLUSION

Public choice analysis, in summary, provides both an explanation of why democratic governments choose a progressive tax structure and a normative basis for the system of taxes and transfers. The most intriguing conclusion of the positive analysis is that the relative stability of actual tax and transfer systems must reflect either some benevolence or the interests of some group that has the authority to set the voting agenda. The normative analysis of tax and transfer systems, in turn, leads to two intriguing conclusions. The optimal tax structure to finance public goods depends on the relative magnitude of the income and price elasticity of demand for these goods; given the crude available estimate of these two elasticities, some progression of both average and marginal tax rates to finance these goods appears to be appropriate. In addition, a constitutional perspective on tax and transfers concludes that some amount of transfers are desirable, average tax rates should increase with income, but that marginal tax rates to finance these transfers should decline over the whole income distribution.

Substantial additional development of these types of analyses would be desirable. Some development of positive public choice is necessary to expand some of the detailed characteristics of actual tax and transfer systems and, most important, why these systems have been relatively stable. Normative public choice should address the nature of the tax system that is appropriate to finance the combination of private goods, public goods and transfers provided by governments.

For those of you who are concerned, as I am, about the absolute size of the state in contemporary societies, I would counsel you not to focus your concern on the progressive tax system. The primary problem of contemporary government is that it does too much, not that it finances its activities, in part, by progressive taxes. My own normative analysis leads me to conclude that the optimal size of government would be smaller than we now observe but would include some amount of transfers targeted to the poor. This government, in turn, should probably be financed by a tax system in which average tax rates increase but marginal tax rates decline with income. The challenge is to design a set of constitutional rules that would make such a tax and transfer system more consistent with the outcomes of democratic processes.

NOTES

1. Several related activities also affect this market. Groups with a relative surplus of votes will attempt to constrain the use of money to influence votes. And groups with a relative surplus of money will attempt to discredit the processes by which people use votes to acquire money. In the spirit of truth in advertising, may I acknowledge that the Cato Institute is financed by this second type of group.
2. A careful reader will observe that the median income in this example is the same as the mean income. For all observed income distributions, in contrast, the median income is lower than the mean income. Since voting is a positive function of income, however, the median income of voters appears to be close to the mean income of the population.
3. The possibility that majority rule may lead to cycles was apparently first discovered by Condorcet in 1785. For an efficient summary of the conditions that lead to such cycles, see Mueller (1979), pp. 38–49.
4. This formula for the revenue-maximizing tax rate applies strictly only when there is only one source of income or if income from all sources is taxed at the same rate. If income from only one source is subject to tax, the revenue-maximizing tax rate is $t_i = (D + S_i / D (1 + S_i)$, where D is the (absolute value of the) elasticity of demand for the factor of production subject to tax.
5. This implication of the 'Lindahl' pricing rule for public goods was first brought to my attention by James Buchanan.
6. The technique for estimating the demand functions for public goods was independently developed and first applied by Borcherding and Deacon (1972) and Bergstrom and Goodman (1973). Both of these articles indicate that the income elasticity of the demand for public goods is higher than the (absolute value of the) price elasticity and that the degree of 'publicness' for most of these services is very low.
7. This 'libertarian' perspective on taxes and transfers is based on my development of the approach first developed by Hochman and Rodgers (1969).
8. This section is based on my own article, Niskanen (1986).
9. Specifically, $U(y, z) = y^{0.5} z^{0.5}$, where y is the level of income after taxes and transfers, and z is the hours of leisure.
10. This example was suggested, but not fully developed by Zeckhauser (1974).
11. This example was fully developed by Zeckhauser (1974). The numbers presented in Table 21.4 are only a scalar change of the Zeckhauser calculations plus the correction of one error.
12. For the symmetric distribution of natural wage rates in this example, the optimal level of taxes and transfers is approximated by the quadratic function

$$T = -a + bE - cE^2; \quad \frac{\partial T}{\partial E} \geq 0,$$

where T is the level of taxes (+) or transfers (−), and E is the observed level of earnings before taxes and transfers.
13. The qualitative effects of changing these other conditions on the level of taxes and transfers were developed by Buchanan (1985).

REFERENCES

Bergstrom, T.C and R.P. Goodman (1973), 'Private demands for public goods', *American Economic Review*, **63**, 280–96.

Borcherding, T.E. and R.T. Deacon (1972), 'The demand for the services of non-federal governments', *American Economic Review*, **62**, 891–901.

Buchanan, J. (1985), 'Coercive taxation in constitutional contract', Working paper, Center for Study of Public Choice, George Mason University.

Hochman, H.M. and J.D. Rodgers (1969), 'Pareto optimal redistribution', *American Economic Review*, **59**, 542–57.

Mueller, D. (1979), *Public Choice*, Cambridge: Cambridge University Press.

Niskanen, W.A. (1986), ' A constitutional approach to taxes and transfers', *Cato Journal*, **6** (1), 347–52.

Zeckhauser, R. (1974), 'Risk spending and distribution', in Harold Hochman and George Peterson (eds), *Redistribution and Public Choice*, New York: Columbia University Press, 206–28.

22. Public policy and the political process*

. . . social functions are usually the by-products, and private ambitions the ends, of human action. (Anthony Downs, *An Economic Theory of Democracy*)

. . . good law is a public good. That is why it is not produced. (David Friedman, *The Machinery of Freedom*)

PERSPECTIVES ON POLICY ANALYSIS

A spectre is haunting policy analysis – the spectre of the Decision Maker. In the 'ideal' form of the conventional myth, the policy analyst is portrayed as a modern Machiavelli advising some Pareto-optimizing Prince. The decision maker is assumed to be beneficent, omnipotent and all but omniscient – lacking only the specialized information that no one but the policy analyst can provide. All that stands between existing conditions and a state of bliss is the heroic act of placing the right analysis before the right decision maker. In the 'realistic' form of the conventional myth, any perceived failure of public policy is explained in terms of personal attributes of the decision maker: he or she is evil or stupid, he or she lacks sufficient authority, or he or she lacks sufficient information. The conventional prescription for good government is to select good men or women for public office and to give them the power and knowledge to do what they believe is in the public interest.

This summary, of course, is a caricature of the conventional view. This description exaggerates but efficiently illustrates the dominant themes of public administration literature from Confucius and Plato to Woodrow Wilson and McGeorge Bundy that are now enshrined in the policy research foundations and other institutional fortresses of the conventional wisdom. The conventional prescription for policy analysis is to identify the objective function of the decision maker, estimate the rela-

* Reprinted by permission from Svetozar Pejovich (ed.), *Governmental Controls and the Free Market*, College Station, Texas: Texas A&M University Press, 1975, pp. 73–93.

tion between action and outcome, and apply the calculus of efficiency. It is all very neat.

An alternative perspective is developing from the harsh lessons of recent history and a rediscovery of another intellectual tradition. For the moment, there is a widespread sense of public failure. Although there are some who maintain a 'devil' theory of public failure, many others have come to recognize that good men or women do not assure good government, high purpose does not assure good law, and good analysis does not assure good policy. This perspective, building on the critical insight of Adam Smith, explains public outcome as the byproducts of actions serving quite private purposes, as organized through the institutions and processes of government. Public failure is thus explained in terms of flaws in the institutions and processes that harness private purpose to public outcomes.

A theory of public outcomes must be based on the distinguishing characteristics of the structure of a specific government. A useful start is to exorcise the spectre of the Decision Maker. For any policy issue, even in the most authoritarian government, there is more than one decision maker. And the set of decision makers are seldom a 'team' in the sense that they have common objectives; there may be as many private purposes as the number of decision makers. No one of the decision makers may have the least personal concern about efficiency or the general welfare (whatever that means), particularly if achievement of these conditions requires any personal diligence and effort. As with businessmen or women, these conditions may be the consequences or his or her personal behaviour, but they are not the purpose of his or her behaviour. The demand for and use of policy analysis depends on how it serves the private purposes of the set of decision makers. And any social function served by policy analysis depends on how the institutions of government are organized to harness these private ends. If the structure of government has serious flaws, one should expect good analysis to have about the same effect as informing a polluter about external costs or arguing with a thief about the inefficiency of theft as a procedure for allocating resources. Many years ago, Madison warned us,

> If the impulse and the opportunity [for the pursuit of private interests at a cost to others] be suffered to coincide, we well know that neither moral nor religious motives can be relied on as an adequate control. They are not found to be such on the injustice and violence of individuals, and lose their efficacy in proportion to the number combined together, that is, in proportion as their efficacy becomes needful.[1]

The conventional model of government decision making and the role of the policy analyst fail to account for the structure of any actual government. The decision maker as a Pareto Prince is just not consistent with the facts.

A useful next step is to recognize that economists generally use different professional tools and perform different professional roles when they address government services than when the same economists analyse private goods and services. The characteristic approach to the analysis of government services is to focus on conditions specific to the producing unit. What is the demand for the service as revealed by the political system? What is the production function for the service? What are the budgetary costs of factors used to produce the service? Some constrained maximization technique is 'then used to calculate the set of factors and activities that minimizes the budgetary cost of meeting a given demand for the service. In this role, the economist is an estimator and a calculator, that is, a 'systems analyst' for the producing unit, taking as given the process by which demands and budgetary costs are established and government decisions are made.

The characteristic approach to the analysis of private goods and services, in contrast, is to focus on the market; that is, on conditions *external* to the producing unit: are there any Pareto-relevant external benefits or costs to the production or use of these products? Are there any taxes, subsidies, or price controls that distort product and factor prices? Are there any barriers to entry in the product and factor markets? Are any such barriers to entry the result of economies of scale relative to the size of the market, collusion among firms or factor owners, or government restrictions? Analysis of these conditions usually leads an economist to recommend government policies to change those market conditions: generalize property rights or use taxes or subsidies to internalize Pareto-relevant externalities; set prices for any related government services at marginal cost; remove the taxes, subsidies and price controls that distort product and factor prices; reduce barriers to entry by penalizing collusion, reducing tariffs and removing government entry controls; and so on. In this role an economist is a social scientist and leaves the systems analysis task to the consumers and producers.

The main argument of this chapter is that economists have a better opportunity to improve public policy by focusing on the political process instead of on specific policies – by asking the same type of questions and using the same type of professional tools that they bring to the analysis of private decisions. The body of this chapter summarizes my perception of those current characteristics of our political processes that most distort the decisions on public policy, given the best possible analyses of specific policies. My main conclusion is that changes in the market for government services in the United States, some quite recent, have substantially weakened the relationship between the personal interests of government officials and the shared concerns of the American population.

POLITICS AND POLICY

My personal perspectives on the major imperfections in the market for government services in the United States are summarized in this section. These perspectives are based on the developing economic theory of public choice, some scattered empirical evidence and personal reflection. After two centuries of our grand experiment with constitutional government, our contemporary political institutions do not seem to serve us very well, and the prospects for the near future are even less encouraging. We seem to be in the early stages of 'the English disease'. Although the facts are not complete, a preliminary diagnosis is more valuable than an autopsy.

The Federal Government

The 'economic constitution'

A political constitution, above all, is a set of rules that limit the nature and extent of decisions that may be made by government officials without widespread popular consent on a change in these rules. Some of these rules may be defined in a formal written constitution. Others that reflect the same extent of popular consent may be defined only in the form of an 'implicit constitution'. Three important rules in our 'economic constitution' have been substantially changed, most rapidly during the past decade, without any formal process of constitutional change: (1) the rule of the enumerated powers and the Tenth Amendment, (2) the fiscal rule, and (3) the monetary rule. In each case the actual process of change is clear: these three rules have collapsed under the weight of a massive assault by the intellectual community and the self-interest of government officials. For several decades most American intellectuals – and economists are the most culpable – have been iconoclasts.[2] A correct observation that such rules are not always optimal, given full information and benevolent officials, has led to an incorrect conclusion that such rules are unnecessary in a world of imperfect information and self-serving officials. And no new rules have been suggested that reflect the consensus for the old rules. Government officials have always had an incentive to break the rules. The intellectual assault on the 'economic constitution', however, provided the necessary opportunity.

Our formal Constitution (Article 1, Section 8) enumerates a small set of powers (or functions) that the federal government may perform. Madison forcefully summarized the sense of the constitutional convention concerning these powers:

> The powers delegated by the proposed Constitution to the Federal government are few and defined. Those which are to remain in the State governments are numerous and indefinite. The former will be exercised principally on external objects, as war, peace negotiation, and foreign commerce, with which last the power of taxation will, for the most part, be connected. The powers reserved to the several States will extend to all the objects which, in the ordinary course of affairs, concern the lives, liberties, and properties of the people, and the internal order, improvement, and prosperity of the State.[3]

Article Ten of the Bill of Rights, added later as a condition for approval of the Constitution, strengthens the limit on the federal powers: 'The powers not delegated to the United States by the Constitution, nor prohibited by it to the States, are reserved to the States respectively, or the people'. The nature and intent of these limits could hardly be clearer. And no subsequent amendment has added to the enumerated federal spending powers.

Today, however, most federal spending programme and many regulatory activities have no formal constitutional basis. Our implicit constitution has been changed to read: 'All powers not formally prohibited to it by the Constitution are reserved to the federal government'. Moreover, this change has been rapid and recent. Although there was some erosion in the Tenth Amendment from the earliest years, total domestic spending by the federal government seldom exceeded 1 per cent of national income through the 1920s. The New Deal, of course, was the first massive breach of this rule. It was rationalized as a temporary necessity in an economic crisis, and in fact many New Deal laws, programmes and agencies expired with the end of the depression. The few new federal functions introduced from World War II through the early 1960s were at least rationalized in terms of the enumerated powers: the interstate highway programme and the first federal education programmes were labelled and advertised as national security programmes. The Great Society began the first massive breach of this rule in a non crisis period. The flood of domestic legislation since 1965 does not even pay lip service to the enumerated powers. The Tenth Amendment, alas, is a dead letter.

Federal spending data reflect a massive change in the federal role in the postwar period. From fiscal year 1947 to fiscal year 1976, total federal spending for national defence, international affairs, veterans and interest increased at an annual rate of about 6 per cent. Total federal spending for all other functions increased at an annual rate of about 13 per cent. Federal spending for these other functions increased from about 17 per cent of total federal outlays to about 58 per cent of the current budget. Most of this current federal spending does not have an explicit constitutional basis in the enumerated powers. Moreover, these spending data do not reflect the recent large federal lending programme or the addition of federal regulatory powers affecting product and occupational safety and uses of the environment. For this chapter, my argument is not that these new federal functions are unworthy, but that the federal government has assumed these functions by an extraconstitutional process of constitutional change.

For most of American history, except during intermittent wars and economic crises, the federal budget had a small surplus. A fiscal rule that federal spending should normally be slightly less than tax revenues, I contend, was part of our implicit constitution through the early 1960s. For the first twenty years following World War II, a period that included a war and several minor recessions, the federal budget had a surplus in eleven years and a cumulative surplus over the period. ˙

After several decades of assault on the balanced budget rule by the economics community, however, a sceptical president endorsed the 'new economics'. A tax reduction was approved in 1964, a prosperous year that, maybe not coincidentally, was also an election year. The murmur of self-congratulation among economists was enough to disguise the fact that the new economics does not suggest a new fiscal rule. Once the nexus between federal spending and revenues was broken, no consensus developed on any other rule to constrain the level of spending and the deficit. In the following eleven years to fiscal year 1976, a period that also included a war and two recessions, the federal budget had a surplus in one year and a huge cumulative deficit over the period, and no balanced budget is in prospect. Some recent evidence confirms the politicians' perception that voters are more averse to tax increases than to deficits.[4] In that case, one should expect a positive relation between the increase in federal spending and the size of the deficit, and federal spending patterns are consistent with this relation. From fiscal year 1947 to fiscal year 1965, a balanced budget period, total federal spending increased at an average annual rate of about 8 per cent. In the later 'new economics' period through fiscal year 1976, federal spending increased at an average annual rate of about 11 per cent. The 1975 tax reduction will probably trigger a new round of demands for federal spending. A tax *increase*, however, by increasing the perceived tax price of federal services, may be a necessary part of a strategy to constrain total federal spending.

For most of American history, federal monetary authorities were constrained to maintain the money supply in some relation to the commodity reserves or, since the 1930s, to maintain the value of the dollar relative to major foreign currencies. These rules, I contend, were also part of our implicit constitution until very recent years. And these rules, however flawed, were usually effective. Price stability was the norm, and inflation was only a wartime condition.

A continuous assault on these rules, again by the economics community, led to a final rupture in 1971, when the dollar was devalued and later floated. Although some of the advocates of floating exchange rates have long promoted a rule of slow, steady monetary growth, there is no consensus on a new rule and apparently no incentive for the monetary authorities to follow a steady-growth rule. Again, the consequences of replacing an imperfect rule with no rule have been dramatic: in the period from 1947 to 1971, a period that included two wars, consumer prices increased at an average annual rate of 2.5 per cent. In the three years after 1971, a period in which the ending of a war and a subsequent recession should have reduced inflationary pressures, consumer prices increased at an average annual rate of 6.5 per cent. For the past several years, the alternative acceleration and braking of the monetary base have destroyed the stability of expectations that is a necessary condition for sustained economic growth. In a world of imperfect information and fallible authorities, any one of several old or new rules would perform better than no rule. A major criterion for choosing among these rules should be a broad consensus for the rule, and for this reason some old rule (such as maintaining exchange rates) may be preferred.

The presidency

The American presidency is a unique institution. In general, I believe, the presidency has served us rather well. Several developing conditions, however, appear to be reducing the responsiveness of the president to the interests of the population. In recent years, several political historians have rediscovered 'the imperial presidency', as if this condition were unnatural or specific to some recent incumbents. Such concerns usually fail to distinguish between the power of the presidency and the conditions affecting the use of power. The presidency was *designed* to be a powerful institution, and any significant reduction of the power of this office would require a restructuring of our whole political system. Several developing changes in the system for selecting candidates and electing presidents, I contend, are responsible for most of the perceived abuses of presidential power.

Our national parties perform only one important function – to select presidential candidates and to organize the campaign to elect a president.

The incentives and constraints facing individual party members, the relative role of the parties and other constitutions, and the 'market structures' of parties will determine how well this function is performed.

Some years ago Anthony Downs demonstrated that a system of two parties, *both* of which are motivated *only* by the rewards of office, will select candidates and implement policies that reflect the preferences of the median voter on every issue.[5] Both parties must be nonideological; that is, they must select candidates and policies to maximize votes. If the entry costs to a third party are high, this system breaks down if one party is an ideological party and the other party acts to maximize votes. (The 1964 and 1972 elections are examples of such a condition.) If both parties maintain their respective ideological and vote-maximizing behaviour, the vote-maximizing party will continue to win by policies that more nearly reflect the position of the ideological party than that of the median voter. The necessary conditions for restoring responsiveness to the median voter are the abandonment of ideology by the opposition party, a revision to ideology by the governing party, and/or the establishment of a major third party.

More recently, Donald Wittman demonstrated that a system of two parties, both of which are concerned only about governmental outcomes, will select candidates and policies that serve only the interests of party members.[6] The governing party selects a policy that maximizes the minimum benefits to its members, given a benefit-maximizing strategy by the opposition. The opposition, knowing the position of the governing party, selects a policy that maximises the benefits to its members. This game is played in front of, and with the nominal participation of other voters, but all of the benefits accrue to members of the two parties. This disturbing result is possible only if the entry costs to a third party are prohibitive.

A critical test of the Downs and Wittman models of party government has not been performed. A few observations, however, are suggestive. In the Downs model, the Republican party could assure a Democratic victory and Republican policies by choosing an ideological candidate and platform. In 1964, however, this Republican strategy led to the Great Society. In 1972 a similar strategy by the Democrats led to a Republican victory and Democratic policies, an outcome more consistent with the Downs model. The important point to explain is why recent presidents of both parties promote the policies of the Democratic party. The Wittman model suggests that these policies – a rapid growth of federal spending, special-interest programmes, regulation and deficits – serve the interests of the officials of both parties, and recent history seems to be more consistent with this model. The current move to establish a third party on the right, for example, suggests that both major parties are identified with policies to the left of the median voter. A perspective that arises from both models is that the responsiveness of party government is critically dependent on either (1) conditions that would lead *both* major parties to pursue vote-maximizing strategies or (2) low entry costs for a third party.

Several evolving conditions, I contend, have led to an erosion of a responsive two-party system. One such condition is the increase in the number of presidential primaries. At present, roughly one-half of the states hold presidential primaries, and for many years the winner of these primaries has won a first-ballot victory at the party conventions. This system strengthens the ideologues in both parties and reduces the opportunity for either party to select vote-maximizing candidates and policies. A second condition is the decline in patronage and the associated growth of the civil service. This change has both reduced the number of people for whom winning the election is very important and increased the number for whom the level of government spending is very important. A candidate cannot now afford to confront the civil service voting bloc on employment and salary issues because he or she cannot promise jobs to a comparable number of voters on the condition that he or she wins. These two twentieth-century 'good government' reforms appear both to have reduced the opportunities and the incentives for the major parties to maximize votes and to have increased the incentives to maximize the benefits to government outcomes, whoever wins the election. A reduction in the number of presidential primaries and the number of government positions filled by civil servants may be essential to assure a responsive presidency.

In the absence of a detailed study, I sense that the entry costs to a third party have always been high. The recent laws requiring contribution disclosure and limiting total campaign expenditures will surely increase these entry costs. Given present conditions, however, the potential entry of a third party is more important. The primary role of a third party is to discipline the governing party. This role is served by a credible threat to split the vote of the governing party. This strategy is risky, however, because a split of the majority can lead to the victory of a minority candidate and policies. The election of 1912 is an example. At present, the interests of those considering a third party on the right are probably best served by a visible effort to organize another party and select a credible candidate, followed by an offer to the Republican party to withdraw the third-party candidate in exchange for a public concession on several major substantive issues.[7] An actual third-party candidacy would probably be counterproductive to the interests of its supporters.

A president has a large vote advantage over any other candidate of the governing party. Some recent evidence, based on the popular vote for president from 1936 to 1972, suggests that this advantage is about 5 per cent of the total major-party vote.[8] Moreover, this advantage would be offset only by a 10 per cent decline in real per capita income between election years, a one-third increase in real per capita taxes, or a war. The effect of this advantage is that a president has a very large range of discretion on major policies that is consistent with his reelection. One or more substantial disasters is necessary to defeat a president who runs for reelection. In this century only William Taft and Herbert Hoover were defeated in such a race, the first because of a split in the Republican party and the second because of a major depression, and no incumbent president has been defeated since 1932.

The source of this advantage is less clear. Since there was no apparent advantage to the incumbent president before 1936, however, it is plausible to attribute this advantage to the president's use of the new media, radio and television. The president's sustained unpaid access to these media contrasts with the high cost of access by any other candidate. If this explanation is correct, the president's advantage could be reduced by restricting his unpaid access to national television to, say, four hours each year, making his party pay for any incremental coverage. Or maybe an incumbent president would be required to win two-thirds of the electoral college votes for reelection. These suggestions may sound rather extreme, but some change appears necessary to induce better performance during the president's first term.

What motivates a president during his second term? More importantly, what would motivate a president to maximize the votes for the successor candidate of his party? Presidents retire to a life of ease, and their reputation seems largely independent of the success of their party. Presidents 'use' their party to secure election and then depreciate the political capital of the party during their term in office. There is no political analogue of the stock option that would motivate presidents to be concerned about their party beyond their tenure in office. This end-period effect increases the president's discretion in his second term; governmental outcomes become entirely dependent on his personal motivations and the constraints on his power. One might hope that a president's concern for his reputation would be sufficient to motivate responsive behaviour, but this concern is a weak reed. Even Hoover's reputation was revived during his years as an elder statesman.

What might be done to reduce the president's discretion in his second term? The Twenty-second Amendment could be repealed, but that action would merely maintain the normal advantage of the incumbent and indefinitely defer the end-period effect. My preferences are to maintain a finite tenure but to use some other instrument to motivate a president to be concerned about the future interests of his party. My own suggestions – to make the president's pension, any public spending for a retirement staff or a library, and the like a function of the percentage of the popular vote for the successor candidates of his party – should not be regarded as entirely fanciful. My ultimate concern, of course, is not the interest of any specific party but the motivation of the president to maximize the votes for himself or a successor candidate of his party. Vote-maximizing behaviour (or profit-maximizing behaviour, for that matter) does not always serve the public interest, but there does not seem to be any feasible attractive alternative.

Congress

Congress is an assembly of special interests. Could it be otherwise? Probably not, as long as congressmen or women are elected from single-member geographic districts. The primary problem of Congress is that individual congressmen or women have very little incentive, inherent in their position, to promote good law. This problem is the result of a massive and pervasive free-rider phenomenon within Congress.

Consider the following example. A congressman or woman faces three actions that would use the same amount of his or her time, staff resources and political capital. One action would generate $2 million of net benefits in his district and net costs of $10 000 in the other 434 districts. The second action would generate $1 million of net benefits in every district. The third action, opposition to the first type of special-interest programme in another district, would save $10 000 in his or her district and 433 other districts and reduce the net benefits in one district by $2 million. The first action thus would generate aggregate net costs of $2.34 million, the second would generate aggregate net benefits of $435 million, and the third would generate aggregate net benefits of $2.34 million. In this case, an individual congressman or woman would choose only the first action. Moreover, he or she would continue to pursue such special-interest programmes for his or own district until the ratio of marginal benefits to his or her district over the marginal input of his or her own time and other resources is less than that for the second type of action.

From his or her perspective, the least productive use of his or her time would be to identify and to organize opposition to special-interest programmes that benefit another district. A recent statement by Senator Edmund Muskie reflects a perception of this problem: 'Everyone recognizes the need for oversight, but other things come along, and it gets pushed further and further down the ladder until it disappears'.[9] An average congressional district bears about 1/435 of total federal taxes. Even if there is a strong relation between district benefits and the perceived rewards of its congressmen or women there is probably no other role in American society for which the decision maker bears a smaller proportion of the total benefits and costs of his or her actions. Congressmen or women are quick to take credit, not surprisingly, for special-interest programmes for their district, for defence contracts awarded to firms in their district, and the like. No congressman or woman, to my knowledge, has ever held a press conference to announce that by great effort on his or her own part he or she has saved ten cents for every family in the United States.

What can be done about this massive free-rider problem? One change would be to elect congressmen or women by a national proportional- representation system, but this solution would be a larger change in our political system than we would be prepared to consider and would create other significant problems of its own. A more important change consistent with our political traditions would be to enforce a constitutional prohibition on special-interest programmes. One part of the free-rider problem is the result of the *combination* of geographic districts and special-interest programmes. A restriction of federal activities to those that promote 'the common Defense and the general Welfare of the United States', a radical eighteenth-century idea that is the only statement of objectives in our formal Constitution, would reduce much of this problem. Even if federal activities are limited to general-interest programmes and policies, there is still a problem of inducing efficient monitoring of federal activities. One suggestion is to create a special prize fund, administered by an independent body, that would provide campaign funds to those congressmen or women who are recognized as especially effective monitors. Another suggestion is to create incentives for private monitoring of federal activities by permitting class action suits against the government for demonstrably inefficient performance.[10] As H.L. Hunt is reported to have said, 'If this country is worth saving, it's worth saving at a profit'.[11] Some such changes are necessary to induce congressmen or women and private individuals to make a living and a reputation by promoting good law and good public performance.

Members of Congress have a great advantage over any other potential candidate. In 1970, for example, 95.2 per cent of incumbent candidates for the House of Representatives and 76.7 per cent of incumbent candidates for the Senate were reelected.[12] Most elections are not even close: only 13 per cent of the elections for both houses were decided by a vote margin of less than 5 per cent. For the House, the proportion of close races has declined from 22 per cent in 1958.[13] A recent study estimates the incumbent's advantage to be about 12 per cent of the major-party vote in House races and about 6.5 per cent in Senate races.[14] The same study estimates the advantage of an incumbent representative to be equivalent to about $200 000 of campaign spending and the advantage of an incumbent senator to be equivalent to about $80 000 per congressional district in his state. Moreover, the incumbent's advantage will surely be increased by the recent campaign finance laws, which establish limits on total campaign spending that are less than the average equivalent value of the incumbent's advantage and are less than was spent by *any* successful nonincumbent running against an incumbent in recent elections. Once elected, members of Congress have a longer potential tenure and as little discipline on their behaviour as, say, university professors.

This great advantage of incumbents has mixed effects. On the one hand it makes them less dependent on serving their district, so it increases their opportunity to serve the general interest. On the other hand, this advantage reduces their incentive to be responsive to anyone. We seem to have created an institution in which we are almost entirely dependent on the personal motivations of its members. This advantage makes a positive model of congressional behaviour more dependent on information about individual congressmen or women and the sociology of the Washington environment. As I observed in an earlier work, 'this condition provides an opportunity for both statesmanship and skullduggery but puts the voter in the unfortunate position of being absolutely dependent on the politician's motivations and the constraints on his power. And one man's statesmanship may be another man's skullduggery'.[15] I cannot believe that representative government with life tenure for our representatives serves the interests of the American population.

Incumbents pass the laws. For this reason it is not clear how or whether the incumbent's advantage can be reduced, and I have no clever solutions for this problem. The first types of actions that should be considered are to strip away those recent contributions to the incumbent's advantage: the campaign spending limits, the increase in the personal staffs, unpaid access to the mails and media, and so on. Public financing of campaigns, if authorized, should be restricted only to opposition candidates. Maybe a change in the election laws should be considered so that incumbents would be required to win, say, 60 per cent of the popular vote. In the absence of a national initiative process or a constitutional convention, however, I do not know how these changes can be effected.

Most of the work of Congress is performed in a set of permanent functional committees. Each of these committees has an effective monopoly of the right to formulate and review legislation and to monitor government performance in a specific area. In other words, no member of Congress, except under special circumstances, may submit a bill for a floor vote or undertake a major policy or programme review without approval of the relevant committee. Members serve on a committee for extended periods, and the composition of most committees does not change much faster than the composition of Congress. Moreover, several recent studies have confirmed that committee members generally have stronger preferences for government action in the area of the committee's responsibility than do other members of Congress.[16] Senator William Proxmire has observed that

> The net result of all of this . . . is that the committee structure develops a built-in bias towards higher budgets. Because the people who serve on each committee have an interest in seeing the budget for which they are responsible increase, they often fail to encourage careful evaluation and analysis of expenditures.[17]

The structure of committees in Congress, as it developed historically, was not anticipated by the constitutional founders, who feared the institutionalization of factions. Some system of committees, however, was made necessary by the growth in the size of Congress and the scale of government. The present system of monopoly committees, however, strengthens the committees relative to the body of Congress, effectively prohibits a fundamental review of existing legislation, reinforces the expansionary interests of the bureaux and regulatory commissions, and confirms the worst fears of the constitutional founders.

Several types of changes in the committee system should be considered. One type of change would maintain the structure of committees; members of Congress, however, would be randomly assigned and periodically reassigned. As an alternative, new bills would be randomly assigned among committees. This type of change would sacrifice the advantages of specialization and expertise to assure that committee decisions would be more representative of the interests of the whole Congress. A more fundamental change would be to allow competitive committees: any group, say 5 per cent, of the members could form an *ad hoc* committee to review a bill or the performance of a specific programme. This committee could then report a recommended bill for a floor vote, possibly in parallel with a bill reported out of the relevant permanent committee. The whole of Congress, then, could choose among two or more competing and considered proposals on a given issue. This proposal is more consistent with the type of *ad hoc* committee of the supporters of a bill that was envisioned by the constitutional founders. Changes in the rules of the House and Senate are sufficient to implement this plan. And most members of a Congress that is concerned about its efficacy may be willing to trade a reduction of their power in one area of federal activities for an increase in their power in all other areas. A fundamental reform of Congress is both feasible and necessary to preserve representative government.

The bureaucracy

The federal bureaucracy has become the fourth branch of government. Since I have written extensively about the problems of bureaucratic supply of government services,[18] this chapter summarizes only the main features of my analysis. The primary problems of the bureaucratic supply of government services are due to the structure of the bureaucracy and the incentives of bureaucrats.

Most bureaux are monopoly suppliers of the services they provide. Competition among bureaux is discouraged and is periodically reduced by organizational reforms that place competing bureaux in a common department. Any form of monopoly creates problems, but monopoly bureaux create distinctively different problems, primarily because bureau managers are not allowed to appropriate any part of the difference between available revenues and costs as personal income. In other words, there is no way to make a buck by maximizing the 'profits' of a bureau; this leads bureau managers to use up the potential monopoly profits in various forms of wasteful activity

The combination of these two conditions leads to the following major types of effects: (1) a bureau's budget will be larger than that desired by a majority of Congress; (2) some part of the excess budget will be used up in production inefficiency; that is, a given level of output will be produced at a higher-than-necessary cost; and (3) some part of the excess budget will be used up in oversupply of the service. Each of these effects, unfortunately, is reinforced by the review of a bureau's proposals and performance by a monopoly committee of Congress. Some empirical evidence is developing about the magnitude of each of these effects, and more needs to be done, but the direction of the effects is clear.

Every president in recent decades has been frustrated by the unresponsiveness and inefficiency of the bureaucracy; it is easy to understand why our chief executives have retreated to golf, images of a new frontier or great society, or foreign adventures. But they have been badly advised. We need more competition among bureaux, not less. We need a system of financial rewards for efficient management, not formula increases in civil service salaries. We need more contracting with private firms for the supply of government services, not the extension of government into private markets. We need more use of vouchers so that recipients can buy services where their interests are best served, not the proliferation of new monopoly bureaux.

State and Local Government

State and local governments manifest most of the types of imperfections shown by the federal political processes. The magnitude of the resulting problems, however, is much less than that of the federal government's problems for three reasons: the absolute level of state and local budgets is lower, the range of authorized functions is smaller, and people have an opportunity to 'vote with their feet', that is, to choose their government by commuting or moving. In general, the more restricted the range of governmental functions and the lower the cost of moving to another jurisdiction, the less important are the characteristics of political institutions and processes. For this reason, for example, consumers are essentially indifferent to the governance of private firms if they have an opportunity to buy other goods and services from a number of local suppliers. The imperfections in the 'market' for state and local government services are intermediate between those of the federal government and those of the commercial market. Most of these imperfections are similar to those of the federal government, they are important, and they deserve special study that is beyond the scope of this chapter. There are two specific and increasing flaws in the market for state and local government service, however, that deserve attention.

State and local governments are increasingly dependent on subventions from the federal government. From fiscal year 1947 to fiscal year 1976, federal grants increased from $1.7 billion to $50.8 billion, an increase from 11 per cent to about 22 per cent of total state and local revenues.[19] Another form of subvention that is not widely recognized as such is the deduction of most state and local taxes from income subject to federal taxes. For fiscal year 1976, personal deductions for state and local taxes on income, sales, property and gasoline are expected to reduce federal tax revenues by $16.1 billion.[20] Total federal subventions to state and local government are thus expected to be $66.9 billion, an amount that is nearly equal to the expected federal deficit.

The primary effect of these subventions is to reduce the perceived tax price of state and local government services. On the average, taxpayers pay state and local governments only 70 to 75 cents for each dollar of state and local spending. Thus, the quantity of state and local services they demand through the political process is increased and their concern about inefficiency in the supply of these services is reduced. It is not surprising why state and local officials are so enthusiastic about these subventions.

These subventions have several other corrosive effects. They have created the new fiscal distinction between 'hard' money and 'soft' money; 'hard' money, in this case, is money that is hard to raise from local taxpayers. The federal subventions have provided the leverage for increased federal intervention in state and local decisions and, to the same extent, have reduced the range of freedom of action by state and local officials. Some federal grants have had an equalizing effect on spending for specific services among state and local governments; this effect has reduced the incentive to vote by moving and the disciplinary effect of potential moves.

There is a conceptual case for federal grants when a substantial part of the benefits of services provided in one state or local government accrue to residents of other states. It is not generally recognized, however, that state and local governments also export a substantial part of their taxes to residents in other states. In the absence of any federal subventions, it is not at all clear that state and local governments would provide a lower-than-optimal level of services in terms of the interests of all affected people. The 'new federalism' has probably contributed to an erosion of a responsive and efficient federal system. Federal officials have an opportunity to improve both federal fiscal conditions and the efficiency of state and local governments by first eliminating both general revenue sharing and the deduction of state and local taxes; as these formula subventions have little appeal in Congress, this seems to be the obvious place to start to restore responsible fiscal federalism.

Counties, cities, school districts, and so on, are, in effect, state-chartered local government monopolies. In the past several decades, state governments have increased the monopoly power of local governments by a massive consolidation of school districts, restrictions of the opportunity to create new cities in unincorporated areas, effective prohibition of the opportunity to secede from an existing local government, and, more recently, encouragement of regional governments in major metropolitan areas. The increasing monopoly power of local government would be appropriate if there were strong economies of scale in the provision of local services and if the political process passed these economies through to residents in the form of superior services or lower taxes. The rhetoric of municipal reform usually emphasizes these potential economies of scale, but the accumulating evidence suggests the contrary: for all major municipal services, all of the potential economies of scale appear to be achieved by cities and school districts with ten thousand to one hundred thousand residents.[21] The monopoly power of larger local governments appears to be used up in the form of higher municipal salaries, wasteful activities and an erosion of service quality. Our major cities and school districts are too large for responsive and efficient government.

Municipal reformers often recommend that the state develop a 'blueprint' for the optimal structure of local government. This plan would surely make matters worse, however intelligent, informed, conscientious and benevolent the planners and legislators might be. The appropriate approach would be to let the structure of local government evolve in response to the preferences of each self-defined community. The first step would be to eliminate those provisions of the state municipal and education codes that effectively prohibit secession from existing units of government. The state should draw up some general guidelines for the process of local government formation and stand out of the way. The state guidelines should specify a voting rule to assure that there is a perceived community of interests and the rules for the disposition of existing assets and debt. The primary effect of this approach would be to permit people, with their neighbours, to have a local government of their own choosing without moving, and the primary beneficiaries would be spatially concentrated political minorities who have strong preferences to live in a given area. Mistakes will be made, but people are less likely to make mistakes in terms of their own interests than any elected or appointed body would be. Moreover, the right to make one's own mistakes is the essence of a society of free people. The experimentation and diversity that would result are the basis for the vitality of a federal system. State governments that face increasing demands to bail out our major cities may soon recognize this approach as a preferable alternative.

PROSPECT AND PROMISE

Two hundred years ago, Americans started a revolution to provide for a government of their own choosing. At that time they were more sure of the form of government they opposed than of the form of government they would put in its place. After eight weary years of war and several years of floundering, a constitutional convention, meeting independently from the Congress, worked out a form of government that has lasted to this day. That was no mean accomplishment. Our government is the oldest surviving republic in the world.

As of 1976, after eight weary years of war and several years of floundering, it is time to reconsider our form of government. Again there seems to be more consensus about the problems of our existing government than about the form of government that would serve us better, but this is the essential basis for an effective dialogue on constitutional change. Our bicentennial celebration could serve no greater purpose than to stimulate a broad national dialogue on the constitution for a society of free people. Although the world has changed a great deal in the past two centuries, it is not clear that our understanding about constitutional government has improved. May I suggest that we start a dialogue on constitutional change by reconsidering those major departures we have made from the formal Constitution developed in Philadelphia in that hot summer of 1787.

NOTES

1. Alexander Hamilton, John Jay and James Madison, *Federalist Papers*, ed. Clinton Rossiter, New York: New American Library, 1961, p. 81.
2. My dictionary defines this term as 'a breaker of icons, of images . . . one who attacks cherished beliefs as shams'.
3. Hamilton et al., *Federalist Papers*, pp. 292–3.
4. William A. Niskanen, 'Economic and fiscal effects on the popular vote for president', Working Paper No. 25, Berkeley: University of California Graduate School of Public Policy, May, 1974.
5. Anthony Downs, *An Economic Theory of Democracy*, Ann Arbor: University of Michigan Press, 1957, p. 29.
6. Donald Wittman, 'Parties as utility maximizers', *American Political Science Review*, June 1973, 490–98.
7. Naming the vice-presidential candidate should be considered a symbolic, not a substantive, issue.
8. Niskanen, 'Economic and fiscal effects on the popular vote'.
9. Allan Otten, 'Oversight', *Wall Street Journal*, 6 March 1975.
10. This prospect excites me. I would be among the first to organize a profit-seeking firm to monitor government performance if some such device for capturing part of the rewards of monitoring were authorized.
11. Quoted in David Friedman, *The Machinery of Freedom*, New York: Harper & Row, 1973, p. 222.
12. US Census Bureau, *Statistical Abstract of the United States*, Washington, DC: Government Printing Office, 1974, Table 694.
13. Edward Tufte, 'The relationship between seats and votes in two-party systems', *American Political Science Review*, June 1973, p. 550.
14. William Welch, 'The economics of campaign funds', *Public Choice*, Winter 1975, p. 95.
15. William A. Niskanen, *Bureaucracy and Representative Government*, Chicago: Aldine Publishing Co., 1971, p. 137.
16. David Rohde and Kenneth Shepsle, 'Democratic committee assignments in the House of Representatives', *American Political Science Review*, September 1973; and others.
17. US Congress, Joint Economic Committee, Subcommittee on Economy in Government, *The Analysis and Evaluation of Public Expenditure: The PPB System*, 91st Congress 1st sess., 1969.
18. Niskanen, *Bureaucracy and Representative Government*; and William A. Niskanen, 'Bureaucracy and the interests of bureaucrats', Working Paper No. 24, Berkeley: University of California Graduate School of Public Policy, April 1975.
19. US Office of the President, *Economic Report of the President*, Washington, DC: Government Printing Office, 1975.
20. US Department of the Budget, *Budget of the United States Government: Special Analysis*, Washington, DC: Government Printing Office, 1976.
21. For a summary of this evidence, see William A. Niskanen and Mickey Levy, 'Cities and schools: a case for community government in California', Working Paper No. 14, Berkeley: University of California Graduate School of Public Policy, June 1974.

23. The pathology of politics*

INTRODUCTION

Capitalism and Freedom,[1] as Milton Friedman explained in the preface, was the product of a series of lectures first given in 1956 and later extended and modified before publication in 1962. On rereading this book in 1972, one is struck by the sense of optimism about the ultimate power of ideas – a faith that closely reasoned argument, an accumulation of evidence and a leavening of wit will persuade most people and that our governmental processes will be responsive to their preferences. In some sense, this book is the 'last hurrah' of the English liberal tradition. Friedman's book is pervasively suspicious of government but its focus is a comparison of actual and desirable outcomes, not the governmental processes that do or would generate these outcomes.

As of 1972, it is difficult to maintain this optimism. *Capitalism and Freedom* has proved to be a near-perfect predictor: almost every type of governmental outcome Friedman criticized has been strengthened and extended.

1. Since 1962, total federal spending has increased from 21 per cent to 24 per cent of net national product, and total government spending has increased from 31 per cent to 35 per cent.
2. Monetary and fiscal policies are still conducted on a discretionary basis.
3. Federal regulation has been extended to a wide range of activities, including international capital flows, employment practices, occupational health and safety, and the uses of the environment.
4. The federal government has conducted a major war which, whatever its merits, was based on questionable constitutional authority.

* Reprinted by permission from Richard T. Seldon (ed.), *Capitalism and Freedom: Problems and Prospects*, Charlottesville, VA: University Press of Virginia, 1975, pp. 20–51.

   This chapter is the text of a paper presented at a conference in Charlottesville, Virginia on 20–21 October 1972 to reflect on the 10th anniversary of Milton Friedman's *Capitalism and Freedom*.

5. The federal government has imposed a comprehensive system of economic controls, in this unique case, after a substantial reduction of war expenditures.
6. The minimum wage has been periodically increased, and its coverage has been extended.
7. Rail passenger transportation has been nationalized.
8. The federal government now finances a substantial proportion of investment for such local services as water and sewerage, urban transportation, and the police.
9. Federal financing of both the demand and supply of health services has increased, and federal regulation has been extended to health services investment and entry control. The major pending health policy debate has been narrowed to the selection of one of several proposals for compulsory national health insurance.
   And so forth . . .

In two cases where Friedman's views have been influential – the negative income tax and tuition vouchers – the bureaucratic and political processes have warped his proposals almost beyond recognition. One important change, the elimination of military conscription in the summer of 1973, may be the sole victory for his reasoning.

One can only conclude, from the experience of the last decade, that Friedman was massively wrong, that the American population does not share his views about the characteristics of a good society or is not yet persuaded by his argument and evidence, or that our political processes do not accurately reflect the preferences of the American community. This chapter does not address either of the first two possible explanations of the general divergence of Friedman's views about desirable governmental outcomes and the experience of the past decade. In addition, I do not have a good understanding of the preferences of the American community or the processes of persuasion. My purpose is to focus on what I believe to be the dominant reason why our political processes, particularly at the federal level, do not reflect the preferences of the American community: the effective federal constitution, I believe, is continually being revised – not by a consensus of the American community but by a consensus of the slowly changing set of government officials.

ALTERNATIVE EXPLANATIONS OF THE GROWTH OF THE FEDERAL GOVERNMENT

As a background for addressing the main thesis of this chapter, it is useful to summarize and comment on a set of alternative explanations for the change in the scope of federal activities that do not premise a change in the effective constitution.

One possible explanation I have suggested earlier is that the income elasticity of demand for federal services is higher than the income elasticity of the effective tax schedule.[2] Although this explanation is consistent with the growth of the federal government during my lifetime, I am not satisfied with this explanation because it is not consistent with other evidence. For all of American history until the 1930s, total domestic spending by the federal government varied little from 1 per cent of national output. The state cross-section samples also suggest that the income elasticity of total state and local spending is around unity. International comparisons do not suggest any simple relation between the proportionate level of government spending and per capita income. Until some method is devised to determine the price and income elasticities of demand for federal services from time-series data, this explanation is not directly testable.[3]

A second explanation is that federal spending increases secularly with income but also increases with cyclical reductions in income. This would lead to a ratchet effect on federal spending, similar to the hypothesized Duesenberry effect on consumer expenditures. This explanation is not appealing (why should the effects of long- and short-run changes in income be asymmetric?) but is roughly consistent with the time-series evidence.

Burton Weisbrod, as part of a valuable developing study of the voluntary nonprofit sector, has suggested that the relative size of government will increase with a reduction of the variance of preferences for collective consumption goods, and his initial tests of this hypothesis, based on a time-series sample of total government domestic spending, are encouraging.[4] Are the preferences for collective goods really becoming more homogeneous, thus leading to an increase in the efficiency of government financing of collective goods relative to voluntary cooperative organizations? On the one hand, the stability of the income distribution and the increased racial consciousness suggest the negative. On the other hand, the combination of ubiquitous television and national programming, increased mobility, the reduction of immigration, and the nearly universal common experience of public education may have increased the homogeneity of the American community. Maybe.

Several possible reasons for a change in the scope of federal government are clearly contrary to the evidence. James M. Buchanan and Gordon Tullock contend that the efficiency and scope of collective activity will decline with an increase in the absolute size of the franchised population.[5] Others have suggested that increasing economies of scale and/or the increasing homogeneity of the population would increase the efficiency and scope of the federal government relative to the state and local governments.[6] The growth of the federal government since 1962, however, although it partially reflects an increasing involvement in state and local functions, has been associated with an increase of state and local spending (net of federal grants) from 10 per cent to 12 per cent of net national product. And the economies of scale explanation may suggest the opposite effect: for the same economies of scale, the absolute growth of the population and income in state and local governments should increase their efficiency and scope relative to the federal government.

Another explanation that I favour is that the recent prevalence of federal deficits has broken the nexus between marginal federal spending and marginal tax revenues.[7] If the cost of federal spending financed by deficits, as perceived by both federal officials and the population, is less than the cost of spending financed by taxes, one would expect a positive relation between the percentage increase in federal spending and the proportionate size of the deficit. This explanation appears to be consistent with both the recent and earlier evidence. Indeed, the major political discovery of the past few years may prove to be the low political cost of federal deficits.

A final explanation, of course, is Parkinson's law – that the relative size of government increases with time. This is not an explanation, however, but an observation; time is a dimension, not a cause, of human activity. For all that, a frustrating personal experience trying to test most of these hypotheses suggests that the variables that manifest the most stable relation with federal spending in the period since 1929 appear to be time and the level of overseas military personnel.

The rapid growth of the federal government – one of the most important phenomena of our time – is not well understood. No one of the above explanations, which assume a stable constitution within which the decisions on government spending are made, is very satisfactory or consistent with the range of evidence. Several groups, to my knowledge, are trying to identify the most important correlates of the growth of federal spending, however, and a sorting out of the conventional explanations of this phenomenon awaits completion of their work.[8]

THE PROCESSES OF CONSTITUTIONAL CHANGE

In another paper prepared for this conference, Buchanan (1975) comes perilously close to asserting that most actions of government, short of changing the constitution or the franchise, are Pareto optimal. In this case, unless the effective federal constitution has been changed without our consent, none of us has any basis for concern about the recent federal actions summarized by Buchanan. Whatever the merit of his analysis, my own thesis is that many of the above actions are the result of evolving changes in the effective federal constitution without our consent. These changes are a legitimate basis for our concern and the most important focus of public policy analysis. As his colleague Tullock has emphasized, the usual response to the threat by a robber (or a tax collector), 'Your money or your life', is Pareto optimal. The more important issue is whether both parties consented to the underlying arrangement.

My own interpretation of the processes of constitutional change developed as a consequence of several recent personal experiences. On first joining the Office of Management and Budget (OMB), I was dismayed to find that no one (other than my staff) ever questioned the constitutional basis for any proposal that came before us, and no proposal ever mentioned a constitutional basis for the recommended action. As late as the mid-1950s, when I first worked for the federal government, there was a general obligation to identify some constitutional basis for new programmes, however orthogonal to the basis for political support. (The national security rationale for the interstate highway programme and the materials stockpile programme come to mind.) At the present time, the enumerated functions do not even command lip service. The US Constitution, in terms of its effectiveness in constraining the functions of the federal government, is a dead letter. I believed at an earlier time that Albert Gallatin did this nation a great disservice by dissuading Thomas Jefferson from proposing the deletion of the general welfare clause; my recent experience suggests that advocates of new federal functions are just as agile without this crutch.

A second conclusion developed more slowly: Congress does not make decisions on most issues by majority rule. The body of Congress itself delegates most decisions to specialized committees and bureaux, even to individual congressmen or women and bureaucrats. The *modus operandi* of Congress is a division of labour based on reciprocal respect for the turf of other members on issues specially affecting their districts or a developed functional constituency. Sometimes this turf is successfully challenged by the larger body, but these challenges, in effect, are constitutional changes in the voting rule – changes made by Congress itself. This understanding led me to recall that the US Constitution, contrary to popular impression, does not specify any voting rule on routine decisions. From the very beginning of the federal government, Congress has selected its own voting rules. On many decisions, the effective passing coalition is a nonrandom minority of the members of Congress, the size of this effective coalition differing on each issue.

A third event helped focus my own developing perceptions. In May 1972 one of the more formidable personalities in the Nixon administration gave a pep talk to the OMB leadership, trying to convince us that a massive effort to reduce the federal budget is good politics, not in Washington, but in the country. He contended that most of the activities of the federal government are a result of the political processes in Washington, not a reflection of the preferences of the population, and that less than fifty of the hundreds of federal programmes would be approved by popular referenda. Most of the discussion at this fascinating session concerned the difficult issue of how to organize the executive budget process to protect it from Washington politics and to be more responsive to the preferences of the population.

A fourth event triggered the development of my new interpretation of the behaviour of representative government. Recently I sold my house in northern Virginia and purchased a house in Berkeley. Midway through the process of negotiating with my selling agent in Virginia, I recognized that my incentives were significantly different from those of my agent. My incentives were to maximize the difference between the sales price and selling costs. His incentives were to maximize the difference between his commission (a constant percentage of the sales price) and his selling costs. Moreover, there was no obvious way that I could structure my contract with the selling agent to induce him to act as if he were selling his own house. A negotiated change in neither the constant percentage sales commission (not legal in Virginia) nor the listed sales price (the primary dimension of bargaining) would have induced him to act in my interests. He wanted to list my house at a significantly lower price than that at which it eventually sold and, if I had fully delegated my decision to him, he would have sold it at this lower price. On reflection, the only obvious form of contract that would have induced him to act as if he were selling his own house would be one with a 100 per cent marginal commission, over some threshold sales price, permitting me to bargain with one or more agents over the threshold price they would accept, in other words, to grant the total residual equity in my house to the agent. Several people have suggested that my problems with my real estate agent confirmed their suspicion that I am a little slow. They point out, quite correctly, that an optimal contract can be written in terms of a percentage commission and a full specification of the selling activities. As an occasional house seller, however, I cannot determine the optimal combination of selling activities. Moreover, the standard real estate sales contract does not provide for specifying the selling activities, and I could not monitor some of these activities. The similar problems of determining, specifying and monitoring the activities by my political agents, of course, are much greater.

For all the problems of the standard real estate contract, this arrangement is far superior to the nature of my contract with my political agents. My real estate agent, for this transaction, had a constituency of one and not the effective coalition of a larger group of which I was a member. Moreover, I maintained the final decision whether to sell the house at a specific price, rather than delegating it to my representative. Both my real estate agent and my political agents, however, are my representatives only in that they act in their own interests as affected by the nature of my contractual relations with them. The most important characteristic of representative government is that one delegates the decisions on collective actions to someone else and this person faces rewards and costs that are different from those faced by the individuals he or she represents.

These several experiences led me to reread one other important book published in 1962, Buchanan and Tullock's *The Calculus of Consent*, the most thorough and incisive book yet on the 'logical foundations of constitutional democracy.'[9] This book represents a rediscovery and revival of a quite different tradition of political economy than does *Capitalism and Freedom*, one that is based on the writings of continental economists dating back into the nineteenth century and that focuses on the processes, rather than the outcomes, of government. The authors summarize this orientation in one sentence: 'It is almost completely meaningless to discuss seriously the appropriateness or the inappropriateness of shifting any particular activity from private to public organization without specifying carefully the rules for decision that are to be adopted if the shift is made' (p. 207). As a convert to this tradition, I had hoped that rereading this book would help explain why the federal government 'went to hell' in the 1960s (although now Buchanan seems to be telling us that nothing went wrong, merely that these actions are the natural dividends from our property in franchise).

The basic model of constitutional processes developed in *The Calculus of Consent* postulates that a group of people convene outside the normal political processes and agree on a constitution that prescribes the decision rules for the normal political processes. At the constitutional stage, a rule of unanimity is assumed. The fundamental hypothesis about the behaviour of the constitution makers is that they select those decision rules that minimize the sum of the external costs of private activities, the external costs of government activity, and the decision costs of government. My expressions for the general functions they describe are:

$$E = a(N - M)^b N^{-b} \quad a, b > 0 \qquad (23.1)$$

and

$$D = c(N - M)^{-d}N^e \quad c, d > 0, e \geq 1. \tag{23.2}$$

E is the sum of the external costs of private activity and the external costs of government activity. N is the number of people in the voting body, M is the minimum number of votes required to initiate government action and D is the total decision cost of government. External costs E are asserted to decline as a function of M and to be zero where $M = N$. Decision costs D are asserted to increase as a function of both M and N. The constitution makers select a value of M which minimizes

$$(E + D) = a(N - M)^b N^{-b} + c(N - M)^{-d}N^e. \tag{23.3}$$

The value of M that minimizes the above function is

$$M = N \left\{ 1 - \left(\frac{cd}{ab} \right)^{\left(\frac{1}{b+d} \right)} N^{\left[\left(\frac{b+e}{b+d} \right) - 1 \right]} \right\}, \tag{23.4}$$

and the voting rule is then,

$$\frac{M}{N} = \left\{ 1 - \left(\frac{cd}{ab} \right)^{\left(\frac{1}{b+d} \right)} N^{\left[\left(\frac{b+e}{b+d} \right) - 1 \right]} \right\} \tag{23.5}$$

The optimal proportion of the voting body required to initiate a government action is seen to be a positive function of external costs, a negative function of decision costs, and a negative function of the size of the voting body.

This is a powerful model for explaining the development of constitutions where the constitution makers and the voting group on routine government decisions are the same people. For example, it explains why most voting bodies require a higher proportion of the body to approve more important changes, why a lower proportion is accepted on more specialized and complex decisions, why the effective voting rule in the House is generally lower than in the Senate, and so on. This model is most directly applicable to direct democracy; indeed, this is the context in which the authors first describe the model.

This is also a powerful model for explaining the rules selected by a representative body for its own routine decisions. At this level, however, the important distinction is that the constitution they select for themselves is based on minimizing the sum of the external and decision costs that they bear, not those costs borne by those they represent. As in the example of a real estate agent, our political agents bear only a small proportion of the total external costs on the population, but they bear most of the decision costs of government. Our political agents face a much lower external cost function than that faced by their constituents; at a minimum, in comparison to function (23.1) above, the value of the parameter a facing the representatives is a small proportion of that faced by the population. Representative democracy shifts most, but not all, of the decision costs from the population to its political agents; as a consequence, the decision cost function faced by these representatives will also be different from that faced by their constituents but, in comparison to function (23.2) above, the value of the parameter c facing the representatives is a high proportion of that faced by the population. This major asymmetry will lead a representative body to select a voting rule with a much smaller proportion of the votes required for approval than the rule they would select if they bore the total costs.

The Buchanan and Tullock model breaks down, most importantly, when it is applied to representative democracy. More specifically, it does not provide either a normative or a positive basis for constitutions developed by one group to specify the decision rules and constraints for another group, acting as representatives of the first group. They explain the general use of representative bodies for the routine decisions of government as a means to economize on decision costs, and this is clearly correct. They also recognize that the reduction in decision costs achieved by delegating routine decisions to a representative body reduces the representativeness of that body, and thus increases the external costs to the population. For example, the effective coalition in a unicameral legislature operating by majority rule and consisting of representatives elected by a simple majority from single-member districts may represent only a carefully positioned $25 + \varepsilon$ per cent of the population. They fail to recognize, however, that the delegation of government decisions to other people, regardless of the representativeness of this body, will lead to selection of a different constitution, based on the costs that these other people bear. Only one form of contract between the individual and his or her political agent, one in which the individual grants all of the residual equity in his or her property in franchise to his or her agent, will make the marginal costs borne by the agent the same as would be borne by his or her constituent. The authors, however, do not explore the nature of this contract. The following sentences summarize their assumption and conclusion concerning the structure of control in representative democracy:

As a first approximation, let us suppose that the representatives, $r_1 \ldots r_5$, simply vote as the majority of their constituents want them to. . . . The result is not precisely equivalent to that which would be expected under direct bargaining, but we do not propose to consider the differences in this work. (pp. 220, 222)

This simple assumption is traditional and understandable, but it submerges one of the main issues of representative democracy – the nature of the contract between the individual and his or her political agent. Unfortunately, almost no one has seriously addressed this issue.[10]

The main thesis of this chapter is that the effective constitution of the federal government represents a continuously evolving consensus of those who have an effective vote in Washington at the time. Some of these people are elected, some are appointed, some are career federal employees, some are nominally outside of government. They select the effective constitution by processes described by the Buchanan–Tullock model but in response to the costs that they themselves bear. The population does not convene outside the normal political processes and agree on the constitution. The only constitutional choice I and most people ever make is the choice of where to live. Representative democracy is best described as government by the consent of the representatives. Once the choice of residence is made, the effective constitution selected by the representative body will reflect the consent of the governed only to the extent that the nature of the contract between the individual and his or her representative induces him or her to act as the individual would act in voting his or her own franchise.

SPECULATIONS ON THE REASONS FOR RECENT CHANGES IN THE EFFECTIVE CONSTITUTION

The Buchanan–Tullock model provides the essential framework for analysing the processes of constitutional change, but attention must be focused on the costs borne by those making these choices. As their model explains, a reduction in the external costs or an increase in decision costs facing the constitution makers will reduce the accepted proportion of the votes required to initiate government action. This, in turn, will lead to an increase in the number of special-interest programmes and the general size of government and to an increase in the external costs of government activities. As these latter conditions reflect the actual recent changes in the outcomes of the federal political processes, an identification of several objective conditions that may have changed the external and decision costs faced by federal officials would lend some credibility to my hypothesis that these changes in outcomes are, in part, due to changes in the effective constitution. What objective conditions in the past decade or so may have reduced the external costs or increased the decision costs faced by federal officials?

The most important evolving condition, I believe, that is weakening the nexus between the external costs faced by the population and those faced by their federal representatives is the increasing professionalization of politicians. The early historical models of representative democracy were groups of merchants who convened on occasion in town councils to further their collective interests as merchants and groups of farmers who convened every winter or so as state legislatures to further their collective interests as farmers. Most of the representatives were occasional representatives. Most of their time, their income, and the social conditions that influenced their behaviour were related to their trade and their home community. Under these conditions, a representative is more likely to act as if he or she is a subject of government rather than as a continuing element of the representative body. The income from serving as a representative was nominal, the entry cost of potential new representatives was low, and there was a substantial turnover of representatives.

The professionalization of politicians has been increasing for a long time, of course, but several events of the past fifteen years probably accelerated this trend. A rapid increase in government salaries and the strengthening of the seniority system has made it more valuable to be reelected. The year-round congressional calendar, in part a function of the growth of government but more directly attributable to air conditioning, has reduced the opportunity for any earnings not attributable to political activity. The increased size of the constituencies and the influences of television have increased the entry cost for potential competitors and have probably increased the incumbents' expectations of reelection. The progressive weakening of the relations of a representative to nonpolitical sources of earnings and with his or her home community increases the relative influence of the esteem of his or her colleagues, the attention of the media and the sociology of the Washington environment. One of the sad comments on this process is that few former representatives return home.

The major condition leading to an increase in the decision costs faced by our federal representatives is the growth and increased complexity of the federal government. This increase in decision costs leads to increased delegation of decisions to committees, to bureaux, and to other sources of specialized understanding and information. Such increased delegations by the representative body, in turn, increase the size and diversification of the federal government. The normal processes of government may not provide for convergence of this phenomenon.

The above speculations and the major thesis of this chapter, of course, may be only personal and *ad hoc* explanations of recent outcomes of the federal political process that I do not like. These explanations, however, are consistent with my experience and are testable by others. If they are wrong, I should be dismissed as a crank. If they are roughly correct, a major rethinking of the processes of constitutional change and the relation between the individual and his political agents in a representative democracy is in order.

WHERE DO WE GO FROM HERE?

One obvious task is to develop and test the major thesis of this chapter. Has the effective constitution of the federal government been changing? What is the process by which these changes are made? How has the nominal rule of majority approval, a long tradition even if not prescribed in the Constitution, been modified – possibly by changes in the rules for a quorum, floor amendments, and so on – to provide more (or less) delegation of decisions within the representative body? What are the processes for enforcing the turf of individual committees and representatives, and what processes lead to a change in these preserves? Do the identifiable changes in the effective constitution explain the recent outcomes of the federal political process?

A second task, if I am correct, is to rebuild our model of the processes of constitutional change. This makes the analysis of public choice more difficult, but at the same time, it reopens this issue to the contribution of other disciplines and the large body of old-fashioned political science. Who has influence in Washington? How is it exercised? What is the sociology of the Washington environment, and how does it affect our political agents?

A third task is to consider seriously the prospects for making more political decisions by some form of direct democracy. Several writers have recently suggested that the dramatic improvements in communications technology have reduced the potential decision costs of national referenda.[11] I have recently proposed an intermediate step that would involve more frequent presidential vetoes of proposals that pass Congress by less than a two-thirds vote, followed by nonbinding national advisory referenda based on a random sample of voters; both the president and Congress could choose to rule against these referenda but at an obvious cost.[12] Several other writers have recently suggested a new type of representative assembly, one that is selected at random and serves for a finite period without reelection.[13] Such a randomly selected assembly would

retain the lower costs of decisions by a representative assembly (and eliminate the decision costs of electing representatives) but would increase the
representativeness of the assembly and assure the amateur standing of
those making our collective choices. Such an assembly could either
replace or complement the elected Congress; the primary role of the
elected professional politicians would be to serve as entrepreneurs, pack-
agers and advisors to the randomly selected assembly, rather than as the
final decision makers. I find this proposal most appealing.

A fourth task is to develop further our understanding of the nature of
the contract between an individual and his or her political agents, maybe
along the lines suggested by Robert Barro.[14] What is the nature of this
contract? How has it changed in recent years? How could it be restruc-
tured so that we can better afford to delegate our franchise to these agents?

And last, I would urge that we retain some of the sense of optimism
reflected in *Capitalism and Freedom*. For better or for worse, ideas are
often powerful, and maybe we are too impatient. There are encouraging
signs that both the intellectual community and the American population
have learned a lot about government in the past decade, most importantly, by unlearning a lot that 'just ain't so'.

After first suggesting the title for this chapter, I had second thoughts.
Our political processes are also being criticized by some with quite different values than those we share – critics who would substitute power for
politics, who would prefer the alternative of rule by specific individuals to
the alternative, wherever possible of rule by each individual. Our present
political processes provide valuable services in a way that diffuses power
and provides moderate protection for minorities – and these values
should be recognized and defended. The. explicit and implicit criticisms
of our political processes in this chapter are offered to stimulate consideration of changes that would further these values. We can do better –
maybe a lot better.

NOTES

1. Chicago: University of Chicago Press, 1962; Buchanan, James M., 'The political economy of franchise in the welfare state' in Richard Seldon (ed.), *Capitalism and Freedom:
   Problems and Prospects*, Charlottesville, VA: University of Virginia Press, 52–77.
2. William A. Niskanen, *Bureaucracy and Representative Government,* Chicago: Aldine-
   Atherton, 1971, p. 170.
3. Theodore Bergstrom and Robert Goodman of Washington University have recently
   developed an ingenious method of estimating the price and income elasticities of
   demand for state and local services, but use of this method requires a cross-section
   sample. See 'Private demands for "public goods" *American Economic Review*, **63**, June
   1973, 280–96.

4. Weisbrod, 'Toward a theory of the voluntary non-profit sector in a three-sector econ-,
   omy,' Institute for Research on Poverty Discussion Paper 132–72, pp. 25–7.
5. Buchanan and Tullock, *The Calculus of Consent,* Ann Arbor: University of Michigan
   Press, 1962, pp. 214–15.
6. This explanation would be consistent with the model developed by J. Roland Pennock,
   'Federal and unitary government – disharmony and frustration,' *Behavioral Science,* **4,**
   April 1959, 147–57.
7. William A. Niskanen, *Structural Reforms of the Federal Budget Process,* Washington,
   DC: American Enterprise Institute, 1973.
8. Groups working on this problem include Otto Davis, M.A.H. Dempster and Aaron B.
   Wildavsky; Burton Weisbrod and his students at the University of Wisconsin; and several faculty members and students at the Center for Study of Public Choice at the
   Virginia Polytechnic Institute and State University.
9. This is the subtitle of their book.
10. One recent exception is Robert J. Barro, 'The control of politicians: an economic
    model', *Public Choice,* **14,** 1973, 19–42.
11. Simon Ramo, address at the University of California at Los Angeles, 1 May 1961,
    mimeographed; J.C. Miller III, 'A program for direct and proxy voting in the legislative
    process', *Public Choice,* **7,** Fall 1969, 107–13.
12. William A. Niskanen, 'Toward more efficient fiscal institutions,' *National Tax Journal*
    25, September 1972, 343–7.
13. Robert Dahl, *After the Revolution,* New Haven: Yale University Press, 1970; Dennis C.
    Mueller, Robert Tollison and Thomas Willett, 'Representative democracy via random
    selection', *Public Choice,* **12,** Spring 1972, 57–68.
14. See n. 10 above.

24. The opportunities for political entrepreneurship*

INTRODUCTION

Some things are not what they seem. A recent story illustrates my point: someone took a drink of 'Billy' beer, noticed its peculiar taste, and sent it off to a chemist for an analysis. The chemist sent back a note, 'I am sorry to report that your horse has diabetes'.

The primary illusion that I wish to address today is the common belief that the problems of government are due to politics. A related illusion – promoted by our civics textbooks, popular histories and the media – is that these problems are due to politicians that are uninformed, unintelligent, unenergetic and/or unprincipled. For today, I have come to praise politicians, not to bury them. For those of you who have just filed your income tax, I ask your special tolerance to hear my case.

Politics is the process of achieving consent on governmental actions. My remarks today make a case that consent is the dominant criterion by which any social action should be judged and summarize the processes by which political entrepreneurs achieve consent on governmental actions.

SOME BASIC CONCEPTS

First, some basic concepts.

Consent, I contend, is the dominant criterion by which any social action, including governmental action, should be judged. In other words, consent should be considered superior to any of the other criteria by which social actions are also evaluated – including efficiency, equity, rationality, comprehensiveness, certainty, simplicity, democracy and, yes, even liberty. Why? I come to this conclusion more or less by default. Consent is an objective criterion for which there is a common measure

---

* This chapter is the text of a lecture presented a the University of Dallas and at Texas A & M University, respectively, on 17 and 18 April 1978.

across people. The other criteria are subjective and differ across people; an action that may be efficient, equitable, and so on for one person may not be for another. Moreover, there are tradeoffs among these other criteria; any one person may resolve these tradeoffs of in terms of his or her personal utility, but there is no criterion, other than consent, to resolve these tradeoffs across people. Even liberty, that precious condition, cannot be a dominant criterion. Most of us live most of our lives in contractual arrangements – such as a job, marriage, and so on – in which we are not free or at liberty to take certain actions without severe cost; the relevant issues are whether a person consents to the arrangement and the conditions under which the consent is granted.

Is there any ethical basis for the consent criterion when consent is not unanimous? Is more consent better than less? The answer is yes, in some conditions, to both questions. For conditions such that people do not know their own circumstances at the time a decision on a specific action is made *or* if the distribution of the effects of the action are not known, there is a conceptual basis, at least, for unanimous consent on a decision rule on that action that involves less than full consent. James Buchanan and Gordon Tullock (1962) describe such conditions as 'the constitutional stage'; John Rawls (1971) describes these conditions as 'behind the veil of ignorance'. The choice of decision rules involves a balancing of two considerations: more consent is preferred to less because each person faces a higher probability on agreeing to the specific action when 'the veil of ignorance' is lifted. On the other hand, the costs of making a decision increase as a function of the degree of consent and the amount of information on personal circumstances and the distribution of effects. Unanimous consent on a decision rule involving partial consent is possible when each person perceives the expected marginal benefits of more consent to be less than the expected marginal costs of making the decision. This method of reasoning, of course, is subject to infinite regress, because there are also costs of making decisions on decision rules, but it does identify an ethical basis for social choice.

More consent is not necessarily preferred to less, however, across actions or, for a given action, when the alternatives differ. An agreement by 90 per cent of the population to enslave the other 10 per cent is not better than an agreement by 51 per cent to levy a small tax on the other 49 per cent, because the costs to the losing group are different. Most people faced by a choice, 'your money or your life', will yield their money; this is not better than a small percentage of the population making a charitable contribution, because the alternatives of not giving are different. Similarly, a 99 per cent vote for the governing party of a state that prohibits opposition parties is not better than a 51 per cent vote in a contested election. The ethical basis of a specific action, thus, must be judged in terms of the degree of consent for the decision rule and the underlying choice conditions rather than the consent on the specific action.

Following Israel Kirzner, I use the word entrepreneur to describe a broker of consensual change. In a market economy, an entrepreneur is one who searches for resources or a combination of resources that are worth more in some use other than their current use; the entrepreneur's profit, in this sense, is a finder's fee. In the government, the entrepreneur is the politician who searches for candidates or governmental actions that are preferred by the relevant consensus to the current official or action. The politician may be a candidate or official but may be the campaign manager, staff assistant and so on; the candidate or official may be only a proxy politician who is selected for his or her reputation, appearance, and so on. The politician's 'profit' takes a number of forms, including preferred jobs, favours, reputation, some preferred governmental action, and sometimes money. The entrepreneur and the politician, thus, perform similar rules – both serving as brokers for consensual change. Their behaviour is different primarily because the decision rules in the market and the government are different. Both the entrepreneur and the politician, unfortunately, are often disparaged by those who do not understand or endorse consensual processes.

THE PROCESSES OF CONSENT

Now I want to turn to the primary processes by which politicians achieve consent on governmental actions.

Information and Analysis

The first process that I shall discuss is a cognitive process, not a political process – the development of information and analysis on the effects of current and proposed government actions. There is a prejudice in the intellectual community that this process – now often called policy analysis – can improve substantially the performance of government; this prejudice is understandable, if somewhat naive, because that is what intellectuals do best. I mention this process first, not because it is very important, but to put it in context. (I do not want to disparage policy analysis; that was my trade for 18 years, and I taught at one of the many new schools of public policy.) In a few cases, more information and analysis will contribute to a consensus on changing some government action. There is no lack of information, however, on the effects of many government actions that most of us would consider wrong. More information is also threatening to those who are promoting some changes, and they have every incentive to suppress such information (the federal administration for example, has recently tried to withdraw from libraries a study that concludes that a large amount of natural gas would be produced at a higher price). More policy analysis, I believe, is likely to contribute to better government only if it is decentralized, uncoordinated, financed by different institutions and reflects a range of ideological positions and methodological approaches.

The more important role of the intellectual community has been to change the way people think about government and to provide rationales for what the politicians want to do anyway. A new theory is often more powerful than any body of evidence. Keynesian economics, for example, has never been supported by any substantial body of evidence, but it has provided a convenient rationale for politicians who want to spend more or reduce taxes. As my example suggests, I do not think this role of the intellectual community is entirely benign. The intellectual community also has a bad record of giving up on the political process of building consent if the government, for whatever reason, is not prepared to accept some fashionable new theory. No tyrant in history has had any problem collecting a stable of intellectuals to rationalize the suppression of political processes in the name of some ideal other than consent. 'Ask not what your country can do for you . . .' and so forth.

Packaging

The most distinctive political process of building consent for a candidate, a party, or a government action is to package or group promises or actions that reflect the interests to enough groups to gain approval. This process is usually called vote-trading or log-rolling. There is no reason for there to be any relation among these actions or any rationale or coherence to the whole package. In a two-party system, a political platform is a political document, not an intellectual document. Almost every major government action reflects a packaging of actions to gain the support of different groups who support the package for different reasons. This is the reason why it is so fruitless to argue about goals. This is the primary reason why those who defend the final compromise package often seem as if they are dissembling.

Let me give you two examples to illustrate how vote-trading works. When Thomas Jefferson came back from France, he found the new federal Congress deadlocked on two actions – whether the federal government should assume the revolutionary war debts of the states and the location of the federal capital. Jefferson quickly recognized that the northern states felt more strongly about the assumption of the war debts than about the capital and that the southern states had the opposite view. Jefferson then promoted a package involving assumption of the war debts and location of the capital in the south, assuring that both groups obtained what they wanted most.

The most important present opportunity for a vote-trade involves the Panama Canal treaty and deregulation of natural gas. Neither action would probably be approved by themselves. The president appears to feel more strongly about the treaty than about opposing deregulation, and many of the treaty opponents have the opposite view. For some months, I have been trying to promote this vote-trade to anyone who would listen. There are some signs that such a trade has been made. This will disappoint the ideologues on both sides, and there will be cries of sell-out, but both groups will achieve what they want most. No effective politician can have an unconditional commitment to more than one issue.

Unpackaging

Strangely enough, one of the important processes of gaining consent also involves 'unpackaging', or breaking down a proposed action into parts. This is usually done to save something rather than to lose everything. Proposals for changing government action are often *too* comprehensive; the package involves proposed actions on which there is no basis for consent. Breaking down the package is often necessary to avoid veto groups on specific actions.

Two recent foreign policy issues illustrate this point. The genius of the initiative by Anwar Sadat last year involved a recognition that most of the issues between Israel and Egypt could be resolved without resolving the Palestinian issue. Similarly, the genius of the recent initiative by Ian Smith was the recognition that there is a basis for representative government in Rhodesia without an exodus of the white community. The US insistence on comprehensive settlements in these areas that involve, respectively, the Palestinian and black terrorists can only be described as criminal.

There are no rules, without knowing the specific circumstances, whether packaging or unpackaging is the best way to achieve consent. It is clear, however, that anyone who says that he or she has 'an unconditional commitment to a comprehensive national pick-your-policy' should not be taken seriously.

Confusion

One of the more effective processes to gain consent is to confuse the issue. It is often easier to gain consent on an action when it is not clear who will be the specific gainers and losers. People will usually support an action if their expected benefits are positive, even if they may end up a loser.

One of the devices to reduce information on the distribution of gainers and losers is to defer implementation of the action, because people are less sure of their personal circumstances in the future than at present. For this reason, for example, some people who are now poor vote against a progressive income tax and some people who are now rich support transfer programmes. Deferral, of course, also serves another purpose by reducing the costs of adjustment to the new action.

Another device is to complicate the package of actions so much that it is not clear who will be the gainers and losers. Most tax legislation seems to have this characteristic.

A final device to reduce information on the distribution of gainers and losers, of course, is to suppress information. Let me give you a hypothetical public health issue. At present, say, a random 10 per cent of the population will die from some disease. A low-cost vaccine is discovered that would eliminate the disease but 1 per cent of the population will die from the vaccine. Almost everyone would support such a vaccination programme *if they do not know* who would die due to the vaccine. Suppose some medical researcher, however, knows which specific people would die from the vaccine, and he or she is not in that group. Should he or she suppress that information? My strong natural inclination would be to support a general rule requiring the release of such information, but I can understand why such information is suppressed. This example illustrates a fairly general type of problem, and I must admit to being less sure about the disclosure issue than I once was. In any case, I do not have any good ideas how to design governmental institutions that would prevent the suppression of such information.

Passing the Buck

The most important of all political processes might be described as passing the buck. I mean this in the best sense. Politicians have devised numerous ways of avoiding endless controversy about some issues by gaining consent at a different level. Ultimately, the government must take some type of action, and politics is the process of building consent for that action.

There is never any reason to argue about goals; there may be as many goals as people, and no consent on goals is necessary. A debate whether the unemployment target, for example, should be 4 per cent or 3 per cent does not provide guidance on specific actions when the current rate is 6 per cent. It is important, however, that the actions taken reflect either direct or indirect consent.

Sometimes when it is not possible to gain consent on a specific action, it is possible to gain consent for a decision rule affecting a class of actions. The politicians may approve a specific set of actions by some bureau or they may allow the bureau to determine the specific actions within broad guidelines. There is no a priori basis for determining the appropriate division of responsibility between the politicians and bureaucrats; the politician has done all he or she can by gaining consent for a decision rule when there is no basis for direct consent on the actions.

Similarly, it is often not possible to gain consent on a specific person for some governmental office, but it may be possible to gain consent on a rule for selecting that person. The only meaningful test whether a government is responsive to the consent of the governed is whether the selection and behaviour of government officials is consistent with consensual rules, not whether each person approves of each official and each action.

CONCLUSION

Most of my writing in recent years has focused on explaining the behaviour and problems of bureaucracy and representative government. The problems are many and are increasing. These problems, however, are not primarily due to politics and politicians, but are due to the rules by which politicians are selected and the authority granted to them. Any one of us would behave much the same as the politicians that we pillory, if we chose to run for reelection. A government with politics is bad enough; a government without politics and effective politicians would be much worse.

We often make heroes of the wrong people. We praise men who stand on principle but who do not have enough patience or conviction to try to convince others. We praise 'leaders' who call for sacrifice, who try to impose their own vision or sense of order, who ride roughshod on consensual processes both in the economy and in government. Beware of such men (and women).

For today, I have come to praise politicians – the trimmers, the compromisers, the vote-traders of the world. We should praise people who are committed to the principle of consent, who work for what they believe but who are prepared to defend the necessary compromise to achieve consent. I may have come to the right place. Winners write history, but losers make the best politicians. At least since the Civil War, something in the Texas air seems to have led to the best of this breed.

REFERENCES

Buchanan, James M. and Gordon Tulloch (1962), *The Calculus of Consent*, Ann Arbor, Michigan: The University of Michigan Press.
Rawls, John, (1971), *The Theory of Justice*, Cambridge, MA: Harvard University Press.

25. Corporations and other large organizations*

INTRODUCTION

For 18 years, I worked for federal agencies and private bureaux. For the past two years, I have worked for a large private corporation. This chapter summarizes some of my observations on 'the differences and similarities between these two types of organizations. My observations are not necessarily specific to the company in which I am employed but are based on conditions that I understand to be common, even if not uniform, among large corporations.

These observations are largely pre-theoretical, because an economist does not approach the study of large organizations with very much useful theory. The 'theory of the firm' in conventional microeconomics is an analytic convenience, a set of assumptions that are part of a theory, not of firms, but of markets. For the most part – with the exception of quite recent work – economic theory does not have much to offer as an explanation of why firms exist, the division of economic activity between markets and firms, and the organization of economic activity within firms. A large and increasing amount of economic activity is beyond the reach of conventional economic theory.

Most people try to fit new perceptions into the mould of familiar perceptions. Business managers understand how to get things done within a firm; many managers seem confused and threatened by markets. Managers are most comfortable with a monopoly in the product market and prefer a competitive product market only to one dominated by another firm. Managers are most comfortable with a monopsony in the factor or supplier market and prefer a competitive supply only to one dominated by a monopoly supplier. A business manager in a government or university position will perceive the organization of these institutions as chaotic, considering the obvious differences from the characteristics of

* This chapter is the text of a lecture presented at the annual meeting of the Public Choice Society in New Orleans, March 1977.

a business firm as institutional flaws (and they may be). Business managers will usually try to reorganize these institutions to be more like the organization they understand, the business firm.

Similarly, economists understand (or should understand) markets. Economists are most comfortable with negotiated decisions under conditions where each party has a wide choice of alternatives. Departures from the market model – such as hierarchy, direction, package deals, and so on – are often viewed as institutional flaws (and they may be). Sometimes trivial events challenge this perspective, but one does not easily override professional prejudice (I am reminded of my irritation with *à la carte* menus, knowing that I usually prefer the chef's judgement about the combination of foods in a meal, but thinking that I *should* prefer my own). An economist in a government or business position will perceive these institutions as overly rigid – too dependent on authority, rules, and so on – and will usually try to reorganize these institutions to be more like the organization they understand, the market. Cognitive dissonance is probably a necessary condition for learning, and I want to testify, on the basis of my experience, that economists have a lot to learn about both government and business firms.

A business firm is not organized like a market. Moreover, business firms are less like markets than they were in the past. A century ago, for example, most American manufacturing firms were organized by an internal contracting system and most labour was paid on a piece-rate basis. The major managerial reforms in American manufacturing involved the substitution of centralized production decisions for internal contracting and the progressive substitution of hourly wages or salaries for piece-rate compensation. Since the firms that pioneered these reforms charged lower prices and paid higher wages, it is hard to contest the efficiency of these reforms at that time. Nevertheless, it is useful to consider whether this development has gone too far in some firms, whether the market model may provide some useful contributions to improve the performance of large modern firms. This chapter organizes some of my own observations about this issue and should stimulate others to flesh out their own skeletal theory of the firm.

DIFFERENCES AMONG LARGE ORGANIZATIONS

The major differences between large private firms and government bureaux are obvious.

External Differences

The most important of these differences are external to the organization. Most large private firms, with the exception of the regulated monopolies, operate in a very competitive product market. These firms sell numerous products to many customers, and most customers of these firms can change their source of supply or defer purchase of the product at low cost. No actual firm has probably ever faced a perfectly elastic demand for its products, and that is usually fortunate because the average cost function for many products is declining over a substantial range. The conventional identification of competitive markets with perfectly competitive firms, unfortunately, has created a lot of confusion and mischievous policy. The only long-term source of financing for a private firm is from the sale of its products; there seems to be an ample supply of equity financing to new firms and an ample supply of debt financing to firms that do not need it, but both of these sources of financing dry up rather quickly when a firm is losing money on its products. The rates of both new business formation and of business failure are comparatively high.

Government bureaux, in contrast, are generally monopoly suppliers of a restricted range of services to a single government. The bureau exchanges a commitment to supply these services for a periodic budget. The government, in turn, is generally a monopoly government in a given area. Some governments, at least nominally, are a 'purchasing agent' for the population, but that is irrelevant to a bureau; a bureau need only satisfy the government, not the population, and any value of a bureau's services to the population depends on the relation between the population and the government. Governments characteristically rely on specialized financial instruments not available to the private firm – taxation, printing money, and, on occasion, conscription and expropriation. The rates of both new bureau formation and of bureau failure are comparatively low.

Internal Differences

The internal differences between a large private firm and a government bureau are also rather obvious. From my perspective, however, these internal differences seem less important. The distinctive internal characteristics of large private firms and government bureaux could be transposed without much affecting the differential performance of these types of organizations. The distinctive internal characteristics of large private firms facilitate survival in a competitive market, but some non-subsidized government or nonprofit firms selling in a competitive market perform quite well. I am also less sanguine that transplanting the distinctive internal characteristics of large private firms on government bureaux would much improve their performance without changing their external conditions. The differences between the internal characteristics still deserve mention, and I may underestimate their importance.

Private firms place substantially greater reliance on financial rewards and employment sanctions. A substantial proportion of the income of higher managers is a residual claim – in the form of a bonus or stock option – based on the firm's earnings or stock performance, and there is no analogue of this type of financial reward in government. In general, the ratio of salary to perquisites is much higher in private firms and would probably be even higher if marginal income tax rates were lower. In addition, it is easier to relieve a manager for poor performance and to lay off a worker because of a decline in demand.

Business accounting conventions are conspicuously flawed but are much superior to that used by government bureaux. Business accounts include both a balance sheet and an accrual-based income statement. Few governments ever draw up a balance sheet, and no decisions are made on balance sheet considerations (what would one do, for example, with information that the net worth of the US federal government is a negative \$4 trillion, ± 1 trillion?). Government budgets, in addition, are usually cash flow statements: capital expenditures are budgeted at the time of purchase and never again; accrued liabilities are budgeted only when payments are made. The business accounting conventions make it easier to gain approval for a new capital expenditure when the expected returns are high and harder to hoard capital in an activity when the expected returns are low. New government activities in contrast, are likely to be capital starved, and older activities are likely to be capital rich. Most important, perhaps, bankers have the power, inclination and information to replace the managers of firms when net worth is negative. Neither elected nor appointed government officials seem much concerned about a similar condition.

SIMILARITIES AMONG LARGE ORGANIZATIONS

I was prepared for the obvious differences between a large private firm and a large bureau; that is, the differences were consistent with my preconceptions. What has most surprised me is how *similar* are the internal organization, incentives and procedures! A good bureaucrat from the Pentagon or the Soviet Union, without any specialized knowledge of production processes or the product market, would perform well in most middle-management positions. The proximate incentive for managers is identical: please your superior; if your superior is in trouble or you have a difficult relation with your superior, try to establish favourable relations with his or her superior or others at that level. The major differences among organizations, I suppose, are reflected in what your superior expects you to do, but the proximate incentive is the same: no one has ever been promoted for serving 'the public interest' or 'the stockholders' interests', whatever that means.

The micro-sociology of large organizations, the games people play, are very similar – the competition for conspicuous perquisites, who answers a phone first, where to sit at a meeting, how to get your job done around the rules established by controllers and personnel officers, how to look busy when you have nothing to do, hoarding slack resources so that you can absorb the next budget cut, who to see socially, the role of the manager's wife, and so on. It is easy to understand why pop sociologists conclude that large organizations are basically alike. This conclusion, supported by any number of anecdotes, is often correct about details and still fails to recognize the important differences.

The basic problem of any large organization is how to translate the incentives of the senior managers into the incentives faced by lower-level managers. In a corporation, resolution of this problem is facilitated, but far from solved, by the combination of financial incentives and business accounting. A description of how the bonus and stock option incentives operate illustrates this situation.

The company bonus pool is usually a significant fraction of the (positive) difference between after-tax profits and some threshold level of profits; the bonus pool, thus, increases more than proportionately with company profits. In many companies, however, the bonus pool for a component is not based on the profits of that component. The distribution of the bonus pool among the managers tend to be progressively distributed relative to a manager's salary with rather small variations based on a review of personal performance. For managers as a group, thus, the bonus formula provides for a rapidly increasing bonus pool as a function of company profits. For the managers in any component, however, the bonus is almost a pure windfall. Managers in a low-profit component receive a large bonus when company profits are high, and managers in a profitable component receive no bonus when company profits are low. In most large companies, managers work in 'teams' that are smaller than the total group of managers; within such teams, there is no possibility of attributing profits to individual managers; employment actions, discipline and praise, and mutual reinforcement are the basic incentive methods. A large company, however, is too large to be a team, too large for these types of incentives to be very effective.

Why do not many companies base the bonus pool for the managers of a component on the profits of that component? The answers are complex and interesting. A part of the problem is the inadequacy of accounting conventions. Capital values are usually based on historical cost and asset-type depreciation rates that only roughly approximate the market value of the assets in the absence of general inflation; in an inflationary period, the book value of capital has only a loose relation to the market value of assets. Some services provided by other components, such as product development, are not charged to the using component. The determination of the correct transfer prices for goods and services provided by another component is very difficult when there is not a developed external market for the good or service provided with the same quality, reliability, timeliness, and so on. A point is also made that it is inefficient to induce managers to spend much time haggling about transfer prices on company-specific goods where there is legitimate difference of views on their value. Economists could make a substantial contribution to business efficiency by developing rules for determining the appropriate transfer prices or by developing procedures for resolving differences between the desired transfer prices between two components in a bilateral monopoly relation.

Another argument that is made against decentralizing the bonus pool is that it would be difficult (or 'unfair') to assign a manager to a low-profit component. One might think that the company would pay a manager a higher salary to take a position with a low expected bonus. The problem is that the salary structure in a large company is like that in the civil service; managers at the same level of responsibility across components are paid the same salary. These salary rules are broken, as in the civil service, only by misclassifying job positions or by creating special job positions.

Public choice scholars will have a special understanding of one other problem. The distribution of managers by the profit rate in their component is skewed to the left; that is, the median manager is in a component with a profit rate that is lower than the average rate. More than half of the managers, thus, would prefer that the bonus pool be based on company earnings rather than component earnings – unless the effect of a decentralized bonus pool on company profits shifts the distribution to the right by enough to increase the bonus of the median manager. A corporation does not use a formal majority rule on this or most other decisions, but the preferences of a majority of managers have a significant effect and are usually supported by the salaried-employee's personnel office.

The stock option is the other major special type of financial incentive in a corporation, but has similar weaknesses. The primary value of a stock option is to motivate managers to be concerned with future profits, and stock options are most important for managers working on long-term projects or those nearing retirement. One problem is that the price of a company's stock is a function of both company earnings and the value of alternative investments; in recent years, increased profits have not been capitalized in higher stock prices with any regularity. As a consequence, I often hear some remark such as 'He is not worried about that problem; it won't be apparent until after he retires'. A stock option also has the same weakness as a bonus pool based on company earnings; the value of the option is based on company performance, not that of the component teams where the manager has worked.

In summary, the characteristic financial incentives used by corporations are not sufficient to assure that the incentives of component managers are consistent with maximizing the objectives of the senior managers or stockholders. As a consequence, corporations rely dominantly on the same type of internal organization and procedures as do large bureaux.

One manifestation of this condition is that managers of major components have surprisingly little discretion on capital spending, staffing and the sourcing of purchases. Managers are expected to minimize costs of meeting a given production schedule, subject to a mix of resources determined by or approved by higher managers; in other words, managers are expected to be managers, not businessmen. The threshold on capital spending that must be approved by the senior company managers is surprisingly low, often about one-hundredth of 1 per cent of total company sales. Managers usually need the approval of the next higher-level managers for the most routine requisitions. These practices are not necessarily wrong. In an older firm with a mature production technology, such practices probably cause fewer misallocation costs than the external costs that are a consequence of decentralized resource allocation decisions. Such practices are most likely to be inefficient when conditions change in a way that is not easily recognized by the senior managers, until a new set of rules are developed.

Another manifestation of this condition is the use of 'tasks' – profit tasks, cost reduction tasks, employment tasks, sales tasks, and so on. At the first stage, these tasks are usually pro-rated among components, regardless of the relative opportunities and costs of meeting the tasks. These tasks are pro-rated because senior management does not have the information to judge the relative difficulty of meeting the tasks, and because of the sense that every manager should make a 'fair' contribution to some company objective. This practice is almost identical to the type of employment reduction or budget reduction tasks used in the government.

The effects of these tasks, of course, are also similar. A manager of a component that is already very efficient in terms of the dimension of the task will have great trouble meeting a task, but a manager that has (consciously or unconsciously) programmed some slack may be able to exceed his or her task. Such pro-rata tasks induce inefficiency in resource use, and they understandably offend the professional sensibilities of economists in both business and government. Information, however, is not free and, more important, managers have a strong incentive not to reveal the amount of slack in their component. Moreover, the short-run effect of such pro-rata tasks is not as inefficient as it may seem; managers that would have an unusual difficulty in achieving their pro-rata task without seriously reducing other dimensions of performance are often able to make a case for an exception. Such managers, however, are best advised to build in some slack to meet the next task, because a manager cannot afford to ask for exceptions on a regular basis.

At the company level, these tasks are often very important to maintain cash flow during a period of declining demand, to probe the organization to determine what is feasible and to identify pockets of slack, and to meet government regulations. The use of pro-rata tasks is often effective and is seldom efficient, and will continue to be used until someone has a better idea.

In summary, the internal organization and procedures of a large corporation are very similar to that of a large bureau. Maybe that is the best feasible structure of large organizations. Maybe not. At the present time, economists do not have a lot to contribute to this issue.

26. Guidelines for delineating the private and the government sector*

This chapter addresses two important choices that must be made in any nation:

- What services should a government finance?
- What services should a government produce?

I do not presume to know a firm answer to either of these questions for any nation, including for the United States but especially for any other nation. At most, this chapter summarizes some of the considerations that bear on these two choices.

My reflection on these issues leads me to the following general conclusions:

1. These two choices are logically and empirically distinct. One should not conclude that all services financed primarily by taxation should be produced by the government. Similarly, there is no strong case that all services produced by the government should be financed primarily by taxation.
2. A constitutional consensus on the set of services that the government is authorized to finance is more important than the specific choices made. A government should finance a specific service only if authorized by the constitution; this restraint is inherent in the general rule that *no government should be allowed to define its own powers*.
3. Economic theory and empirical evidence is now moderately helpful in advising the choice of which services the government should finance but a sufficient consensus, by the rules prescribed by the constitution, is the only normative basis for judging whether the government has made the correct choice. Among the few general rules that are especially valuable is that the set of services that a government is

---

* Reprinted by permission from Horst Siebert (ed.), *Privatization*, Tübingen: J.C.B. Mohr, 1992, pp. 217–25.

authorized to finance should be smaller the lower the effective voting rule on legislation is, the higher the variance of preferences among the population is, the lower the mobility of people and their assets is, and the larger the area served by the government is. In addition, expenditures for a specific service should be lower the larger the total expenditures for other services are.

4. There are no strong reasons, at least no reasons obvious to me, why the constitution should prescribe or restrict the set of services *produced* by the government.

5. Economic theory provides little guidance about what services should be produced by government or, more generally, by nonprofit organizations. The overwhelming empirical evidence, however, suggests that there should be a presumption, but not an exclusive presumption, in favour of production by profit-seeking private firms. For example, I know of no government enterprise that has survived without subsidy, preferential taxation or regulation, or entry restrictions. On the other hand, the survival of a small private nonprofit sector in most nations suggests that this organizational form may be preferable for the production of some services.

These conclusions, I suggest, are helpful but not sufficient to choose what services should be financed or produced by the government. For those of you who may not already be persuaded, let me put some meat on these bones.

WHAT SERVICES SHOULD A GOVERNMENT FINANCE?

The Primacy of Constitutional Consent

My first response to this question is that a government should finance only those services authorized by the constitution. Some of you may respond that this is obvious, but this response overlooks the dominant political development of our lifetime. Some of you may regard my first response as begging the question, because it does not address what services the constitution should authorize. One issue at a time.

Consider a club in which you are a voluntary member. The club may approve some activity with which you disagree. If both the activity and the decision process by which this activity is approved are consistent with the club's bylaws, however, your only recourses are to accept the result, persuade enough of the members to change the decision, or to leave the club; in this case, there is no normative basis for concluding that the specific decision of the club was wrong. If either the activity or the decision process is not authorized by the bylaws, however, you have the additional recourse to take the club to court to enjoin the activity or to seek compensation. In this case, the primary issue before the court is not whether you were harmed by the decision of the club but whether the decision was consistent with the bylaws.

A government is best described as a special form of club that has universal membership and a monopoly on the right of legal coercion in a specific area. Most of the advantages and disadvantages of government, in either financing or producing a specific service, derive from these two characteristics (Stiglitz 1989). One is more likely to be harmed by the legal actions of a government than of a club, primarily because the number of people who must be persuaded and the costs of leaving are much higher. But the decisions of a club and a government should be judged by the same standard – whether the decisions are consistent with the bylaws or the constitution. And the recourse available to the individual should be the same. The primary problem arises when the courts, a part of the government, are not willing or able to enjoin the government from an action that is a clear violation of its constitution.

The primary intellectual development in the nineteenth century has been described as the death of God – the concept of a higher being to whom we must all someday answer. In a similar sense, the primary intellectual development in the twentieth century is the death of the constitution – the concept of a higher law that the government itself may not change. Let me illustrate this point based only on the fiscal history of the United States.

The US Constitution authorized the federal government to exercise only 18 rather narrowly defined powers, only a few of which – such as the authority to 'raise and support Armies' and to 'provide and maintain a Navy' – involve the potential of substantial expenditures. For the first 140 years of our constitutional history, these limits on the enumerated powers were an effective brake on federal spending. In 1929, for example, the federal budget was 2.6 per cent of GNP, almost all of which was spent for the military or the deferred costs of prior wars. Over roughly my lifetime, however, the federal budget share of GNP has increased nearly tenfold, most of which now finances new services, without a single amendment to the Constitution that would authorize these new services. The Great Depression and the New Deal, of course, were the primary events that led to this massive breach in the fiscal constitution. And the first judicial rationalization of this breach was a Supreme Court decision, US v. Butler, in January 1936 (five months after congressional approval of the social security programme) in which the Court ruled that 'the power of Congress to authorize appropriations of public money for public purposes is not limited by the direct grants of legislative power found in the Constitution'. In effect, each Congress may now write its own fiscal constitution, subject only to the restraint that the appropriations must serve some vague concept of public purpose. The fiscal constitution of the United States is now only a 'parchment barrier', and Americans have no legal recourse to enjoin a continued expansion of the services financed by government. The demand for some of these new services may have been sufficient to meet the test of constitutional consent, but that is not obvious. My primary point is that, without a test of constitutional consent, Congress may now authorize many services that would not meet this test.

Theory and Evidence

So far, I hope that I have convinced you that the government should finance only those services authorized by its constitution. But that begs the question of what government-financed services are likely to be preferred by a sufficiently broad share of the population to meet the test of constitutional consent. The test of 'public purposes' should be shifted back from the legislative stage to the constitutional stage but cannot be avoided. What 'public purposes' merit government financing? My first answer to this question is that there is no general answer to this question. The set of services a government should finance may differ both among nations and over time and will depend importantly on other features of the constitution.

Economic theory has developed by fits and starts to a point, I suggest, that it now provides some limited useful guidance to addressing this question. John Maynard Keynes, of course, made the most expansive claim for government spending, almost coincident with the Butler decision that destroyed the US fiscal constitution. In a period of involuntary unemployment, Keynes argued, government spending on any service would increase total spending and output, whatever the direct value of the service financed. This assertion was an important part of the rationalization of increased government spending for the next 40 years but finally fell victim to inflation, common sense, and the developing empirical evidence. (My own development as an economist was marked by three stages of my views about the balanced budget multiplier. On first hearing this concept in college, my reaction was 'that's crazy'. On learning the algebra, I concluded 'that's wonderful'. Only in graduate school did I learn the reasons to conclude 'that's crazy'. This experience also taught me that, although the most important concepts in economics are nonintuitive, most nonintuitive concepts are wrong.)

The micro foundations of the modern theory of government spending were first developed in the 1950s by Samuelson (1954) and others, based on the concepts of public goods and positive externalities. Public goods (or services) are those for which one person's use of a service does not fully displace the amount used by others. This condition presents the same potential problems as private goods for which the average cost declines over the full range of effective demand; private firms were believed to supply an insufficient quantity of these goods or services. The concept of public goods first seemed to provide a 'bright line standard' to delineate the private and government sectors. This concept, however, has proved to be both normatively incomplete and empirically misleading. Many services provided by the private sector have this characteristic of a public good and are supplied in nearly optimal amounts by multipart pricing and exclusion of nonpaying would-be customers. And the concept of public goods has not proved to be very descriptive of the actual services financed by government, few of which appear to reflect economies of scale as a function of the size of the population served. We are left with the more limited conclusion that the government should finance only those public goods for which the total value is higher than the cost and nonpaying beneficiaries may not be efficiently excluded. These conditions probably apply only to a few services such as national defence, basic research and uncongested highways.

The concept of positive externalities (or 'merit goods') has proved more valuable (Musgrave 1959). There is a reasonable case, for example, that some amount of physical infrastructure and education increases the productivity of people other than those who make the direct investment in these goods and services. The primary conceptual qualification is that only those externalities that are positive at the margin of the level of private investment provide a rationale for some amount of government financing of these services. Measurement of these externalities is often difficult, and this concept is subject to abuse, but there is increasing evidence, for example, that the United States may have underinvested in physical infrastructure in the past two decades (Aschauer 1990).

There is also a reasonable case that people might approve some types of social insurance at the constitutional stage, even with full recognition that transfers and taxes bias the choice of hours worked and occupation in the post-constitutional stage (Zeckhauser 1974; Niskanen 1986). This type of analysis suggests that the amount of such social insurance would increase with the variance of the distribution of natural endowments and would decline as a function of the substitution between income and leisure (or the nonpecuniary benefits of specific occupations) and the level of taxes to finance the protective and productive services of the government. (This analysis also leads to the intriguing conclusion that average tax rates should increase but that marginal tax rates should decline over the whole distribution of pretax earnings.)

The choices whether to authorize each of these types of services, moreover, are related, because the marginal cost to the economy of each service is a function of the total tax rate. At the margin of current conditions in the United States, for example, the cost to the economy of an additional $1 billion of government spending is now about $1.5 billion (Jorgensen and Yun 1990) and would be even higher in nations with higher tax rates. One implication of this relation is that the probability of a constitutional consensus on authorizing the government to finance a new service would be a negative function of the total tax rate for services previously authorized.

The three above types of analyses, often termed 'welfare economics', make a positive case for some types of government spending based on the analysis of market failure. Welfare economics has proved valuable but is clearly one-sided, based on the implicit assumption that governments are run by benevolent dictators. The necessary complement to welfare economics is the analysis of government failure, a body of analysis that developed beginning in the 1960s and is now usually termed 'public choice'. For this chapter, the most important general conclusion of public choice is that the structure and decision rules of any government leads it to finance some services that would not meet a test of constitutional consent and, more generally, to choose nonoptimal service levels and inefficient production processes. 'The recent essay by Stiglitz (1989), for example, suggests that this perspective is now shared by the broader community of American public finance specialists. Many services of modern governments are the contemporary equivalent of bread and circuses, both of which are supplied by the private sector in quite adequate amounts. At the constitutional stage, the choice of what services the government should be authorized to finance should be based on a recognition that both markets and governments are subject to various types of biases. Economic theory and the developing evidence can now provide some useful guidance to identifying these biases but is not a sufficient basis for making these constitutional choices.

Public choice analysis also provides some useful guidance about the relation between the set of services a specific government should be authorized to finance and the structure and decision rules of that government. In the limit, there is no reason to constrain the authority of a government in which every decision must be approved by the entire population. Most democracies have chosen a representative government and a majority voting rule to economize on decision-making costs, but it is more important to constrain the powers of these governments. The polar alternatives are to authorize a narrow range of services and a majority voting rule or a broader range of services and a more constraining voting rule. The formal structure of the national government of the United States and Switzerland are examples of the first alternative. The structure of the American states, Swiss cantons, and the national government of Finland are examples of the second alternative. Many American states and Swiss cantons, for example, may not borrow to finance their operating budget and require either a supermajority or a referendum to increase taxes. Finland's constitution requires a two-thirds vote of their parliament to increase taxes for more than one year and a five-sixths vote to approve any measure that restricts property rights. One should not be surprised that the relative size of government is generally lower in federal systems, although governments have grown rapidly everywhere. Among the democracies, the worst alternative is a national government with plenary powers and a majority rule, but the effective structure of most national governments, including the United States, is unfortunately evolving in that direction.

None of the above, I remind you, is sufficient to determine what services should a government finance. But it may help build a consensus on this issue.

WHAT SERVICES SHOULD A GOVERNMENT PRODUCE?

The Constitutional Issue

No one, myself included, appears to have thought very much about whether the constitution should specify what services a government should produce. The US Constitution, for example, authorizes the federal government to 'establish Post Offices and Post Roads, raise and support Armies, and to provide and maintain a Navy', but these powers are clearly permissive rather than prescriptive. Over time, the federal government has used a combination of government agencies and private contractors to carry the mail, build and maintain roads, develop and produce weapons and munitions and even, in the early years, to provide naval forces. Moreover, the Constitution authorizes Congress to approve any measure that is 'necessary and proper' to implement the enumerated powers. There is no apparent reason for the constitution to constrain the combination of private and public production of services financed by the government.

There is more reason to question whether the constitution should authorize the government to produce services that are entirely financed by the sale of the services. The US Constitution, for example, does not authorize the federal government to build and maintain ports, canals, electric utilities, recreation areas, airports and various types of specialized insurance, but the federal government has produced such services for many years. There is reason to question whether the federal government should finance these services, provide preferential taxation or regulation, or restrict entry of private competitors, all of which the government also does. Consider, however, the following case: a government issues a bond to finance some project against which only the earnings of the project are pledged, builds and operates the project with government employees, and provides no subsidy or other preferential treatment. In this case, there is no apparent reason for the constitution to restrict the government from providing this service. And some general supporters of a market economy, such as Henry Simon, have argued that government production of services that are natural monopolies is preferable to the combination of regulation and private monopolies.

The above case, however, is purely hypothetical. As far as I know, every service produced by the government has had some government financing or preferential treatment. The case for a constitutional prohibition on government production of services other than those 'necessary and proper' to implement their enumerated powers must be based on the consistent pattern of preferential treatment for such government-produced services. This is an empirical judgement but, none the less, is an appropriate consideration at the constitutional stage.

Theory and Evidence

Much current attention is focused on the opportunities, problems and methods of selling government-owned assets or enterprises to the private sector. We should recognize, however, that we have almost no theory that bears on how far a nation should go down the road to privatization and what remaining services should a government produce. We have a rich theory of the behaviour of private firms with the important conclusion, in the absence of marginal externalities, that both productive efficiency and allocative efficiency are the usual characteristics of equilibrium in a competitive market. We have a still inchoate theory of the behaviour of government bureaux that suggests that the market for the services produced by bureaux does not generate either of these desirable efficiency properties (Niskanen 1971, 1975). The combination of our refined theory of private firms and our crude theory of government bureaux, thus, suggests that all services should be produced by private firms, even those financed by government. In this world, the executive branch of government would be limited to dispensing vouchers, negotiating contracts, and reviewing the performance and costs of the private firms producing the government-financed services – or maybe even these instrumental services could be privatized. But I doubt whether this conclusion is correct.

In this case, I suggest, the best guidance is provided by investigating the distribution of organizational forms in the private sector. Almost all firms financed exclusively by the direct sale of services to customers are profit-seeking corporations, partnerships or individual enterprises. Most firms that are substantially financed by contributions from private 'sponsors', however, are nonprofit firms. Such firms provide a substantial part of the charitable, cultural, educational, hospital, recreational, religious and research services in many nations and are especially important in the United States where they now produce about 3.7 per cent of the GNP (Weisbrod 1988). Sponsors who are concerned about the level of such services make contributions to these firms to expand their output beyond the level that could be financed by the direct sale of these services to customers. In turn, the sponsors who dominate the board of trustees of these firms, make three distinctive decisions, each designed to expand the output of these services. They choose a nonprofit form of organization to induce the expansion of output beyond the profit-maximizing level of service. They require board approval of the salary schedule. And, to reduce the relative productive inefficiency that is characteristic of this form of organization, the sponsors select managers who have a reputation as 'zealots' for the supply of the specific services. (This perspective is derived primarily from trying to understand my own experience as both the chairman and a manager of nonprofit policy institutes.)

This experience, I suggest, is the best guide to what services the government should produce. Services financed exclusively by the direct sale to customers should probably be supplied by profit-seeking, investor-owned private firms. This conclusion should also apply for those services for which the consumer payment is partly or wholly compensated by any government-financed vouchers for education, energy, food, medical care, rent, and so on. Services that are substantially financed by direct private contributions should probably be supplied by private nonprofit firms, even if such firms receive some direct grants from the government or government-financed vouchers. All other services financed by the government, however, should probably be produced by the government, at least at the final stage of production. This should not preclude contracting with private firms for a wide range of inputs to the production of these services, but the final services should be produced by government bureaux responsive to the government sponsors. For these services, the relation between the bureaux and their government sponsors presents a range of problems, but it is not obvious that this institutional relation can be substantially improved.

In summary, my suggested delineations of production between the private and the government sector, my suggested answers to what services should a government produce, should be regarded as presumptions rather than firm conclusions. The theory that bears on these questions is still quite weak but the evidence, I suggest, is quite strong.

REFERENCES

Aschauser, D.A. (1990), 'Is government spending stimulative?', *Contemporary Policy Issues*, **8** (4), 30–46.

Jorgensen, D. and K.-Y. Yun (1990), 'Tax reform and US economic growth', *Journal of Political Economy*, **98** (5), Part 2, S151–S193.

Musgrave, R.A. (1959), *The Theory of Public Finance*, New York: McGraw Hill.

Niskanen, W.A. (1971), *Bureaucracy and Representative Government*, Chicago: Aldine-Atherton.

Niskanen, W.A. (1975), 'Bureaucrats and politicians', *Journal of Law and Economics*, **18** (4), 617–43.

Niskanen, W.A. (1986), 'A constitutional approach to taxes and transfers', *Cato Journal*, **6** (1), 347–52.

Samuelson, P.A. (1954), 'The pure theory of public expenditure', *Review of Economics and Statistics*, **36**, 387–9.

Stiglitz, J.E. (1989), *The Economic Role of the State*, Oxford: Basil Blackwell.

Weisbrod, B.A. (1988), *The Nonprofit Economy*, Cambridge, MA: Harvard University Press.

Zeckhauser, R. (1974), 'Risk spreading and distribution', in H. Hochman and G. Peterson (eds), *Redistribution and Public Choice*, New York: Columbia University Press, 206–28.

27. The soft infrastructure of a market economy*

A Western economist's first visit to a socialist nation is an eye-opening experience. One's first impressions are rather like those from visiting the poorer regions of our own economies – most visibly the lower levels of creature comforts, health and environmental conditions. It would be a mistake, however, to explain the differences between the market and socialist economies in terms of the conditions that explain the differences over time or among regions in the productivity and average income within a market economy.

An economist studying a market economy, for example, is most likely to focus on the differences in human skills, private and public investment, and natural resources, and the incremental or small differences in government policy. We are less likely to study the basic institutions of a market economy, because they have changed only gradually over time and are common across the nation. Indeed, our standard graduate training in economics hardly mentions these institutions, and few economists have more than a shallow understanding of their importance.

The most important differences between the market and socialist economies, however, are the less-visible or quantifiable differences in these basic institutions. I am not a specialist in the socialist economies, so my understanding of the Soviet economy is necessarily secondhand. For the past several years, however, the inchoate reforms in the socialist economies and my own brief visits to several other socialist economies have led me to reflect on the basic institutions, or 'soft infrastructures', of a market economy. The present chapter gives me an opportunity to share my reflections in a systematic way.

THE LEGAL SYSTEM

One of the three basic institutions of a market economy is the legal system. Specifically, a market economy is dependent on a comprehensive

* Reprinted by permission from *Cato Journal*, **11** (2), Fall 1991, 233–8, Cato Institute. This article is the text of a lecture presented in Moscow in September 1990.

commercial code and a system of commercial courts to adjudicate disputes. A modern commercial code includes the laws bearing on property, contracts, torts and those laws specific to the several major types of business enterprises. For this system to be fully effective, property rights should be

- *exclusive* – to provide clear title for the authority to use or sell specific rights;
- *alienable* (sellable) – to permit market exchanges of specific rights;
- *partitionable* (separable) – to permit the separation of a specific right from a package of rights; and
- *extensive* (universal) – to permit market exchanges of all valuable resources, a necessary condition to avoid the abuse of 'common pool' resources that is characteristic of environmental problems.

In effect, the political economy of a nation is defined by the nature and distribution of these rights. The distinctive principle of a market economy is that any *change* in the distribution of rights must have the consent of *all* those who own the affected rights.

An American economist is reluctant to conclude that any nation might have too few lawyers. Our army of lawyers is about as large as the US Army and is almost as dangerous. The socialist economies, however, clearly need to extend and refine their commercial codes. The following examples might be helpful.

Although most property in a socialist economy is nominally owned by the state, it is often not clear whether the workers, the local manager, some party official, or the relevant minister has the authority to sell the property and who is to receive the proceeds. This ambiguity has already created cases in which two firms have purchased the same property from different officials, with no clear process for adjudicating the title dispute. The important but necessarily complex process of privatization will be undermined if the general population perceives the initial distribution from the sales to be unfair. A strong assertion of clear title by the state may be the necessary, but somewhat ironic, first step to effective privatization.

In some cases, rights have been granted to farmers or cooperatives to use property but not to sell it. This situation generally leads to inadequate maintenance of the property, most visibly demonstrated by the Yugoslav experience. In other cases, rights have been granted as a package but without the authority to sell specific rights to others. This condition leads to an underutilization of those specific rights that the owner is less qualified to use. In all nations, the most egregious environmental offenders are state firms, primarily because governments have exempted these firms from legal suits or from the regulations that apply to other firms.

A closer look at the Soviet economy would surely produce more examples. My main point is that many of the apparent problems of the socialist economies could be reduced by extending and refining their commercial codes. The Soviet Union should not try to copy the Western commercial codes; the US code specifically, is too complex and involves too much litigation. Nevertheless, there is a rare opportunity to learn from both our successes and problems. President Mikhail Gorbachev has pledged to restore the rule of law in the Soviet Union. That task will not be complete until it is extended to the full range of economic rights and relations.

THE ACCOUNTING SYSTEM

The second basic institution of a market economy is the accounting system. Specifically, a market economy is dependent on the broad use of a common set of financial accounting rules and an independent system to audit financial reports. The two common reports are a balance sheet (a statement of the value of a firm's assets and liabilities at the end of the prior period) and an income statement (a record of the receipts and expenditures during the period). These reports, with additional internal information, are used by a firm's directors and managers to determine the costs and profits on specific products and the financial performance of component divisions. More important, these reports are critical to a bank or other firm that is considering a loan to or investment in the firm. The accounting rules and auditing systems have evolved over the many years and are not perfect, but one cannot imagine a market economy without a similar set of financial records.

My conversations with Western entrepreneurs who have considered joint ventures with socialist firms, however, indicate that the accounts of these firms are almost worthless, either for internal management or external monitoring. In most of the socialist nations, the accounts of state firms are designed and maintained to provide the insatiable data demands of the state planning system. Most of these data bear on physical flows and are of little use to estimate the costs or profits of individual products or the financial status of the firm, even if the input and output prices were closer to market rates. Indeed, I am informed that the balance sheets of many state firms do not include a measure of net worth. At an earlier, more innocent, time, computers were expected to solve the massive data-processing problems of a socialist economy. The problems of a socialist economy, however, are not from the lack of data; indeed, socialist economies are drowning in data. The problem is that these data convey so little relevant information.

One of the major advantages of a market economy is that it minimizes the necessary data flow, since prices convey most of the information necessary to coordinate economic activity among firms and with consumers. A financial accounting system, in turn, provides the information necessary for firm managers to respond correctly to the market prices of inputs and outputs. A major programme to train accountants and develop modern financial accounts would be among the highest return investments in the Soviet economy.

CULTURAL ATTITUDES

The third basic institution of a market economy is the set of cultural attitudes. Again, this institution is one that Western economists take as given and, as a consequence, have often not understood its importance. The German liberal Wilhelm Röpke (1954) may have best expressed the importance of a specific set of cultural attitudes in concluding that

> An intensive and extensive economic exchange cannot exist or last very long without a minimum of natural trust, confidence in the stability and reliability of the legal–institutional framework (including money), contractual loyalty, honesty, fair play, professional honour and that pride which makes us consider it unworthy of us to cheat, to bribe, or to misuse the authority of the State for egoistic purposes.

In turn, the single condition that most distinguishes a modern market economy from an oriental bazaar is the mutual desire for continued relations. I learned this lesson late. As chief economist of the Ford Motor Company, I was surprised to learn that Ford made billions of dollars of purchases a year from regular suppliers over the telephone with only the skeleton of a contract and with few contract disputes. The mutual desire for continued relations was what enforced the performance of both parties in each transaction. At any time that either party expected to end the relation or expected the other party to end the relation, moreover, the primary remaining discipline on the immediate transaction was the value of the firm's reputation with other parties, not the protection of the formal contract. Only when Ford made a major purchase without the expectation of a future relation was the contract extensive and often disputed. The cultural attitudes that contribute to this 'evolution of cooperation' are subtle but simple: a mutual commitment to *exchange* (rather than threat) as the primary means to coordinate economic activity, the self-restraint to leave something on the table for the other party in each transaction, and the use of the authority of the state only to discipline gross or repeated breaches of contract.

Röpke was most perceptive about the requisite cultural attitudes for a market economy. But he did not develop on those attitudes that would prevent or destroy a market economy. The one attitude most incompatible with a market economy is a profound and pervasive sense of envy. A society can survive pervasive egoism; indeed a market economy relies on it. A market economy, however, cannot survive the levelling instinct, the concern that your neighbour or former schoolmate might be doing better than you are. One should not be surprised that all of the major religious traditions regard envy, covetousness or resentment as a major sin. Envy is a human condition, but it is most destructive of social organization. Envy, combined with the erosion of the constitutional limits on the powers of government, has progressively weakened the Western market economies. And envy may prevent the development of stable market economies in some of the current socialist nations. I am disturbed to hear of old Russian folktales in which the peasants prayed, not for a good harvest or a fecund herd, but for their neighbour's barn to burn or for their neighbour's goats to die. As Röpke observed, it is important not to 'misuse the authority of the State for egoistic purposes'. It is also important not to misuse the powers of government as an instrument of envy.

CONCLUSION

In summary, the three basic institutions – the requisite soft infrastructure – of a market economy are the legal system, the accounting system and the cultural attitudes. I have purposefully avoided a ranking of the importance of these three institutions. In combination, these institutions are rather like a three-legged stool, in that any one short or weak leg seriously reduces the stability of the stool. Individual and state investment in these three institutions is far more important than the other elements of a radical perestroika; indeed, these three institutions are requisite to the success of the other measures.

REFERENCE

Röpke, Wilhelm (1954), 'Economic order and international law', *Recuil des Cours*, Academie de Droit Internationale, **86** (2), 207–71.

28. Conditions affecting the survival of constitution rules*

INTRODUCTION

James Madison's noble objective was

> so to modify the sovereignty as that it may be sufficiently neutral between different parts of the Society to control one part from invading the rights of another, and at the same time sufficiently controlled itself, from setting up an interest adverse to that of the entire society. (Madison 1787)[1]

By that high standard, the Constitution that Madison worked so hard to shape and defend has proved, at least, to be insufficient. The *structure* of the government authorized by the Constitution has proved to be remarkably stable for 200 years. That structure, however, has not proved to be sufficient to avoid a massive change in the effective constitution, especially as it bears on the economic powers of the government.[2]

The seeds of this change were planted many decades ago, but most of this change has occurred in the past 60 years. Over this period, the federal budget share of our national output increased about ninefold, real per capita federal debt increased about eightfold, federal regulatory powers were massively expanded, and the general price level increased about tenfold – without any formal amendment to authorize an expansion of these powers. Moreover, the US experience is unique only in that the massive expansion of government powers began later and has been relatively smaller than in most other countries.

In the absence of a revolution, most changes in the structure of government have been authorized by a change in the formal constitution. But most constitutions, whether written or unwritten, have proved to be only 'parchment barriers' to the expansion of the economic powers of governments, whatever their structure. In other words, constitutions have proven to be moderately effective in preserving political property rights,

* Reprinted by permission from *Constitutional Political Economy*, **1** (2), 1990, 53–62, George Mason University.

but they have proved to be relatively ineffective in protecting economic property rights against 'extraconstitutional' processes of changes in the effective constitution.

The focus of this chapter is *not* on the conditions that have led to the relative growth of government in all countries; that is an important related topic that we also do not understand very well. Rather, the focus is to understand why some types of constitutional rules have proved to be relatively stable, that is relatively immune to change except by constitutional processes, and why other rules have been progressively eroded.

On several occasions, I have agreed to write a paper primarily to force myself to think through an issue that I believe is important but do not understand very well. That provides an opportunity, of course, for both creativity and failure. On beginning this task, I did not understand the conditions that affect the survival of constitutional rules. My conclusion is more disturbing; after some months of reading and thinking about this issue, I still do not understand it very well. That may be only my problem, but I think not. My sense is that we do not yet have an adequate theory of constitutional maintenance. My purpose will be served if this chapter leads others to recognize and address this important issue.

PROBLEMS OF THE CONVENTIONAL THEORY

The conventional American civic textbook explains that the Supreme Court is the guardian of the Constitution. There are at least three major problems with this conventional explanation.

First, there is no plausible theory to explain why the Supreme Court would have either the authority or the incentive to fulfil this role. The Constitution itself does not clearly authorize the Court to resolve constitutional disputes, and the first assertion of this role by the Marshall Court was strongly disputed. Congress has the authority to confirm appointments and approve the budget for the entire federal judiciary and to establish (or abolish) the lower federal courts. The president has the authority to nominate replacements to the federal courts, and he directly commands the resources necessary to enforce the orders of these courts. Why would either Congress or the president tolerate a role for the Supreme Court that does not serve their expected interests? And if the Court had such authority, neither the selection process nor the reward system of the Court appears to reinforce an incentive to maintain constitutional rules that do not serve the interests of the more powerful branches of government.

The controversy surrounding the nomination of Robert Bork to the Supreme Court illustrates this point. Bork was strongly critical of 'judicial activism', primarily by the Warren Court, reflected by the changes in the effective constitution initiated by the Court. On the other hand, Bork was most deferential to majoritarianism, suggesting that the Court should never challenge Congress's interpretation of its own powers. For that reason, it is most ironic that Bork was not confirmed, because liberals are more likely to dominate Congress and conservatives the Supreme Court, at least in the near future.

My colleagues at the Cato Institute, in contrast, have promoted a 'principled judicial activism'. Consistent with this perspective, the Court would refrain from initiating changes in the effective constitution by its own decisions (a position consistent with Bork) but would strike down any attempts by Congress or the presidency to expand their own powers beyond those enumerated in the Constitution (a position not shared by Bork).[3]

My own views are strongly sympathetic with those by my Cato colleagues. I would prefer a Supreme Court that would defend the Constitution against all parties, including itself, thus forcing the pressures for constitutional change through the formal Article V process for amending the Constitution. This position – a rather heroic 'Horatio-at-the-bridge' stand – however, is probably unrealistic. The Court will ultimately respond to political pressure, as illustrated by 'the switch in time that saved nine' in the middle 1930s. My preference is that the Court would have declared most of the New Deal legislation as unconstitutional, as it surely was (and is) on any consistent interpretation of the constitutional language, but I am not surprised that they caved. If they had not Franklin D. Roosevelt and Congress would surely have packed the Court until they had a majority of their choosing. The Supreme Court is somewhat like the Federal Reserve Board: both groups maintain their independence only by responding to political pressure at the worst possible times. The type of 'principled judicial activism' that Cato has promoted is probably unrealistic, but one might hope for an occasional 'principled judicial resignation' rather than the more frequent, and unseemly, conversion to a new, more politic interpretation of the Constitution.

Landes and Posner (1975) provide the most plausible hypothesis about the behaviour of the Supreme Court. They postulate that the Court serves the weighted interests of the current and past Congresses. The current Congress tolerates the role of the Court as an 'anchor' on constitutional change because it increases the durability of current political contracts against changes in the preferences of a future Congress. In this sense, the effective constitution is what the Court decides, but the

Court acts as an agent, albeit imperfect, of a succession of Congresses – not, as in the conventional myth, as an agent of the general population against threats to the Constitution by the other branches of government.

The second problem with the conventional explanation is the accumulating history of cases by which the Court has either initiated or ratified changes in the effective constitution. Indeed, most American courses and textbooks on constitutional law focus on the major cases by which the Court has changed the effective constitution, not on the language and internal logic of the Constitution.

The third problem of the conventional explanation is that it is specific to the United States. In most other countries, the highest court has no constitutional role. What institutions and processes maintain or change the effective constitution in these other countries? Even if the conventional explanation fits the US experience, it fails to provide a general theory of constitutional maintenance and constitutional change.

Although the conventional explanation, I suggest, is wrong, I understand its appeal. Like most of our civic textbook perspectives on political processes, the conventional explanation of the constitutional role of the Court is simple and romantic, appealing to those who look for heroes and villains, not systems and processes, to explain the history of constitutional change.

TOWARDS A THEORY OF CONSTITUTIONAL MAINTENANCE

A small but growing number of scholars have recognized the problem of maintaining the constitutional contract.[4] Most of the recent contributions are based on a model in which some dominant coalition receives all of the net revenues from the supply of government services. The contributors then explore the effects of several conditions that limit the potential of the dominant coalition to exploit people who are not in this coalition. Grossman (1989), for example, explores the effects of political competition and insurrection. Epple and Romer (1989) evaluate the effects of individual mobility. And Buchanan and Faith (1987) evaluate the effects of secession. These new models of what Grossman describes as 'proprietary' government provide fascinating insights about the limits on the exploitative power of government and may soon be accepted (by economists) as the dominant paradigm of the behaviour of government. However, they are not specifically designed to explain why any constitutional rule has survived or to identify the types of rules that are likely to be broken and under what conditions. So, let us start from scratch.

First, it is important to recognize that a constitution is a unique form of contract. A regular contract is an agreement between two parties in a broader legal environment that provides an authoritative independent dispute settlement process. A constitution is a contract among various parties to form a government in which the government – the object of the contract – has the dominant power to interpret the rules and resolve any disputes in its favour. The conditions that maintain a constitution are not legal conditions; they are more like the conditions that maintain the relations among primitive tribes or modern nations. One learns less about constitutional maintenance from reading constitutional law than by understanding how Switzerland, for example, has preserved a prosperous independence in a continent of sometimes-malign much-larger neighbours.

Second, it is useful to understand why most market exchanges involve no formal contract or few contract disputes. I learned this lesson late. As chief economist of the Ford Motor Company, I was surprised to learn that Ford made billions of dollars of purchases a year from regular suppliers over the telephone with only the skeleton of a contract and few contract disputes. The mutual desire for continued relations was what enforced the performance of both parties in each transaction. At any time that either party expected to end the relation or expected the other party to end the relation, moreover, the primary remaining discipline on the immediate transaction was the value of the firm's reputation with other parties, not the protection of the formal contract. In contrast, when Ford made a major purchase without the expectation of a future relation, the contract was most extensive and often disputed.

The processes that lead to 'the evolution of cooperation' in repeated prisoners' dilemma games of uncertain duration are now understood even by academics. Robert Axelrod (1984), for example, has demonstrated that an initial cooperative move followed by a tit-for-tat rule is the dominant strategy in such games. For such relations, the value of a contract is limited to defining what both parties regard as cooperative behaviour, to reduce the probability that a specific move would be mistakenly interpreted by the other party. For such relations, contracts can stabilize 'the evolution of cooperation' but are not necessary to this outcome. It is less clear, however, whether a tit-for-tat strategy is dominant when there are many dimensions of the contract or many parties to the contract.

These observations lead me to a rather spare 'model' of constitutional maintenance summarized in the following propositions:

(1) The effective constitution is the set of rules that serves the interests of the current dominant coalition. A specific constitutional rule, thus, will

be maintained only if it serves the interests of a succession of domi-
nant coalitions.

For this purpose, I define the dominant coalition as the smallest group
that commands the allegiance of the military forces. (If the allegiance of
the military forces is divided, there is no dominant coalition.) In a representative democracy, I suggest, the dominant coalition is the majority of
the lower (popular) house of parliament.

This proposition should be regarded as more general and wholly consistent with the Landes and Posner proposition about the behaviour of
the US Supreme Court. The current dominant coalition will tolerate a
Court that serves as an 'anchor' on changes in the effective constitution
only when the benefits of the increased durability of new political contracts are higher than the costs of restrictions on the authority to make
these contracts, both benefits and costs being measured in terms of the
interests of the dominant coalition. The effective constitution, thus, is
most likely to be changed in crisis conditions, because the demand for
new political contracts increases and the future benefits of existing contracts are discounted at a higher rate.[5]

(2) The effective constitution will change in response to changes in the
  dependence of the dominant coalition on cooperative behaviour by
  those not in this coalition.

This proposition has a rich set of implications:

- An oligarchy is more likely to exploit labourers the smaller its
  dependence on a resident army.
- A government is more likely to renege on the terms of its outstanding debt the smaller its dependence on new loans.
- A government is more likely to break the terms of contracts with
  those not in the dominant coalition the smaller its dependence on
  revenue from foreign trade. (In the *Merchant of Venice*, for example,
  Shakespeare made the case that Venice, as a commercial republic,
  could not afford the precedent of ruling against Shylock, even
  though the contract with Antonio was unreasonable and Shylock, as
  a Jew, was an alien.)
- A government is more likely to exploit the residents of a border
  region the smaller the threat from the adjacent government. (The
  Sudetan Germans, for example, had some tensions with the Czech
  government before 1938 but they were not expelled until after
  Germany was defeated.)

- A government is more likely to exploit the residents of any region the smaller the threat of secession. (The Civil War, by demonstrating the very high costs of secession, may have been the primary condition that enabled the relative growth of the US federal Government.)
- A government is more likely to exploit individuals outside the dominant coalition the lower the mobility of their capital (including human skills) or the lower the value of this capital in regions ruled by other governments. A related implication is that those with the least mobile or most site-dependent capital have the highest relative incentive to be included in the dominant coalition.

(3)   The effective constitution will change in response to changes in the probability that members of the dominant coalition will be replaced.

As Peter Aranson (1988) has observed in a related context, 'It is difficult to overstate the central place of uncertainty in the constitutional construction'. This proposition also has a rich but complex set of implications:

- A government's incentive to exploit individuals outside the dominant coalition increases with the probability that it will be replaced, by reducing the present value of the future benefits of a less-exploitative tax rate. As Grossman and Noh (1989) have demonstrated, however, this is a complex relation, because the equilibrium tax rate also increases, with the cost to replace the dominant coalition. The least exploitative government appears to be one with a long expected tenure despite a low cost of being replaced, but it is not clear that these are compatible conditions.
- The rules enforced by the dominant coalition will depend on the probability that members of that coalition may ever be subject to these rules. This applies to both structural rules and substantive rules.

A concern about the possible loss of membership in the dominant coalition will limit severe violations of civil rights to those groups who are not likely to be part of a future dominant coalition. Such groups are likely to be minority races, such as the blacks following Reconstruction and the Californians of Japanese background during World War II.

Similarly, an interest in a possible opportunity to advance one's status in the dominant coalition will limit the erosion in the powers of superior groups in this coalition. Members of the House of Representatives, for example, are more likely to reduce the powers of the Senate the less likely that members of the House might be selected or elected to the Senate. Political theorists have long recognized the value of a bicameral legislature where the members of the two houses are selected from different bases, but they failed to recognize that this structure is unlikely to survive.[6] In almost all representative democracies, the powers of the upper house have been gradually eroded until or unless the base for the upper house was changed to permit election of those from the lower house. The necessary condition for the survival of a bicameral legislature probably reduces its value. For similar reasons, Congress is more likely to erode the powers of the presidency the less likely that members of the dominant coalition in Congress might be selected for senior positions in the presidency.

An uncertainty about future status also affects such substantive rules as criminal law. It has now become commonplace, for example, to observe that a conservative is a liberal who has been mugged and that a liberal is a conservative who has been arrested.

SOME CONCLUDING THOUGHTS

The several propositions discussed above, I suggest, should be the core of any theory of constitutional maintenance and are probably sufficient for a much richer set of implications. At the same time, we are a long way from a satisfactory theory of constitutional maintenance. For my part, the major puzzle is why many constitutional rules last as long as they do. Why, for example, has there seldom been any substantial reduction in the franchise? Why did most of the economic rules in the US Constitution survive for nearly 150 years and then change dramatically in one lifetime? My sense is that Buchanan and others are right that we have lost a 'constitutional perspective' of a higher law that constrains the scope of laws approved by the contemporary majority. But why did the changes in the effective constitution happen when they did? Why have other rules survived? And where do we go from here? On this issue, the beginning of wisdom is to recognize how little we know.

NOTES

1. James Madison, *Letter to Thomas Jefferson*, 24 October 1787.
2. For efficient summaries of the massive expansion in the economic powers of the US federal government, see Anderson and Hill (1980), Dorn and Manne (1987), Epstein (1985), Gwartney and Wagner (1988), Lee and McKenzie (1987), Niskanen (1988) and Siegen (1980).
3. For an efficient summary of this perspective, see Macedo (1986).
4. Among those who have addressed this issue recently, see Aranson (1988), Buchanan (1975, 1977), Buchanan and Faith (1987), Epple and Romer (1989), Grossman and Noh (1989), Wagner (1987) and Wagner and Gwartney (1988).
5. On this point, see Higgs (1987).
6. For the most analytic development of this point, see Buchanan and Tullock (1962).

REFERENCES

Anderson, T.L. and P.J. Hill (1980), *The Birth of the Transfer Society*, Stanford: Hoover Institution Press.

Aranson, P.H. (1988), 'Procedural and substantive protection of constitutional liberty', in James D. Gwartney and Richard E. Wagner (eds), *Public Choice and Constitutional Economics*, Greenwich: JAI Press, 285–314.

Axelrod, Robert (1984), *The Evolution of Cooperation*, New York: Basic Books.

Buchanan, J.M. (1975), *The Limits of Liberty*, Chicago: University of Chicago Press.

Buchanan, J.M. (1977), *Freedom in Constitutional Contract*, College Station: Texas A&M Press.

Buchanan, J.M. and R.L. Faith (1987), 'Secession and the limits of taxation', *American Economic Review*, **77**, 1023–31.

Buchanan, J.M. and G. Tullock (1962), *The Calculus of Consent*, Ann Arbor: University of Michigan Press.

Dorn, J.A. and H.G. Manne (eds) (1987), *Economic Liberties and the Judiciary*, Fairfax: George Mason University Press.

Epple, D. and Th. Romer (1989), 'Mobility and redistribution', *Working Papers in Economics E–89–26*, Stanford: Hoover Institution.

Epstein, R.A. (1985), *Takings: Private Property and the Power of Eminent Domain*, Cambridge, MA: Harvard University Press.

Grossman, H.I. (1989), 'A general equilibrium model of insurrections', Unpublished Manuscript, Department of Economics: Brown University.

Grossman, H.I. and S.J. Noh (1989), 'Proprietary public finance, political competition, and reputation', Unpublished Manuscript, Department of Economics: Brown University.

Gwartney, J.D. and R.E. Wagner (eds) (1988), *Public Choice and Constitutional Economics*, Greenwich: JAI Press.

Higgs, R. (1987), *Crisis and Leviathan: Critical Episodes in the Growth of American Government*, New York: Oxford University Press.

Landes, William N. and Richard A. Posner (1975), 'The independent judiciary in an interest-group perspective', *Journal of Law and Economics*, **18**, 875–901.

Lee, D.R. and R.B. McKenzie (1987), *Regulating Government*, Lexington: Lexington Books.

Niskanen, W.A. (1988), 'The erosion of the economic constitution', in J.D. Gwartney and R.E. Wagner (eds), *Public Choice and Constitutional Economics*, Greenwich: JAI Press, xi–xiii.

Siegen, B. (1980), *Economic Liberties and the Constitution*, Chicago: University of Chicago Press.

Wagner, R.E. (1987), 'Parchment, guns, and the maintenance of constitutional contract', in Ch.K. Rowley (ed.), *Democracy and Public Choice*, New York: Basil Blackwell, 105–21.

Wagner, R.E. and J.D. Gwartney (1988), 'Public choice and constitutional order', in J.D. Gwartney and R.E. Wagner (eds), *Public Choice and Constitutional Economics*, Greenwich: JAI Press, 29–56.

29. The case for a new fiscal constitution*

For the first 140 years of US history, the federal budget was effectively constrained by two fiscal rules: the formal limits within the Constitution on the enumerated spending powers and an informal rule that the government could borrow only during recessions and wars. At the end of the 1920s, federal expenditures were 2.6 per cent of GNP, most of which was for the military and the deferred costs of prior wars. And a budget surplus, characteristic of peacetime recovery years, constrained the federal debt to an amount equal to 16 per cent of GNP. The constraints on federal expenditures and borrowing also contributed to the conditions that led to a roughly stable general price level over this long period.

Over the past six decades, however, federal expenditures have increased to nearly 25 per cent of GNP, most of which is for new forms of services and transfer payments. Larger and more frequent budget deficits (continuous since 1969) have increased the federal debt held by the public to an amount equal to about 50 per cent of GNP. And the general price level is now about nine times the level at the beginning of this period. This dramatic change in fiscal and monetary conditions occurred without one amendment to the Constitution to authorize a change in the fiscal rules. Our effective fiscal constitution has been transformed into one in which Congress and the president may authorize any type or amount of expenditures and taxes, subject only to the voting rules for routine legislation.

How did this happen? Should economists be concerned about this change in the fiscal constitution? What, if anything, should be done about it?

THE EROSION OF THE FISCAL CONSTITUTION

The Constitution (Article 1, Section 8) grants to Congress only 18 rather narrowly defined powers, only a few of which – such as the powers to establish Post Offices and post roads, raise and support Armies, and to provide and maintain a Navy – involve the potential for substantial

* Reprinted by permission from *Journal of Economic Perspectives*, **6** (2), Spring 1992, 13–24.

expenditures. There were numerous minor breaches of these limits from the earliest years, but the aggregate effect of these activities was not substantial. For example, the Constitution does not authorize the federal government to build and maintain ports and canals, develop national forests and parks, or provide veterans' benefits and workers' compensation – all of which were approved prior to World War I. In addition, the federal government levied an income tax during the Civil War, a clear breach of the prohibition against direct taxes prior to approval of the Sixteenth Amendment.

The Great Depression and the New Deal, of course, were the primary events that led to a massive breach in the fiscal constitution. After the Supreme Court ruled that some of the major regulatory initiatives of the early New Deal were unconstitutional, Congress and the Roosevelt administration switched to a transfer payment strategy. At the time that the Social Security Act was approved in August 1935, however, there was still considerable doubt whether the Court would rule it unconstitutional. This issue was indirectly resolved by the Court's decision in *United States v. Butler*, in January 1936. Although this decision ruled, on narrow grounds, that the Agricultural Adjustment Act of 1933 was unconstitutional, it provided the judicial opening for the developing welfare state by asserting that 'the power of Congress to authorize appropriations of public money for public purposes is not limited by the direct grants of legislative power found in the Constitution.' This first major accommodation to the New Deal saved the Court from Franklin Roosevelt's threat to pack it with more acquiescent justices, but it effectively destroyed the fiscal constitution. In effect, each Congress may now write its own fiscal constitution, subject only to the restraint that the appropriations must serve some vague concept of public purpose.

The rest is history. The major new spending programmes of the New Deal were not challenged on constitutional grounds. As late as the Eisenhower administration, there was still some deference to the enumerated powers but only to justify new activities; the first major federal highway and education programmes for example, were both rationalized on national security grounds. Starting with the Johnson administration in the 1960s, however, the enumerated powers have no longer commanded even rhetorical deference. There is no longer any basis for rejecting demands for new federal services (or transfer payments) on the basis that the federal government has no constitutional authority to finance these services, a condition that makes federal politicians appear hard-hearted if they fail to respond to these demands.

The fiscal constitution of the United States is now only a parchment barrier, and Americans have no legal recourse to enjoin a continued expansion of the services financed by government. The demand for some of these new services, probably including social security and unemployment insurance, may have been sufficient to approve amendments to the Constitution to authorize these services. However, without any such test of constitutional consent, Congress may now authorize many other services as well. The substantive limits on federal expenditures are no longer binding.

The conditions that led to the erosion of the informal but effective rule on federal borrowing were similar, except for the absence of any role by the Supreme Court. Politicians have long had an incentive to borrow to finance current expenditures, primarily because the interests of children and future generations are not adequately represented in legislatures. However, the folk wisdom supporting balanced budgets has been and remains quite strong. In this case, the economics profession must bear part of the blame for undermining the borrowing rule. For about 40 years, from the second Roosevelt administration to the Nixon administration, Keynesian macroeconomists provided a rationale for increasing spending without increasing taxes as a means to reduce involuntary unemployment. The federal budget had a surplus in only twelve years during this period, but economic growth and increasing inflation reduced the ratio of the public debt to GNP from World War II to the mid-1970s. The amount and frequency of federal borrowing during this period may have been undesirable, but it was at least sustainable. This perspective finally fell victim to the new classical macroeconomics, the developing empirical evidence, and a confusion about the appropriate Keynesian response to the stagflation of the late 1970s.

Soon after, the new supply-siders provided a rationale for reducing taxes without reducing expenditures as a means to increase the incentives to work, save and invest. The fiscal and economic record during this period has included continuous large deficits, lower economic growth and inflation, and a continuous increase in the ratio of the public debt to GNP. The record of federal borrowing during this period was and is clearly unsustainable.[1] At some time, some action will be necessary to stabilize or reduce the ratio of the federal debt (and interest payments) to GNP.

On two occasions during this period, Congress bound itself by new fiscal rules in an attempt to reduce the deficit: the Gramm–Rudman rules approved in late 1985 and the budget agreement approved in late 1990. The Gramm–Rudman rules proved to be moderately effective for several years but finally fell victim to the explosion of the savings and loans (S&L) bank deposit insurance liabilities, the increased demand for domestic spending, and the 1990–91 recession. The rules approved by the budget agreement in 1990 seem unlikely to survive beyond 1992. Congress appears unable to bind itself to a sustainable borrowing rule, at least one that is sustainable in a low-inflation environment.

THE CASE FOR A NEW FISCAL CONSTITUTION

Should the erosion of the fiscal constitution be a cause for concern? My answer is 'yes', because majority rule is not a sufficient constraint on the decisions affecting federal expenditures, taxes, and borrowing. A new set of rules for an explicit fiscal constitution is surely one plausible answer.

At the extreme, one sort of constitution would simply require the unanimous consent of all individuals affected by a specific decision. Such a constitution need have no other provisions – no enumeration of authorized powers or protected rights. Most such organizations, however, are not viable; the costs of making decisions and bargaining with others to achieve unanimous consent are usually higher than the potential value of the group activity. Moreover, such organizations are subject to strategic behaviour; an individual may have an incentive to withhold approval of a decision to gain an even larger personal benefit from subsequent bargaining.

All of us are willing to delegate many decisions within a family, firm and other voluntary organizations to realize the benefits of comparative advantage and the reduction of decision-making costs. For this same reason, many nations have chosen a representative government with a majority voting rule. Such delegations, however, are almost always subject to substantive, quantitative or procedural constraints on the group to which the decisions are delegated. Moreover, there is an important relation between the voting rule and the several types of constraints: the lower the voting rule, the lower the probability that a specific decision will serve one's interests, the more important are the constraints on the authorized powers of the organization.[2]

For governments, the realistic alternatives are to authorize a narrow range of powers and a majority voting rule or a broader range of powers and a supermajority rule. The formal structure of the national government of the United States and Switzerland are examples of the first alternative. The structure of the American states, Swiss cantons and the national government of Finland are examples of the second alternative. Many American states and Swiss cantons, for example, require either a supermajority of the legislature or a referendum to increase taxes or to issue new debt. Finland's constitution requires a two-thirds vote of their parliament to increase taxes for more than one year and a five-sixths vote to approve any measure that restricts property rights. One should not be surprised that the relative size of government is generally lower in federal systems, although governments have grown rapidly almost everywhere. The alternative most likely to lead to fiscal trouble in a democracy is a national government with plenary powers and a majority rule, but the effective structure of most national governments, including the United States, is unfortunately evolving in that direction.

In the United States, the erosion of the fiscal constitution has made the federal government more powerful, and the progressive broadening of the franchise should have made it more responsive to the interests of the majority. There is reason to question, however, whether the growth of government has served even the interests of the majority. This conjecture can be tested by estimating the marginal effect of increased expenditures and taxes on conditions such as votes and migration.[3] A broadly popular fiscal programme should lead to an increased vote for the candidate of the incumbent party and net migration into the area served by the government; a fiscal programme that does not serve the interests of the majority should have the opposite effects. The evidence from both voting and migration studies suggests that government budgets are larger than are consistent with a majority-rule equilibrium.

The regressions presented below are only illustrative of a larger body of voting and migration studies. The results presented in Table 29.1 consider the results of fiscal decisions on voting outcomes.[4] A common form for these regressions is to use the popular vote margin (measured as the log of popular vote for the candidate of the incumbent party minus the log of popular vote for the candidate of the major opposition party) as the dependent variable. The independent variables then include a constant term, which reflects the vote advantage of the candidate of the incumbent party; a war dummy, set as 1 for elections in war years 1944, 1952 and 1968, and 0 in other years; a term for economic growth, measured as the log of real GNP per capita minus the log of real GNP per capita in the prior election year; a term for the change in federal tax burden, measured as the log of real federal taxes per capita minus the log of real federal taxes per capita in the prior election year; and a term for the growth of federal expenditures, measured as the log of real federal expenditures per capita minus the log of real federal expenditures per capita in the prior election year.

Table 29.1 presents the results of two regressions of this form, one using taxes and one using expenditures as the fiscal variable. The sample is the 24 presidential elections from 1896 through 1988. The marginal effects of each variable on the percentage of the total popular vote for the candidate of the incumbent party are about one-fourth of the

Table 29.1 Economic and fiscal effects on the popular vote for the president

Constant	0.100	0.099
	(0.043)	(0.041)
War dummy	−0.341	−0.278
	(0.130)	(0.129)
Change in real GNP per capita	2.171	1.573
	(0.375)	(0.308)
Change in federal tax burden	−0.489	
	(0.118)	
Change in federal expenditures		−0.250
		(0.056)
$\bar{R}^2$	0.600	0.624
SER	0.185	0.179
DW	2.255	2.327

estimated coefficients. The standard errors are the numbers in parentheses below each coefficient.

The general results of these tests, roughly consistent with that from other studies, are that incumbency and economic growth favour the candidate of the incumbent party and that a war and higher taxes favour the opposition candidate. Candidates of an incumbent party have generally survived an increase in taxes only because the voters have a strong preference for continuity and credit the incumbent party for general economic growth. For the argument here, the most important result is that a 10 per cent increase in real federal tax revenues per capita since the prior election year appears to have reduced the popular vote for the presidential candidate of the incumbent party by about 1.2 percentage points. The negative effect of higher taxes is stronger than that of higher expenditures, probably because future taxes are more closely related to current taxes than to current expenditures.

People also react to government tax and spending policies by moving. Again, a majority-rule equilibrium should have no marginal effect on net migration; higher government expenditures and taxes should lead to net immigration if this fiscal programme is broadly popular and net outmigration if it does not serve the interests of the majority. The recent pattern of net migration among the states, thus, provides a basis for testing whether state and local fiscal programmes serve the interests of the majority.

For this purpose, the sample is the 48 contiguous states. The regressions presented in Table 29.2 are of a common form for such analyses. The dependent variable is net migration between 1980 and 1988, mea-

Table 29.2 Economic and fiscal effects on interstate migration

Constant	62.960	53.378
	(22.022)	(24.274)
Unemployment rate in 1980	−1.134	−1.350
	(0.396)	(0.385)
Percentage of population in	0.104	0.068
metropolitan areas in 1980	(0.041)	(0.036)
Population density in 1980	1.392	
	(0.757)	
Share of income from agriculture, 1980		−0.139
		(0.059)
Share in income from minerals, 1980		−0.141
		(0.040)
Manufacturing shipments as share		−0.036
of income, 1980		(0.024)
Log of state and local taxes, FY 1981	−8.651	−6.323
	(3.202)	(3.438)
Migration from 1970–80	0.400	0.314
	(0.056)	(0.052)
$\bar{R}^2$	0.687	0.753
SER	3.935	3.496

sured as a percentage of the population in 1980. Independent variables include a constant term; the unemployment rate in 1980; the percentage of the population living in metropolitan areas in 1980; the log of population density in the state in 1980; gross farm income as a share of total personal income in 1980; the value of mineral production as a share of personal income in 1980; the value of manufacturing shipments as a percentage of personal income in 1980; the log of state and local tax receipts per resident in fiscal 1981; and net migration from 1970 to 1980 as a share of the 1970 population. Thus, regressions of this sort attempt to explain interstate migration patterns during the 1980s entirely in terms of the economic, demographic and fiscal conditions at the beginning of the decade.

As shown in Table 29.2, migration patterns during the 1980s appear to have been a positive function of the percentage metropolitan, population density and the migration patterns during the 1970s and a negative function of the unemployment rate and state and local tax revenues per capita at the beginning of the decade. Population density, in turn, appears to be a (negative) proxy for the relative importance of agriculture and mineral production in a state. (One of the surprising results of this regression, not shown here, is that personal income per capita does not appear to have had a significant effect on migration patterns in the 1980s.) For the argument being made here, the most important result is that a 10 per cent higher level of state and local tax revenues per capita in fiscal 1981 appears to have reduced the net migration rate (from 1980 to 1988) by 0.6 to 0.9 percentage points.

Apparently, something is wrong with the fiscal rules that bear on the level of expenditures and taxes, both at the federal and the state and local levels. Both the voting data and the migration data suggest that government expenditures and taxes are higher than would be approved by a majority of the population.

NEW FISCAL RULES TO LIMIT FEDERAL BORROWING AND TAXES

The case for a new fiscal rule affecting the authority of the federal government to borrow is based on three observations. First, the current pattern of federal expenditures and receipts is not sustainable. Second, it is preferable to stabilize the ratio of the federal debt (or interest payments) to GNP sooner than later, at levels of this ratio closer to the present level than at a higher level; net interest payments, already the third largest component of federal expenditures, are also among the most rapidly growing components. Third, Congress has demonstrated no ability to bind itself or a subsequent Congress to a sustainable borrowing rule.

Economists should have learned from the experience of the 1980s that the short-term economic effects of federal borrowing are much weaker than most of us had previously expected. The large federal deficits, for example, had no apparent effects on inflation rates, interest rates or exchange rates, although we have yet to sort out why this was the case. The primary effect of the increased deficit appears to have been a reduction in the net US foreign investment, but most of this effect appears only after a lag.[5] And the level of the deficit seems to be more of an effect than a cause of changes in employment, domestic investment, or total output. None of David Stockman's apocalyptic visions about the adverse consequences of higher federal deficits has proved accurate. There may be some 'cliff' out there, beyond which additional federal borrowing would have severe economic effects, but the much larger relative deficits by the government of Italy, for example, reduce the credibility of a conjecture that the United States risks such effects in the near term.

The absence of obvious near-term adverse effects of the federal deficit, moreover, has contributed to the erosion of the political discipline necessary to enforce a sustainable fiscal policy; if some adverse effects had been more apparent, the normal political incentives of Congress would probably have been sufficient to reduce the growth of the federal debt. The primary problem of federal borrowing is a moral problem: we are passing an increasing part of the cost of current government services to our children – without their consent. Federal net interest payments are now about $2000 per taxpayer; each new generation of voters and taxpayers would clearly prefer that less borrowing had been authorized in prior years. The case for a new constitutional rule on the authority to increase the federal debt is to protect our children from our own lack of fiscal discipline.

The design of the US Constitution was to limit federal expenditures to the enumerated powers defined in Article 1, Section 8, with the amount of such expenditures to be determined by the normal voting rules for appropriations. There is a reasonable case that such substantive limits may be preferable to a supermajority rule on the budget totals. Such substantive limits, for example, permit a federal politician to respond to constituent pleas by saying, 'I would like to help you, but the Constitution does not authorize Congress to finance this service'. But that genie is already out of the bottle. Most of the current activities of the federal government have no constitutional basis in the enumerated powers, and there is no prospect of a constitutional consensus on the original substantive limits or on some new set of substantive limits

Thus, the appropriate response to the erosion of the substantive limits on federal fiscal powers is to approve more constraining voting rules on decisions affecting the budget totals. One should reject out of hand the argument that such rules are inherently inconsistent with democratic government. The US Constitution requires a supermajority to approve several measures. Congress has established a supermajority rule for several other types of measures, now including proposals to *reduce* taxes. Almost all of the states have some form of special rule on the issue of new debt. Many of the states require a supermajority of the legislature or a referendum to increase taxes. And the constitution of other countries, such as Finland as mentioned above, require a supermajority to increase taxes or restrict property rights. Majority rule has instrumental value – it is the minimum voting rule that avoids inconsistent decisions on the same vote – but it does not have normative value in and of itself.[6] There is a strong case for requiring a higher voting rule on more important decisions, such as the overall levels of federal taxation and the public debt.

For those who accept the analysis to this point, there are still two other important questions: what new fiscal rules merit considerations? Is there a potential constitutional consensus for these rules?

The arithmetic of the federal budget indicates that two new fiscal rules would be sufficient: total outlays minus total receipts equals the deficit, which in turn equals the increase in the outstanding debt. Rules that limit any two of these variables also limit the others. The considerations that bear on the design of a proposed amendment include the choice of which two variables to limit, whether the limits should be direct or indirect, whether the limits should be on the expected or actual levels of these variables, and the vote ratio required for approval.

The most efficient way for me to summarize my views on these issues is to start with my preferred version of a proposed fiscal amendment and then to explain my reason for choosing this specific form. I have been involved in the design of proposed fiscal amendments (a few of which have been approved) at both the state and federal level for 20 years, and my currently preferred version of a federal amendment reflects some evolution of my views. Here is my proposed amendment:

Section 1 Congress may increase the limit on the public debt of the United States only by the approval of two-thirds of the members of each House.

Section 2 Any bill to levy a new tax or increase the rate or base of an existing tax shall become law only by the approval of two-thirds of the members of each House.

Section 3 The above two sections of this amendment shall be suspended in any fiscal year during which a declaration of war is in effect.

Section 4 This amendment shall be effective beginning in the second fiscal year after ratification.

The primary consideration that leads me to prefer a focus on debt totals and increases in tax rates is to avoid the problems of a direct vote on the budget totals. Congress does not (and should not) vote to approve the actual levels of total outlays, receipts and the deficit, because each of these variables is subject to both estimation errors and forecast errors. Since 1976, based on the Congressional Budget Act of 1974, Congress has voted to approve a budget resolution establishing target levels of total outlays, receipts and the deficit and the allocation of outlays among the major programmes. This resolution, however, has no force of law and has not been sufficient to constrain the growth of the budget totals. Requiring a supermajority rule to approve the budget resolution would only increase the controversies about possible biases of the forecasts of outlays and receipts. My preference is to focus the supermajority votes on two types of bills that Congress has addressed since the dawn of the Republic: the bill to authorize an increase in the limit on the public debt and on any bill to increase any tax.

A firmer limit on public debt would constrain the increase in the public debt without requiring either an estimated or actual balance of outlays and receipts in any fiscal year. Moreover, this approach would ease the problems of transition from the current large deficit to an expected balance; prior to the effective date of the amendment, Congress could set a limit on the public debt that would permit a transition to an expected balance over a period of years. At such time that an expected balance is in prospect, the limit on the public debt should be set to permit borrowing to finance the unexpected increase in outlays and decline in receipts that has been characteristic of US recessions. There is a legitimate concern, in the absence of a limit on the expected deficits, that a limit on the public debt would be 'gamed' by declaring some types of borrowing to be outside the limit or by forcing an increase in the limit to avoid an outlay reduction or tax increase during a recession, but this problem is at least smaller than our current deficit problem.

My proposed tax limit would require a supermajority vote to increase any tax, which would avoid the controversies about whether a specific tax change or set of tax changes would increase total receipts. Of course, the federal tax code is far from perfect, and this proposed rule would also increase the vote required for a revenue-neutral tax reform. This seems like a small price to pay, however, to reduce the continuous rent-seeking and rent-defending costs of a tax code that is subject to frequent revision. This proposed limit would provide a much needed stability to the structure of the tax code. My preference would be to include tariffs in this limit, but not user fees. This limit would also be subject to some gaming, primarily affecting the definition of user fees, but again this problem should be relatively minor.

There is a legitimate concern that supermajority rules would lead government towards an increased use of mandated benefits and, thus, shift more of the cost of government decisions from the general tax base to the regulated parties. My own concern about this condition leads me to conclude that some additional constitutional rule to limit the conditions under which regulations are imposed should also be considered. This problem, however, may not be as serious as one expects; regulations are a quite imperfect substitute for expenditures and taxes, because the benefits and costs of these two approaches accrue to a different mix of interests.[7]

The case for the last two sections of the proposed amendment is simpler. Any potential aggressor should be warned that these limits would be suspended upon the declaration of war; this would also increase the incentive to force a declaration of war as a condition for authorizing a major military activity. And some lag between ratification and the effective date of the amendment is necessary to permit the administration and Congress to adjust to the new fiscal rules.

Is there a potential constitutional consensus for a change in our fiscal constitution? The following evidence is offered to suggest the potential for such a consensus. Public opinion polls have long indicated about 80 per cent support for a balanced budget amendment. The legislatures of more than 30 states have endorsed a resolution requesting Congress to approve a balanced budget/tax limitation amendment and authorizing a constitutional convention to draft such an amendment if Congress fails to act. More than two-thirds of the Senate approved a balanced budget/tax limitation amendment in 1982. (Our current fiscal problems would be substantially smaller if this amendment had been ratified and become effective in the mid-1980s.) And a similar amendment, with a stronger balanced budget provision and a weaker tax-limit provision, failed to pass the House by only seven votes in 1990. Both of the proposed amendments considered by Congress were crudely drafted, unduly complex and far too wordy. This history provides a plausible case that Congress would approve binding itself by a new set of constitutional fiscal rules, especially if the proposed amendment were better drafted and supported by the legislatures of a few more states.

WHAT ARE THE ALTERNATIVES?

Of course, the concern about the fiscal condition of the federal government is much broader than the consensus on whether any new fiscal rules would be desirable, and no change in fiscal rules would resolve all of America's fiscal problems. It may also be true that some change in the fiscal rules proposed above may be preferable. Suggestions are welcome.

The American economics community has long criticized the fiscal policies of the federal government. Criticism is useful, but it is not enough. If economists believe that the current fiscal problems are so large as to pose a threat to our future standard of living, they should either defend the ability of the current political system to reduce those problems, or evaluate and make clear their views about the case for a new fiscal constitution.

NOTES

1. The strongest direct evidence of the unsustainability of recent fiscal policy is the progressive increase in the ratio of federal net interest payments to GNP. For a more technical analysis, see Hakkio and Rush (1991).
2. See Buchanan and Tullock (1962) for the first formal development of the relation between the authorized powers of a government and the voting rule. Mueller (1991) recently extended this approach to the analysis of constitutional rights.
3. The share of a group that receives some net benefit from the decision of the group, however, will usually be higher than the share required to approve the decision.
4. See Niskanen (1979) for a set of prior estimates of this relation, based on the presidential elections from 1896 to 1972.
5. See Niskanen (1991) for my own estimates of the effects of the combined government sector deficit on the US foreign investment balance.
6. Of course, majority rule is not sufficient to assure consistent decisions on the same issue over a series of votes.
7. For two perspectives on this issue, see Wildavsky (1980) and Flowers (1992).

REFERENCES

Buchanan, James M. and G. Tullock (1962), *The Calculus of Consent*, Ann Arbor: University of Michigan Press.

Flowers, Marilyn R., (1992), 'The political economy of mandated spending,' *Cato Journal*, **12** (2), Spring–Summer, 337–48.

Hakkio, Craig S. and Mark Rush (1991), 'Is the budget deficit "too large"?' *Economic Inquiry*, 29 July, 429–45.

Mueller, Dennis (1971), 'Constitutional rights,' *Journal of Law, Economics, and Organization* **7** (2), 313–33.

Niskanen, William A. (1979) 'Economic and fiscal effects on the popular vote for the president', in Douglas W. Rae and Theodore J. Eismeier (eds), *Public Policy and Public Choice*, Beverly Hills: Sage Publications pp. 93–117.

Niskanen, William A. (1991), 'The determinants of US capital imports', *Annals of the American Academy of Political and Social Science*, July, **516**, 36–49.

Wildavsky, Aaron (1980) *How to Limit Government Spending*, Berkeley: University of California Press.

30. The reflections of a grump*

Over time, maybe a consequence of ageing, I have become somewhat of a grump. I have increasing difficulty with child-proof packaging. As my eyesight has weakened, I am only partially comforted by the illusion of greater strength: when I was child, for example, I could hardly lift $10 worth of groceries; now I can hardly see $10 worth of groceries.

More to the point of this chapter, presumably, the simple models of early public choice now seem to be romantic rationalizations of democratic theory. Much of the subsequent literature is a collection of intellectual games. Our speciality has developed clever models that predict the signs of first and second derivatives but cannot answer such single questions as 'Why do people vote?'. More important, we have no satisfactory explanations of the major political developments of our lifetime:

- the massive expansion of government budgets and regulation,
- the erosion of the economic constitution, and
- the progressive spread and recent collapse of communism.

Public choice has now become a recognized field of academic study. It is not clear, however, that we have much of interest to tell the rest of the world.

Our system of representative democracy may be the best conceivable form of government, maybe, as Fukuyama (1992) suggests, 'the end of history'. The accumulating evidence, however, suggests that the outcomes of representative democracy are only loosely related to the preferences of the population.

Studies of the popular vote, for example, indicate that an increase in real per capita government spending (or revenues) reduces the popular vote for the candidate of the incumbent party (Niskanen 1979; and Peltzman 1987). Similarly, studies of migration patterns indicate net migration from states with high government spending to those with lower spending (Niskanen 1992). These types of results are strongly inconsistent with our standard models of vote-maximizing behaviour by incumbent politicians. Other types of evidence only add to the confusion;

* Reprinted by permission from *Public Choice*, **77**, 1993, 151–8.

estimates of the demand for government services based on cross-section data, for example, explain only about one-half the increase in real per capita government spending over time (Borcherding 1977). Many national and regional governments have pursued destructive economic policies for decades without a substantial reversal of these policies short of a near collapse. I read the broad body of evidence to suggest that the processes of representative democracy lead to a higher level of government spending and regulation than is preferred by a majority of the voters or the population. Much of the resulting redistribution, in turn, is not from the rich to the poor but from the general population to those to whom the agenda setters are most responsive.

A PERSONAL PERSPECTIVE ON THE REALITY OF AMERICAN POLITICS

Figure 30.1 summarizes my rather grumpy perspective on contemporary American politics. The vertical axis measures the number (or percentage) of voters who favour a specific level of government spending. The horizontal axis (from right to left) measures the level of real government spending per capita. This distribution of preferences at any specific time, in turn, is a function of the distribution of expected tax payments and the level and distribution of current spending. My judgement, in

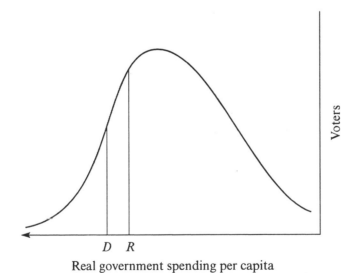

Real government spending per capita

Figure 30.1 Distribution of voter preferences for government spending

addition, is that the characteristic position of Republican candidates is somewhat closer to the most preferred level of spending but that the characteristic positions of both major party candidates is to the 'left' of the most preferred level.

All right, Niskanen, your perspective seems plausible, but it raises some very awkward questions:

1. Why do the Republicans lose so many elections? The simple but incomplete answer is that the Republicans, as in 1992, are often 'the stupid party'. A more informative answer is that the popular vote is also a function of conditions other than the level of government spending and that the Republicans have often not been as effective in promoting or identifying with these other conditions.

   A function of the following form explains most of the variance in the popular vote:

$$LVR = \propto - \beta DLS + \Sigma \gamma_i O_i,$$

   where LVR is the log of the ratio of the popular vote for the candidate of the incumbent party over the popular vote for the candidate of the other major party, DLS is the change in real per capita government spending since the prior election, and O_t are the several other conditions that most affect the popular vote. For the elections for the president and for a governor, the other major condition in this function is the change in real per capita income since the prior election, and the coefficient on this variable is substantially larger than the (absolute) value of the coefficient on government spending. As a consequence, a substantial increase in government spending is consistent with the election of the candidate of the incumbent party if general economic conditions are satisfactory.

   Similarly, for the elections for Congress and the legislatures, the other major condition in this function is the effectiveness of the incumbent as an intermediary with the bureaucracy and in securing preferences for interests in his or her district. Again, a substantial increase in spending is consistent with the election of the candidate of the incumbent party if the incumbent has been effective in these roles. The 1992 election reflected both a broad discontent with the general performance of Congress and an endorsement of the performance of most individual members. Although congressional term limits were approved in every state on which this issue was on the ballot, almost every incumbent member of Congress running in the general election was reelected.

In summary, the popular vote is a vote for (or against) a *package* of conditions specific to each candidate and party. Voters do not appear to have endorsed a higher level of government spending, but politicians and parties that approve higher spending can usually be elected if their performance or position on other important conditions is satisfactory.

2. Why don't the Republicans move to the right? The simple answer is that the Republicans can win elections without endorsing lower spending as long as the Democrats are a high spending party. The more complex answer is that almost all the agenda setters in American politics – the interest groups, the bureaucracy, the intellectual community and the media – have a stake in big government, and any move to the right on spending issues is broadly described as unrealistic, reactionary, unfeeling, and so on. The political calculus of concentrated benefits and diffused costs will assure that the advocates of big government will continue to dominate the 'culture of spending'.

3. Why don't the Democrats endorse lower spending? The simple answer is that the Democrats can win elections as long as the Republicans make serious mistakes on other major issues. The more complex answer is that the Democrats are more dependent on party activists who have an ideological or pecuniary stake in big government. Similarly, the role of party activists has led the Republican party to endorse a position on abortion that is substantially different from the vote-maximizing position. The role of both party activists and money in elections restrains the opportunity for a party to choose a vote-maximizing position on the issues. There have been very few major shifts in party positions in American history, but it would be useful to study the conditions that led to these shifts. The Democrats, for example, were generally the small government party through the nineteenth century and were the low tariff party until the 1980s. And in this century, the Republicans were generally the small defence party until the 1980s.

4. Why doesn't a third party arise on the right'? In fact, the largest third party votes in the period since World War II were for candidates on the right, George Wallace in 1968 and Ross Perot in 1992. The American electoral system, however, is strongly biased against third parties. The only condition in which a third party can be successful is when one or both of the major parties splits on a major issue, such as slavery. As a rule, the two major parties can move substantially apart from a vote-maximizing position without significant risk from a third party. Ross Perot, for example, won 19 per cent of the popular vote in 1992 without winning one electoral vote.

IMPLICATIONS FOR FUTURE RESEARCH

Our simple models of public choice suggest that the issue positions of political candidates will converge on the vote-maximizing position. That is the only basis for a conclusion that the outcomes of the political process reflect the revealed preferences of a majority of the voters. My perspective, as summarized above, suggests that there is no basis for this conclusion. Our research agenda for the next 25 years should focus on the effects of several characteristics of the political process that may and, I believe, often do lead to very different outcomes.

1. More than one issue is important Voters face two (or more) *packages* of issues positions and candidate characteristics and vote for the package that most closely reflects the weighted average of their preferences. When more than one issue is important, a candidate may be elected without choosing a vote-maximizing position on any issue. The more extreme the position of one candidate on one important issue, the more extreme the other candidate may be on other issues. We need better empirical research on the relative importance of a range of issues and better analysis of the effects of 'package voting' on the choice of candidate positions on specific issues.
2. The role of party activists and financial contributors is important The 'production function' of votes for a specific candidate includes their package of issue positions, the activities of party activists, and the amount of financial contributions. As a consequence, the choice of issue positions will be dependent, in part, on the interests of both party activists and financial contributors, as well as on the issue positions of the opposing candidate. The dependence of any candidate on both party activists and financial contributors seriously constrains the opportunity to select a vote-maximizing position on issues of special importance to these groups. We need better empirical research on this production function and better analysis of the effects of the election resources on the choice of issue positions.
3. Voters are 'rationally ignorant' One of the few conclusions of early public choice that have survived subsequent analysis is that voters have very little incentive to invest in information about the political choices. Most of the information on which they base their choices is a byproduct of other activities, such as work and entertainment. We need better empirical research on the types of information that voters receive as a byproduct of these activities and better analysis of the effects of this information on voter choices.

4. Much voting may be 'expressive' rather than 'consequentialist'. As a registered Republican in the District of Columbia, I find it especially difficult to explain why I vote, but this is only an extreme example of the difficulty of explaining, by consequentialist reasoning, why anyone votes. If the decision to vote is primarily an expressive act, such as an endorsement of the democratic process, is it reasonable to believe that the choices in the voting booth are based on consequentialist considerations? Maybe so, but even in this case the outcome of the vote is decided by the group that makes the initial expressive decision to vote at all. We need better empirical research on the conditions that affect voting participation and better analysis of the effects of voting participation on the political outcomes. What are people doing when they vote? If this sounds like an appeal for some careful political psychology, so be it.

5. Agenda setters are important Maybe I have worked in Washington too long. My impression, however, is that the focus of political debate and the range of the alternatives considered are almost entirely determined by the 'inner circle' of players in the political process. Congress and the president, of course, have the authority to make all of the political decisions, but the issues that they choose to address and the options considered are strongly shaped by the interest groups, the bureaucracy, politically active intellectuals and the major media. And many of the detailed political choices are finally made by nonelected officials in the bureaux, regulatory agencies and courts.

Most political choices by the federal government are strongly affected by a 'Beltway mentality' that may have little relation to the preferences of most voters. Almost all witnesses at congressional hearing on spending issues, for example, favour higher spending for the specific programme being reviewed. Congressional votes for higher spending increase as a function of tenure in office. All presidents elected since 1968 have 'run against Washington', but the relative federal fiscal and regulatory burden has continued to increase.

Who decides, for example, whether we have a 'health-care crisis'? Why does Washington now perceive a health-care crisis when 86 per cent of the population has health insurance and the average life expectancy at birth is 75 years, whereas there was no such perceived crisis in 1940 when only 10 per cent of the population had limited health insurance and the average life expectancy was 63 years? At a time when the relative price and expenditures for medical care are increasing at a rapid rate, however, Washington will soon approve some measure that will further increase the demand for medical care, with the attendant effects on relative prices and expenditures. The mindset that will shape this decision, like that which led to the Maastricht agreement in the European Community, was nurtured by the political élite with little apparent basis in popular concerns.

This perspective suggests the following types of research: who are the agenda setters? How does one become an agenda setter? How does this group decide on the focus of political action and the range of relevant options? How and how much are their decisions ultimately constrained by the electoral process? If this sounds like an appeal for some careful political sociology, so be it.

6. The constitutional limits on the powers of the federal government are no longer binding   Public choice has made a major contribution to the importance of constitutions and the effects of various types of constitutional rules. We have almost no theory, however, about how constitutional rules are sustained when they conflict with the interests of the current government (Niskanen 1990). Over my lifetime, the effective powers of the federal government have been massively increased without one amendment to the Constitution that would authorize an increase in these powers. The democratic provisions of the Constitution have been sustained, but the limits on governmental power have not.

A political scientist (without apparent exposure to public choice) recently summarized the effects of this constitutional revolution as follows:

> In a constitutional system, the powers of government are thought to be limited; in the administrative state only resources are limited. In a constitutional regime, the most important political questions are those of principle or public right; in an administrative state they revolve around money and finance. ... The administrative state has undermined the capacity of the institutions to pursue a public interest. It reflects a concern about administrative detail rather than principle, rule making rather than law making, and the attempt to placate every private interest, rather than the obligation to pursue a common good. (Marini 1992, p. xiii)

The most important part of the research agenda for public choice may be to address the following questions: what conditions sustain any constitution? What conditions led to the progressive erosion of the limits on powers in the US Constitution? How might some limits on the powers of government be restored? What are the long-term outcomes of a democratic government with no limits on its powers? Are there any corrective processes short of a revolution or financial collapse? These are pretty heady questions for public choice scholars but are probably our most important challenge.

Over time, I have come to share the pessimism about an unlimited democracy most forcefully expressed by Alexander Fraser Tytler, Joseph Schumpeter and Mancur Olson. Maybe there is reason to be a grump. Tell me, please, that I am wrong.

REFERENCES

Borcherding, T. (ed.) (1977), *Budgets and Bureaucrats: The Sources of Government Growth*, Durham: Duke University Press.

Fukuyama, F. (1992), *The End of History and the Last Man*, New York: Free Press.

Marini, J. (1992), *The Politics of Budget Control*, London: Taylor & Francis Ltd.

Niskanen, W. (1979), 'Economic and fiscal effects on the popular vote for the president', in D. Rae and T. Eismeier (eds), *Public Policy and Public Choice*, Beverly Hills: Sage Pubfications.

Niskanen, W. (1990), 'Conditions affecting the survival of constitutional rules', *Constitutional Political Economy*, **1** (2), 53–62.

Niskanen, W. (1992), 'The case for a new fiscal constitution', *Journal of Economic Perspectives*, **6** (2), 13–24.

Peltzman, S. (1987), 'Economic conditions and gubernatorial elections', *American Economic Review*, **77** (2), 293–7.

31. The moral case for bourgeois democracy*

We gather today to honour the 100th anniversary of Berner Ltd, a distinguished and successful business firm. Success itself, however, is not a cause for honour because it may be achieved by accident or expropriation. There is more reason to honour noble failure than ignoble success. The reason why we honour Berner is that its success derives from the actions of a family of entrepreneurs in an economic system in which their personal success has also increased the well-being of others. One of the great tragedies of modern life, however, is that the reasons for the success of specific people and institutions are more clear, at least in retrospect, than are the reasons for the success of the general economic, political and cultural systems in which we live. We need to understand these reasons to determine whether the success of these systems should also be so honoured.

THE CRITICS OF BOURGEOIS DEMOCRACY[1]

Only a European intellectual can distinguish the many shades of contempt in the word 'bourgeois'. Popular films, television and novels mock bourgeois manners and values. Serious theatre from Henrik Ibsen to Bertolt Brecht has scorned bourgeois culture. Novelists from Charles Dickens to Jean-Paul Sartre have been among the strongest critics of the social role of the bourgeoisie. For more than a century, Marxist philosophers and Catholic theologians have hurled competitive anathemas against the liberal individualism of bourgeois society.

What is the basis for this extraordinary contempt for for the bourgeois role in modern societies?

For the most part, this criticism is not based on the general economic performance of bourgeois economies. Karl Marx and Friedrich Engels

* This chapter is the text of a lecture presented at the University of Helsinki, 15 September 1983.

were among the first to recognize that 'The bourgeoisie, during its rule of scarce one hundred years, has created more massive and more colossal productive forces than have all preceding generations together'. (*The Communist Manifesto*, New York: International Publishers, 1948, p.13) For the next century, of course, Marx and his followers maintained that a socialist economy could perform even better, but that promise, at best a Faustian bargain, has proved to be empty. The record of the past half-century suggests that the economic conditions in market economies are almost uniformly superior to those in nations (with a similar culture and resource base) in which the government has the dominant economic role. I invite any of you to compare economic conditions in West and East Germany, in South and North Korea, in Taiwan and China, in Puerto Rico and Cuba, or in Finland and the former Baltic states to challenge this conclusion. A variety of dirigiste proposals maintain a certain romantic appeal but they have lost their revolutionary flavour.

Nor have the critics, for the most part, alleged that market economies are inconsistent with constitutional democracy. The development of market economies and constitutional democracies in the same countries and during the same period was not a historical accident. These parallel developments evolved from many of the same values and motivations and nourished each other. Marx recognized this relation in the term 'bourgeois democracy', a term that he created and used as a term of contempt. In the modern world, a market economy appears to be a necessary (but not sufficient condition) for democratic government. The evidence is striking. All nations that have broad-based representative government and civil liberties have most of their economic activity organized by the market. No nation in which the government has the dominant economic role has maintained broad political freedom. Voluntary migration, sometimes at high personal risk, is uniformly to those nations with both more economic freedom and more political freedom.

The reasons for these relations between economic and political systems are simple but are not widely understood. Everyone would prefer higher prices for goods they sell and lower prices for the goods they buy. Since the farmer's wheat is the housewife's bread, however, both parties cannot achieve all that they want. The most fundamental difference among economic systems is how these conflicting preferences are resolved.

A market economy resolves these conflicts by allowing the seller to get the highest price at which others will buy and the buyer to get the lowest price at which others will sell, by consensual transactions from which both parties expect to benefit. Any attempt by one party to improve his or her outcome relative to the market outcome requires a coercive activity at the expense of some other party. The politicalization of price decisions

– whether of wages, commodities or interest rates – tends to reduce both the efficiency of the economy and the breadth of popular support for the government. A rich nation can tolerate a good bit of such mischief, but not an unlimited amount. One should not be surprised that all nations in which the government has dominant control over the economy are run by narrow oligarchies and, in most such countries, economic conditions are relatively poor. In the absence of limits on the economic role of government, the erosion of economic freedom destroys both political freedom and economic performance.

Only a few dozen nations, with about one-quarter of the world population, now guarantee their citizens both broad economic and political freedom. By any standard other than military conquest, these are the most successful nations in the human experience. For all that, many of our leading intellectuals are either critical or pessimistic about bourgeois democracy or the equivalent concept, as used in the United States, democratic capitalism. This concern has been most eloquently expressed by Michael Novak, an American Catholic theologian:

> Democratic capitalism seems to have lost its spirit. To invoke loyalty to it because it brings prosperity seems to some merely materialistic. The Achilles' heel of democratic capitalism is that for two centuries now it has appealed so little to the human spirit.
> This failure is not commanded by stars conjoining in the sky. It is a failure not of iron necessity but of intellect. If the system in which we live is better than any theory about it, as Reinhold Niebuhr has suggested, the guardians of its spirit – poets and philosophers and priests – have not penetrated its secret springs. They have not deciphered or taught its spiritual wisdom. They have not loved their own culture. (1982, p. 31)

THE CHARACTERISTIC INSTITUTIONS OF BOURGEOIS DEMOCRACY

An understanding of the moral case for our social system must be based on a recognition of its characteristic institutions.

The characteristic institutions of a market economy are private property, competitive firms, free unions and the entrepreneur. For the system to work well, property rights should be as extensive as are mutually consistent and should be exclusive, partitionable and tradeable. Some of the problems of market economies, such as protection of the environment, are the result of insufficiently exclusive or extensive property rights. Many of the political tensions of a market economy are a consequence of the mutually inconsistent attempt of sellers and buyers to protect the prices at which goods are sold. Competition among firms is necessary to protect the consumer and, probably, to induce production efficiency. Only a few firms in a given industry are unusally sufficient to assure effective competition in the absence of collusion, high transport costs or governmental barriers to international trade. The opportunity to form and join a union has become one of the more distinctive features of market economies and is wholly compatible with efficiency if one union is not the sole bargaining agent in an industry. The most distinctive role in a market economy is that of the entrepreneur. Any type of economy involves the joint inputs of workers, managers and investors. The key role of the entrepreneur in a market economy is to identify some new product or some new organization of the factor inputs that serves the interests of all of the affected parties. In a technical sense, the entrepreneur is the agent that moves a market economy from disequilibrium to equilibrium, and the importance of innovative entrepreneurs is a function of the rate of change of tastes and technology.

The characteristic institutions of a constitutional democracy are the constitution, a broad franchise, competitive parties and the politician. The effective constitution, whether written or unwritten, represents the set of constraints on the powers and functions of the state and the procedures for selecting the government. A viable constitution should be changeable but only on the basis of a much broader consensus than the rule for approving routine legislation. A democracy without an effective constitution is prone to either instability or tyranny. Constitutional democracies have experienced a progressive broadening of the franchise and, contrary to the concern of conservatives, this broadening has strengthened these nations by giving more of the population a voice and a stake in the political process. The only important test for participation in the franchise should be a commitment to the constitution and to the processes of constitutional change.

The right to form and join any party committed to the constitution provides the essential discipline on the behaviour of the governing party. A wide range of procedures for selecting party candidates and forming a government have proved to be consistent with this critical role. The politician is the entrepreneur of the democratic process. As in a market economy, the entrepreneurial role of a politician is to identify some new policy that is preferred by some effective coalition – to move the government to a new political equilibrium. This central role of the politician may not lead to policies that all prefer, but this important role should not be disparaged. If the outcomes of the political process are undesirable, something is wrong with the effective constitution. The essential distinction between a politician and a statesman is whether the policy initiative serves some narrow constituency or most of the affected population.

A bourgeois democracy, however, is not a two-legged stool. The relation between man (or woman) and the state is protected by a rich set of intermediate and mediating institutions – the family plus the whole array of social, cultural, professional and religious institutions. These institutions are the third leg that provide the stability to a free society. The strength of the set of these institutions is *pluralism* – no one institution, especially the state, is the sole authority for determining what is true and what is right. Any one person may choose to accept the authority of a specific institution but has no right to insist that all people accept the authority of the same institution. This pluralism of truth-determining and value-setting institutions is, at the same time, one of the three pillars of strength and the primary target of the critics of a free society. Cultural aesthetes disparage bourgeois tastes without recognizing that a tolerance for the tastes of others is a necessary condition for their own artistic freedom. Socialists rage against inequality without acknowledging that some inequality of economic rewards appears to be a necessary condition to increase the expected well-being of everyone. A succession of popes have condemned liberalism and individualism as if there were no risk that some other institution might gain absolute authority. The final irony is that the arts are most creative, socialist theory is most vigorous, and the church is strongest in those liberal bourgeois democracies that are the target of all this criticism.

CHOICE AND CONSENT

The moral case for bourgeois democracy and our many other institutions, unfortunately, is not well understood or articulated.

What is the moral case for a society that tolerates poverty, that restricts the authority of the government to serve the interests of even the majority, that permits the expression of bad taste, that does not reenforce the authority of some true church? In comparison with the economic, political and social outcomes of authoritarian societies, there is no reason to apologize for the outcomes of a free society. The moral case for a free society, however, is based on the *process* by which outcomes are decided. In brief, the outcomes of a free society are based on the best deal that each of us can make with our neighbours.

The moral case for a free society is based on *choice* and *consent*. Both characteristics are essential. Choice without consent – an awareness of otherwise feasible alternatives from which one is not allowed to choose – destroys the human spirit. Consent without choice is tyranny – the choice of a worker who may only work for one employer, of a housewife who may only buy from one store, of the voter in a one-party state, of the devout who may worship at only one church.

The central elements of choice in a market economy are the freedom to select your occupation and employer, to invest in or borrow from a number of independent sources, to buy from a number of independent stores, to market a new product and to form a new business. The central elements of choice in a constitutional democracy are to vote for alternative parties, to form a new constitutional party, and to emigrate from any political jurisdiction. The central elements of choice in the social environment are the freedom to select your forms of expression and types of association.

The exercise of this choice in a free society should be bounded only by the consent of others who have affected rights. It is important to recognize the limits of consent that are inherent in mutually consistent rights. In a market economy, for example, each exchange requires the consent of both the seller and the buyer. Some other seller may object that the price is too low, and some other buyer may object that the price is too high, but the consent of these other parties cannot be required, because it is not possible to define mutually consistent rights in the price at which goods are exchanged. In a constitutional democracy, the right to form a new majority implies that each voter cannot be assured of being in the effective majority on each policy. In a pluralistic culture, one's freedom of individual or group expression, of course, implies that others may exercise their freedom in different ways. A free society, a bourgeois democracy if you will, can provide economic efficiency, political stability and cultural diversity but cannot assure happiness, particularly if one is strongly motivated by the sin of envy. The best deal we can make with our neighbours is to build a free society, in the language of the US Declaration of Independence, on a mutual respect for the rights to 'life, liberty, and the pursuit of happiness'.

The free nations of the world are stronger than is our understanding of their success. One of the many ways in which our freedom is expressed is the criticism of our basic institutions. That is a small price for freedom. We have many remaining problems, most of which can be resolved without using the powers of the state, some of which may require national action, a few may require the concerted action of a group of nations. But no one has made an effective case that a fundamental change in the basic institutions of a free society is necessary to resolve these problems. A free society will evolve in ways that cannot be anticipated. We do not have the luxury of delaying a moral judgement of our own society, based on some distant outcome. The survival of our free societies may well depend on a better understanding of the moral basis for defending freedom. I am not asking you to accept a moral rationalization of success. I am asking you to consider the idea that the success of these nations is based on a fundamentally moral order, the morality of social processes based on choice and consent, the only moral basis that will distinguish us from the animals and ultimately, the machines.

NOTE

1. This section draws extensively from: Michael Novak, *The Spirit of Democratic Capitalism*, New York: Simon & Schuster, 1982, and *Economic Report of the President*, Washington, DC, US Government Printing Office, 1982, Chapter 2. (*The Communist Manifesto*, New York: International Publishers, 1948, p. 13.)

32. The prospect for liberal democracy*

> ... the government created by this compact was not made the exclusive or final judge of the extent of the powers delegated to itself, since that would have made its discretion, and not the constitution, the measure of its powers.[1]
>
> (Thomas Jefferson 1798)

INTRODUCTION

Is a liberal society compatible with democratic government? Can democratic states survive in a world of hostile governments? What individual and collective actions would improve the prospects for liberal democracy?

For the first 150 years of the United States, few Americans would have asked these questions, and the answer would have been self-evident. In the 1830s, a sceptical Alexis de Tocqueville asked whether democracy was safe for the world and received the characteristically pragmatic American reply, 'It works!' Fifty years later, James Bryce reported that 'What do you think of our institutions?' is the question addressed to the European traveler in the United States by every chance acquaintance'.[2] A flood of immigration testified to a worldwide perception that America was the land of the future. The American experience, for better or worse, has a way of transforming German socialists into midwestern Republicans.

American self-confidence probably peaked when the United States entered World War I to 'save the world for democracy.' Since that time, the prospect for liberal democracy has been progressively eroded by both external and internal conditions – the most important of which include the success of communist armies, the Great Depression, and the progressive increase in the relative role of government in the democratic states. Only a few of the many national states formed since World War II have maintained a constitutional democracy. Only 20 per cent of the world's population now live in the two dozen or so constitutional democracies.

* Reprinted by permission from James Buchanan and Richard Wagner (eds), *Fiscal Responsibility in Constitutional Democracy*, Dordrecht, Netherlands: Kluwer Academic Publishing, 1980, pp. 157–80.

On the 200th Anniversary of both the political and economic blueprint for a free society, more Americans are questioning the viability of our institutions than at any previous time.

Analysis must precede prescription. But the perception of a problem must precede analysis. American political analysis atrophied as a consequence of the unrivalled success of the American experiment. As problems accumulate, however, pragmatism is not enough. As a political community, we are at sea without a rudder; we do not share a theory that explains both our success and the reasons for our developing problems,

The primary conclusion of this chapter is that there is a fundamental flaw in the Constitution of the United States and of other constitutional democracies. If this flaw is not recognized and repaired, the processes of democratic government will probably destroy the basis for both a liberal society and democracy. And, finally, the 'constitutional revolution' that is necessary to preserve liberal democracy must transfer the distribution issue from the political agenda to the constitutional agenda.

Some definitions are in order at this stage. A society is defined as a group of people subject to a common set of rules or laws. A liberal society is characterized by a set of rules that minimize the sum of the costs of coercive actions by individuals, by the agent enforcing the rules, and by individuals and agents 'outside the rules', subject to the equal application of the rules among individuals in the society. The primary role of government in a liberal society, in the words of the US Constitution, is to 'secure the Blessings of Liberty to ourselves and our Posterity'. A democracy is defined as a society in which the population has the fundamental authority to select the rules and the enforcing agent. A liberal democracy, thus, is a society in which liberal rules are selected by democratic processes. A liberal society requires some government but does not imply a specific form of government. A democratic government does not assure the selection of liberal rules. As it turns out, a liberal society is compatible with democratic government only under a very special set of conditions and the prospect for liberal democracy is dependent on a recognition and reenforcement of these conditions.

THE DEMOCRATIC LEVIATHAN

What are the consequences of unconstrained democratic politics? Are these consequences even consistent with preserving the basic democratic processes? Alexander Fraser Tytler, an eighteenth century Scot historian, anticipated our contemporary concerns with gloomy prescience:

A democracy cannot exist as a permanent form of government. It can only exist until the majority of voters discover that they can vote themselves largesse out of the public treasury. From that moment on, the majority always votes for the candidate who promises them the most benefits from the public treasury, with the result that democracy always collapses over a loose fiscal policy, always to be followed by a dictatorship and then a monarchy.[3]

It is interesting to reflect that Tytler's conclusion was based on his analysis of the democratic experiments in classical Greece, prior to any history of modern democracies.

The primary internal threat to liberal democracy is a totalitarian democracy. For our purpose, a totalitarian democracy is defined as a government in which a majority of the voters (or their representatives) may change any provision of the effective constitution other than the franchise and the election rules. In earlier articles, I have made the case that the primary political event of the past decade or so was the dramatic change in the effective constitution.[4] The democratic character of our institutions has proved to be remarkably invulnerable to oligarchic threats. The limits on the functions and powers of government that are a requisite for a liberal society, however, have been rather rapidly eroded by democratic processes.

It is useful to estimate the consequences of a totalitarian democracy for several reasons – to provide a base case against which to judge the present conditions, and to identify those processes that limit the democratic leviathan. The major unique process that limits the potential of a democratic government to exploit the minority is voting. The other major types of individual behaviour that limit the exploitative potential of any form of government are the reduction of taxable income and exit. These processes are explored below in this order.

Voting

Voting provides substantial protection for any group included in the franchise, if their interests are effectively represented. First, consider the redistributional consequences of the following conditions:[5]

- All heads of households are included in the franchise and are equally represented in government decisions.
- All voters vote their own economic interests; that is, they have no marginal benevolence (or malevolence) to others. (The assumption that there is no malevolence is important: Lebanon, Cyprus and Northern Ireland are examples of the consequences of democracy with malice.)

- All government decisions are made by majority rule.
- The effective constitution allows collective transfers, subject to the constraints that transfers to lower-income families can be no lower than to higher-income families and the marginal tax rate on lower-income families can be no higher than on higher-income families.

And, in the first case to be considered,

- The elasticity of supply of taxable income is zero.

Table 32.1 presents the consequences of democratic redistribution under these conditions, given a pretax distribution of income that roughly representative of the United States. The first row presents the distribution of income in the absence of any taxes or transfers.[6] The second row presents the post-tax and transfer distribution of income resulting from a coalition of the lower three income groups. This coalition generates a transfer budget of 19 per cent of total income and marginal tax rates of 100 per cent in the top two income groups. The relative size of the transfer budget would increase as a function of the inequality of the pretax income distribution.

For these conditions, however, transfers are a zero-sum game, and there is no dominant coalition if all groups are equally represented. The two higher-income groups can break the (3,4,5) coalition by offering to increase the transfers to the lowest-income families. This reduces the transfer budget to 6.5 per cent of total income and reduces the marginal tax rate of the highest-income group to 38.2 per cent. The lower-middle-income groups, in turn, can break the (1,2,5) coalition by a further reduction in the transfer budget and the marginal tax rate. And the (1,3,4) coalition can be broken by the original (3,4,5) coalition. Any majority coalition favours some redistribution of income, but no majority coalition dominates all other majority coalitions. The potential circularity

Table 32.1 Democratic redistribution given pre-tax income

| Coalition | Percentage of money income by quintile | | | | | Transfer budget % |
	1	2	3	4	5	
(0,0,0)	41.0	24.0	17.5	12.0	5.5	0.0
(3,4,5)	23.4	23.4	23.4	18.0	11.7	19.0
(1,2,5)	34.5	24.0	17.5	12.0	12.0	6.5
(1,3,4)	39.8	23.7	18.0	12.5	6.0	1.5

of majority voting, of course, is neither a surprise nor a general problem, because the consequences of different coalitions are usually similar. In this case, however, the consequences of the several potential coalitions are very different, so one should expect continuous political controversy on transfer issues.

This example may raise more questions than it answers about observed government transfers. Total government social welfare expenditures in the United States are now about 20 per cent of national income, but marginal tax rates are not 100 per cent; this suggests that many social welfare programmes should not be regarded as transfers among income groups but as tax-financed services to people in the same income group. We do observe that redistribution is a periodic (and often poisonous) political issue, but we do not observe enormous instability in the level of the transfer budget. Why have the higher-income groups not been able to form a (1,2,5) coalition that would both reduce the transfer budget and increase the transfers to the lowest-income families? This is the potential coalition for a negative income tax, but there seem to be no early prospects for a break of the currently effective coalition. One possible explanation is ideological resistance on the part of both the rich and the poor to form a coalition on this issue. Another explanation is that both the rich and the poor are effectively disenfranchised by the geographic basis for representation, since the variance of the median incomes among congressional districts is much smaller than among the population. This explanation suggests that proportional representation would increase the potential for a (1,2,5) coalition on distribution issues only at the cost of reducing the stability of any coalition. The primary lesson of this example is that voting protects the interests of the rich only when they are able to form an effective coalition with the poor. Any effective coalition that excludes the rich should be expected to extract from them the maximum potential tax revenue. The primary revolutionary threat to an unconstrained democracy is likely to be a 'rightist' coalition of the rich and the poor.

The Supply of Taxable Income

The supply of income subject to taxation by a specific government, of course, is not invariant to the marginal tax rate. The generation of income is the result of individual actions and a social process, and tax rates influence income generation in several ways. An increase in the marginal tax rate should be expected to reduce hours worked, the formation and maintenance of human and physical capital, the relative employment in more onerous occupations and regions, the relative employment and investment in activities subject to low-cost monitoring by the tax authorities, and the relative employment and investment in the taxing jurisdiction. Any one of these effects may be small, but the combined effects are likely to be substantial. Moreover, the aggregate elasticity of supply of taxable income is likely to increase over time. The potential reduction of taxable income is the primary limit on the exploitative potential of any form of government.

For any individual, the tax rate that maximizes (gross) tax revenues is equal to $1/(1 + E)$, where E is the elasticity of supply of taxable income by that individual (the tax rate that maximizes revenue net of collection costs is slightly lower). If the elasticity of supply of taxable income by some individual is 1, for example, a marginal tax rate of 50 per cent maximizes the gross revenues the government can collect from that person. A government is unlikely to set a higher rate except by mistake or malevolence.

In addition, we are protected by the differences in the elasticity of supply of taxable income among individuals. All of us who enjoy our work earn more than our reservation wage because others have a higher reservation wage. A government cannot know the elasticity of supply of taxable income of individuals; at most, a government can set rates based on an estimate of E by income groups and sources of income. As a consequence, most individuals in a tax rate group will be subject to a tax rate less than the revenue-maximizing rate, because others have a higher elasticity of supply of taxable income. In a state with an exploitative government, the enjoyment of the finer (nontaxable) things in life is a public good. The rhetoric of all totalitarian governments is filled with exhortations against the 'shirkers' and the 'malingerers'. Our liberty, however, is a function of our differences; both the puritans and the flower children should recognize how much they need each other.

Table 32.2 presents the consequences of democratic redistribution in a state where the supply of taxable income is a function of the tax rate. The conditions that generate these consequences are the same as those

Table 32.2 Democratic redistribution given maximum tax rates

Coalition	Percentage of money income by quintile					Transfer budget %
	1	2	3	4	5	
(0,0,0)	41.0	24.0	17.5	12.0	5.5	0.0
(3,4,5)	29.9	21.4	21.4	16.5	10.7	17.4
(1,2,5)	36.7	22.8	17.5	12.0	11.0	5.5
(1,3,4)	39.8	23.7	18.0	12.5	6.0	1.5

described above, except that the revenue-maximizing marginal tax rate is assumed to be 50 per cent. The first row again presents the assumed pre-tax and transfer distribution of income. A (3,4,5) coalition, in this case generates a maximum transfer budget of 17.4 per cent of total income; the effect of a limit on the marginal tax rate on the high income group is to reduce the post-tax and transfer income of each other group. Although the maximum tax rate is limited by the elasticity of supply of taxable income, the rich still have an incentive to vote if they can form a coalition with the poor. These other coalitions reduce the total transfer budget but, again, there is no dominant coalition on transfer issues.

The potential for democratic redistribution is further limited by the demand for government services. If transfers absorb the total revenues generated by the maximum marginal tax rate, for example, any expenditures for defence and other services must be financed by either reducing transfers and/or increasing the middle-income tax rate. A demand for both transfers and services, of course, will generate lower levels of both transfers and services than if one or the other demand was not effective.

Table 32.3 presents the consequences on the distribution of money income and the level of the government budget in the United States for several combinations of transfers and services, given a maximum marginal tax rate of 50 per cent. The first two rows are identical with those in Table 32.2. A (3,4,5) coalition is assumed to be effective on each issue. Both the level of services and the middle-income tax rate will be determined by the demand for services by the middle-income group.

For this case, the demand for services by the middle-income group is assumed to be

$$Q_3^D = 15 (1 - C'S_3),$$

Table 32.3 Democratic financing of transfers and services

	Percentage of money income by quintile					Budget	
	1	2	3	4	5	Transfers (%)	Services (%)
Pre tax	41.0	24.0	17.5	12.0	5.5	0.0	0.0
Transfers only	29.9	21.4	21.4	16.5	10.7	17.4	
Services only	29.3	20.8	17.5	12.0	5.5		15.0
Transfers and services	27.8	19.3	19.3	14.2	8.3	9.8	11.3

where

$C' \equiv$ marginal cost of services, assumed $\equiv 1$
$S_3 \equiv$ marginal tax share of middle-income group.

For the assumed pre-tax distribution of income, a marginal tax rate of 50 per cent on the two high-income groups would generate tax revenues of 15 per cent of income. If the *total* government budget is less than 15 per cent of income, thus, the tax share of the middle-income group is zero. For any budget larger than 15 per cent, however, the marginal tax share of the middle-income group is 25 per cent. For the assumed demand function for government services, thus, the budget for government services would be 15 per cent of total income in the absence of any transfers and 11.25 per cent of total income if tax revenues must cover both transfers and services. Similarly, the transfer budget would be 17.4 per cent of total income in the absence of any services and 9.8 per cent of total income if the government provides both transfers and services. A tradeoff between transfers and services is forced by the fact that any government budget above 15 per cent must be financed by increases in the tax rates on incomes up to the level of the middle-income group.

This example has been designed to illustrate recent and present conditions in the United States. Twenty years ago, the federal budget was less than 20 per cent of national income, most of the budget was spent for defence and other services, and the federal tax rates on lower-income groups were minimal. Since that time, the 'transfer revolution' has increased the federal budget share of national income by about 40 per cent, reduced the share for government services, and increased the tax rates on the lower-income groups. The increase in transfers has been financed primarily by reducing the relative expenditures for defence and reducing the relative income of those middle- and low-income families not eligible for transfers.

This example, and my reading of present conditions, leads me to believe that the federal budget is about in equilibrium. A further increase in the relative transfer budget appears unlikely unless the demand for government services is reduced (or the revenue-maximizing marginal tax rate is increased, possibly by a deterioration of conditions in other nations). Any increase in government services would probably be financed by a reduction of transfers and an increase in the middle-income tax rate. The 'transfer revolution', I believe, has about run its course. The major present concern is whether democratic politics will generate a sufficient level of defence spending which, given the present transfer budget, must be financed by increases in the middle-income tax rate.

One interesting option suggested by this analysis involves breaking the (3,4,5) coalition on transfer issues. A (1,2,5) coalition would make possible an increase in the defence budget, a reduction in the middle-income tax rate, and an increase in the transfers to the lowest-income group. My guess is that this will be the platform of the next major political entrepreneur. This change necessarily involves a reduction in the transfers to middle-income families, but this may be the cost of maintaining an adequate defence in a hostile world. A democratic government can probably not finance both an adequate defence and a broad-based welfare system. There appears to be no fundamental incompatibility, however, between democratic politics, an adequate defence, and even more generous care of the poor.

Exit

The ultimate individual defence against a totalitarian government is exit. The opportunity to emigrate limits the power of a government to exploit any individual, even if he or she has no vote and he or she has a high preference for income subject to tax. The following relations hold for any individual:[7]

$$G_A + P_A + M_{AB} \geq G_B + P_B$$

$$G_A \geq G_B + P_B - P_A - M_{AB},$$

where

$G_A \equiv$ value of government services in state A
$P_A \equiv$ value of private services in state A
$M_{AB} \equiv$ costs of moving from state A to state B
$G_B \equiv$ value of government services in state B
$P_A \equiv$ value of private services in state B

All variables are in present value terms. An individual will remain in state as long as the sum of the value of government and private prices plus the costs of moving are greater than the sum of the value of government and private services in the most attractive alternative state. For some people, the opportunity to emigrate is not very valuable; the second relation suggests that an individual may remain in a state even if the value of government services in the state of residence is zero or negative.

Some further elaboration on several of the above variables is valuable. An individual's valuation of private services in state A (P_A) is a function of the after-tax real income in state A, relations with family and friends, and attributes of the social and physical environment. And, similarly for P_B. The costs of moving from state A to state B (M_{AB}) will be a function of the physical distance and transportation costs, the quantity of unmovable physical capital and selling costs, the absolute difference between the language and culture of the two states, any exit controls in state A, and any entry controls in state B.

Table 32.4 summarizes the directional effect of these conditions on the value of government services to each individual. The opportunity to emigrate, of course, provides the most discipline on the performance of a local government or state within a federal union in which there is a common language and culture and there are no controls on the movement of population and capital.

The opportunity to emigrate provides the least discipline on the government of a large rich nation in which family relations and private ownership of capital are important such as, for example, the United States. Most economic and social phenomena, however, appear to be changing in a direction that would make emigration a more attractive option and a more effective discipline on the US government – the increasing relative income in other countries, the spread of an international English- speaking culture, the erosion of family ties, the reduction in transportation costs and the increasing efficiency of the capital market. Governmental actions offset some of these effects: a reduction in the performance of government in other nations and the spread of movement

Table 32.4 Conditions affecting the value of government services

Direction of effect on G_A	
Favourable	Unfavourable
Government services in B	
Income in B	Income in A
Tax rates in A	Tax rates in B
Attachment to B	Attachment to A
	Distance from A to B
	Transportation costs
	Difference in language and culture
	Ownership of physical capital
	Selling costs of capital
	Exit controls in A
	Entry controls in B

controls reduces the discipline of the emigration option. Controls on immigration and capital exports, unfortunately, are very attractive to democratic governments, and such actions reduce the performance of all governments. Liberal government is a public good among nations, and some form of international constitution on population and capital movements could improve the performance of all governments.

THE CONSTITUTIONAL CHALLENGE

How did the problems of our constitutional democracy develop? Where do we go from here?

The primary contemporary problems of constitutional democracy, I contend, are the result of an extraconstitutional process off constitutional change. The national governments of the democracies now define their own powers, in response to the political processes affecting the decisions of these governments. The potential problems of a democratic government that defines its own constitution have long been recognized. Seth Low, writing to James Bryce, observed:

> When . . . all men . . . are politically equal, and all men equally enjoy the right to take part in the government of a country, the experience of the United States would indicate that an omnipotent parliament would then be full of peril. The United States have enjoyed the measure of prosperity which they have had by trusting completely the whole of society. But written constitutions, in the nation and in each of the States, protect at once the individual, the State, and the nation, from hasty and ill-considered actions on the part of the majorities as to matters fundamental. Laws may be passed by majorities and may be removed by majorities, but majorities cannot change, in a moment, the fundamental relation of government to the people. . . . To the American mind, it seems as though England's omnipotent parliament, which has been to her so valuable during this period of change from the feudal to the democratic ideal, may before long become an instrument full of danger to the state, unless, in some way, checks producing the same effect as those which have been found necessary in the United States are placed upon the exercise of its omnipotence.[8]

In the late nineteenth century, neither Low nor Bryce could conceive of the same problems developing in the United States, because of the American commitment to a formal constitutional process of constitutional change.

A century later, however, without any change in the enumerated federal spending powers, the powers of the US federal government are almost unlimited. Congress has proliferated transfer, grant and regulatory programmes that have no formal constitutional basis. The flood of domestic legislation since 1965 has not even been rationalized in terms of the enumerated powers. The Tenth Amendment, alas, appears to be only a 'parchment barrier' to the extension of federal powers. All of Low's concerns about an 'omnipotent parliament' have been realized in the birthplace of constitutional democracy.

For most of American history, liberal constitutional theory has held that the exercise of undelegated powers by any government is null and void. Several quotations illustrate this tradition:

> whensoever the general government assumes undelegated powers, its acts are unauthoritative, void, and of no force.[9] (Thomas Jefferson 1798)

> the powers of the federal government as resulting from the compact to which the states are parties, as limited by the plain sense and intention of the instrument constituting that compact, as no further valid then they are authorized by the grants enumerated in that compact.[10] (James Madison 1798)

> the government it created was formed to execute, according to the provisions of the instrument, the powers therein granted . . . that its acts, transcending these powers, are simply and of themselves null and void.[11] (John Calhoun 1832)

> if the subordinate body attempts to transcend the powers committed to it, and makes rules for other purposes or under other conditions than those, specified by the superior authority, these rules are not law, but are null and void. . . . They ought not to be obeyed or in any way regarded by the citizens because they are not law.[12] (James Bryce 1888)

The spirit of this tradition is that the language of the Constitution is clear and that every citizen has the right to interpret 'the plain sense and intention of the instrument'. The essence of a constitutional democracy is that the whole of the people is the superior authority and that the government is subordinate to the fundamental law defining the relation between the people and the government.

Against the background of this tradition, how have the several institutions created by the Constitution (Congress, the presidency and the federal courts) been jointly able to assume almost unlimited power to change the effective constitution? The powers of any one of these institutions have been quite successfully limited by the 'checks and balances' of the other federal institutions, but there appears to be no effective limit on the combined powers of these institutions. My own reading of American political history leads me to conclude that this problem reflects a fundamental flaw in the Constitution, a flaw that has led to periodic problems that were resolved in the past in an *ad hoc* manner that deferred a more general recognition and correction of this flaw.

The Constitution, in brief, does not establish an adequate procedure for forcing a constitutional test of the assumption of undelegated powers by the federal government. The Constitution (Article V) provides an adequate procedure for testing the consensus on any formal amendment proposed by Congress or a convention. Reflecting Madison's vision of a 'compound republic', the Constitution also grants powers to the federal government (Article IV, Section 4, and the Fourteenth Amendment) to guarantee a republican form of government and the civil rights of individuals in each state. The only procedure by which an individual or state can test the constitutionality of a federal action, however, is in a case brought before the federal courts. No procedure is established for forcing a constitutional test on issues for which the Supreme Court is unwilling or unable to enjoin the actions of Congress or the presidency or of a decision by the Court itself. The Constitution establishes the Court as the only arbiter of constitutional issues, short of the formal process of constitutional amendment. The Constitution of our 'compound republic' is asymmetric: a vote of the legislatures in one-fourth plus one of the states can block a formal amendment. There is no corresponding procedure for the same number of states to force a formal constitutional test by enjoining a change in the effective constitution.

The procedural solution to this asymmetry is as old as the Magna Carta and has been circulating in the backwater of American political theory since the beginning of our republic: some proportion of the parties to the constitutional contract must be able to enjoin the actions of the government established by the contract in order to force a formal constitutional test of the actions. Clause 61 of the Magna Carta established a group of 25 'guardians of the charter', any four which could notify the king of violations of the charter and, if not resolved within 40 days, bring the matter to the other guardians.[13] This famous clause, probably the contribution of Stephen Langton, was subject to continuous attack by defenders of the royal prerogatives, and was omitted from later versions of the charter when the king gained power.

The Kentucky and Virginia resolutions, written respectively by Jefferson and Madison, tried to establish a similar procedure in 1798. These resolutions articulated the concept that the exercise of undelegated power had no force of law, but proposed nothing more than a common appeal by the states to Congress to repeal the Alien and Sedition laws. The election of Jefferson and a Republican Congress in 1800 led to early repeal of these laws but deferred consideration of the basic constitutional issue. The South Carolina Ordinance of Nullification, written by John Calhoun, raised the issue again in 1832. This ordinance, declaring that the selective tariff on manufactures was unconstitutional and would not be enforced in the state, was designed to force a constitutional test on this law. This issue was resolved by Congress in the compromise tariff legislation of 1833. Although Calhoun recognized that some form of sanction was necessary to force a constitutional test, his argument, unfortunately, misdirected the earlier concept. Jefferson and Madison resisted the action by any one state to nullify a federal law; Calhoun declared the right of every state to nullify a law which it regarded as unconstitutional. Madison regarded the United States as a 'compound republic' in which the states and the national government have a mutual responsibility to enforce the constitution of the other government; Calhoun declared the states to be 'free, independent, and sovereign communities'. Calhoun, unfortunately, confused the case for a collective responsibility of the states to enforce the federal Constitution with an unviable concept of 'states' rights'. The State of Wisconsin next raised this issue in 1859 to force a constitutional test on the Fugitive Slave Law, which required the return of slaves that had escaped. The Wisconsin confrontation with the Supreme Court was resolved only when a newspaper editor who had been arrested was pardoned a few days before the start of the Civil War.

The doctrines of 'nullification' and 'interposition' have been criticized or dismissed by later political theorists, primarily because they were later used to defend the institution of slavery and the continued denial of civil rights to negroes. Americans have an unfortunate habit, however, of evaluating a legal concept by the motivations of its advocates. Most contemporary Americans probably regard the Alien and Sedition laws, the protective tariff and slavery as repugnant. The doctrine of nullification, however, should not be evaluated by the fact that it was first developed to attack bad law and later used to defend other bad law, but rather whether it would, in general, have promoted law that reflects the broad consensus of the population. The Civil War was the first major tragic result of the failure to correct the constitutional flaw to which this doctrine was addressed. The 'constitutional anarchy' of our time, I suggest, is the result of the same problem.

The prospect for liberal democracy, I contend, will be dependent on some constitutional reform that would enforce a constitutional process of constitutional change. This reform should build on Madison's concept of a 'compound republic'. The federal government is now an effective guardian of the constitutions of the states. The state governments, correspondingly, should constitute the 'guardians of the charter' of the federal government. Andrew Jackson's response to Calhoun was correct in stating that the federal union could not survive if each state could nullify federal law. It is also important to recognize that a constitutional democracy cannot survive the subjugation of any substantial minority. The general nature of the constitutional reform that derives from this analysis would be to authorize a group of states to enjoin any federal law, executive action or court ruling within some specified period. A specific amendment to the Constitution, consistent with these principles, would provide for the nullification of any federal action by the vote of more than, say, one-third of the state legislatures within one year after the date of the last vote. Such an amendment would be designed to force a constitutional test on any action, and would be nearly symmetric with the present provision for approving constitutional amendments. Such an amendment would provide a considerable period for both reasoned evaluation of the federal action and continued federal abuse of its constitutional powers, but it should protect the nation against both an ephemeral whim and an indefinite extension of federal power. The primary expected effect of such an amendment would be to force a compromise that would avoid exercise of the nullification authority on most issues.

A broad coalition, of course, is required to approve any constitutional amendment. The federal government has abused its powers, however, because the actions serve the interests of a substantial part of the population. The central problem for the advocates of constitutional reform to restrict the powers of the federal government is to gain the approval of those who now benefit from the abuse of these powers. Whether or not the federal actions that created these benefits are regarded as constitutional, the beneficiaries of these actions must also be included in any new constitutional consensus. The redistributive genie is out of the bottle, and no amount of wishful thinking will convince people to relinquish the transfer dividends from their voting rights, without compensation. A constitutional consensus must be based on the status quo, not some status quo ante. For this reason, any constitutional reform to restrict the powers of the federal government, I believe, must be paired with a constitutional agreement on transfers and taxes. The amount and character of the redistribution that is, in some sense, 'right' from a moral or efficiency perspective is irrelevant in this case. The necessary distribution is that which will achieve a constitutional consensus on both constitutional process and redistributive issues. The prospect for liberal democracy is dependent on moving both the process of constitutional change and redistributive issues from the political agenda to the constitutional agenda. Neither the tory sceptics nor the romantic democrats are right; democracy is not doomed to either failure or success. Our collective future as a political community will be of our own making.

Public choice

NOTES

1. Thomas Jefferson, 'The Kentucky resolution', *The Annals of America*, Vol. 4, Encyclopedia Britannica, Inc., 1968, p. 62.
2. James Bryce, *The American Commonwealth*, Vol. 1, London: Macmillian, 1888, p. 1.
3. Quoted in Sir John Glubb, *Soldiers of Fortune*, London: Hodder and Stoughton 1973, pp. 229 – 30.
4. W.A. Niskanen, 'The pathology of politics', in Richard Selden (ed.), *Capitalism and Freedom: Problems and Prospects*, Charlottesville: University of Virginia Press, 1975, pp. 20–35, and W.A Niskanen, 'Public policy and the political process', Graduate School of Public Policy Working Paper No. 29, June 1975 1975, Berkeley, California.
5. These are essentially the same conditions explored by James Buchanan, 'The political economy of franchise', in Richard Selden (ed.), *Capitalism and Freedom: Problems and Prospects*, pp. 52 –77.
6. The numbers presented are the estimated percentage of pre-tax, post (money) transfer income of families in the United States in 1973. For this analysis, the pre-tax, pre-transfer income distribution would have been desirable but is not available. US Bureau of the Census, 'Money income in 1973 of families and persons in the United States', *Current Population Reports*, Series P–60, No. 97, 1975, Table 22.
7. This is a slight modification of the analytic framework in James Buchanan and Charles Goetz, 'Efficiency limits of fiscal mobility: an assessment of the Tiebout model', *Journal of Public Economics*, 1, 1972, 25–43.
8. James Bryce, *The American Commonwealth*, Vol. 1, London: Macmillan, 1888, pp. 567–8.
9. Thomas Jefferson, 'The Kentucky Resolution', *The Annals of America*, Vol. 4, Encyclopedia Britannica, Inc., 1968, p. 62.
10. James Madison, 'The Virginia Resolution.' *The Annals of America*, Vol. 4, Encyclopedia Britannica, Inc., 1968, p. 66.
11. John Calhoun, 'Address to the People of the United States', *The Annals of America*, Vol. 5, Encyclopedia Britannica, Inc., 1968 p. 577.
12. James Bryce, *The American Commonwealth*, Vol. 1, London: Macmillan, 1888, p. 326.
13. *Encyclopedia Britannica*, 1972 edition, Vol. 16, p. 579.

33. The erosion of the liberal economic order*

Our lesson for the day is from Adam Ferguson (1792), one of the principals, along with David Hume and Adam Smith, of the Scottish Enlightenment:

> Liberty or Freedom is not, as the origin of the name may seem to imply, an exemption from all restraints, but rather the most effectual application of every just restraint to all members of a free society whether they be magistrates or subjects.

My brief remarks make four simple points.

First, a social order is best defined as a group of people who live by the same rules. At any place and time, thus, each person lives in a number of social orders, depending on the extent of shared rules. Over time, in turn, the size and composition of a social order changes in response to the effects of the shared rules.

Second, the personal, social and political rules that contribute most to a social order cannot by derived by deductive reasoning but may be inferred from the relative success of different orders. The laws of physics, for example, are presumably constant but are only sequentially revealed by experiment and evaluation. The rules of just conduct, I contend, have the same objective character. Sometimes history provides dramatic natural experiments, such as the division of Europe and Asia between capitalist and socialist economies after World War II, from which the lessons are, or should be, obvious. More often, sorting out the rules that contribute most to a social order requires a more discriminating analysis and any conclusions will be subject to more dispute.

At this stage, I must acknowledge my own cranky perspective on this issue. My judgement is that *the rules of the bourgeois liberal social order* (in Europe, the US and a few other countries through about 1914), with a

* Reprinted by permission from *Atlantic Economic Journal*, 23 (1), March 1995, 1–8. This article was my presidential address to the Atlantic Economic Society, Montreal, Canada, October 1994.

few important exceptions, *are our best guide to the rules of just conduct*. My focus is on the economic order but it is important to recognize that the social and political orders involve the same people.

The German liberal Wilhelm Ropke (1954) may have best summarized the personal rules that best contribute to the economic order:

> A minimum of natural trust, confidence in the stability and reliability of the legal-institutional framework (including money), contractual loyalty, honesty, fair play, professional honor and that pride which makes us consider it unworthy of us to cheat, to bribe, or to misuse the authority of the State for egoistic purposes.

To that, I would add only that the condition that most distinguishes an extended-market order from an oriental bazaar is the mutual desire for continued relations. The rules that contribute to the 'evolution of cooperation' over time are subtle but simple: a mutual commitment to *exchange* (rather than threat) as the primary instrument to coordinate economic activity, the self-restraint to leave something on the table for the other party in each transaction, and the use of the authority of the state only to discipline gross or repeated breaches of contract.

The one attitude most incompatible with a market economy is a profound and pervasive sense of envy. A society can survive pervasive egoism; indeed, a market economy relies on it. A market economy, however, cannot survive the levelling instinct, the concern that your neighbour or your former schoolmate might be doing better than you are. (Intellectuals may be the most prone to envy, for never having an answer to their mother-in-law's question that, 'If you are so smart, why aren't you rich?') One should not be surprised that all of the major religious traditions regard envy, covetousness or resentment as a major sin. Envy is a human condition but it is most destructive to the social order.

In the same liberal tradition, Frederick Hayek (1984) writes that, 'the coercive activities of government should be limited to the enforcement of such rules [of just conduct], whatever other services government may at the time render by administering those particular resources which have been placed at its disposal for those purposes'. Hayek does not suggest what other services government should provide. (Even Ludwig von Mises favoured government support of the opera.) The common principle in this tradition dates from James Madison and the American Constitution: a government should not have the authority to define its own powers but should be limited to those powers enumerated in the Constitution.

Third, every social order contains the seeds of its own destruction. At any time, some people, even a majority, may have an incentive to break or change the rules that sustain the social order.

George Will (1993) recently summarized a conventional concern that 'capitalism requires thrift, discipline, industriousness, and deferral of gratifications; but capitalism by its prodigal success in making Americans a people of plenty, may be subverting these very virtues, making us soft and indulgent'. This concern, I suggest, is misplaced. The American employment rate and average hours of work per year are among the highest in the world, and productivity growth continues to be high in those sectors most subject to foreign competition.

There is more reason to be concerned about Will's (1993) other concern that 'the very virtues that democracy presupposes – individualism, self-restraint, and self-reliance – are subverted, over time, by the very solicitousness of democratic government'. A government that is responsive to the demands of most any group invites an increase in demands by other groups. That is the reason why government budgets are now perceived to be so tight, even though real per capita government spending has never been higher.

My own view is much more grim, *Most of the major changes in personal, social and political rules in roughly our lifetime*, I suggest, *have undermined and will continue to undermine the liberal social order*. Let me count the ways.

1. *The erosion of responsibility* The confusion of sex with love or causes with responsibility have seriously undermined the family and the firm. The percentage of American babies born to single mothers has increased from 5 per cent in 1960 to 29 per cent and is now 68 per cent for blacks. Parents who neglect their children in favour, for example, of saving the rain forest, have misdirected their caring. Businesses that serve various stakeholders at the expense of their stockholders will not prosper and may not survive.
2. *The erosion of rights* The confusion of interests with rights has substantially eroded our rights and changed the role of government. In the liberal concept embodied in our founding documents, people have rights to life, liberty and their own property, and the primary role of government is to *secure* these rights. The contemporary concept is that people have rights to food, housing, education and now medical care – even at the expense of the liberty and property of others – and the role of government is to *provide* these rights.
3. *The erosion of civility* The civility of public discourse has been substantially reduced by the increasing practice of impugning motive. This reduces both the scope of public discourse and the potential for a consensual resolution of differences.

4. *The erosion of language* Words that imply value judgements previously served an important role of reinforcing rules that contribute to the social order. Such words, however, have been progressively replaced with words that either neutralize or reverse the initial value connotation. What was once called bastardy became illegitimacy and now single motherhood. Charity becomes welfare, then entitlements, and now human rights. Those who were once called tramps, hobos, bums or beggars became itinerants and are now homeless. Those who disrupt public life became demonstrators, criminals became victims, terrorists became freedom fighters. The effect, of course, has been to reduce the opprobrium of those activities that undermine the social order and the esteem of those who nurture it. Senator Pat Moynihan has described this process as 'defining deviancy down'.

5. *The socialization of risk* Most of us are risk averse and will buy insurance against some types of risk. Moreover, there may be some types of desirable insurance that are best supplied by the government. What we have lost is the principle that insurance should be limited to conditions that are substantially invariant to personal behaviour. The progressive socialization of risk has substantially reduced the returns to responsible behaviour. Welfare increases illegitimacy. Unemployment insurance increases unemployment. Social Security reduces private saving. Disaster insurance increases the costs of disasters. Deposit insurance increases bank failures. Pension insurance increases pension failures. Chapter 11 of the bankruptcy code increases the cost of bankruptcy. Assigned risk policies for auto and health insurance increase accidents and the demand for medical care, and so on. Our shared problem is that it seems easier to create new forms of social insurance than to unravel the web of existing social insurance that is probably already too extensive

6. *The erosion of the moral order* The most dangerous idea of the nineteenth century was Friedrich Nietzsche's arrogant statement that 'God is dead'. A shared belief in a higher being to whom we must each answer has strengthened the rules of just conduct in all cultures. The role of taboos in primitive cultures had a similar effect.

I do not assert that a shared religious belief is necessary for a moral order. My concern is the erosion of the concepts of sin and virtue. A liberal social order involves multiple rule-setting bodies, with the government setting only the outer limits of acceptable behaviour. Conservatives, however, are now too prone to making a crime out of every sin; liberals, to making a requirement of every virtue. The proliferation of laws has reduced the authority of the rules of just conduct within other social units.

7. *The erosion of the political constitution* Similarly, the most dangerous
idea of the twentieth century is that there should be no limits on the
powers of a democratic government – a view promoted by the
Progressives, legitimized during the New Deal, and largely accepted
by the 1960s. A shared commitment to a higher law that the government may not change is the central political foundation of a liberal
social order.

The Constitution of the United States established the structure of the
federal government, limits on the powers of the federal and state governments, the procedures for amending the Constitution, and a partial listing
of the rights of individuals. The objective of the Constitution was to
define the islands of government powers within the ocean of individual
rights. The distinctive American contribution was to assert the supremacy
of individual rights over governmental powers and, in the Declaration of
Independence, 'That to secure these rights, Governments are instituted
among Men, deriving their just powers from the consent of the governed'.

Although the US is one of the youngest major nations, it is the oldest
surviving republic. In general, the Constitution has served us very well.
For two centuries, the structure of government has been remarkably
stable. Our civil rights have been strengthened by the extension of the Bill
of Rights to limit the powers of state governments. There is no need for
me to elaborate on the strengths of our Constitution, other than to reaf-
firm my loyalty and thankfulness for the wisdom of its framers.

At the same time, we should recognize that whole sections of the
Constitution bearing on the economic powers of the government and the
economic rights of individuals have been seriously eroded, for the most
part in our lifetime and without any formal amendment. Those who are
surprised by this observation may not recognize the many provisions of the
Constitution that bear on economic powers and rights. Others dismiss any
concern for this condition on the basis, in the language of Justice Holmes,
that 'a constitution is not intended to embody a particular economic
theory'. Giving the benefit of the doubt to the learned Justice, one wonders
whether these commentators have read the Constitution or the deliberations that led to its numerous fiscal, monetary and economic rules. The
fiscal rules include the enumerated spending powers and the limitations on
federal and state taxing powers. Specific monetary rules are prescribed. The
major economic rules include the interstate commerce clause, the patents
and copyrights clause, the contracts clause, and the rights to property.

Any reading of the deliberations that led to the Constitution and several amendments should lead one to recognize that these rules were
specifically designed as part of the larger set of rules to secure individual

rights. The framers may not have shared a common vision about the economic system. There should be no doubt, however, that the Constitution was designed to provide a strong but limited federal role, free trade among the states, the enforcement of contracts and the security of private property.

Most of these rules, unfortunately, have now been stretched beyond recognition. Only a partial listing of the changes in the effective economic constitution is sufficient to make this point.

- The few spending powers enumerated in Article I, Section 8 were expanded without limit by a 1936 ruling of the Supreme Court that 'the power of Congress to authorize appropriations of public money for public purposes is not limited by direct grants of legislative power found in the Constitution'. One can state with assurance that the initial Constitution would not have been ratified if this later interpretation had been anticipated.
- The requirement that 'all duties, imposts, and excises be uniform throughout the US' has been interpreted to permit a differential windfall profits tax on oil and the complex web of internal tariffs that is implicit in environmental regulation.
- The power 'to coin Money' has been broadened to permit a federal monopoly of paper money.
- The power 'To regulate commerce ... among the several States' has been progressively broadened to permit federal regulation of any form of commerce within individual states.
- The rule that 'No state shall ... pass any ... law impairing the obligation of contracts' has been interpreted to permit several types of contractual impairments, including debt moratoria.
- The 'public use' test for the exercise of eminent domain has been expanded to a 'public purpose' test to permit the use of eminent domain for urban renewal and land redistribution among private parties.
- The 'just compensation' test for the exercise of eminent domain has been restricted to preclude compensation for regulations that substantially reduce, but do not eliminate, the value of the property to the private owners.

In these cases, the language of the Constitution is clear and specific. The effective economic constitution, however, has been changed substantially in response to political pressure, and these changes have been ratified, not by formal amendment, but by creative and compliant decision of the Supreme Court. There is a reasonable case that some of these changes in the effective economic constitution may have been appropriate. My primary point is that these changes in the effective constitution were made by extra constitutional procedures, by compliant courts, rather than by the Article V procedures for formal amendments that would have provided a test of whether these changes were supported by a broad consensus.

The effects of this erosion of the economic constitution have been dramatic. For the first 140 years under the Constitution, the federal budget share of national output was roughly constant in peacetime, there was no cumulative inflation, and there was little federal regulation. Since 1929, however, the federal budget share of GDP has increased from less than 3 per cent to more than 23 per cent, and the price level has multiplied tenfold. A similar quantitative measure of the breadth and cost of federal regulation is not available but indirect measures, such as the number of lawyers and the number of pages in the *Federal Register*, indicate an explosion of regulation and litigation in the past 30 years. The powers of the federal government have expanded enormously in our lifetime without one amendment that would authorize these expanded powers. The central political foundation of a liberal social order has been perilously weakened.

There is one bright exception to this grim litany. The personal, social and political rules of American life, at least until about 1965, reflected a progressively shared commitment to judge people by their ability, character and behaviour, rather than by their race, religion or gender. Even this profound strengthening of the rules of just conduct, however, has been more recently eroded by new forms of discrimination in the name of affirmative action and diversity.

My general conclusion is still quite grim. Most of the major changes in the rules of American life in our lifetime will continue to reduce our freedom, civility and economic growth. We are using up our stock of moral capital. One might hope this would induce a change in the rules, but there are too many examples of organizations and societies maintaining self-destructive rules for decades with little pressure for change short of imminent collapse. We might choose better rules if there were a discernable 'cliff' in the near future, rather than to continue to act like the Gadarene swine. James Q. Wilson (1993) recently observed that:

> The kind of culture that can maintain reasonable human commitments takes centuries to create but only a few generations to destroy. And, once destroyed, those who suddenly realize what they have lost will also realize that political action cannot, except at a very great price, restore it.

Fourth, most contemporary proposals for changing social rules would contribute to a continued erosion of the liberal social order. The most deceptive illusion is that egoism is an inadequate basis for organizing an increasingly complex society. Egoism, operating through exchange, is the *only* motive that is sufficient to coordinate an extended economic order. Love is a noble motive like gold is a noble metal – beautiful but rare; contrary to the popular song, there is not enough love to make the world go around. For that reason, it is important to substitute a base motive like egoism wherever possible, avoid disparaging a social process just because it relies on a base motive, and focus the limited supply of caring on those social relations for which it is most important. What we need is institutional creativity to make better use of self interest, not Rousseauian fantasies that the mix of human motives can be modified to serve the public interest. Again, Hayek's (1984) perception is apposite:

> the order of the market, in particular, rests not on common purposes but on reciprocity, that is on the reconciliation of different purposes for the mutual benefit of the participants. The conception of the common welfare of the public good of a free society can therefore never be defined as the sum of known particular results to be achieved, but only as an abstract order which as a whole is not oriented on particular concrete ends but provides merely the best chance for any member selected at random successfully to use his knowledge for his own purposes.

The language of the contemporary debate, however, only confuses the issues. Coordination does not require cooperation towards a common end. A responsive social order does not require a commitment to social responsibility by individuals and firms. The public interest is not a set of aggregate social objectives. The primary alternative to exchange as the means to coordinate the extended social order is not love but is threat. The liberal social order is being destroyed, not so much by the greedy, but by those who are most generous at other people's expense.

REFERENCES

Ferguson, Adam (1792), *Principles of Moral and Political Science*, II, Edinburgh: A Strahan T. Caddell.
Hayek, F.A. (1984). 'The principles of a liberal social order', *The Essence of Hayek*, Chicago: University of Chicago Press, 365–6.
Ropke, Wilhelm (1954), 'Economic order and international law', *Recuil des Cours*, Academic de Droit Internationale, **86** (2), 207–71.
Will George F. (1993), 'Mr Jefferson comes to town', *Public Interest*, **112**, Summer, 58.
Wilson, James Q. (1993), *The Moral Sense*, New York: Free Press, p. 234.

34. Growing up*

Some people grow older without growing up. What a tragedy!

Growing up is a *humbling* experience. A school can transform natural ability into job skills, some appreciation of our history and culture, and a confidence to take on larger tasks. And I am sure that your experience at Suomi has done all that and more. But the beginning of wisdom is to recognize what one does *not* know. And even more humbling is to recognize that some of what one knows is just not so.

You have reason to ask what all this humility has to do with growing up. Isn't surviving the teenage years enough? The primary reason that growing up is a humbling experience is that people learn more from mistakes than from successes. For growth to be a continuing process, people must be willing to risk mistakes and to learn from them. The timid, who do not risk mistakes, deny themselves the opportunity to learn and grow. The foolish, who do not learn from mistakes, will repeat the same mistakes.

Several experiences from my professional life illustrate these observations:

1. After being selected for my first position as a manager, I sought the counsel of some older friends about how to deal with employees. The most frequent advice was to ask employees to perform only those tasks that I already knew how to do. After completing a number of solid but not-very-creative projects, I realized that this advice was almost wholly wrong, because it restricted the division of labour between the manager and employees. I learned that a better rule was to hire the employees who were better at their jobs than I could be and specialize in my own job as a manager. My professional training in economics should have given me that insight, but I did not learn this lesson until after my first mistakes. Some of those older friends from whom I sought counsel later worked for me.
2. The standard practice of young economists is to bring advanced techniques to bear on established problems. After some years of doing this, I realized that these techniques did not address several important

* This is the text of a graduation address given at Suomi College, Hancock, Michigan, on 24 April 1983.

dimensions of economic behaviour, most importantly the behaviour of governments. My one major scholarly contribution developed from that recognition and led to the application of a rather crude technique to explain the behaviour of government bureaux. Several younger scholars have since improved substantially on my initial formulation. In general, the major contributions in my field are the result of recognizing what we do not know and trying to sort out these puzzles, initially by rather simple techniques. As a rule, it is better to be roughly right rather than precisely wrong.

3. As a young man, I had a rather heroic perspective on human behaviour. Most of the great contributions to the human conditions were attributed to people perceived to be 'larger than life'. Conversely, most major problems were attributed to people who were dumb, lazy or evil. My experience has substantially changed this perspective. I have had the occasion to meet many of the leading public figures of our time. None of them 'is quite larger than life'. All of them, as far as I know, put on their pants one leg at a time. Most of them attained their position by using skills that are not much beyond the reach of most of us at a time and place where such skills were most valuable. It has also become clear that most of the major problems of our time are also attributable to this same group of the 'best and the brightest'. This does not deny the presence of evil, even great evil. But the sad fact is that most of the major errors in human judgement that have affected all of us are made by bright, hard-working people with the best of intentions. The difference between great error and great success is often the difference between training and learning, between cleverness and wisdom.

All in all, these experiences have led me to believe that the differences in natural ability are not that great, that the differences in acquired skills are the result of personal effort, and the differences in wisdom cannot be taught but can be learned. These observations are meant to be both encouraging and humbling (there's that word again). Although chance conditions affect all of us, our individual futures are not pre-determined. Most success is the result of personal effort. Most of us have no one to blame for failure but ourselves.

For those of you who want to continue to grow up, rather than grow older, my advice is the following:

- recognize your natural ability;
- reenforce that ability by acquired skills;

- be willing to risk error at a time and in ways where the costs of error are not too large to you and others;
- learn from those errors;
- be humble about your successes and don't blame failure on others;
- maintain a sense of humour; and
- develop a respect, but not a fear, for the many mysteries of life.

For this honoured class, this occasion is both a graduation and a commencement – a graduation from your rich-shared experience at Suomi and a commencement of your many different journeys on that long road called growing up.

God bless you and keep you.

Index

processes 310–16
speculations on reasons 316–18
constitutional consent (primacy of)
338–40
constitutional issue (government
services) 343–4
constitutional maintenance (theory of)
355–9
constitutional perspective
(taxes/transfers) 280–81
constitutional rules, survival of
(conditions) 352–9
consumption 268–9
goods 309
services 142–3, 193
Coolidge administration 232
copyright law 187, 188
corporations
federal chartering of 11–15
large organizations and
(differences/similarities) 329–36
corrections
District of Columbia expenditure
83–5, 93–4
employees 26–8, 30–32
cost differences (environmental
quality) 263–6
Council of Economic Advisers (CEA)
6, 163–6, 168–9, 177, 180, 203
Council for Environmental Quality 164
countervailing duties 195
courts, District of Columbia
expenditure 83, 93–4
Craig, Steven 22
Crane, Ed 6
'creative destruction' 173
crime
drug enforcement and 113–14
prevention programmes 33
rate (District of Columbia) 83, 96–8
reported 19–27, 29, 31–3, 82–3, 85,
93–4, 114
root causes 16–34
supply of 22–29
see also property crimes; violent
crimes
Crime Control Institute 17
Crocker, T.D. 135
cultural attitudes (in market economy)
350–51

cultural conditions (crime rate) 23–4,
28–29
cultural indicators (poverty) 216–17
culture of poverty 212–26

Dam, Ken 4
Danzig, George 1
Deacon, Robert 127
deaths
drug-related 118–19
of infants (District of Columbia)
87–8
debt 169
fiscal constitution and 361, 363–4,
369–71
illusion 249
international 210
decision costs 313–19 *passim*
decision makers 288–90
decision rules 258, 267, 272, 315, 322,
327
Declaration of Independence 387, 409
defence 2–3, 4
buildup (for smaller forces) 58–75
problems (proposed solutions) 48–56
programme (recent history) 35–43
programme-change process 43–8
resource allocation process 35–56
spending 171, 174, 193–4
Defense Reorganization Act (1958) 38
Defense Reorganization Act (1986) 74
Defense Resources Board 72
Delaware 13–14
demand
price elasticity of (illegal drugs)
107–8
rule (monetary policy) 155–7
target path of total 155–6
'demand for alcoholic beverages'
(Niskanen) 8
democracy
bourgeois (moral case for) 382–8
liberal (prospect for) 389–403
democratic government, progressive
taxation and 271–86
democratic leviathan (totalitarian
democracy) 390–99
democratic liberalism 384
Democratic Party 235, 241–2, 251–2,
295, 377

monopoly power of local government
304
moral case for bourgeois democracy
382–8
moral dilemma (in culture of poverty)
225–6
moral order, erosion of 408
Moynihan, Pat 408
Mueller, Dennis 165
Multifiber Agreement (MFA) 184
Murphy, K. 105–8
Musgrave, R.A. 341
Muskie, Edmund 298
national ambient standards
(environment) 263–4
National Criminal Victimization
Survey (NCVS) 19, 21, 27, 29,
32–3, 216
*National Drug and Alcoholism
Treatment Unit Survey* 106
*National Household Survey of Drug
Abuse* 100, 104
National Institute on Alcohol Abuse
and Alcoholism 106
National Institute on Drug Abuse 100,
106
National Longitudinal Survey of Youth
(1984) 112
national security 45
defence buildup and 58, 59, 68–70,
72–4
NATO 59, 66, 69, 73–4, 194
natural monopolies 344
Navy 37, 38, 42, 63–4, 67, 69, 71
near-term defence budget and
programme 71–2
net import of capital (1980s) 200–210
net US foreign investment 197–200
New Deal 250, 292, 339, 354, 362, 409
Niebuhr, Reinhold 384
Nietzsche, Friedrich 408
Nisbet, C. 107
Niskanen, William A. 237, 245, 341,
345
professional and academic career
1–7
reflections (on public choice theory)
374–81
Niskanen – Levy study (school district
size) 124–33

Nixon, Richard 233
Nixon administration 4, 165, 169, 312,
363
Noh, S.J. 358
nonemployment rate 212, 214, 221–4,
223, 225
normative public choice analysis (of
taxes and transfers) 271, 275–85
Novak, Michael 384
Novick, David 1, 39
nuclear weapons/materials 54, 55, 70
nullification doctrine 401–3

Office of Information and Regulatory
Affairs (OIRA) 176–7, 180–81
Office of Management and Budget 4,
177, 311, 312
Office of National Drug Control
Policy 117
Office of the Secretary of Defense 2–3,
41, 46–8, 49–50, 52, 55
Office of Systems Analysis 2
oil consumption 268–9
Olson, Mancur 259, 381
Omnibus Trade Act (1988) 183, 189,
192
opportunity cost of capital 136–7
Ordeshook, Peter 3
organizations, corporations and
(differences/similarities) 329–36
out-of-wedlock births 212, 214, 221,
222, 225, 226
outlays by appropriation, defence 61

packaging (consent process) 324–5
Packard, David 75
Panama Canal treaty 325
parental choice (education) 92, 133
Pareto-relevant externalities 290
Pareto changes 257, 260, 261
Pareto optimality 288, 310, 311
Parke-Davis 110
party hypothesis 235–6, 242, 251–2
party system 294–8
passing the buck 326–7
patronage 296
Peltzman, S. 374
Perot, Ross 377
Phillips curve 248
planning (defence programme-change